D0081540

RONALD PAULSON

Sin
AND Evil

MORAL VALUES IN LITERATURE

YALE UNIVERSITY PRESS   NEW HAVEN & LONDON

Published with assistance from the Mary Cady Tew Memorial Fund.

Copyright © 2007 by Ronald Paulson.

All rights reserved.

This book may not be reproduced, in whole or in part, including illustrations, in any form (beyond that copying permitted by Sections 107 and 108 of the U.S. Copyright Law and except by reviewers for the public press), without written permission from the publishers.

Set in Scala and Scala Sans by Duke & Company, Devon, Pennsylvania.
Printed in the United States of America by Thomson-Shore, Inc.

Library of Congress Cataloging-in-Publication Data
Paulson, Ronald.
Sin and evil : moral values in literature / Ronald Paulson.
p. cm.
Includes bibliographical references and index.
ISBN: 978-0-300-12014-1 (alk. paper)
1. Evil in literature. 2. English literature—History and criticism. 3. American literature—History and criticism. 4. Sin in literature. 5. Religion in literature. I. Title.
PR149.E87P38 2007
820.9'38—dc22

2006022021

A catalogue record for this book is available from the British Library.

The paper in this book meets the guidelines for permanence and durability of the Committee on Production Guidelines for Book Longevity of the Council on Library Resources.

10 9 8 7 6 5 4 3 2 1

ei de ti presbuteron eti kakou kakon
tout' elakh' Oidipous

      (Sophocles, *Oedipus tyrannos*, ll. 1365–66)

    If there is evil beyond evil,
that is the lot of Oedipus.

      (trans. David Slavitt)

If there is any ill worse than ill,
that is the lot of Oedipus.

      (trans. David Grene)

If there be yet a woe surpassing woes, it hath become
the portion of Oedipus.

      (trans. R. C. Jebb)

What grief can crown this grief?
It's mine alone, my destiny—I am Oedipus!

      (trans. Robert Fagles)

Is there any horror deeper than other horrors,
This Oedipus has inherited.

      (trans. Philip Vellacott)

CONTENTS

EVIL IS A TERM of particular poignance in our time. The blatant (or unarguable) evil of the twentieth century has been followed by an evil that is more subjective in the twenty-first, more reliant on one's point of view and, significantly, on the distinction between sin and evil. The confusion of sin and evil, of religious and moral transgression, is the subject of this book.

"Evil," as distinguished from evil, is evil aggravated or exacerbated, and one way of placing the scare marks has been to add the vocabulary of sin. The probable reason for this goes back to the so-called Problem of Evil. The originary sense of evil(s) as *suffering*-evil (death, disease, pain) in a god-created world was the basis for our understanding of *doing*-evil as well: to do evil is to make a sentient being, human or animal, suffer. Sin then involves a transaction between a human and his or her god; evil between humans, or between gods and the humans on whom they impose evils. The fires of hell, of course, are the ultimate evil consequent upon sin.

The evils that were thought to follow from the Original Sin were, in Christian theology, redeemed by Christ's Incarnation, which provided, in compensation for death and suffering here, eternal life and happiness in the hereafter—the notion that a more satisfactory life begins after death. Deriving as it does from the justification for evil in Original Sin, the apparatus of salvation has (or has often had) the effect of sidestepping the issue of evil(s) in this world in favor of focusing the attention on one's own personal salvation, which is, as Swift for example showed in his *Tale of a Tub*, self-centered and ultimately, in terms of everyday life, destructive of self and others.

By the twentieth century the emphasis of mainstream theology had largely shifted from personal salvation to acts of charity and love, from religion as soteriology to a concern with living in this world. This was often referred to as Christian Humanism. Toward the end of the century, however, the pendulum had swung back to the salvationist position, and the latter has taken a prominent place in American political discourse.

Sin is, in one sense, internal—if not between oneself and God ("just between me and my Savior"), then between oneself and one's conscience, or one's id or ego and superego. This contrast, between internal and external evil (or sin and evil), distinguishes those who believe that wrongs and evils are due to our common Original Sin from those who blame these evils on society (church, state, family, the burden of the past). The external equivalent of sin is the legal classification of the Ten Commandments, the Seven Deadly Sins, and the laws of Leviticus; sin as offense to God finds its human equivalent in the English Common Law's treason against the monarch.

What then are "moral values"? Moral values are based on custom, and so sins based on the Old Testament laws can be construed to be moral failures; in fact, however, they are largely (what in Leviticus are called) abominations—prostitution, single-sex marriage, abortion, stem cell research, showing one's breasts on TV. I take *morals* to be a word that refers to the study of the relationship of good and evil—the complex meaning and significance of evil, as in the novels I deal with, which also examine the relationship of sin and evil.

The twentieth century—and so far the twenty-first—has, as Gertrude Himmelfarb and others claim, abandoned moral values for the *evils* of genocide, serial killings, predation of innocent children, and so on; but not for the *sins* on which the advocates of "moral values" focus their attention. We recall the placard-bearers at the funeral of the homosexual Matthew Shepard showing satisfaction in the murder and the victim's anticipated punishment in the hereafter ("Matt burn in Hell," "Kill the Fags," etc.)—which, in reality, is an obvious case of moral evil. Christian fundamentalist leaders claimed that AIDS was the divine punishment for the evil of homosexuality, 9/11 for the evils of American liberal secularism; and, more recently, Pat Robertson has written that environmentalists are "the evil priests of a new paganism that will become the official state religion of the New World Order." These are all cases of evils that are really sins; Robertson's statement, in the context of Katrina, for example, is itself evil.

A consequence of this confusion of sin and evil is that sin is punished, evil rewarded, as in recent times one president is impeached for a sexual indiscretion and another is reelected for getting thousands of soldiers and civilians killed under dubious or false premises. The latter event depends upon a constituency—an association of the Christian Right with chauvinist nationalism, fundamentalist authoritarianism—that, while talking of "Evil," is more concerned with sin than evil, with theology than morality.

I begin with the assumption that evil is now a cultural construct. Evil is in the eye of the beholder. The corollary is that evil to one person may be good to another, but also what is evil to one may be merely wrongdoing to another. I would argue that this particular situation is most clearly seen in the context of the history of sin and evil. After the Second World War large events begin to appear from alternating points of view: the Allies are good, the Axis (Germany, Japan) are evil—and in the death camps there is much evidence to prove the point; but then one of the Allies, the USSR, proves to have killed more innocent people than Germany and Japan put together; and, as people begin to point out, the atom bomb and saturation bombing could also be called evil. Again, in Vietnam the United States is good, the Vietcong evil—but we massacre innocent Vietnamese.

Evil is in the eye of the beholder, but evil is not just what is *called* evil. Evil and good have to be opposed in some absolute sense, as in the evil of Hitler and his Holocaust, to which all except some Palestinians, some Muslims, and some remaining anti-Semites would agree. But in many cases evil is merely designated by the emphasis assigned by the enemy, as in "Axis of Evil" or the "evil" Muslims or "the great American Satan." There is little disagreement that genocide, torture, and defilement (especially of children, in both third world countries and at the hands of Roman Catholic priests) and terrorism all fit into a certain conception of evil based on excess, the gratuitous, and the incomprehensible (*this* has never happened before). Now, in the twenty-first century, we in

America can agree that 9/11 was an act of evil. Al Qaeda killed 3,000 innocent, randomly chosen Americans. But Al Qaeda believed Americans are "devils"—capitalist Christians who are occupying Arab lands (in Palestine by supporting the Israelis, in Saudi Arabia, etc.) and are corrupting the purity of the Muslim world. There had been, however, no clear signs of "evil" actions like that of 9/11 (random death, suffering, cruelty) on the part of the American sinners. (Though Muslim extremists pointed to the evils of "colonialism," the support of torture, murder, etc. in American-supported dictatorships.)

Some Americans believed Iraq was evil because it had connections with Al Qaeda and the 9/11 bombings and stored weapons of mass destruction awaiting deployment. But, it having been proved that Iraqis had neither ties to Al Qaeda nor WMD, they were not in fact "evil"; unless one focused on non-9/11 related matters such as the torture chambers and rape rooms of Saddam Hussein. But after thousands of Iraqis were killed by the U.S. invasion and occupation troops, some Iraqis (and some Europeans as well) believed that the United States was, as Al Qaeda believed, evil. We might recall that the Resistance in France in 1944 was seen by the Germans as insurgency, by the occupied French as heroic resistance to the occupying Germans.

President George W. Bush named Iraq as part of the Axis of Evil, a concept applied to a country whose "evil" was at best intentional (as in the heinous crime of "imagining the death of the king"). In fact, to President Bush evil was essentially sinners who were neither Christian nor "democratic," and evil, in the eyes of Islam, was what resulted from the American invasion to eradicate sin and institute "torture rooms" at Guantánamo and Abu Ghraib.

Of the tsunami of 2004, a "natural evil," all we can say is that it happened. Iraqi Muslims spread the story that the real cause was nuclear tests the United States and Israel were carrying out in the Indian Ocean. A geologist might have some explanation for how and why. Americans of the Religious Right believed that it was significant that it hit and killed mostly Muslims (this was before Katrina and Rita). God, they implied, had once again visited an evil upon his enemies, the sinners.

All of these issues—endlessly rehearsed following the debacle in Vietnam and recovered for the catastrophically dubious war in Iraq and since then tsunamis, hurricanes, natural and human disasters—have rendered the whole issue of evil ambiguous, and ambiguity appears to be what distinguishes our sense of evil. This book sets out to show some of the literary precedents for the difficulty we now experience telling who is good and who evil, and who is evil and who a sinner. These precedents begin with classical and Christian fictions of sin/evil, pivoting first on the Enlightenment phenomenon and second on the twentieth-century world wars and genocides, "war crimes" and "crimes against humanity."

My examples are taken from the Anglo-American tradition because the tradition of Protestant sin connected the mother country with its colonies. (If the Cavaliers instead of the Puritans had settled New England—if the Merry Mount colony had wiped out Governor John Endicott's neighboring colony—the fictions would have been different.) In no other area with which I am familiar has the polarity of sin and evil, or religion and morals, church and state produced such an interesting confluence, recently confused by the term *moral values*. There are, so to speak, two traditions in Anglo-American literature, whether Christian or deist or atheist—that of sin and that of evil. Each uses the cultural capital of the other to make its points.

ACKNOWLEDGMENTS

While conditioned by a historical moment, and with some relevance to contemporary affairs, this book took off from the last pages of my *Hogarth's Harlot: Sacred Parody in Enlightenment England* (2003), in which I concluded that the line connecting the satirists William Hogarth and William Blake, pointing toward Charles Dickens and Nathaniel Hawthorne, was based on the distinction between sin and evil—the refusal by these artists to confuse evil with the very different concept of sin. I am particularly indebted to Susan Neiman, whose *Evil in Modern Thought* got me started on the investigation of the Problem of Evil; and, of course, Paul Ricoeur's seminal *Symbolism of Evil*. The many other works upon which I have drawn will be acknowledged in the text. I wish to thank personally Colin Dayan, who introduced me to the legal concept of cruel and unusual punishment, on which she has written eloquently, and shared with me that other interesting legal concept, moral turpitude; Richard Macksey and Paul Arnold, with whom I have had many conversations and e-mails on the subject; also John Hollander, John Irwin, Neda Salem, Harry and Claudia Sieber, Ann Stiller, David Wasserstein, Brenda Wineapple, and

Larzer Ziff; at Yale University Press, Lawrence Kenney for copy-editing and Enid Zafran of Indexing Partners LLC. for indexing.

In general I use whatever text I have in my library; therefore, for the benefit of the reader I have indicated, when possible, both chapter and page number (i.e., 4.34).

SIN AND EVIL

CHAPTER ONE

Evil, Sin, and Wrongdoing

1. EVIL

Evil and "Evil" ("Evil With a Very Big E")

> Mr. Hyde was pale and dwarfish, he gave an impression of defor-
> mity without any nameable malformation, he had a displeasing
> smile, . . . all these points were against him, but not all of these to-
> gether could explain the hitherto unknown disgust, loathing, and
> fear with which Mr. Utterson regarded him. "There must be some-
> thing else," said the perplexed gentleman. "There is something
> more, if I could find a name for it."
>
> —*R. L. Stevenson,* The Strange Case of Dr. Jekyll and Mr. Hyde

RADICAL EVIL IS A TERM we often hear: evil at its root, its ultimate
source; fundamental, basic, and essential. (In politics it suggests an extreme, evil of the far left or far right.) *Absolute evil* is another: perfect, unqualified, pure, and unmixed, without a trace of mitigation. These refer
to our rock-bottom definition: harm to another human being. But there
are also forms of *added* charge: "beyond limits" or "beyond the line,"
meaning beyond *the acceptable,* as in "a strong case could be made that the
killing of tens of thousands of civilians within a little more than twenty-
four hours, as at Dresden, should also go *well beyond the line*" (emphasis
added.).[1] What we call evil is wrongdoing plus *n,* or wrongdoing raised to
the *n*th power (above or beyond the ordinary norm). As Henry James has
a character put it in *The Golden Bowl:* The "very, *very* wrong" is "what's
called Evil—with a very big E."[2]

Evil can be approached by an analogy with tragedy. Tragedy is to pathos as evil is to wrongdoing. When a child is run over by a car and killed,
bystanders say this is a tragedy, but the child's death, however closely it
touches us, is not tragic but sad and pathetic. There must be something in

excess in various ways of the sad accident of the child's death. *Peripeteia,* a reversal of fortune, derives from a human *hamartia* (a tragic flaw) and must be, in Aristotle's terminology, "of a certain magnitude"—we might say a wrongdoing by a wrongdoer great enough to "inspire pity and fear," of a dignity that renders his fall terrible; and this must be followed by an *anagnorisis,* a climactic recognition of something he had not previously realized. The *pathos* of the scene involves "suffering . . . a destructive or painful action, such as death on the stage, bodily agony, wounds and the like"—by "those who have done or suffered something terrible" (in S. H. Butcher's translation of the *Poetics*). And what are these acts? For example, "a brother kills, or intends to kill, a brother, a son his father, a mother her son, son his mother. . . . Medea slay[s] her children."[3]

In the same way, the murder of a person is a crime or a wrongdoing. It may never be in any real sense more than a felony or assault, manslaughter or homicide, but as the circumstances are aggravated in one way or another it becomes, in the eyes of many, evil or even Evil.

To correct Henry James: Evil is wrongdoing with a capital W; "Evil" is evil "with a very big E." Which means in the twentieth century *plus* dimension (6 million), intention (genocide, "racial cleansing"), or the gratuitously cruel (forcing a child to mutilate or kill its parents); in short, whatever is worst, or is unthinkable or even unimaginable. But also, a more artificial strategy, *plus* the scare quotes of religious discourse (of sin, as both one of the sources of evil and itself one of the evils) with the effect of deepening the sense of evil. We can say that evil has been theologized, then heightened for the purposes of rhetoric ("Evil Empire," "Axis of Evil") or of aesthetics (obscurity, power, sublime terror).

The root of Old English *yfel,* according to the *OED*, "usually referred to the root of *up, over;* on this view the primary sense would be either 'exceeding due measure' or 'overstepping proper limits.'"[4] This can refer to a person as being beyond the normal human limits and/or an act that is what I have referred to as evil "with a very big E."

Suffering-Evil and Doing-Evil

The *OED* senses of *evil* fall roughly into two categories: *suffering*-evil and *doing*-evil. Suffering-evil is the condition of being unfortunate, miserable, wretched (as in evil health), a victim of calamity and misfortune. Under misfortune are also included the bad, wicked, inferior, offensive, and disagreeable agents who cause discomfort or repulsion. "In quite familiar speech," the *OED* adds, "the adj. is commonly superseded by *bad;* the sb. is somewhat more frequent, but chiefly in the widest senses, the more specific senses being expressed by other words, as *harm, injury, misfortune, disease,* etc." This is the significant root. The earthquake and tsunami that ravaged the Indian Ocean on Christmas Day in 2004 claimed some 220,000 lives and was, in the original sense of the word, evil. The Holocaust, involving the systematic murders of 6 million Jews, was also an evil but with a human, not natural, origin. The second sense of evil, doing-evil, is being morally depraved, bad, wicked, vicious; doing or tending to do harm; causing discomfort, pain, or trouble, arising from bad character or conduct.[5]

The Greek *kakia,* with its excremental root, refers to suffering-evil, "what is bad" in the sense of "ill" or "ill-ness"—"what one desires to avoid, such as physical pain, sickness, suffering, misfortune, every kind of harm."[6] The translations of the word in Sophocles's *Oedipus tyrannos* range from *evil* to *ill, grief,* and *horror.* The "French Evil" denoted syphilis; the Latin equivalent, *malum* (the noun or *malus-a-um* the adjective—bad, evil, wicked as well as unfortunate, weak, cowardly), like the French *mal,* denoted sickness as well as bad or evil. The Old Testament also presents evil as pain, sickness, suffering, and misfortune: doing-evil and suffering-evil (or moral evil and calamity) are covered by the same Hebrew root (*ra'*). When God decides to destroy his unsatisfactory creation in Genesis 5:6, the words ordinarily translated into English as "wickedness" and "evil," both words based on the root *ra',* are rendered literally by Robert Alter: God sees that "the *evil* [wickedness] of the human creature was great in the earth and that every scheme of the heart's devising was only perpetually *evil* [evil]."

The agency of evil, called natural evil, is ordinarily attached to God. As Samuel E. Meier puts it, in the *Oxford Companion to the Bible,* "Since God was the undisputed master of creation, it was assumed that every occurrence was through his explicit command." Isaiah's God speaks: "I form the light, and create darkness: I make peace, and create evil: I the Lord do all these things."[7] In 1 Kings 14:10 Jehovah vows to "bring evil upon the house of Jeroboam" because of his sins (worshiping "other gods"). Amos's rhetorical question is, "Shall there be evil in a city, and the Lord hath not done it?," and Job's, "Shall we receive good at the hand of God, and shall we not receive evil?" (Isa. 45:7; Amos 3:6; Job 2:10).[8] These evils can be neutral dangers or calamities—"A prudent man foreseeth the evil, and hideth himself" (Prov. 22:3)—but when they are disastrous they are attributed to the deity (originally, we may suppose, to natural forces, animistic then deified).

The Old Testament references gravitate toward a Genesis sense of evil summed up by the Christian theologians in the Problem of Evil (*unde malum?* whence and why evil?). The "evils" that entered the world with Adam's Fall were death, strife, and labor—disease, pain, and natural disaster, and all those effects people have found inexplicable given the belief in an all-powerful and benevolent deity.[9] These are presented throughout the Old Testament primarily as punishments inflicted by God. Amos's rhetorical question, "Shall there be evil in a city, and the Lord hath not done it?" reminds us that when evils happen they are attributed to God's wrath, and in this case "evil in a city" conflates the evil done by men and the reciprocal evil imposed by God.

When evil in the Old Testament does refer to injuries or wrongs done by one man to another (murder, fratricide), he is warned: "Whoso rewardeth evil for good, evil shall not depart from his house" (Prov. 17:13).[10] This is doing-evil, moral or criminal evil based on *lex talionis* (the law of retaliation), which is also the basis for the evils God administers; as we read in 1 Kings 16, when Jezebel had Naboth killed to secure his vineyard, it was evil in the sight of the Lord, and this justified her punishment at the hands of Jehu (2 Kings 9:30–39).

An extension of suffering-evil (death, pain, natural disaster, murder), doing-evil has tended to designate the suffering of one sentient being imposed by another; it is the *pain* that matters and the fact that it is deliberately inflicted (as opposed to a natural disaster or an accident). The words "deliver us from evil" in the Lord's Prayer encompass both meanings, natural and moral (Mat. 6:13). But suffering-evil is natural evil plus moral or doing-evil insofar as both were included in what Adam's Fall brought into the world, that is, God's doing, God's punishment for sin. Doing-evil (as in Cain's murder of Abel) ordinarily refers to the suffering inflicted only by one man or woman on another. And yet when God punishes the family of Jeroboam he is also doing-evil to human beings.

Suffering-evil is the whole world of death, disease, pain, and so on, that is the basis for the Problem of Evil; which should perhaps more accurately be the plural *evils,* sometimes called sorrows, sometimes woes, but comes down finally to death, in Søren Kierkegaard's words, "what human-ity normally calls the greatest evil."[11] Evil is what the psychiatrist C. Fred Alford has called "an experience of [existential] dread"—that combination of natural and moral evil, of meaninglessness and victimhood which is the world; in short, "the dread of being human, vulnerable, alone in the uni-verse, and doomed to die."[12] All goes back to this sense of evil as suffering and misfortune or victimhood and loss. *Pace* the story of Eden, existential evil would appear to have preceded the Problem of Evil and called for the "attempt to master the experience," to explain and hopefully alleviate it, by the invention of a god.[13] To begin with, there was existence—Hobbes-ian, nasty, brutish, and short, involving two parties, the stronger and the weaker—and then the need to cope with these facts, first physically and then psychologically; and so one posited forces of nature and/or gods and created the discourse of evil and the Problem of Evil.

One answer, in many ways the most obvious (with the Zoroastrians, Manichaeans, Bogomils, and Albigensians), was to premise two gods, an evil god who, responsible for the evils, counteracts a good god. Only with the premise of a monotheist god did it become necessary to explain why he, if omnipotent and all good, permits evil; and so were postulated crimes/sins for which god has punished us with misfortunes—crimes against each other, sins against god himself. And with offenses/crimes/sins arises the principle of rewards and punishments, either in daily life or, more significantly, in an eternal afterlife promised in recompense for the evils of a transitory life here, either (depending on the criterion of acts or of faith) in heaven or hell. And not only the hope in a life after death but the Christian belief, expressed here and there in the New Testament (e.g., the Magnificat), in a hereafter where the last will be the first.

2. SIN

Disobedience/Offense to the Deity

> If one man sin against another, the judge shall judge him: but if
> a man sin against the Lord, who shall entreat for him?

> —*1 Samuel 2:25*

The first is evil, the second sin. Genesis says only that following the Fall women will suffer in childbirth and be ruled over by their husbands (because, eating the apple, Adam had subjected himself to Eve), and Adam will have to "till the ground" and labor for a livelihood. Most important (the *felix culpa* aspect), he will now "know good and evil." The idea of "evils" (death, suffering, and the rest) is introduced by the Christian interpreters. "Evil" as the evils of existence was implied by Paul and made explicit by Augustine, whose primary religious problem—at the beginning of his career, following his eating of the pears (see below), and at the end as he battled Pelagius—was the Problem of Evil, which first drew him to the Manichaean solution and then, in violent reaction, to the monotheist god and the conclusion that God created all things good, and therefore "there is no such entity in nature as 'evil' [*malum*]; 'evil' is merely a name for the privation of good."[14] Augustine says *malum* and clearly means the evils of the world ("distress, like fire, cold, wild animals, and so on"), privations which he regards as "deserved punishment" for sin.

The two great subjects for Augustine were the Problem of Evil and the nature of sin and the ineradicable human sin that came with the Fall. His answer was that evil was the consequence of, the punishment for, the one sin of our remotest ancestor, which, in John Milton's words, "Brought Death into the World, and all our woe" (*Paradise Lost*, 1.3)—disobedience, the Original Sin of Eve and Adam in Eden.[15] God made man in his own image, allowing man a share in Creation by giving him free will. Man abused this gift by disobedience followed by punishment (natural evil, moral evil), saved only through a miracle, God becoming man and suffering—taking upon himself evil—vicariously for Adam/man.[16]

Suffering-evil precedes and, with a monotheist god, gives rise to the concept of sin. The religious term in English for doing-evil is *sin*, from Old English *synn*—an offense against God; disobedience against a God who commands, exacts obedience, punishes, and rewards (as laid out in Genesis, Exodus, and Leviticus); willful violation of the divine order by presuming the pride of judgment, to choose whatever one wills for oneself. The concept of Old Testament sin (which Alter, in his translation of the epigraph for this section, renders "offend")[17] has its linguistic root in the Hebrew verb *chattat*, missing the mark or target (or *'awon*, a tortuous road, or *shagah*, losing one's way or—a synonym for sin—trespassing). The Greek word used to translate the Hebrew *chattat* was *hamartia*, also the missing of a mark with bow and arrow (see below, chapter 2).[18]

Paul Ricoeur has noted that sin "does not so much signify a harmful substance as a violated relation," a "personal relation to a god," what is in the Old Testament the violation of a Covenant, thus a lawbreaking, but of a religious bond, of a contract with the deity himself.[19] The Prophets introduced the senses of sin: Amos defined sin as essentially evil deeds, the exploitation of the poor and lowly, traffic in slaves, cruelty to enemies at war, and luxury among the great, and Hosea defined it as adultery; but Isaiah extended the betrayal of the conjugal bond to revolt against God (as we shall see, adultery becomes a form of treason), by which man becomes "unclean in lips and heart," and, as Ricoeur notes, "Henceforth sin is represented by the figure of violated suzerainty; sin is pride, arrogance, false greatness."[20] Sin is in fact transgression (L. *transgredior, transgressus,* to step beyond or across, i.e., trespass), and at this point evil and sin may overlap in the etymological sense of *yfel* as *up, over.*

After the covenant with Moses, sin was a violation of the Ten Commandments, the first five of which concerned man's relation to God (No. 5, Honor thy father and thy mother, is "as the Lord thy god hath commanded thee"). These sins are victimless crimes, not harmful to anyone except the deity; the second five involve harm done to human beings—Shalt not murder, steal, or commit adultery. All do have affect and effect, but they follow from the first Commandments, where injury is to God and the surrogates of God, and within that context they deal not with the victims so much as the authority of God, father, or husband and his property rights.

Sin is established on a level with holiness, not with ethics or morality, which has to do with the rights or wrongs of men and women. Sin, as opposed to immorality, is disobedience to God but in the specific form of the first five Commandments: Do not worship other gods and, in more general terms, Do not violate ritual. Mary Douglas's example is the need "to reconsecrate a church if blood has been shed in its precincts." "St. Thomas Aquinas explains that 'bloodshed' refers to voluntary injury leading to bloodshed, which implies sin, and that it is sin in a holy place which desecrates it, not defilement by bloodshed,"[21] that is, not the murder itself but the sacrilege, analogous to the capital crime of shedding blood in the royal presence.

Evil with a capital E is often called a sin; sin hypes evil. The book of Revelation ends with the image of evil as sin: "For without are dogs, and sorcerers, and whoremongers, and murderers, and idolaters, and whosoever loveth and maketh a lie." Aside from the last obscure phrase, of these only murderers would in my formulation qualify as evil.

The Seven Deadly Sins, a staple of medieval Christian theology, were lust, sloth [acedia], pride, anger, greed, gluttony, and envy.[22] The number seven was adapted by the Christians from Mithraism (an elitist religion that competed with early Christianity), which saw mystic significance in the number and applied it to soteriology. Ascending toward salvation, the dead soul rises through seven spheres, in each shedding one of the seven vices: the sun is pride, the moon envy, Mars anger, Mercury greed, Jupiter ambition, Venus lust, and Saturn sloth. The Christians (who also mystified the number seven in Revelation) leveled the hierarchy, labeled them sins, and defined them as fallings away from, preferring something else to, the deity.

Geoffrey Chaucer's Parson enunciated the orthodox Christian sense of sin in his sermon on the Seven Deadly Sins: "Sin is of two kinds; it is either venial or mortal sin. Verily, when man loves any creature more than he loves Jesus Christ our Creator, then is it mortal sin. And venial sin it is if a man love Jesus Christ less than he ought."[23] What then is sin? In Augustine's terms, referring in the *Confessions* to his theft of the pears, sin (*peccatum*) is "committed, while through an immoderate inclination towards these [pears], which are goods but of a lowest allow, better and higher are left out; even thou, our Lord God, thy Truth and thy Law" (II.v.81).

The rock bottom definition of evil has emerged from the contrast with sin, which is being interested in something more than (other than) God. If sin is about man's relationship to God, evil is about the relationships between men. Evil—moral evil—is of the secular social order, one's effect on the other (or folly, on oneself, or incidentally/accidentally on others). We may conclude that evil equals the pain and suffering consequent upon natural death or the act of murder or theft; and the cause of this evil in Judeo-Christian theology is sin. As these ideas become secularized, sin becomes associated with God's surrogates, with church dogmas and rituals, the priests.[24] It was Friedrich Nietzsche who drew the connection between sin and the priests' "exploitation of the sense of guilt": "the reinterpretation [by the priests, by religion] of suffering as feelings of guilt, fear, and punishment."[25] I have suggested that it was the suffering of evils that led to feelings of guilt and, through the creation of a god who punishes and rewards, to the concept of sin. Sin, as opposed to evil, is a fabrication, a myth that explains evil; but since it is essentially about our relation to a god, it is about obedience, worship, and offense. If you subtract sin you have evil without rewards and punishments; you have an interpersonal relationship, a subject of morality.

There is a real entity that corresponds to "sin": the sense of personal unworthiness, of guilt and "the darkness of the human heart." In William James's terms in *Varieties of Religious Experience* (1901), there is theological and there is existential sin: the latter, "the feeling of unwholeness, of moral imperfection, *of sin, to use the technical word*"; "the present incompleteness or wrongness, *the 'sin'* which [one] is eager to escape from." So there is sin in quotes and sin as "want and incompleteness," or mere self-centeredness; sin as loving something more than God is the equivalent of existential alienation. And "the dread of being human, vulnerable, alone in the universe, and doomed to die" (above, 5) is an "evil, *as made up of ills and sins in the plural*" (emphases added).[26]

Another mechanism for dealing with the experience of evil was the preemptive strike, to become the predator you fear; to blame not the deity but another human, a scapegoat for your misfortune, making misfortune into evildoing. As Alford postulates, "When we are faced with intolerable, uncontainable dread, the natural tendency is to identify with the persecutor, becoming the agent of doom, as the only way of controlling it. Evil is the attempt to inflict one's doom on others, becoming doom, rather than living subject to it. . . . *Doing* evil is an attempt to evacuate this experience [of dread] by inflicting it on others, making them feel dreadful by hurting them. Doing evil is an attempt to transform the terrible passivity and helplessness of suffering [evil] into activity . . . we defend ourselves against unbearable experience by projecting it into others."[27] Being active rather than passive helps to alleviate the dread of meaninglessness and victimhood. Suffering is coped with by attributing it to the malevolence of an other (whether human or divine), by demonizing the other, and by doing evil to the other (when not worshiping him).

Sometimes the inflicting of one's evil on others is justified by giving it the name of morality, and Alford, among others, has noted "how much evil has been done in the name of fighting evil" (67). The alternative was to accept the fact that suffering has no meaning and the world and everyone in it are indifferent—but that has proved an intolerable, or intolerably difficult, alternative.

Abomination

In the Levitical laws sin/offense takes the form of abomination. *Abomination* (L. *abominari*—adj. unspeakable, detestable, loathsome, vile, odious; —antonym, attractive, lovely) refers to unclean animals or foods, blemished sacrifices or priests, anomalous mixtures; to overturning, rebelling, fornication, harlotry, worshiping false gods; applied in the New Testament Revelation to the Antichrist (vs. the true Christ); in anthropology to taboos such as incest, cannibalism, patricide, fratricide, and matricide.

As opposed to holiness, which is oneness or purity, sin is impurity, a hybrid or mixture, something that does not conform to the system of classification (to the class to which it belongs), a confusion of things that should be separate or pure. In short, ambiguity, anomaly, and contradiction are to be abominated (according to Douglas, *to abominate* is simply to avoid). So worshiping a golden calf is an abomination (and worshiping an abomination) as well as a case of disobeying a Commandment. In the case of adultery, the sin is the violation of order and classification; not the rights and wrongs of husbands and brothers. As Tony Tanner puts it, "Lover, mistress, whore . . . are all at least recognized as having an existence and a definition that is not incompatible with the social terminology and economy within which they live. But the very word *adulteress* is close to a contradiction in a single term. *Adulteration* implies pollution, contamination, a 'base admixture,' a wrong combination"—in short, a Levitical abomination.[28] Of course, one can define adultery as an evil as well as a sin when it involves and affects innocent people, and some people regard abortion as murder. Though gay marriage remains victimless, in Levitical terms it is a sin because it is an abomination. Here is another example: "Pope Gregory I codified liturgical singing in the sixth century—hence Gregorian chant. As part of that codification, he forbade use of an augmented fourth, a dissonant, unresolved harmony that became known as *diabolis in musica.*"[29]

Besides *abomination* the Levitical terms describing sin are *defilement, profanation, uncleanness, iniquity, trespass,* and *unrighteousness.* Ricoeur has shown that "the stain is the first 'schema' of evil," by which he means sin-prior-to-evil.[30] The sacred object is defiled (or made impure) by a defiler, someone unsanctified or unqualified (Uzzah's well-meant steadying of the Ark of the Covenant) who thus creates a stain or blemish on the object—on the other, God, or the person stolen from or murdered; as opposed to defilement of oneself by the act of stealing or murdering. Impurity can also apply to either the subject or the object.

Referring to the distinction between sin and evil, Douglas points out how simple versus complex are the categories of pollution and wrong: "Pollution rules, by contrast with moral rules, are unequivocal. They do not depend on intention or a nice balancing of rights and duties. The only material question is whether a forbidden contact [a defilement] has taken place or not" (162). She adds that "the moral code by its very nature can never be reduced to something [as] simple, hard and fast" as the rules of sin/pollution. It should be evident by now that sin, more obviously than evil, is a cultural construct.

Corruption

Paul simply defined evil against good—like light vs. darkness, spirit vs. flesh, inner man vs. outer man—supporting the Manichees' belief in two independent and opposing realms, locked in cosmic conflict; so also Paul's belief in the hierarchy of the body metaphor—the "law of my members . . . warring against the law of my mind, and bringing me into captivity to the law of sin which is in my members" (Romans 7:23). This was the position Augustine originally took up from the Manichees but later repudiated by way of the late Platonists, monists who held that evil does not exist, as darkness or silence does not exist; darkness is simply the absence of light, silence of sound, and so evil of good.

Augustine formulated the monotheist doctrine of doing-evil as the corruption, in the sense of the negative, of good (*corruptus, putridus, parvus, impurus,* words that include seduction and bribery as well as putrefaction). He wishes, first, "to prevent anyone from supposing, when we speak of the apostate angels, that they could have another nature, derived, as it were, from some different origin, and not from God." Second follows the assumption that God "makes a good use even of [these] evil wills. Accordingly, He caused the devil (good by God's creation, wicked by his own will) to be cast down from his high position, and to become the mockery [i.e., parody] of His angels—that is, He caused his temptations to benefit those whom he wishes to injure by them."[31]

Augustine's term is *vitium,* a fault, failing, deformity, that is, corruption of a good. "To vitiate" is to contaminate or pollute, debase, weaken (another synonym for "defile" from Middle English *defilen,* to make dirty, to corrupt the pure). Vice is an evil in the sense that it vitiates or corrupts the good and brings evil (pain, suffering, punishment) only on the vicious. C. S. Lewis put the matter with characteristic pith: No one is *evil* for its own sake; even evil acts give some sort of satisfaction or one wouldn't do them ("money, or power, or safety" are in themselves good). Evil is "the pursuit of some good in the wrong way." So "badness is only spoiled goodness," a "corruption of goodness," as darkness is simply an absence of light. In the terms of his friend J. R. R. Tolkien, evil "mocks" and does not "make."[32]

But *to corrupt,* the turning of something from a sound to an unsound condition (a rotten vs. a ripe apple), is both intransitive and transitive: intransitive in that it is limited to the subject, a vice or a sin; transitive in that, as in Satan's corruption of Eve, it is passed on to another person, rendering her morally unsound, in effect defiling (or vitiating) her.

Concupiscence

> Sin, taking occasion by the commandment, wrought in me all manner of concupiscence.
>
> —*Paul,* Romans 7:8

> Just thus does the soul commit fornication [*fornicatur anima*], when she turns from thee, seeking those things without thee, which she can nowhere find pure and untainted, till she returns again to thee.
>
> —*Augustine,* Confessions, II.6:86–87

Augustine describes his famous sin in *The Confessions* as gratuitous: "Yet had I a desire to commit thievery; and did it, compelled neither by hunger nor poverty; but even through a cloyedness of well doing, and a pamperedness of iniquity. For I stole that, of which I had enough of mine own, and much better. Nor when I had done, cared I to enjoy the thing which I had stolen, but joying in the theft and sin itself." That last word, the "sin" (*peccatum*), opens up the truth behind the gratuitousness of Augustine's act: "And all this we did because we would go whither we should not. . . . Now, behold, let my heart tell thee, what it sought for there, that I should be thus evil [*malitia*] for nothing, having no other provocation to ill [*malus*], but ill itself [*malitia*]. It was foul [*foeda*], yet I loved it, I loved to undo myself, I loved mine own fault [*defectum*], not that for which I committed the fault, but even the very fault itself." He refers to his "base soul" (*turpis anima*) (II.4.78–79).[33] Augustine's interpretation of his eating of the pear was, in short, the same as Eve's eating her apple—disobedience, defiance, rebellion against authority; it was also, like Eve's, substituting a pear for an apple, an act of preferring the lesser to the greater good, the sin of preferring something else to God.[34] But, as he continues to think about it, he comes up with what was probably the psychologically true answer: He acted as part of a gang. He would not have done it if he had been alone in the orchard.

A page later in the *Confessions* Augustine admits the impossibility of an evil act that is gratuitous: "Would any man commit a murder upon no provocation, but only upon a delight he takes in murdering? Who will believe it?" He cites Catiline, who was "said to be so stupidly and savagely cruel for cruelty's sake [*gratuito potius malus atque crudelis*]." But even there a cause was assigned: "Lest (says himself) my hand or heart should grow unactive with idleness" (II.v.81–83).

For Augustine, sin was rebellion, which he dissociates from taste or gluttony but in general associates with concupiscence (*concupiscentia carnalis*). As a way of answering Pelagius's argument that God created men with the capacity for either good or evil (put simply, one can win salvation by being good, unassisted by divine grace), Augustine, searching for compelling arguments, found his unanswerable case in Adam's Fall, which must be attributed to man's inability to control his sexual organ. Man's will is helpless against his concupiscent body. From his Manichaean days Augustine carried the belief that Eve (according to Tertullian, "the Devil's doorway")[35] tempted Adam to go along with her sin by seducing him, her weapon his lust. As Augustine explained it (I am quoting Lewis), "Since the fall consisted in man's Disobedience to his superior, it was punished by man's loss of authority over his inferiors; that is, chiefly over his passions and his physical organism (*De Civ. Dei*, xiv, 5)."[36] In short, Eve's original sin was disobedience, and Adam's was the concupiscence God imposed on man (along with death) for Eve's first sin. The sin of lust is bad in excess, but officially (to Augustine) it is, of course, bad because it prefers and substitutes a human being for God.

In the Septuagint Pentateuch sexual intercourse was condemned as a way of seducing an Israelite into the worship of foreign gods (i.e., to fornicate with a Moabite woman) or participate in orgiastic fertility rituals, a concept foundational to the Christian sense of sin as being led to prefer, in a way obviously stronger than most others, someone else to God: "Neither shalt thou make marriages with them [aliens]; thy daughter thou shalt not give unto his son, nor his daughter shalt thou take unto thy son. For they will turn away thy son from following me, that they may serve other gods; so will the anger of the Lord be kindled against you, and destroy thee suddenly" (Deut. 7:3–4). Rebellion was the essential element—"the danger of men or women making love and reproducing with partners who worship gods other than the Lord," which will produce abominations. This was what Kathy L. Gaca in her scholarly work *The Making of Fornication* says was regarded as "religious treason" or "sexually fornicating rebellion," an act which, above all others, elicited God's wrath. Thus "religious treason" is the "sexual transgression of God's laws."[37]

Paul shared with the Old Testament prophets two metaphors for religious disobedience: sinning as "spiritual fornication" and as "spiritual adultery." As Gaca points out, to say that a dissident "fornicates with" or "whores around with" (etymologically cognate words in Greek) religion is simply a somewhat stronger metaphor than our contemporary "screw with," but the metaphor had significant consequences for religious thought: "If, for example, the poetic emblem were the sacrifice of animals to alien gods, then disobedience would be a symbolic act of 'slaughter' rather than 'fornication' against God. The poetic aura of wrongdoing would cling to animal sacrifice as a paradigmatic sign of the forbidden, not to acts of sexual intercourse, and early Christians might have turned out to be ardent vegetarians with a happy sex life. As things stand in biblical poetics, however, sexual fornication is the chosen one of all wickedness; the sin of sins is sexual" (165). To commit fornication or spiritual adultery against God (Numb. 15:34) meant any religious disobedience, both sexual and nonsexual. To "live in sin" refers specifically to sexual cohabitation outside the bonds of matrimony.

The sexual element in the forbidden, in defilement, was already evident in the taboos against incest, sodomy, and abortion. As Ricoeur notes, "The inflation of the sexual is characteristic of the whole system of defilement, so that an indissoluble complicity between sexuality and defilement seems to have been formed from time immemorial"; this as opposed to "the silence of the same ritual codes with regard to lying, theft, and sometimes homicide," the areas one might be more inclined to think of as transgressions between humans.[38]

The sexual abomination goes back to the association of purity and virginity, defilement and violation or rape or contamination; which, however, was capable of becoming the basis of morality, or what Ricoeur calls "an ethics of relations to others . . . , an ethics of justice and love, capable of turning back toward sexuality, of re-evaluating and transvaluing it" (29). Grounds for such a religion of morality were found in Jesus' teachings, which reduced the Ten Commandments to the Golden Rule, *Do unto others as you would that they do unto you* (Matt. 7:12), and *Love thy God and thy neighbor* (Matt. 22:37–39). Love was primary: "This is my commandment, that ye love one another, as I have loved you" (John 15:12), a subject developed by Paul in his Epistle to the Romans. Writers of the Enlightenment also noted Jesus' attack on the moneychangers in the Temple and on the Pharisees and priests, and Paul's arguments against the Old Testament Law. In the Gospel according to Matthew Jesus condemned the lawyers and Pharisees to hell for their hypocrisy, greed, and corruption of others (23:33). Jesus intruded between the Judeo- and the Christian traditions. And, of course, he defended the Woman taken in Adultery, keeping company with such as Mary Magdalen, the penitent harlot.

In the Pauline Epistles love is associated with *caritas* rather than *eros,* and what is uniquely Pauline is the belief that "sexual fornication is the most profound possible betrayal of God." Thus Paul "vilifies the Gentiles' sexual heritage as wicked and deadly fornication against God, and portrays his new order of virginity or marriage in the lord as the sole path to salvation and immortality."[39] (Even reproduction, the end of sexual intercourse in marriage, was only to further glorify God; Plato put it plainly when he noted that "one ought to beget children, for it is our duty to leave behind, for the gods, people to worship them."[40] Paul himself was not terribly concerned about reproductive sex because, like our contemporary chiliasts, he believed the Last Days to be at hand.)

As context, not only for Paul and Augustine but for their Puritan descendants, we might recall the violence and specificity—the prurience—of the Prophets' imagery of adultery, which returns in the polemics of Jerome and Tertullian: Hosea is speaking as both betrayed husband and as the Lord: "And now will I discover her lewdness in the sight of her lovers" (literally: "I shall strip her as naked as she was on the day of her birth. . . . I shall expose her sexual defilement to her male lovers" [2:10]); as is Ezekiel when he cries, "Thou . . . pouredst out thy fornications on every one that passed by . . . and hast opened thy feet to every one that passed by. . . . Thou hast committed fornication with the Egyptians thy neighbors, great of flesh; and hast increased thy whoredoms, to provoke me to anger" (literally: "You offered yourself freely to every passer-by. . . . You spread your legs for any man who came along. . . . You committed fornication with well-hung Egyptians who copulated with you. In many ways you fornicated so as to provoke me" [16:15, 25–26]).[41] The references are to a community or country as a body politic, which in the Pauline Epistles becomes the metaphor of "the members of Christ" that can be corrupted into "the members of a harlot," meaning: "Now the body is not for fornication, but for the Lord; and the lord for the body" (1 Cor. 6:15, 13).

Thomas Aquinas's example is based on the sick body: the bad (or crippled or deformed) leg equals evil, as opposed to the act of limping, which equals sin;[42] deformity is evil, a deformed act is sin. Man's inability to control his sexual organ is based on the evil that follows from the Original Sin, and his lust in action is the sin. The evil is concupiscence and the sin is fornication. So *evil,* distinct from and contrasted with *sin,* remains a word that refers to death and disease, and so to the innate depravity that resulted from Original Sin. Sin is first anterior, as the cause of evil, and then posterior as the consequence; or, in my earlier more secular formulation, evil first, then the concept of sin becomes attached to the fact of evil by religious belief.

Demonology

In the Old Testament evil was the province of God: "Since God was the undisputed master of creation, it was assumed that every occurrence was through his explicit command." Although it was sometimes carried out "through the mediation of supernatural beings who afflict, deceive, bring harm, and do evil in general at God's command" (1 Sam. 16:14; 1 Kings 22:19–23; Job 1:12; Ps. 78:49), in the New Testament these figures were detached from God and lodged in a figure called the "Evil One" (Eph. 6:16; 1 John 2:13–14).[43]

"Satan," the original sinner, in Hebrew meant simply "adversary"—one who opposes or obstructs. The term *satan* evolved from an agent of God to his opponent (as, by contrast, an angel was a messenger). Initially God's agent was not malevolent, though sometimes dispatched by God to block human plans and desires. In 2 Samuel and 1 Chronicles he visited a plague on Israel, presumably at God's command, to punish David's sin.[44] In Numbers 22 he harassed Balaam; in Job he began as a secret intelligence officer, the "king's eye and ear," but became a tempter—of Job and, in one possible interpretation, of God himself: tempting Job to curse God, but also leading God to impose the many evils on Job. Later he tempts King Saul (1 Sam.) and Ahab (2 Chron.).

In Zechariah 3:1–2, he speaks for the disaffected, and unsuccessful, party against another party of Israelites. In Isaiah 14:12–15 the angel Lucifer, with whom Satan will be associated, makes his first appearance:

> How art thou fallen from heaven, O Lucifer, son of the morn-
> ing! How art thou cut down to the ground, which didst weaken
> the nations! For thou hast said in thine heart, I will ascend into
> heaven, I will exalt my throne above the stars of God: I will sit
> also upon the mount of the congregation, in the sides of the
> north: I will ascend above the heights of the clouds; I will be
> like the Most High. Yet thou shalt be brought down to hell,
> to the sides of the pit.

Presumably basing the figure on the king of Babylon in his splendor and in his fall,[45] Isaiah made Lucifer a "bright star," an angelic power with associations of beauty but swollen with pride and arrogance, who fell from heaven. Created during the Babylonian Captivity from the Persian Ahriman ("Evil Spirit"), a dualistic figure of evil, this Lucifer was neverthe-less subordinated and inferior to the "good" deity. This is the Lucifer that Augustine and Milton use to figure the idea of evil not independent of good—as spoiled goodness—and therefore a perversion or a corruption, Satan the "fallen angel" or angel perverted.

Around the time of Christ, however, he began to recover his dualist roots, becoming God's antagonist, his enemy, even his rival, introduced by such splinter groups as the Essenes into tales of the sons of light battling the sons of darkness. People are now accused of having been seduced by the power of evil, whom they name—Satan, Beelzebub, Semihazah, Azazel, Belial, and the Prince of Darkness; in other words, they are turning to, sinning with, false gods. Satan is the most dangerous, being one of God's angels—superhuman beings with superior qualities and insider status. The Greek *satanas* has become an enemy of God by Revelation (12:9), where the forms attributed to him—Rahab, Leviathan, and the Red Dragon—are adapted from animalistic, monstrous creatures of the Old Testament.

The connection with the glamorous Lucifer was made by Christ's words (Luke 10:18) to Satan: "I beheld Satan as lightning fall from heaven" and by Paul's warning in 2 Corinthians against false prophets: "Satan himself masquerades as an angel of light" (11:14). Satan had become associated with false-seeming, beauty concealing deceit, treachery, betrayal, treason—a figure attached by Judaism to idolaters, by the Gospels to the Jews, and by the Christians to heretics and apostates: all sinners.

The word *devil* derives from the Greek *diabolos* (accuser): Close to the sense of Satan, derived from *dia-ballein,* to tear apart, it refers to one who throws something across one's path; to the endeavor to break the bonds between others and "set them at variance," bonds of communion between God and man, and the bonds of truth and love between men; to which common usage adds the special idea of "setting at variance *by slander*" or perjury.[46] In the New Testament the devil (in the King James Version of 1611 he is called Satan) appears as a tempter of Jesus and prince or ruler of the "demons" (Greek *daimon* or *daimonion*). He tempts Jesus immediately after his Baptism with the sins of pride and earthly power; he reappears in the legalist Pharisees, Scribes, and priests and, above all, in the betrayer of God, Judas. The latter, of course, leads to the final evil, the crucifixion. The devil's appearance in these stories is suggestive of Manichaeism, but, in fact, he is presented as offering only a preliminary skirmish, which will lead up to the final ones in Revelation.

In the Gospels the devil is internalized; the *forces* of evil (as consequent upon sin) are shown to act through *certain people* to effect violent destructions of someone—as with Judas/Jesus. Jesus' ethical function in the Gospels is to cast out demons that possess (energize) men, to heal the sick, and to proclaim the coming of God's kingdom. In the stories of his miracles there is precedent for the idea of being possessed by demons (or madness, e.g., Matt. 12:24–26); and in the Epistles Paul tells us that Satan will tempt us to fornication (1 Cor. 7:2–6). Tempting to fornication—which expands in Revelation into the rule of the Whore of Babylon—is of course "sexual rebellion" and "rebellious sexual fornication." Following the demonizing of Satan-Lucifer in the Gospels (especially John), Revelation presented a demonology, *cosmic* as opposed to mere earthly forces, at war with an angelology. The idea emerges that there are incarnations of influence toward sin and evil actions in the world, as in the Seven Deadly Sins who tempt people, taking allegorical form or embodied, on the one hand in heretics, on the other in witches and sorcerers. These helpers of Satan are fiends—Anglo-Saxon *féund,* the devil or any demon—a person of diabolical wickedness, especially with cruelty or excessive cruelty ("fiendish tortures")—a term applied to Grendel and his mother.

There are those who read the stories of the Fall and the devil literally (from the Genesis serpent to Job to Isaiah and Revelation); then there are those, from Origen on, later from the Renaissance and then the Enlightenment, who interpreted the stories symbolically. As Denis de Rougement put it in *The Devil's Share,* "A myth is a story which describes and illustrates, in dramatized form, certain deep structures of reality."[47] Another way of putting it is to say that the anthropomorphic, the allegorical and symbolic figure—the surface meaning—expresses truths: Satan is a fallen angel, therefore evil is a corruption or perversion of good; a "devil" is in us, or is external to us—versions of (aspects of) the devil that range from deeply evil to comic. These describe realities. The same is true of the most basic of all problems, the literal reading of an anthropomorphic God, from which most disagreements of the holy texts derive. The problem is with the literal-minded, the Inquisitors and Puritans who punished in the name of the myth and ignored the reality.

Sin Up, Evil Down

When he introduces the example of Catiline, Augustine is confusing sin and evil—his stealing pears, which is more between him and God than between him and the owner of the orchard, with Catiline's cruelty to his subjects. He was committing an offense to God but not an injury. It is hard to think of an injury (in the sense of pain, cruelty), as opposed to a wrongdoing, directed upward from low to high, or at any rate from a position of less power to one of more: Was Augustine's stealing a pear an infliction of pain on the property owner? Does one injure (inflict an evil upon) the person from whom one steals? Is it not possible that evil is ordinarily downward directed, whether (as in the Problem of Evil) from God the creator or from men in power—or simply armed, empowered men—against people without power, ultimately the innocent and powerless, innocents, children, animals—all the objects of evil; while sin is always *lèse-majesté* or high treason (directed, in John Bunyan's term, "Godward"). This is confirmed by Dante's punishment of sinners, the worst of whom are traitors and betrayers of their masters. Evils are imposed usually downward as the consequence of sin, primarily of the upward-directed treason. The worst evildoer in the Torah, according to the rabbinical scholars, was Amalek, who fought the Israelite army by killing the weak and exhausted stragglers (Exod. 17:8–16; Deut. 25:17–18).

There are, of course, instances of the powerless killing the powerful, but the sense of "evil" does not as often adhere; part of the evil seems to include the idea of power exerted on the powerless—the reverse is a turning of tables which, in some cases, could be regarded as justice—until, of course, the excess carries wrongdoing by humiliation and torture to the level of undeniable evil. Or take the case of David and Goliath, in which evil in the sense of injury goes the other way, upward to the giant Philistine; evil becomes at least potentially a matter of perspective: David and Goliath seen from the perspective of the Israelites or of the Philistines.

In short, evil as harm was originally imposed by God on Adam and Eve—who sinned against him; and so while harm can be done horizontally, person to person, it tends to become evil or "evil" when it is done from an agent with power, from above, whether that agent be, as originally, God, or his vicegerent the monarch or any person with power over other people. The response of these injured people to such evil is rebellion, or treason, or in God's terms *sin*. Evil(s) originate with God, and it can be said that humans who do harm so great as to qualify for the term *evil* are usually attempting to play God. Thus not only a Hitler or Stalin or Pol Pot but the priest's power, as God's surrogate, over an altar boy. Lord Acton's *bon mot* was that power corrupts, absolute power corrupts absolutely: *Evil* tends to apply most unequivocally to power plus terror or cruelty. In any case, power and authority are of primary importance to the question of evil as well as sin, only operating in different directions—and by implication

the supreme duty of power and authority, which should be the minimiza-
tion of suffering, is often its maximization.[48]

3. WRONGDOING

The Law: Treason and Original Sin

I have polarized sin and evil as god-oriented and man-oriented. But we
need another term such as *wrongdoing* or *wickedness* or *crime*.[49] *Wrong*,
from the Middle English, is "not in accordance with law, morality, or
with people's sense of fairness, justice, and what is acceptable behavior"
(*OED*). Wrong is what is not right or proper according to a code, standard,
or convention (i.e., law). In the legal discourse of William Blackstone's
Commentaries on the Laws of England (1765–69) a wrong is a crime, an act
or omission forbidden by law and punishable upon conviction. Wrongs
(private or public—robbery, murder, or treason) are "crimes" which involve "injury": "In all cases the crime includes an injury" (4.1.5). *Injury*
is defined as an act that damages or hurts. Wrongs are divided into (1)
misdemeanor—a crime less than a felony; (2) *felony*—an offense—theft,
murder—which occasions a total forfeiture of either lands or goods, at the
common law, and to which capital or other punishment may be added,
according to the degree of guilt; and (3) *treason*—overthrow of the constituted government, killing the sovereign.

"Law courts," writes Lance Morrow, "cannot judge good and evil; they
must deal with lawful and unlawful, right and wrong":

> A crucial difference between wrong and evil is that people are
> implicitly in charge of the universe in which rights and wrongs
> are discussed; people have systems of laws to right wrongs.
> But evil implies a different universe, controlled by extra-human
> forces. Wrong is a human offense that suggests reparation is
> possible and deserved. Wrong is not mysterious. Evil suggests
> a mysterious force that may be in business for itself and may
> exploit human agency as part of a larger cosmic conflict—
> between good and evil, between God and Satan.
>
> Evil has the dark old majesty, and belongs to the realm of
> the sacred. "Wrong" is a utilitarian word employed in the pro-
> fane transactions of human life.[50]

Morrow reflects the confusion between evil and sin, which may be a sense of evil that, in order to raise itself above wrongdoing, draws on the discourse of sin; which is precisely what Blackstone does, basing his (and Englishmen's) concept of law on their concept of religion, thereby mystifying the law, especially as it applies to the monarch.

Blackstone is referring to natural evil when he writes of "the infirmities of the best among us, the vices and ungovernable passions of others, the instability of all human affairs, and the numberless unforeseen events, which the compass of a day may bring forth"; these natural evils he opposes to moral evil, those acts "which the laws of our country have forbidden, and the deplorable consequences [i.e., evils] to which a wilful disobedience may expose us" (4.1.2). The equivalent of natural and moral evil reappears in his distinction between *mala prohibita* and *mala in se*—wrong in "municipal law" versus the "law of nature."[51] The term *evil* itself is first introduced as punishment, "the evils or inconveniences [pain, suffering, and death] consequent upon crimes and misdemesnors . . . in consequence of disobedience or misbehaviour in those, to regulate whose conduct such laws were respectively made" (4.1.7), as in Original Sin.[52] The next appearance of the word applies it to a wrong, but specifically to treason (4:1.15).

There are distinctions between qualities of a crime, elevating the status of the crime in the direction of evil: It is worse for a servant to rob his master than for a stranger—"if a servant kills his master, it is a species of treason," as opposed to mere murder (16). Punishment also reflects the degree of the crime, and this is based on the Old Testament *lex talionis*—an eye for an eye—but supplemented by Solon's stipulation that "he who struck out the eye of a one-eyed man, should lose both his own in return." The death of a "needy decrepit assassin" is inadequate punishment for "the murder of a nobleman in the bloom of his youth, and full enjoyment of his friends, his honours, and his fortune" and calls for "the highest penalty the law can inflict" (13). The greater the object of an injury, the greater the punishment—above all in the case of the monarch. Thus for treason (a crime "the most destructive to the public safety and happiness" [16]), the penalty is symbolic: beheading or being hanged, drawn, quartered (punishing all the parts of the offending body); plus attainder, by which the guilt (as with Original Sin) is transmitted to all the sinner's descendants.

To summarize, sin is basically disobedience, and the analogy (as the Commandment's equation of God and father and mother suggests) extends down from God to civil authority, to the death of the king; in English law to the distinction between the Court of King's Bench, which deals with crimes against monarch or state, and the Court of Common Pleas, which handles crimes between subjects (the Court of Chancery handles cases of conscience). This is essentially the distinction I have established between sin and evil. There is theological evil, which is largely *sin*—mortal sin being one that leads to damnation, and so the evil of burning eternally; then there is evil as wrongdoing; and finally "evil," or evil to the nth degree, which subsumes, or rather appropriates, the aura of sin—a melodramatic or Satanic term, carrying some of the religious associations, not only of sin but of abomination and uncleanliness and taboo.

Murder is to treason as evil is to sin—rebellion against the monarch threatens civil order as rebellion against God or the church threatens religious order—the royal or religious hierarchy. In treason and heresy the concepts of sin and evil join, for the sin has the gravest consequences—the evils of disorder, murder, patricide, etc. The distinction I have noted is between sin and evil (vs. holiness and goodness), law (sacred and secular) and morality. Cain committed murder, but one suspects he was punished according to the law of high treason for killing God's surrogate, Abel, whose sacrifice was more acceptable than his.

Wrongdoing, we might conclude, becomes evil when it goes so far as to seriously hurt another person—literally inflict "evils" upon another human; manslaughter (killing under provocation, unpremeditated) becomes murder (premeditated, deliberate and wholly inexcusable), and murder becomes (to use Senator Jacob Javits's words, applied to the Holocaust) "murder and more."[53] An example is the legal term *moral turpitude,* which refers to what is also called *aggravated,* added to the offense.[54] The Latin verb *turpo* is to make ugly, defile, pollute, and disfigure (recall Augustine's *turpis anima,* "base soul"); the noun *turpitudo* designates ugliness, foulness, and baseness (related to *infamis,* infamy). Moral turpitude designates something beyond the law or crime: If one were convicted of murder, the aggravated aspect, which the judge would take into consideration in sentencing him, would be, for example, gratuitous cruelty. In the law dictionaries the sense of moral turpitude is dependent on the customs of local society: In some societies consensual sex between males would be moral turpitude; in others only pederasty would qualify. Nevertheless, as with the definition of *morals,* the definition of *turpitude* returns us to custom and the "evil" that is in the eye of the beholder.

The *OED* cites from 1659: "Those which have a natural turpitude and indispensable sinfulnesse in them!"[55] *Sin* itself is another such addition in that it carries the connotations of the *ungodly* and of abomination—and "sin," like "moral turpitude," is factitious, when examined signifying only to religious believers of a certain stamp. One example is in works like Hogarth's *Harlot's Progress* and Dickens's *Oliver Twist,* in which evil is done by someone who precisely does not break the laws but represents them (as well as God's commandments, equating religion and law).

Cruel and unusual is another term that adds to an act of wrongdoing, in this case emphasizing an aspect that is inseparable from "Evil."[56] *Cruel and unusual,* like *moral turpitude,* signifies an excess, but also an act not covered by a legal statute; it applies, as in Hogarth's *Stages of Cruelty,* to the sense of excess in both the crime and the law's brutal punishment.

Sin Internal, Evil External

Sin is an act of a defective will; there are what Aquinas calls the "interior act" and the "exterior act," which he believes are both necessary for the commission of a sin. Intention is a consideration in the legal judgment of a wrong: According to Blackstone, it "requires more obstinacy in wickedness to *perpetrate* an unlawful action, than barely to *entertain the thought*"; a crime is alleviated by "the violence of passion, or temptation . . . as theft, in case of hunger" as opposed to sheer avarice—a "cool deliberate motive." In the law, murders "which consist *merely* in the intention, and are not yet carried into act" are condemned only as "conspiracy," but there is one exception: "imagining the king's death"—"in case of a treasonable conspiracy, the object whereof is the king's majesty, the bare intention will deserve the highest degree of severity: not because the intention is equivalent to the act itself; but because the greatest rigour is no more than adequate to a reasonable purpose of the heart, and there is no greater left to inflect upon the actual execution itself" (4:1.15).

In Matthew 5:27–28 Jesus, in the Sermon on the Mount, notes of the Commandment "Thou shalt not commit adultery," "But I say unto you, That whosoever looketh on a woman to lust after her hath committed adultery with her already in his heart." He has, in a sense, only updated or clarified Moses' God's "covet thy neighbor's wife," but it proved significant that he applied the internalizing to lust, that most fraught of sins.

Augustine's analysis of his "gratuitous" sin of stealing pears was an internalizing, a moving back from a trivial action to a serious motive. The Augustinian sense of sin was based on the insight that one's relationship with God is finally internal; replacing Manichaeism, he internalized God as conscience, the devil as sin and feelings of guilt, and this was the seed of the Protestant Reformation and its emphasis on internal sin, that is, one's personal relationship with the deity.

In Romans Paul internalized sin as ungodliness and unrighteousness, an in-turning against nature and (at least as interpreted by the Protestant reformers) unsalvageable by works: since any work is marred by sin, sin is an inclination to *unrighteousness*—"there is none that doeth good, no, not one" (Rom. 3:12)—words interpreted by Augustine, later by Martin Luther and John Calvin, to mean that no Commandments can be properly kept. One can roughly know when he has committed a crime or a wrong of some kind to his fellow men, but one's relation with God is more mysterious, as Luther realized when he returned to Romans and justification by faith only. Sin is, it is true, an internalizing of evil; its effect is to make you look inward to examine your motives, to judge your thoughts in terms of the Seven Deadly Sins: They do have external manifestations (active or passive—lust in the sexual act, gluttony in obesity, illness, and death), but they are essentially internal; these thoughts are on the cusp of sin and evil, the inner states that can be manifested in evil deeds or misfortunes, both characterized by pain and suffering, to others or to oneself.

T. S. Eliot summed up the issue of sin and evil, or "evil" and evil, for the modern period when he noted that Ezra Pound's Hell in his *Cantos* "is a Hell for the *other people,* the people we read about in the newspapers, not for oneself and one's friends."[57] Elsewhere he writes,

> One reason why the lot of the secular reformer or revolutionist
> seems to me to be the easier is this: that for the most part he
> conceives of the evils of the world as something external to
> himself. They are thought of either as completely impersonal,
> so that there is nothing to alter but machinery; or if there is evil
> *incarnate,* it is always incarnate in the *other people*—a class, a

race, the politicians, the bankers, the armament makers, and
so forth—never in oneself."[58]

Eliot is describing the tradition I ascribe to Hogarth, Henry Fielding, and
Dickens that sets sin against true evil, which is in the destructive force
of social structures. Eliot represents the contrary tradition that demonizes and internalizes sin, reducing evil to banal crimes. Eliot reverses my
hypothesis, which is that sin is used to hype evil; he argues that sin *is* evil
with a capital E.

Original Sin was, in Jackson Lears's words, "a tendency toward es-
trangement from all creation—rooted in every human soul, which could
only be transcended with the aid of divine grace, another way of putting
the definition of sin as preferring something to God."[59] The alternative to
this inward turning was "the notion that evil is a palpable entity outside
the self"—whether a Manichaean devil or, with the organized Church,
witches or Jews—or, with most of the writers with whom we shall be
concerned, symbols or elements of society, ascending to and including
God himself.

There are stories in which the evil is internal, coming from inside,
as in sin or in the Commandments' "covet" or Jesus' "thoughts" (vs. the
act) of desiring your neighbor's wife; it remains between you and God
(or your conscience) rather than, if in action, between you and another
human. Then there are stories in which evil comes from outside, and
these begin with the evils of the Fall and the book of Job.[60] Satan's first
test—or temptation—gets God to agree to impose suffering that covers
everything except Job's person: but Job will not sin, will not curse God;
then Satan asks God to let him try Job's person as well. Job still will not
curse God but insists he did no wrong and asks for God to admit that
"maybe there's such a thing as innocent suffering, maybe suffering does
not result [the common assumption] solely from divine retribution for
evil."[61] God's response, out of the whirlwind—"Where were *you* when
I laid the foundation of the earth? . . . When the morning stars sang together and all the heavenly beings shouted for joy?" (38:4, 7)—contrasts
his power to Job's: "Can *you* draw out Leviathan with a fishhook? . . . Who
determined its [the earth's] measurements—surely you know!" (41:1; 38:5).
As Augustine or Calvin would have answered, God's irony draws Job's attention to the unbridgeable chasm between divine and human. There is

no way a human can comprehend God's ways: "Therefore have I uttered that I understood not; things too wonderful for me, which I knew not" (42:3). We are left to conclude that Job's "sin," his hubris, retrospectively explains the "evil" God visits upon him.

God punishes Job with evils (destroys his properties, kills his children, covers his body with boils)—why? Job has not, like Eve, committed a sin. Only to respond to Satan's test (or temptation or jest) or, since he must, at least in the Christian ontology, control Satan, to "test" Job as he had tested Abraham? It is possible to see the bet with Satan as a trivial whim; the return of Job's fortune and a new generation of children hardly compensate for the losses. Evil can be interpreted as what was done to Job by Satan; or what was done to him by God, projecting the two senses of *evil*, as suffering and doing, and two senses of God, as the God who *permitted* the evil and the God who *caused* it, who shows Job to be a "sinner."

My point is that the tradition of evil/sin depends upon the Problem of Evil, evil as death and suffering at the hands of a legal power, which traces its power back from the local magistrate to the king and to God, internalized as an Original Sin, as the intention to do evil to others, as turning away from God to some other, as desiring abominations, as pride or envy or the other "sins" before being externalized in actions, gestures, or attire. But as in Job, external evil originates in God and the Problem of Evil—interpretable either as a contest between the Manichaean forces of good and evil or simply as a punishment by God; and so later by the ruling order in Hogarth's or Dickens's London, the vampires of nineteenth-century horror fiction, ultimately aliens from outer space.

We keep coming back to the Problem of Evil and so, in the terms of theology (of religious belief), to the responsibility of God. Original Sin was translated into the more secular concept of innate depravity, which Thomas Hobbes could have accepted—the idea that people are basically evil; not that they are suffering evils for Adam's sin but that they are, as Adam apparently was, basically evil. Though in fact since Adam's problem was sin, his punishment evil, we have to say that innate depravity, theologically understood, is sin—problems about man's relation to God—and not evil.

Sin and Morality

> The terror of society, which is the basis of morals, the terror of God,
> which is the secret of religion—these are the two things that govern
> us. And yet—
>
> —*Lord Henry Wotton, in Oscar Wilde,* The Picture of Dorian Gray

To think that your good and bad deeds will be rewarded or punished in the
afterlife is soteriology, the theology of salvation and sin. To do good out of
a sense of what is (or is deemed by custom or conscience) right or wrong
is morality. As we have seen, the category of sin is often appropriated for
the term *morality*, which already has about it the associations of custom
(*autre temps, autres moeurs*).

Etymologically, *morality* and *morals* (L. *moralis*) refer to the study of
right conduct, but right conduct based on custom, manners, usage, and
habit—in practice, customs of the country. As J. B. Schneewind summa-
rizes Aquinas, "The moral virtues, Aquinas holds, are habits enabling us
to control the passions and desires that tend to lead us away from our true
good."[62] Hobbes's sense of custom and manners as a social contract—his
assumption that "there are no authentical doctrines concerning right and
wrong, good and evil, besides the constituted laws in each realm and government"—would seem to place ethics/morality on a level with religion
and law, which are also sets of mutually accepted customs. Morality as
custom in practice is essentially the law.

Cicero's *On the Good Life* laid out the divisions of moral goodness:
the ability to distinguish truth from falsity and to understand the relationship between one phenomenon and another; the ability to restrain the
passions; and finally to behave considerately and understandingly in our
associations with other people.[63] Morality, as contrasted with religion,
deals with human-to-human relationships, just as the Court of Common
Pleas relates to the Court of King's Bench. (A more precise equivalent of
religion is perhaps "moralism," or the habit or practice of moralizing.) But
there is a further distinction—between canon law (Roman law, still taught
in the eighteenth century at Oxbridge), based on a priori codification, and
common law, based on precedent, custom drawing on experience in England (taught in London in the Inns of Court). The first was theoretical,
the second practical.

Luther and Calvin, the theologians closest to the Anglo-American tradition, followed Augustine in distinguishing the City of God from the City of Man—two kinds of rule, spiritual and secular, divine and earthly, corresponding to the two tablets of the Law (re God and re man), which correspond to the two realms of sin and evil. The second tablet, though negative in its commandments except for "Honor thy father and thy mother," was interpreted to include Jesus' "Love thy neighbor as thyself." The two governances were defined by Luther as "the spiritual, which by the Holy Spirit under Christ makes Christians and pious people, and the secular, which restrains the unchristian and wicked so that they must needs keep the peace outwardly, even against their will. . . . [T]hese two kingdoms must be sharply distinguished, and both be permitted to remain; the one to produce piety, the other to bring about *external* peace and prevent *evil deeds; neither is sufficient *in the world* without the other."[64] The key words are italicized: Piety is internal; this, which involves sin and salvation, is what matters. Morality keeps "external peace" and "prevent[s] evil deeds . . . in the world." In Schneewind's words, "For both Luther and Calvin, then, morality as such concerns human life on earth. It extends no further" (36).

So in *Pilgrim's Progress* Bunyan has the town of Morality inhabited by Mr. Legality, associating the law with good and bad deeds, dissociating the law from faith, and internalizing what mattered—sin. Religion and morality share an origin in law (in, for example, the laws of Leviticus) and share such specific abominations as fornication, sodomy, and abortion, which have been called but are not moral values, as opposed to genuine moral values—issues of right and wrong, good and evil. In his satire of Bunyanesque theology, *The Confessions of a Justified Sinner,* James Hogg has the evil Parson Wringhim sum up a good man, John Barnet: "A morally good man John is, but very little of the leaven of true righteousness, which is faith, within. I am afraid old Barnet, with all his stock of morality, will be a cast-away."[65]

The philosophical placement of morality in relation to theodicy and the Problem of Evil was based on the principle of voluntarism: in Luther's words, "What God wills is not right because he ought or was bound so to will; on the contrary, what takes place must be right, because he so wills." "It is not for us to inquire into these mysteries, but to adore them."[66]

"It is agreed," wrote G. W. Leibniz of voluntarism at the end of the seventeenth century, "that whatever God wills is good and just. But there remains the question whether [1] it is good and just because God wills it or whether [2] God wills it because it is good and just."[67] We cannot ask why God has willed as he has: to ask that is to suppose something higher than God, which Calvin and Job took to be absurd. To take this position is to "destroy the justice of God. For why praise him because he acts according to justice, if the notion of justice in his case, adds nothing to that of action?"[68] Voluntarism was a case of defining moral concepts in terms of nonmoral ones, evil in terms of sin: what the gods want, what the Christian God commands, which with time becomes, for example, what evolution leads to.

Antivoluntarists sought to show how we can be sure that morality— thus an external rule—applies both to God and to humans. Is God essential to morality or is morality wholly independent of God—as would appear, intuitively, to be the case—because *his judgment* appears to be at odds with the Christian moral teachings that centered on love. Antivoluntarists attacked what they took to be a degrading view of human beings, based on the idea that God is a tyrant whose commands seem wholly arbitrary because they do not have to be guided by independent standards of goodness or rightness: If God ruled as a despot, why might not earthly rulers do the same?

In the seventeenth and eighteenth centuries two conceptions of morality still coexisted—morality as obedience and morality as self-governance. Obedience meant, first, obedience to God and, second, to civic authority, both based on the principle of punishments and in some cases rewards. Self-governance meant that "we may each rightly claim to direct our own actions without interference from the state, the church, the neighbors, or those claiming to be better or wiser than we are."[69] Most claims of self-governance in our examples stop with state and church, though state or church usually absorbed the others—morality as obedience to a social elite. Like voluntarism, self-governance found its authority, divine and secular, in the moral teachings of Christianity and in the Renaissance idea of human dignity. The extreme position—caused by religious dissension and the desire for wider participation in politics and governance—was that all ties between religion and morality be severed.

Niccolò Machiavelli's secularized discourse was of the just and unjust, honorable and disgraceful, *virtù* and corruption. For Michel de Montaigne evil was the torture and killing that followed from the religious wars of the sixteenth century, the burning of people said to be witches, and so (the cause of such actions) perjury. For Hobbes, who lived through the English Civil Wars, the word *evil* referred to what he had experienced: "Now, all such calamities as may be avoided by human industry, arise from war, but chiefly from civil war."[70] And it was civil war and chaos that represented evil to John Dryden and Jonathan Swift, who were following the example of Virgil and Horace, who had lived through the Roman Civil Wars. For Swift evil(s) are the consequence of sin and heresy (Gk. root, *hairetica,* simply one who chooses)—the evils are civil dissension and war.

In the recent words of Lears (to which I have already referred), "The Augustinian strain of piety dissolved the comforting delusion that evil could be situated outside the self." Reacting against the Reformation's emphasis on faith over works, belief over morality, soteriology and heaven over "a righteous community on earth," the Enlightenment rationalists have dominated, according to Lears, too much of modern Christianity by replacing the sense of sin with the efficacy of works and a religion of piety with one of mere morality. And so, weakening the sense of Original Sin, moving evil ever outward from the self, we attribute it to "a poor environment or a weak character, which [the obvious corollary] could be strengthened or improved." Thus Lears, who finds it a deplorable situation to be more interested in one's fellow man than in one's soul, believes that "Protestant theology gave way to Protestant ethics, which in turn became barely distinguishable from bourgeois conformity and respectability—a self-satisfied moralism that has shaped our public discourse down to the present, though it would have appalled Augustine." The consequence is that sin is punished, evil rewarded—social progress is secondary to simple soul conversion (based on *sola fide* and *sola scriptura*), which did little to help the wretched of the world.

The Part and the Whole: Sin and Evil Reconciled?

A "middle way," exemplified by the Anglican church (the historic capaciousness of the religion of Richard Hooker and Swift), sees morality as consisting of three aspects, (1) decent relations between people—"fair play and harmony between individuals,"—mutual "kindness"—which we would call morality; (2) the same harmony within the individual, internal as opposed to external or social relations, which we can call ethics;[71] and, finally, (3) between man and God, which is religion. The Christian believes that without (2), (1) is impossible—(3) is essential *because* one is not one's own property but the Creator's; also because (1) is momentary and temporary (covering seventy or eighty years only), whereas (2) and (3) involve the assumption that one is going to live forever—the result being "a creature that is in harmony with God, and with other creatures, and with itself."[72] This formulation makes sense in that it offers a choice: We can take (3) or leave it.

Is it possible then to reconcile sin and evil—God-directed and human-directed, divine and worldly, internal and external phenomena? Sin and evil might be reconciled if (3) God is regarded as simply the good, the whole of Creation against whom one "rebels" when one prefers something else, some part to the whole, and acts upon one's preference. In the words of Leopold Sabourin, S. J., though sin is "an offense against God," one can also sin "by injuring others (or themselves), since the person injured is also an object of divine providence and protection."[73] In Aquinas's rationalist terms, sin is what "is discordant with [i.e., equated with] the due rule of reason or of the law of God,"[74] which need not be different.

Reinhold Niebuhr attempted to recover sin for the evil twentieth century by making the terms interchangeable: "Evil is always the assertion of some self-interest without regard to the whole." This is an evil that can be brought into line with the concept of sin if God is replaced by *some other*—the world, other men, Christ's "Golden Rule," or Immanuel Kant's "categorical imperative."[75] The last two are examples of morality as self-governance, which would interpret sin as self-interest that excludes everything from God (sin) to his creatures and the whole of which this man is only a part (evil). Thus Jesus' two laws, "Love thy God" and "Love thy neighbor as thyself," can be taken to mean "Do not prefer anything else (such as thyself) to God or to thy neighbor."

But if we mean by the whole God's creation, we are broaching pantheism; and if we mean God's creatures, we must recall Blaise Pascal: "'Granted that,' they say, 'let us delight in creatures.' It is a second best. But if there were a God to love they would not have reached this conclusion."[76] For many rigorist Christians the world of morality is an infinitely second best to the world of grace.

If we substitute for God the nation-state, then the evil, more closely equivalent to sin, becomes, as we have seen, treason; if ideology, then deviation. The sense of *sin* in the twentieth century was alienation of the part from the whole (the iconic image being Edvard Munch's *The Scream*), the whole retaining associations of the divine but less and less an anthropomorphic god. But then the world from which one is alienated (whether nature, god, or "party") is the evil (suffering-evil) with which it all started. In these terms, evil (as opposed to sin) is a lack, a taking away of life and ease, an area where God is not involved (in which, Christians believe, he can intervene). Evil is essentially that barren area in nature defined by Hobbes (the secular equivalent of life after the Fall) as nasty, brutish, and short—to be recovered not by Redemption but, if at all, by social contracts.

CHAPTER TWO

Classical and Christian Equivalents of Sin and Evil

1. GREECE AND ROME

Tragedy: Curse and Revenge

The Greek word used to translate the Hebrew *chattat* (sin) was, we saw, *hamartia*, referring to the missing of a mark with bow and arrow: a lack of skill, not a morally culpable act. One scholar writes, "*Hamartia* (error) and its concrete equivalent *harmartema* (an erroneous act) and the cognate verb *hamartanein* seem to connote an area of senses shading in from a periphery of vice and passion to a center of rash and culpable negligence," and notes "a passage in *Oedipus at Colonus,* ll. 966ff., where *hamartia* and *hamartanein* shift in successive lines from the connotation of the voluntary to that of the involuntary."[1] *Hamartia* is an unfortunate mistake, a misfortune, closer to suffering-evil than to doing-evil (*kakia*).

I have quoted Aristotle on tragic heroes, "those who have done or suffered something terrible": "a brother kills, or intends to kill, a brother, a son his father, a mother her son, son his mother. . . . Medea slay[s] her children."[2] These are evils equivalent to the killing of Abel by Cain, but their point of origin is traced back to an initial transgressive act, a curse, and revenge. To take the example of Aeschylus's *Oresteia:* first Tantalus challenged the gods by feeding them the body of his son Pelops—thus prompting the curse on the House of Atreus. His was incidentally an

34

act of filicide, but first an act of impiety, testing the gods to see whether they can tell the difference between celestial and human meat, trying to bring them down to the level of humans. The result is the gods' curse on the House of Atreus. Pelops then, resurrected with the exception of the shoulder eaten by Demeter, grows up to cheat and kill King Oenomaus, his prospective father-in-law, in a chariot race; and he kills his accomplice, the king's driver, who had removed the chariot's linchpin, which caused the death: a crime and another reason for, or an extension of, the curse on the house of Atreus. Pelops's sons are Atreus and Thyestes. Thyestes seduces the wife of his brother, who in revenge serves him a dish containing the flesh of Thyestes' children. Thyestes utters another curse, and subsequently his son Aegisthus seduces Clytemnestra, the wife of Atreus's son Agamemnon while he is away at the Trojan War, and when Agamemnon returns the two kill him. What all of these curses have in common is an act of revenge, whether human or divine. At this point the revenge of Thyestes-Aegisthus merges with the revenge of Clytemnestra for Agamemnon's sacrifice of their daughter Iphigenia in order to recover the winds that drive his ships to Troy. Then, of course, Agamemnon's son and daughter avenge the murder of their father by murdering their mother and Aegisthus.

In short, *kakia* is patricidal or fratricidal, or (as in Agamemnon's case) a choice between two evils—sacrificing your daughter or failing in your duty, or (as in Antigone's case) being loyal to your dead brother or to your city. But the ultimate source is a curse, the work of the gods who are avenging themselves on a human who has disobeyed or offended. Greek evil is not that far from Hebrew evil—man's natural suffering and death at the hands of fate or unpredictable gods or forces of nature. But as filicide, Tantalus's act was in one sense a sin (offense to the gods), while in another—as the killing and eating of his son—it was an evil. The story begins with the challenge of a god—a version of the Christian Original Sin, though in this case it is not suggested that all the people of the earth are Tantalus's descendants, and the evils are more precisely designated than in Genesis: they are not only evil (suffering) acts but also taboo acts such as incest, patricide, matricide, and filicide. These are liminal situations, more complex if not more disturbing than the Old Testament ones, the simple disobedience of God's command or law or behaving badly toward the Israelites (as with Amalek and the Amalekites).

It is sometimes only a human curse (or at least its source is not traced back as far as the gods), as in the case of Oedipus: His father, Laius, exiled as a youth from Thebes, had taken refuge with Pelops, repaying his hospitality by making off with his son Chrysippus; thus Pelops cursed the descendants of Laius. The prophecy that his son would kill him led Laius to expose the baby, Oedipus, with a spike driven through his feet, to die on Mount Cithaeron. So a hero violates the host-guest relationship, and a curse is placed on him and his descendants. The curse leads to both further sins (abominations such as parricide and incest) and evils, such as the *kakia* of the Theban plague (suffering and death).

But in Aristotle's *Poetics* Oedipus's *hamartia* is not his unfortunate killing of Laius or incest with Jocasta; it is his *hubris*—his belief, following his success with the Sphinx's riddle, in his powers of ratiocination—that leads him to pursue the question of the plague to its bitter end, the discovery of his patricide and incest. The only way he could have avoided his fate was to avoid all skirmishes with older men and never marry, but because of his *hubris* he ignores the prophecy—is ignorant of the curse.[3] When Oedipus kills his father and marries his mother, he has no idea that he is doing wrong—only later, when he seeks out the truth does he reveal his *hamartia* and suffers *kakia*—and indeed it is the *hubris* that makes (proves) him a hero and makes his suffering/punishment inevitable, as his ignorance proves him human.[4]

In the Greek New Testament *hamartia* was used to translate all three of the Hebrew terms and carried some of the associations with *hubris;* and in the Vulgate the more neutral Latin words *peccatum* (*pecco,* to err, offend, or commit a fault) or *culpa* then assumed the connotations of *hamartia.* In the New Testament context, read back into Greek tragedy by Christian interpreters, the appropriateness of the punishment was attributed to culpable weakness on the part of the heroes. In Christian terms—the terms with which Christians read Aristotle and the Greek tragedies—the curse initiated a series of evils as punishment for a sin or *hamartia,* but whereas the Christian evil (suffered for the original *hamartia*) is redeemed by the Incarnation and Redemption of the son of God, the Greek equivalent was for the hero *anagnorisis,* or self-knowledge, and for the state—when the curse has proceeded for a number of generations—resolution by the creation of a new civic institution. Vendetta and *lex talionis* were replaced by judicial review, as in Aeschylus's *Eumenides,* or by the *anagnorisis* of Oedipus and his absorption into the society of Colonus.

Epic and Georgic: Civic Disorder

The Roman ethos took up where the *Eumenides* left off, pointing toward the civilizing structures of law and order. In Latin the adjective *malus-a-um* included unfortunate, weak, cowardly, or physical disability (sickness, misfortune); which, carried into English, became *malevolence*—the result of a defective will, as in malice and malpractice.[5] The Latin word used by Christians for "to sin" was *pecco*, to err (or *culpa*, or *delictum*, fault, offense, crime). Related Latin terms include *transgressus*—the step beyond or across a boundary, waywardness; *vitium*—a favorite word of Augustine's—denoted fault or failing. In a naturalistic, social pre-Christian world these words described greed, disloyalty, envy, self-indulgence, disrespect—vices that threaten the social order (opposed by the virtues of courage, justice, practical wisdom, which preserve and enhance a community and a political system).

The Roman ethos was summed up in Virgil's *Aeneid. Pius Aeneas* was essentially good or dutiful Aeneas, where *pius* meant loyalty to family, friends, homeland, and not *piety* to Christ alone. In the Aeneas-Dido story, from Virgil's perspective, *malum* and *peccatum* are embodied in Dido's passion, *virtus* in Aeneas's devotion to duty. Dido is the sinner (fornicator) who is trying to prevent Aeneas from carrying out his mission of founding Rome, thereby defying the providential pattern ordained by the gods, and (as if Virgil were anticipating Augustine) in the process she destroys not the Romans but both herself and her city, Carthage (clearly *malum*).[6] If the equivalent of sin is the defiance of the gods' decrees, there are also the evils that accompany the following of duty: the abandonment and the fate of Dido being one of these, something like a recollection of the sacrifice of Iphigenia in order to get the Greek troops to Troy. These evils are accompanied by the sense of loss that goes with the carrying out of duty.[7]

Virgil's conclusion is that evil, in both senses of the term, as natural and as moral, can be contained by civilization, culture, and in particular art. In *Aeneid* I his paradigm is the paintings of the Trojan War that cause Aeneas to weep at the memory (*lachrymae rerum*) but feel consoled by the transformation of this bitter experience into lasting art. In his *Georgics* Virgil designates as evils the storms, plagues, animal combats (based on lust), and civil wars that are recovered by the stability of peace and the nascent empire; the assumption was that order can be recovered out of these evils as a ruined beehive can be regenerated by religious ritual and wise husbandry. The word *religio* denominated the cult of the gods, the precise ways of worshiping the gods (via ritual and priests) as opposed to the practical rules of husbandry; as opposed also to morals and philosophy, upper-class pursuits which were supplementary to *religio*. Something like sin did exist—as contamination of the temple; for example, for a Vestal Virgin to have sex was a capital crime. But, as in both *Georgic* IV and *Aeneid* I, it is the poet's art that supplements and informs the work of the farmer and priest. As aesthetics replaces religion and beauty replaces God, so sin (the disobedience to God) and evil (human doing- and suffering-evil) are in a secular or classical sense redeemed by art.

Virgil's was the solution to the evils of the time—primarily civil war— on which the English Augustan satirists modeled their works. Beginning with Milton in *Paradise Lost,* either Christian redemption or Virgilian recovery on the georgic model defined the aesthetic solutions of John Dryden, Swift, Alexander Pope, and John Gay. In the second book of *The Dunciad,* a parody of *Aeneid* V, the heroes' games, the goddess Dulness's reward to Curll, who has won the booksellers' race against Lintot, is none other than a shaggy blanket, a demotic equivalent of the paintings Aeneas saw in the temple of Carthage that tell the story of the Fall of Troy and include the *lachrymae rerum* passage: The evils/sufferings of the dunces have been redeemed, insofar as they can be redeemed, by Pope's art. The image, and the power of pleasurable vision it confers, console for the pain of what it represents. And so Mother Dulness shows Theobald a blanket on which are stitched representations of the defeats of the dunces—Defoe in the pillory (with fictional cropped ears) and Curll's own humiliations, his blanket-tossing by the Westminster boys, ending with: "And oh! (He cry'd) what street, what lane, but knows / Our purgings, pumpings, blanketings and blows? / In ev'ry loom our labours shall be seen, / And the fresh vomit run for ever green!" (2.145–48). The blanket itself is a travesty of those great paintings in the Carthaginian temple, Curll is a burlesque Aeneas, but the beautiful lines of poetry (the order of the couplets, the assonance and consonance, the "for ever" of the "fresh" green of the vomit) in which these things are represented, are the poet's—Pope's—and the process described is the conflation of Miltonic-Christian redemption and

Virgilian renewal, as of the empire of Troy, the georgic landscape, and the poet's transforming art. This is what Pope means in the "Advertisement" to *The Dunciad* when he writes that "it is only in this monument that they [the obscure and wretched dunces] must expect to survive, (and here survive they will, as long as the English tongue shall remain such as it was in the reigns of Queen ANNE and King GEORGE)."

The Gods: Ovid, Metamorphoses
The origin of Old Testament evil found its classical equivalent in the myth of Pandora, who like Eve released the evils (suffering-evil) into the world, according to one version by way of curiosity (disobedience [don't open the box] or sin). In Hesiod's version in his *Works and Days* and *Theogony* she is simply an evil woman, created at Zeus's command to avenge himself on Prometheus, who had created men and women, stolen for their benefit the gift of fire, and tricked Zeus into letting them keep the better parts of their sacrificial animals for themselves. The motive of curiosity and the equation of Pandora and Eve was introduced by the Church Fathers, especially Origen, who "explicitly compares the story of the forbidden pithos [jar or box] with that of the forbidden fruit."[8] Origen shifted the emphasis from the selfish Zeus to the fallible young woman.

A selfish god, a benevolent subgod whose sin (befriending man) is punished, and a bad woman: It seems strange that Ovid omitted this story from his *Metamorphoses*. Writing in the world of imperial Rome, Ovid polarized the poet and the whimsical gods (for whom read: the imperial family), who now see his georgic recovery of evil into art (of civil war into peace) as only another Promethean transgression to be punished. The *Metamorphoses* is in fact a skeptical revision of the Virgilian story of *Georgic* IV, the beneficial metamorphosis of the hive. If Virgil's bees are good Romans of the Republic who "take no pleasure in the body's joys, / Nor melt away in love" (IV.212–14), Ovid's story is of the unruly passion of love or concupiscence; in Ovid's story, Rome begins with the rape of the Sabine women, not with Aeneas's dutiful rejection of Dido. The georgic's natural catastrophe of storm or plague is replaced by the disastrous meddling of the gods, far worse offenders than the gods of *The Aeneid*. Their absolute and arbitrary power, no doubt embodied in the established order of Augustus and his family (vs. the Octavius of Virgil), could be read as Ovid's real subject.

Ovid (who formally parodies the Virgilian georgic in his *Ars amatoria*) transvalues two aspects of the fourth *Georgic:* pursuit and metamorphosis. From the pursuit of Eurydice he turns to Daphne, from the beekeeper Aristaeus to the god Apollo: Fleeing, "her soft hair streaming," which makes her "more beautiful than ever" to Apollo, Daphne is saved by being transformed into the laurel. This metamorphosis confines Daphne within a tree, her heart still beating under the bark—to all human purposes, dead. Thwarted of his sexual end, Apollo converts her resistant frozen chastity into a work of art—immortal, but strictly speaking no longer living. In Ovid's words, "Let the laurel / Adorn, henceforth, my hair, my lyre, my quiver: / Let Roman victors, in the long procession, / Wear laurel wreaths for triumph and ovation."[9] This is the version of metamorphosis celebrated by Andrew Marvell in his "Garden," the reference being to Adam and Eve:

> The *Gods,* that mortal beauty chase,
> Still in a tree did end their race.
> *Apollo* hunted *Daphne* so,
> Only that she might Laurel grow.
> And *Pan* did after *Syrinx* speed,
> Not as a Nymph, but for a Reed. (ll. 27–32)

In fact (as Marvell shows in his "Horatian Ode"), it is not so much art as the celebrating and immortalizing of art in the service of the state: Apollo uses the laurel crown for the Roman victor in a military Triumph *and* for the poet (himself).

But Daphne's fate—the etiology of the laurel crown—begins not with her pride (in her chastity) but with Apollo's bragging and with Cupid's revenge and victimization of the innocent Daphne as well as of the culpable Apollo. The result of Cupid's two arrows is Apollo's lust and Daphne's chastity—consequently her flight and her metamorphosis (by her father) into a laurel tree. It is Cupid's fault. Daphne is the innocent victim of the quarrel between Cupid and Apollo. She asks for an escape from Apollo's "love" and receives the enclosure/obliteration of her body—of use now only to Apollo, though elevated from sexual desire to the cultural celebration attendant upon the laurel wreath. A woman is metamorphosed into tree, insect, stone—escape into the life-death of a plant; the rape is transfigured by the plucking of leaves or cutting of reeds in order to make a laurel crown to wear and, in the case of Pan and Syrinx, an instrument to play.[10]

Ovidian metamorphosis reveals the punishments for resisting the desires of the powerful (a classical analogue of the Christian doctrine of rewards and punishments), as opposed to Virgil's positive interpretation of change as recovery-redemption. (Virgil began *Georgic* IV with Aristaeus's sin, not the gods'.) In the story of another artist, Arachne, the human not only challenges Minerva, the divine weaver, but portrays the scandalous loves of the gods (and their own metamorphoses in order to obtain their human objects). Her rival, Minerva, produces a self-serving portrayal of herself and the other gods. Arachne wins the challenge ("Neither Minerva, no, nor even Envy / Could find a flaw in the work; the fair-haired goddess / Was angry now" [133]), and yet she is punished for the hubris of challenging and depicting satirically the gods by being beaten and, when she tries to hang herself, metamorphosed into a spider.[11] In short, in a rehearsal of Ovid's own story, Arachne portrays an unjust (or "evil") world characterized by the crimes of the gods pursuing their sexual desires, based on metamorphosis, and is punished for her offense (sin). Minerva's *epic* poetry, like Virgil's, offers a laudatory account of the gods that recalls the newly established Roman empire according to Virgil, founded on duty, not (as Ovid's *Metamorphoses* suggests) sexual desire.

Thus, in Christian terms as in Ovidian, humans all sin because, in one way or another, they defy the wishes of a god and suffer for it (die), and yet they do achieve a kind of immortality or transcendence by being turned into a form of art—a symbol (Daphne), an instrument (Syrinx), a producer (Arachne), or an object of art (Niobe).

Both georgic and metamorphosis deal with the inevitability of change; but in the georgic the farmer shows how to utilize change in the service of repetition and order, helping to retard degeneration and circumvent death. The Ovidian poet, in a kind of desperation, shows that the only metamorphosis beyond the reach of the gods is the poet's; and Ovid, for being this kind of poet, was exiled to the distant shore of the Black Sea. Milton is, in this sense, an Ovidian poet insofar as he describes himself in *Paradise Lost* as the disgraced and oppressed poet who does his best in a fallen world (Ovid was one of his favorite poets).

Moral Satire: Horace and Juvenal

Ovid introduces satire, the genre that ignores the god-man relationship and deals instead with deviations from moral rectitude—socially accepted values. "Satura," as Quintilian wrote, "tota nostra est."[12] Writing in the generation preceding Ovid's, Horace, in his satires (which he called *sermones,* or conversations), considers what the Christians would later call the individual sinner—the individual whose personal salvation was in question. In Horace's terms, however, it was not sin and damnation but folly, the self-destructive nature of men's attraction to extremes, though this proved to be roughly a secular approximation to the Christian idea of sin—lust, sloth, wrath, and so on—as preferring something else to the good, some part to the whole. Horace, in his orderly dialectic, divided vices into opposites: avarice became miserliness and prodigality. He would have agreed with the Church Fathers that it was the excess that turns love into lust and the active will that turns the inclination into the vice, which implies both excess and obsession. Always, however, between the extremes Horace situates (briefly in the *Sermones,* at great length in the *Epistolae*) a golden mean (*aurea mediocritas*), his secular equivalent of the God from which Christians, when they sin, allow their attention to wander.

Horace's point is that suffering-evil follows from allowing oneself to succumb to one of the extremes; this *malum* is a form of punishment that extends from the hatred and abandonment of your children to such fatal disasters as being "divided . . . squarely in two with an axe" by your wife. Not satisfied with a cupful of water, you (the "you" Horace habitually addresses) seek water from the flood-raging Aufidus River, which sweeps you away "with its crumbling bank," while "he / Who wants only what he needs neither drinks water / Churned up with mud nor loses his life in the waves." As Horace concludes, "There is still room for us in between."[13] Exceptions appear in his *Epodes,* a more melodramatic genre in which torture and murder take place: a witch starves to death innocent boys in order to make a love potion. Evil in the *Epodes* is imposing suffering on others—doing-evil—but the idea that evil is itself a suffering of consequences for a folly is Horace's in his *Sermones,* and one that was shared by Augustine, who knew his works well. (Augustine seems not to have known the works of Ovid.)

As an image of society, the *Sermones* are Virgilian: The social unit is Augustan, society in place and impregnable, a symbol of order; outside is chaos, possibly another civil war. And if like Virgil he implies problems with imperial authority, they are glancing, worth accepting to stave off disorder. His satiric object is the outsider who tries unsuccessfully to break into the charmed circle of the elite, where Horace (with self-irony) sits un-easily with the emperor himself, with Maecenas, Virgil, and a few others. The principle of exclusion is, of course, excess, and the ideal represented by the inner circle is moderation: Augustus is the figure to whom one does not prefer something else. Whereas the outsider is too boorish, too eager and assiduous, too avaricious to fit into this charmed circle.

In his poetics, *De Arte Poetica,* Horace abstracts from the morality of the *sermones* aesthetic principles. In his initial example, an artist paints "what began as a lovely woman at the top / Tapered off into a slimy, discolored fish," which, he says, will (like the figures of his satire) pro-voke the spectator's laughter (ll. 3–5). Hogarth will take his epigraph for *A Harlot's Progress* from Horace's *De Arte Poetica* ("license is given on condition that you use it with care," ll. 48–49) and reproduce Horace's grotesque mermaid as Sin in his painting *Satan, Sin, and Death* (below, fig. 16). Horace is, most significantly for Hogarth, aestheticizing a Leviti-cal abomination—and, significantly for the whole tradition of aesthetics (from Shaftesbury to Hogarth and on), positing the same harmony of the subordination of part to whole as in his *Sermones:* "Make what you want, / So long as it's one and the same, complete and entire" ("simplex dumtaxat et unum," l. 23)—and as in the theology of Augustine and the Christians. Horace shows the way to aestheticize, in effect to secularize (more specifically, to classicize), sin.

If Horace's satire, written in the age of Augustus, is about folly (and beauty), Juvenal's satire, written in the time of the bad emperors, is con-cerned with what I have referred to as evil. This satire, he explains in Satire I, is heroic or, more precisely, tragic, concerned with emperors and great men and the evil they do. His word in Satire I is *culpa:* The persons satirized "tacita sudant praecordia culpa," they sweat with the secret consciousness of *culpa,* a word the Christians would translate as sin. Juvenal's *culpa* is primarily the corruption of an ideal, by characters whose actions are judged in the diminishing shadow of that ideal. Satire VIII, for example, contrasts degenerate Romans of the present with the busts of their illustrious ancestors of the Republic. In Satire III Rome has de-generated from its Republican ideals into a city of foreigners. Umbricius, the last Roman, leaves Rome, now totally un-Roman, to return to the country, specifically to Cumae, where Aeneas first landed and consulted the oracle, descending into the underworld to receive his vision of the Rome he will found—the Rome that is now totally corrupted. In Satire VI Juvenal contrasts the women of Aeneas's time with the masculine women and effeminate men of the present, the husband-dominated marriage of then with the wife-dominated marriage of now. These serve for Juvenal as corruption, the negation, deflection, degeneration of *pietas* into unnatural lusts.

Juvenal and Augustine would have agreed that evil was merely the negative of an ideal and its manifestation was civil disorder. Perhaps *culpa* leads to *malum* as sin, according to the Church Fathers, leads to evil; but with social rather than religious values, except insofar as Juvenal cites as one of many examples a decline from traditional piety. To judge by his historical situation in the fifth century with the fall of Rome, Augustine in *The City of God* also opposes chaos—disintegration and disorder, in other words, *un*righteousness—to a Platonic God who is perfect and *un*-changing (in terms of predestination, cannot change his mind, and so our salvation or damnation was decided at the beginning of time and cannot be changed by our acts).

The basic polarity of an ideal (ordinarily in the past) and a degenerate (defiled, vitiated, corrupted, perverted) present provides a useful frame for the argument of a satire; but the only comment it has to offer, unless it carries the religious context of sin, is, "Alas, what a falling away!" A merely static contrast cannot demonstrate other areas of satiric subject matter, folly and knavery on the part of the degenerate. In order to portray these subjects the satirist must present (or at least imply) an act of some kind, ordinarily a physical encounter which ends in violence—in dire consequences either to oneself (Horace's folly) or to another (knavery). The satiric scene is a shockingly violent concatenation of action and consequence.

Corruption is a victimless crime, except, we might say, against nature. But corruption has a transitive verb, to corrupt, implying a corrupter and his victim, as in the case of Satan and Eve. Corruption is not, in Juvenal's satires, victimless. Those who have remained in corrupted Rome are in danger of anything from destitution to the burning of their homes and the mangling of their bodies. These poor innocents are in constant danger of injury and death at the hands of the knaves who now control Rome and, in Juvenal's terms, represent a corruption of an ideal in the past; this corruption is primarily of the ideal relation of patron and client that Horace had celebrated in the Maecenas circle (his own term was *amici*, friends), now degenerated into the relation of a fool and a knave. The decent client—poet or artist—is excluded and starves; but his degenerate replacement, the fool who sells out to the knave, is seated at a remote table and eats the rotten scraps from the patron's table. The patron—the knave—in Juvenal's satire never receives punishment; he flourishes, degrades his clients, and rules the roost.[14]

The innocents suffer pain, deprivation, humiliation, often death, but the fools, who contribute to their pain, also suffer punishment for their folly. In Satire VI, the Roman wives who have grown masculine, whores or gladiators, not only dominate their husbands, who permit this outrage, and humiliate them, but betray and ultimately kill them. The vocabulary is of *monstrum* and *scelus*, great crime or enormity, as in the woman "quae conputat et scelus ingens / sana facit" (who calculates and commits a great crime in cold blood).[15] These effeminate husbands are fools who have abdicated their rightful position. Even in Satire X, Juvenal's most Horatian satire (translated by Samuel Johnson as "The Vanity of Human Wishes"), the consequences of the foolish wishes for riches, fame, power, and beauty are murder, confiscation, and rape at the hands of the knaves who are in power.

The effects of corruption are reciprocal, on both the innocents, who are destroyed, and the fools, who try to cooperate with the knaves—and presumably even on the knaves themselves, fish who devour smaller fish but will themselves be devoured by a larger fish. One man's knave becomes another man's fool, and only the emperor is finally—or for the moment, before the assassins strike—safe.

2. CHRISTIAN SATIRE

Punishment

Satire's ritual origins are in the curse—the curse on the forces of sterility that complements the prayer to the forces of fertility;[16] and the curse of the ancient satirist Archilochus demonstrates the interdependence of crime and punishment. He asks that the culprit be shipwrecked: "Shivering with cold, covered with filth washed up by the sea, with chattering teeth like a dog, may he lie helplessly on his face at the edge of the strand amidst the breakers—this 'tis my wish to see him suffer, *who has trodden his oaths under foot, him who was once my friend.*"[17] Helplessness and isolation are not an arbitrary curse; they describe the character of the turncoat who has cut himself off from human loyalties. The curse derives from the notion that external appearance must correspond to inner reality, a diseased body to a diseased soul. Satire has this in common with the law: it externalizes internal states in crimes and follies and their consequences in suffering and punishment, to others and the self. Punishment presents the psychological inner reality of the evil action.

In the case of Apuleius's Lucius, turned into an ass, punishment adjusts the appearance until it reveals the inner reality. Peregrine's self-immolation in Lucian's dialogue proves his self-consuming folly; Ben Jonson's Volpone, pretending to be sick to cheat fools of their fortunes, is made really sick by being bedded in a dungeon loaded with chains, and Mosca, the wily plotter, is confined to a life at the oars of a galley; Mr. Bumble, in Dickens's *Oliver Twist,* ends a pauper in the same workhouse where "he had once lorded it over others." Milton's Satan, at the end of his project for corrupting humankind, is turned by God the Father into a serpent, groveling on the floor of Pandemonium and hissing out his words of "triumph."

The marks of punishment will suggest the quality of the soul within that merits such punishment. Punishment can take the form of legal-penal or of therapeutic suffering—the consequence of crime is the pillory, whip, or strappado (metaphors of laceration, flogging, and so on), or of disease is the scalpel, blister, purge, and phlebotomy. A pox, with all its symptoms (as outlined in Swift's account of the Banbury Saint) is both a painful punishment for transgression and an externalization of an internal corruption.[18] The scalpel defines the distemper as it removes it; the mercury cure for the pox—which produces intense sweating and the loosening of teeth—defines the disease through its "cure." The legal equivalent, whip or strappado, however, may define the punisher as much as the punished; the scalpel or purge may, in the age of dubious physicians, do the same—as satire in general may contaminate the satirist himself, producing a more complicated satire that cuts both ways. The punishment takes on an independent reality or status—the punisher made by his act another agent of evil, as most obviously in the act of revenge.

In classical mythology, the good souls went to the Elysian Fields, the bad to Tartarus, the pit into which the Cyclopes were thrown by Uranus when they rebelled; inside the abyss of Tartarus was the house of Hades, guarded by the Hound of Hell: Here, among the bad souls, were a few emblematic figures being punished by everlasting torture: Tantalus, who tricked the gods into eating his son, is punished by hunger and thirst; Sisyphus, who attempted to escape from Hades, must endlessly roll a boulder up a hill only to see it roll back down again; Tityus, for attacking Leto, has his liver eaten by vultures; Ixion, for the attempted rape of Hera, is bound to a fiery wheel. All, we note, were crimes against the gods (sins). Even the Danaides, who murdered their husbands and are in some stories condemned to draw water from a lake with sieves, had rebelled against authority. Also present in the Greek-Roman underworld were some demons—Alastor and the Furies (the Erinyes)—to fill the role of punishers for the gods. In the underworld Aeneas visits he hears the sounds of the lash and chains and human groans; he glimpses the suffering Titans, Tityus, Ixion, and others. What one sees therefore is the powerful doing evil to the weak, however guilty or innocent, however much the punished qualify as sinners or as evildoers—and they are mostly the former.

Christian theology, like satire, is eschatological in that it has to do with ends, with the end of things, with judgment and primarily punishment. The Christian religion, with its emphasis on the afterlife, added to its vision of a heaven that compensated for the evils of this life a hell for those who misbehaved. Hell was at bottom the anguish of permanent separation from God, that is, the punishment (the evil) for desiring something more than God (the sin)—like the anguish Horace attributed to those who prefer extremes to the golden mean.

Hell defines evil actions by their punishments. Only in hell—in the agony of punishment—is it possible to see that sinners *are* (spiritually) splitting open with their excesses, or that their sin is actually consuming them, not they it. Hell is about sinners, even when they commit evils; it is the sin that is emblematized in punishment because sin is a state of mind—evil is the suffering that follows. Hell shows what it *is*, to oneself, to be a hypocrite, a lustful person, or a traitor. Thus treason freezes, lust aimlessly blows one around and around, and hypocrisy weighs one down with a bright-colored robe made of lead. When a second party is needed, it is a demon whose acts materialize the self-flagellation of the sinner—or who merges with the sinner in a double monster, another abomination.

Dante's highly structured hell consisted of concentric circles narrowing as they descend to Satan, at the bottom, locked in ice—the constriction and ultimate immobility of sin. Fire is above, in the higher circles, but at bottom darkness and cold, deprivation and negation. Hell is both the place where sinners are punished and a place where sinners *punish;* they kill, torture, and mutilate others. It is therefore a place where evil is illustrated or, we might say, permitted; theologically evil, the negation of good, is the inevitable consequence of sin. The question, as a scholar notes, is, "Are the demons in hell keepers or inmates? Eventually they came to be both" is his answer.[19] As the examples suggest, evil is both the suffering (punishment) of evil and the *doing* evil. The Hebrew word for sin, *'awon,* a tortuous road, can refer equally to the offense, the consequent guilt, and punishment—suggesting the concurrence of all three (e.g., Gen. 4:13).[20]

Hell is the interface of suffering-evil and doing-evil. The damned committed sins and/or did evil and are punished with suffering so as to emblematize the nature of their sin/evil. The demons who punish them are doing evil as punishment. Sinners are alone, isolated in their folly, but as Dante's circles descend from sins into acts of evil they are accompanied by other forces that impose suffering on them, until the punishment involves evil upon evil. In the ninth circle Ugolino and the Ghibelline archbishop Ruggieri are symbiont: Ugolino betrayed his city, Ruggieri betrayed Ugolino and forced him to choose between starvation and the devouring of his own sons, and now one gnaws on the head of the other. The devouring denotes the pain of both Ugolino's hunger and Ruggieri's retributive devourment. Much the same applies to Satan and Judas, Cassius and Brutus—though punisher and punished, they are equally implicated as evildoers. In hell the sinners become (like Horace's fools) the sufferers of evils. If, as in some cases (Brutus, Ruggieri), they were evil to begin with, they are nevertheless punished for sins with evils, precisely as Adam was; evils imposed by God and demons.

Dido, of course, suffers for her passion for Aeneas (she "killed herself for love"), but specifically for her adulterous betrayal of her husband Sichaeus, not for the obvious (Virgilian) consequence of the Punic Wars and the destruction of Carthage. Paolo and Francesca are simply adulterers, who have already suffered death at the hands of the betrayed husband, who himself appears nowhere in Dante's hell. Sin is disobedience to God, at worst rebellion against him, supported by the analogy to rebellion against the monarch and, in Dido's and Francesca's cases, their husbands. Dante punishes betrayal of one's master in the lowest circle of hell: drawing on the classical evil of the betrayal of host by guest, of guest by host, but in this case only one way, from guest to host. Betrayal of God is, of course, a sin, but Dante makes it evil as well by using the examples of men who betrayed by killing their masters—Brutus and Cassius as well as Judas; which relates them to the archsinner Satan, who holds all three in his mouth.

When Francesca describes her adultery she spreads the blame, attributing the first kiss to Paolo and attributing their act to the story they were reading of the adulterous passion of Lancelot and Guinevere. The latter anticipates the explanation for Don Quixote's being rendered a madman and attacking sheep and windmills—he read romances of chivalry. The situation involves prototypes, themselves evil, that are imitated (Francesca would say) by relative innocents. In Francesca's case, she hopes the book will serve as mitigation of her crime. But she has rewritten the story, in which Guinevere first kisses Lancelot; now Lancelot and Paolo make the first overture.

Like the story of Lancelot and Guinevere, sin and its consequent evils are contaminants that rub off, even on the pilgrim Dante, who takes on the characteristics of the damned he encounters. The virtues of pity and mercy are replaced by their negatives: while he fainted at seeing the pain (evil suffered by) Paolo and Francesca, as he descends he grows increasingly indifferent to suffering, his language coarsens, and at the bottom of hell he carelessly kicks the head of a sinner who is encased in ice up to his neck. When he recognizes the man as a traitor to Florence, he grasps him by the hair and threatens to pull it out if he does not tell him what he wants to know. The sinner refuses and Dante carries out his threat, becoming just another inflicter of pain on the damned. But Dante's actions may more accurately be interpreted as a progress toward righteous anger at what he sees; his initial pity (regarding what he sees as cruel) is, in Christian terms, merely naive. It is, after all, Virgil, the pre-Christian resident of Limbo, who expresses pity for the damned, an inappropriate response for a Christian. The Christian reading was of punishment as *lex talionis*, whether God's rendering of strict justice to sinners or Dante's to the Ghibellines of Florence who drove him into exile, a personal settling of scores.

Another version of hell, more easily available to the English,[21] was Lucian's, hell-as-Saturnalia. In the subversive underworld of Lucian's *Dialogues of the Dead*, Alexander the Great is now a cobbler living in what is essentially a reversal of the living world, servants are now masters, masters servants—power is reversed and tyrants brought down. In the biblical equivalent, Isaiah's curse on the king of Babylon (where he calls him Lucifer) is, "Thy pomp is brought down to the grave, and the noise of thy viols: the worm is spread under thee, and the worms cover thee. How art thou fallen from heaven, O Lucifer" (Isaiah 66:23–24). The writers with whom we are concerned will have their choice of the two hells, Dante's and Lucian's.

Christian-Humanist Satire: Erasmus, The Praise of Folly

> What is "humanism"? The measure of man. It holds that the individual is the measure of all things. . . . The human attitude which does not hope for a supernatural reply to the problem of death and does not expect solutions to human problems from supernatural powers.
>
> —*Sándor Márai*, Memoir of Hungary 1944–1948

Passing over Christian satire prior to 1500—the Juvenalian satire of Tertullian and Jerome, largely misogynist, and medieval complaint satire (we shall, however, return to the second-century satire of Irenaeus)—I take as my example Erasmus, the first modern Christian satirist, who, not coincidentally, published his *Praise of Folly* (1509) just eight years before Luther introduced the Reformation. Erasmian satire is anticlerical, pitting the ideal of simple faith and the teachings of Jesus and the Apostles against the Church, the fellowship of love against the reliance on compulsion by the pope, the priesthood, and the authority of Scholasticism. He sets the primacy of the subject of man against not God himself but God's usurpers, the clergy. *The Praise of Folly*, though Erasmus keeps its assumptions within the limits of orthodoxy and the Church as he understood it (and refused to follow Luther into a break with the Church of Rome), is essentially Antinomian, or *against the law*. Luther, by his Reformation, simply canceled the options Erasmus entertained; but Erasmus's anticlericalism was censored in some quarters, called by some the egg that Luther hatched.[22]

To judge by its title, *The Praise of Folly* would appear to be Horatian and outside the range of evil. But folly for Erasmus is a double- and triple-edged concept. Folly is both a good and a bad thing, and as the latter, its ultimate object is not folly but knavery, or rather the knavery that results from folly: one face of folly is the corruption of the simple apostolic ethos (the innocence of children, the warmth of lovers, the simplicity of the saint) by the pope, the cardinals of the Church, monks, and priests. At its worst (its highest level), this folly, aimed to obtain and extend power, produced wars, persecutions, and the burning of heretics. As Robert M. Adams writes, "Erasmus was addressing himself to an audience which, if schooled in the quite usual medieval patterns of thought, customarily regarded war (like the plague) as caused by man's sin and God's answering justice, yet at the same time (since St. Augustine) as an action approvable as just and Christian." Erasmus's satire is on the warmongering of a pope like Julius II and the "theologians who falsify Christ and the scriptures to justify war."[23] This ideology Erasmus attacks as folly expanding into the cruelty and murder that are the ultimate case of suffering-evil.

The evils (of the Problem of Evil) that Folly considers are the "many misfortunes" to which "the life of man [is] subject": "How miserable, to say no worse, our birth, how difficult our education; to how many wrongs our childhood exposed, to what pains our youth; how unsupportable our old age, and grievous our unavoidable death? As also what troops of diseases beset us, how many casualties hang over our heads, how many troubles invade us, and how little there is that is not steeped in gall? To say nothing of those evils one man brings upon another, as poverty, imprisonment, infamy, dishonesty, racks, snares, treachery, reproaches, actions, deceits."[24] But, she adds, "for what offenses mankind have deserved these things, or what angry god compelled them to be born into such miseries is not my present business"; rather it is how to deal with them. If all men were wise, Folly tells us, they would kill themselves. She, however, "partly through ignorance, partly unadvisedness, and something through forgetfulness of evil, [does] now and then so sprinkle pleasure with the hopes of good and sweeten men up in their greatest misfortunes that they are not willing to leave this life, even then when according to the account of the destinies this life has left them." Folly's solution to the Problem of Evil is "to remove the trouble of the mind" by illusion: "But tell me, by Jupiter, what part of man's life is that that is not sad, crabbed, unpleasant, insipid, troublesome, unless it be seasoned with pleasure, that is to say, folly?" (49, 8, 17). From the dread of age and death, which constitute "so great an evil" (22), Folly "redeems" us. Erasmus does his best to suggest that Christian redemption is not simply another illusion (as Folly might seem to be saying) by offering folly's other sense as Christian faith, simplicity, and good conduct.

During the early part of the *Praise* Erasmus keeps his figure of Christian Folly safely concealed among a plethora of classical gods ("Death—no small evil, by Jupiter!"), associating her with "the spring [that] breathes afresh on the earth," when "all things immediately get a new face, new color, and recover as it were a certain youth again" (7–8). And when the imagery becomes overtly Christian he sharply distinguishes the good folly of the true Christian simplicity of the Gospels from the bad folly of "feigned miracles and strange lies . . . ghosts, spirits, goblins, devils, or the like" as well as the rituals of "mass priest and pardoners," the "wooden or painted images of saints," the "counterfeit pardons," and the "magical charms and short prayers" with their promises of "wealth, honor, pleasure, plenty, good health, long life, lively old age, and the next place to Christ in the other world." The sense of *folly* develops from the virtues of illusion to the evils of "wisdom" in the hands of grammarians, logicians and sophists, philosophers, and finally, the end to which Folly has been leading us, the divines, who, she tells us, "straight pronounce me a heretic" (91).

Ultimately it is the popes who "supply the place of Christ," who "govern all by the sword," who terrify with "interdictions, hangings, heavy burdens, reproofs, anathemas, executions in effigy, and that terrible thunderbolt of excommunication" (116, 119, 118). Erasmus is implicitly connecting the pope, as Protestants would, with the Antichrist, contrasting this abomination with the life of the true Christ, "His poverty, labor, doctrine, cross, and contempt of life," which of course is in papal terms "folly."

Approaching the end of her oration, Folly makes the connection with Christ explicit: "And what does all this drive at," she says, "but that all mankind are fools—nay, even the very best?":

And Christ himself, that he might the better relieve this folly,
being the wisdom of the Father, yet in some manner became
a fool when taking upon him the nature of man, he was found
in shape as a man; as in like manner he was made sin that he
might heal sinners. Nor did he work this cure any other way
than by the foolishness of the cross and a company of fat apostles, not much better, to whom also he carefully recommended
folly but gave them a caution against wisdom and drew them
together by the example of little children, lilies, mustard seed,
and sparrows, thing senseless and inconsiderable. (139)

Original Sin was the folly, wars and the rest were the evils, which Christ
became man (another aspect of folly) in order to redeem, through another
act of folly, his crucifixion. Folly, significantly a woman, with her good
and bad faces, remains part of nature and (as Erasmus emphasizes) the
human body; whereas there is also what is not of the body—spirit, with
heaven and the results of Christ's Incarnation, Atonement, and Redemption.[25] What lies at the bottom of *The Praise of Folly* is the distinction
between sin (man's supposedly original sin and all the legal structure
of church and state, in particular pardons) and the evil that results from
the same—which Erasmus comes close to designating as embodied in a
religion of sin.

3. CHURCH OF ENGLAND SATIRE: SWIFT

Credulity and Curiosity (Fools and Knaves): A Tale of a Tub
In *A Tale of a Tub* (1704) Swift repeats Folly's solution to the Problem of
Evil but only in order to discredit it, indeed to discredit *both* alternatives,
illusion as well as reason:

Those Entertainments and Pleasures we most value in Life, are
such as *Dupe* and play the Wag with the Senses. For, if we take
an Examination of what is generally understood by *Happiness*,
as it has Respect, either to the Understanding or the Senses, we
shall find all its Properties and Adjuncts will herd under this
short Definition: That, *it is a perpetual Possession of being well
Deceived.* . . . Such a Man truly wise, creams off Nature, leaving
the Sower and the Dregs, for Philosophy and Reason to lap up.

> This is the sublime and refined Point of Felicity, called, *the Pos-*
> *session of being well deceived;* the Serene peaceful State of being
> a Fool among Knaves.[26]

The alternative?—"and then comes Reason officiously, with Tools for cutting, and opening, and mangling and piercing," ultimately flaying and
dissecting, exposing defects—whereas illusion finds "an Art to sodder and
patch up the Flaws and Imperfections of Nature" (9.173–74).

Swift adopts the opposition between curiosity and credulity, which
Erasmus sees only from the point of view of the latter,[27] and makes it
central to his *Tale* and in particular to the chapter called "A Digression
on Madness," in which one alternative is as mad as the other. But at the
center of this chapter, as in the *Praise*, is the equation of war, evil, and
philosophies and religions—though in the latter case newly invented and
proliferating (Protestant) sects, not the hardened tradition of the Church
of Rome (which he satirizes elsewhere in the figure of Peter).

Swift adopts Erasmus's idea of Folly speaking an encomium on folly
(a false encomium—the old Cretan liar paradox), presupposing as *his*
"author" a Grub Street hack who retains something of Folly's ambiguity—"some grains of sense / Mixed with whole volleys of impertinence."[28]
He is writing a book in praise of those exemplars of both illusion and
skepticism whom he admires, the Moderns; his folly rises, as it does in
the *Praise*, to madness, and the conclusions Swift draws (or has his hack
draw) are, aside from the devastating severity of the satire, very similar
to those drawn by Folly.

Erasmus's "several sects" were the Schoolmen, "the realists, nominalists,
Thomists, Albertists, Occamists, Scottists"; Swift's are the post–civil war
enthusiast sects of England; but both are opposed to an ideal, a distant
memory in the past, of "the apostles" (93–94). Both are set off in different
ways from the "heretic" Folly—in Erasmus by their theologizing, in Swift
by the "author's" naive imitation, himself regarded by the very philosophers
he admires and tries to emulate as something of a heretic, certainly a fool.

Whereas, however, the ironic "heretic" Erasmus attacked the Church
and Scholasticism in the name of apostolic Christianity, Swift attacks the
true heretics and schismatics; though, as he explains in the "Apology"
attached to the 1710 edition, his book has itself been accused of heresy by
the Church of England.

Heresy

The evils (civil war, revolution) in the satire of *A Tale of a Tub* follow from sin, but sin in the particular form of heresy. The context was the post–civil war period in which diverse religious sects and factions, deviations from civil and ecclesiastical orthodoxy, appeared to threaten church authority, alongside that of the king. Swift invokes the idea of heresy, not only as a crucial term on both sides of the Reformation (for which a great many died), but also in its early Christian sense, which referred primarily to the Gnostic sects of the second century CE. (Gnostic = *gnosis,* or knowledge, that is, *secret* knowledge, known only to the Gnostics.)[29]

The first indication is on the title page, where one of the epigraphs, "Basima eacabasa eanaa," etc., is a meaningless formula of initiation re-cited by the Gnostics; the sense was apparent only to (because invented by) themselves. Swift is quoting from the five-volume *Adversus Haereses* (*The Destruction and Overthrow of Falsely So-called Knowledge*) of Irenaeus, bishop of Lyon c. 180 CE, which, the title page claimed, "set forth the views of those who are now teaching heresy . . . to show how absurd and inconsistent with the truth are their statements. . . . I do this so that . . . you may urge all those with whom you are connected to avoid such an abyss of madness and of blasphemy against Christ."[30] Irenaeus attempts to show that the Gnostics' claims of spiritual communication with Christ were only "madness and . . . blasphemy."

The epigraph shows that Swift had read Irenaeus's great compen-dium, which helped to establish Christian orthodoxy by discrediting al-ternative doctrines (he also included it in a list of books he had read in the years preceding the publication of the *Tale*). Swift follows Irenaeus's argument but adds his own analogy between the Gnostic enthusiasts and the Moderns (of the "Battle of the Ancients and Moderns"), who, in the field of learning, believe they have improved upon the Ancients, claiming that recent discoveries in science and philosophy surpass earlier ones. The list of "Treatises wrote by the same Author" sums up the interrelation —or rather unity—of religion and learning, sacred and secular in the thematics of the satire.

One aspect of, and criterion for, heresy is its novelty: Irenaeus writes that "every one of them generates something new every day, according to his ability; for no one is considered initiated among them unless he develops some enormous fictions!" (1.18.1). Drawing also on the literary "newness" advocated by another model, Mr. Bayes of Buckingham's farce, *The Rehearsal* (1670), Swift connects the affected newness and the endless proliferation of secular with religious fictions.

Irenaeus's *Adversus Haereses* served as his formal as well as ideological model: Irenaeus's method was parody, first quoting the Gnostics' works (in fact, until the discovery of the codices of Nag Hammadi, he was the chief source of our knowledge of Gnostic texts) and then drawing out, expanding, and playing with their words and notions. His basic assumption, like Swift's, was that the only source of religious knowledge was the original teachings of the Apostles, who had the doctrine from Jesus' lips, and he attempts to show that the heretics' aim was to replace the Apostles with themselves. As he puts it, "They imagine that they themselves have discovered more than the apostles, . . . that they themselves are wiser and more intelligent than the apostles."[31] The Gnostics, Irenaeus argues, were attempting to pass off as "apostolic" doctrines that were in fact derived only from their own experience, intuitions, inventions, imaginings, and fantasies.

Tertullian also scored both the "deviation" from the apostolic tradition and the diversity of the Gnostic teachings: "Every one of them, just as it suits his own temperament, modifies the traditions he has received," the results of which "each individual of his own mere will" advances.[32] What they attempted most dangerously to demonstrate, in Elaine Pagels's words, was that "the structure of authority can never be fixed into an institutional framework: it must remain spontaneous, charismatic, and open" (25).[33] Direct access to God was subversive of order in church and state; and the situation in first-century Christianity (perhaps read back from the fourth century when church and state began to join) could be applied to the aftermath of the English Civil Wars, when bishops, priests, and deacons along with king, Lords, and Commons, appeared to be in the process of being subverted by the idea of every-man-his-own-church and the memory of the monarch's beheading.

In the *Tale* the evil (what the "author" calls knavery)—the Moderns themselves, Descartes, Bacon, Bentley, Dryden, and Wotton—is supplemented by the folly or banality of the imitator, praiser, and follower. Swift's Grub Street hack is a sort of naive Irenaeus retelling what he has gathered from his "Masters the Moderns," for which read the Gnostic heretics. Swift's terms are credulity and curiosity, fool and knave—a fool lives on illusions, a knave (a skeptic, freethinker, atheist) destroys these illusions of beauty, faith, heaven, etc. And in the larger context of Irenaeus's *Adversus Haereses* there is the distinction between the heresiarchs (and the evils they produce, corruption of ideals and disordering of society) and their followers: between Valentinus and Marcian and the Gnostic sects they spawn, or Jack (or Calvin) and the enthusiast sects he spawns. The *Tale* demonstrates the knavery—the self-sufficiency (the sin) of the Moderns and its consequences (evils)—being *recounted* by a disciple, the "author" of the book *A Tale of a Tub:* he, like Don Quixote, is transmitting the doctrine, which is demonic and in its way monstrous, but he is the less successful imitator (poor, living in a garret, suffering beatings, poxed, and not even acknowledged by his models the Moderns), roughly equivalent to Juvenal's fools who support and make possible his knaves.

A heretic, in Pagels's terms, "may be anyone whose outlook someone else dislikes or denounces. According to tradition, a heretic is one who deviates from the true faith" (whatever the "true faith" may be, according to the party of the Church who turned out to be victorious).[34] In Swift's case, heresy is the proliferation of diverse—often odd, even actively individualist and so seditious—beliefs: not one true church (Horace's "simplex dumtaxat et unum") but many. Throughout his works it is sedition (faction, division, treachery) that Swift regards as the ultimate knavery—or, presumably, what we would call evildoing: the man who measures all mankind by his own length and breadth (prefers something else to God) is evil *because* this leads to sedition—to the formulation of a new religion or philosophy or government, and so treason.[35]

Soteriology and Self-Sufficiency: Crusoe and Gulliver

> The Church taught that it was every man's first duty to save his own soul.
>
> —*Graham Greene,* The Power and the Glory

For Irenaeus and the Church Fathers, outside orthodoxy there was no salvation and no order, only chaos, disorder, and treason.[36] For Swift only the latter mattered; he shows no concern in the *Tale* for personal salvation. The development of theology in England was from the primary emphasis on soteriology—on Christ's Atonement and Redemption, which led to the

Grace and Justification that assured one of an eternal life in heaven (in compensation for the evils of the Fall)—to the emphasis on Incarnation, that is, to Christ's whole life, his triumphant mission, and his teachings, not only his suffering and death. Christian satire from the sixteenth century, but strongly from the 1660s, was anti-Puritan, which meant, among other things, antisalvationist. It regarded people who talk of sin and holiness as hypocrites—and hypocrisy was the chief vice or evil attacked by the major English satirists culminating in Swift: they attacked Puritans and enthusiasts who talk only about their own salvation, while in secret they cheat, steal, and in particular fornicate.

In that prime text of soteriology, Bunyan's *Pilgrim's Progress* (1678), Evangelist admits to the Everyman named Christian that "life is attended with so many evils," which include the burden of Original Sin; therefore, the alternatives would seem to be simply to die or to seek salvation in the hereafter.[37] But there is a third possibility, which is quickly discarded: In the city of Morality, Mr. Worldly Wiseman and Mr. Morality can "help men off with such burdens as thine are, from their shoulders; yea, to my knowledge he hath done a great deal of good this way: and besides, he hath skill to cure those that are somewhat crazed in their wits with their burdens" (19). Morality can rid you of your guilt, give you a feeling of false security, and divert you from what should be your chief concern, which is your salvation. Thus *Pilgrim's Progress* begins with the vivid image of Christian fleeing his wife and children, who "began to cry after him to return: but the Man put his fingers in his ears, and ran on crying, Life, Life, eternal Life" (10).

In Daniel Defoe's *Robinson Crusoe* (1719) evil as misfortune appeared in the "punishment" Robinson suffered for his original sin of disobedience and selfhood, denying his father and leaving home; he was consequently (like the object of Archilochus's curse) cast away and isolated on an island. Or at least that is the way Robinson, in his memoir of his adventures, interprets the evils he suffers for twenty-eight years. During that time he has two tasks to fulfill—conversion to the will, to accept the grace, of God, and so be rewarded with the compensation of everlasting life in heaven; and, a more pragmatic task, reconstruction of what he requires in order to live on the island, creating a simulacrum of what he has lost because of his sin. One is theological, the other existential.

Later Robinson encounters something he thinks of as evil: He discovers, in the evidence of the cannibals' feast on the other side of his island, the presence of an independent force of evil in the world, one that threatens his ease and existence. Evil takes the form of the scattered body parts, which indicate actions that are melodramatically evil, evil of a demonic sort (possibly reflecting vaguely the radical Protestant Defoe's abhorrence of the Roman Eucharist and its "cannibalistic" devouring of the "real body" of Christ), based on the "sins" of abomination and uncleanliness as well as (perhaps for Robinson more than) the facts and threats of murder, death, and pain. These are external evils, Satanic in the sense of Satan the Adversary, as opposed to the internal sin of his own quest for salvation. These cannibals Robinson combats and kills, as many as he can, and converts one of them, Friday, and later Friday's father, to Christianity.

However, other forms of evil—as wrongdoing, injury to others—are overlooked, in Crusoe's retrospective soteriological narrative of events: for example, his selling of his helpmate, the black boy Xury, into slavery and the casual treatment of his wife and family—cases that Swift critiqued in *Gulliver's Travels* (1726) from a moral perspective. To paraphrase Emile Durkheim, religion (the ritual and the system of classification that must not be violated) exists either for the saving of souls or for the preservation of society. Defoe appeared in *Robinson Crusoe* to choose the former, and Swift in *Gulliver's Travels* plainly chose the latter.[38]

Gulliver's Travels is a demystification (by way of the Church of England) of the soteriological narrative Defoe used in *Robinson Crusoe*. Swift will have none of the Reformed Protestant worries about personal salvation, which he focused on with a cold eye in *A Tale of a Tub;* his concerns are resolutely social, his "evil" about withdrawal from and division and subversion of the social unit, by which he means church and state, religion and learning, in short, civilization. Gulliver, who has spent scant time with his wife and family in any case, ends his voyages living in his barn, unable to stand the smell of his family, while consorting with his horses, who are his memories of the rational Houyhnhnms. He recalls Ulysses in Dante's hell, who, though consigned among the bad counselors, also deserted his wife, his son, and his aged father, who had all faithfully waited twenty years for him to come home from the Trojan War. Unlike *pius* Aeneas, the hero of Virgil's *Aeneid,* Ulysses shows no familial piety but only a fatal desire for personal glory.

Gulliver's Travels is primarily concerned with moral matters—the gamut of exploitation of others and the fear of the exploitation of oneself *by others*. In the transitions between his voyages Gulliver is forced to descend from natural evil to moral: (1) a storm, a "natural evil," leaves him stranded in Lilliput; (2) he is abandoned in Brobdingnag when he insists on accompanying the sailors, who must replenish their water supply and are confronted with giants, an action which would qualify as morally neutral or a reflection on Gulliver himself, whose own motive is merely to gather specimens (he thinks he has found another Lilliput); (3) he is cast adrift with provisions by the villainy of pirates, who seize his ship; and finally (4), now the captain of his own ship, he is betrayed by his sailors, who mutiny and cast him out to die on the ocean. He has experienced a descent like Dante's to the Ninth Circle.

In Voyage 3 Gulliver is momentarily required to desecrate a Bible and refuses, but otherwise the evil into which he descends is associated with one of the Seven Deadly Sins, pride. Gulliver is guilty of pride in Voyage 2, but he has just left the island of Lilliput, where he may have learned a thing or two about pride, and his pride in Brobdingnag has no consequences/effects on anyone but himself, while the Lilliputian empress's pride and Flimnap's sins of pride and envy threaten Gulliver with blinding, starvation, and death.

Gulliver himself is a secular-sacred case of soteriological obsession and solipsism (Protestant "calling," business sense). The Master-Bates joke with which *Gulliver's Travels* opens ("Mr. James Bates," "Mr. Bates," "Master Mr. Bates," "Mr. Bates, my Master," and "My good Master Bates"), which Phyllis Greenacre interpreted as Swift's mischievous subconscious at work, is rather Gulliver's first revelation of self-enclosure.[39]

Gulliver's Travels was published a few years after the publication of the notorious *Onania; or, the Heinous Sin of Self Pollution, and all its Frightful Consequences, in both SEXES Considered, with Spiritual and Physical Advice to those who have already injured themselves by this abominable practice*. The message of *Onania* was that masturbation, the "filthy Commerce with oneself," was "man's vice of vices, sin of sins." The three "core horrors" of solitary sex, in Thomas Laqueur's words, in his magisterial *Solitary Sex*, were "its claim on the imagination and fancy, its secrecy and solitude, its tendency to excess."[40] This was primarily the fantasy stimulated by solitude, one form of which was the erotic fantasy, thought to be "more seductive than the objects themselves," and the outlet of masturbation with its Old Testament sense of sin and abomination in the story of Onan, who "spilt his seed."[41] The closed circuit of masturbation that excluded all the needs and feelings of others was the very symbol of solipsism and Augustine's definition of sin. (Robinson Crusoe himself confesses, recalling his life of solitude on the island, "A man may sin alone in several ways.") Gulliver's "masturbation" cuts him off from the classics, the Church Fathers, the textual tradition, the outside world (*incurvatus in se*, he is turned in on himself).[42]

In *A Tale of a Tub*, published twenty-three years before *Gulliver*, the satire was on self-sufficiency and self-absorption. The symbol there (in the supplementary *Battle of the Books*) was a spider, who "Spins and Spits wholly from himself, and scorns to own any Obligation or Assistance from without," as opposed to his enemy the bee, who flies from flower to flower producing "Sweetness and Light." Also implicit in masturbation was transience—"If," says the bee, "the materials be nothing but Dirt, spun out of your own Entrails (the Guts of Modern Brains) the Edifice will conclude at last in a Cobweb: The Duration of which, like that of other Spiders Webs, may be imputed to their being forgotten, or neglected, or hid in a Corner" (*Tale*, 234).

As the play on "mastur-bates" shows, for Swift self-exposure is characteristically in language, which, as in Irenaeus, is a normative medium; evil can try corrupting language but only to reveal its (and God's) true purpose. The Gnostic epigraph tells the reader that the book will be about self-enclosed language regarded, in a religious context, as heresy; in the case of the *Tale*'s "author," self-sufficiency or self-enclosure amounts to his demand that his audience must *be* the author in order to read his book. At the same time, like the objects of anti-Puritan satire, Swift's protagonist, while concerned only with his self-sufficiency, keeps talking about his projects "for the universal benefit of mankind."

Abomination/Corruption

In at least a few places in Romans, which Swift appears to have noticed, Paul replaces the Prophets' metaphor of sin as rebellious heterosexual fornication with homosexual union, assuring gentiles who worshiped other gods that therefore God "gave them up to uncleanness, through the lusts of their own hearts, to dishonor their own bodies between themselves . . . gave them up unto vile affections: for even their women did change the natural use into that which is against nature: and likewise also the men, leaving the natural use of the woman, burned in their lust one toward another; men with men working that which is unseemly, and receiving in themselves that recompense of their error which was meet" (Rom. 1:24–27). Whereas in the Old Testament God punished the rebellious by subjugating them to enemies like the Babylonians, Paul supposes that God punishes Christian sinners by stimulating forbidden homosexual desires, turning them into "a society of deviants."[43]

Sodomy and forms of sexual perversion like masturbation are crimes against the social order, the kingdom, and the family; while there was no victim, in the sense of some one person injured, there was a corruption of the whole body politic. Sodomy is implied in the author's reference in the *Tale*'s "Preface" to the "large *Pederastick* School, with *French* and *Italian* Masters" in the academy proposed by the Moderns (along with schools for swearing, criticism, and salivation—the last for syphilis). Sodomy is what connects Richard Bentley and William Wotton, the two originary figures of the *Tale* insofar as it derived from the "Battle of Ancients and Moderns"—the unity, even tautology, of the "love Pair," as they are called (on the page preceding, Bentley is also called Wotton's "Lover" and elsewhere "beloved"). At the end of *The Battle* "this [i.e., modern] Pair of Friends compacted . . . close Side to Side" is skewered on a lance, "their Legs and Wings close pinion'd to their Ribs; So was this pair of Friends transfix'd, till down they fell, joyn'd in their Lives, joyn'd in their Deaths; so closely joyn'd, that *Charon* would mistake them both for one." Swift is evoking Numbers 25:8, where Phineas kills Zimri and the Midianite woman, Cozbi, his lover, and indeed the baby in her womb, with a single spear—the punishment for an abomination.

Sin as impurity, a hybrid or mixture, something that does not conform to the classification system: this sense of sin of course applies primarily to Pope's *Dunciad,* which carries an almost Levitical sense of "abomination" in its hybrids and monstrous amalgams, but it applies as well to the strange deformations of Swift's *Tale*—to the coats of Peter and Jack, and their bodies as well as those of the Aeolists and the moderns in general and the books they produce (heavy bottoms, predominant digressions and indices): All this is sin rather than evil. Sin becomes evil only when Peter imposes his wishes (his doctrine or dogma) on his brothers; but when Jack creates endless sects, their divisiveness is sin. It creates dissension that essentially supplies impure alternatives to the one church and one state, and specifically in the image of the body. Pollution is again evoked: As Mary Douglas puts it, the "kinds of social pollution" are em-bodied, referring to the human body: "The first is danger pressing on external boundaries; the second, danger from transgressing the internal lines of the system; the third, danger in the margins of the lines. The fourth is danger from internal contradiction . . . so that at certain points the system seems to be at war with itself."[44] All of these threats apply to the body politic and private in Swift's *Tale*.

A final aspect of the body metaphor is the notion of the part outgrowing and superseding the whole. Bad things are good things perverted; perversion is a creature becoming more interested in itself than in God, wishing to exist "on its own" (*esse in semet ipso*); and, finishing the argument, permitting the part to exceed or replace the whole.[45] Swift's underlying assumption is that "all Catholics are one body in Christ"—and therefore the disaster of the body's deformity or dissolution.[46] In the *Tale* sin is not merely disobedience to God, preferring something else, but preferring oneself to others, that is, to the world, and the part to the whole; most dramatically, it is preferring the index and digressions to the text of the book, and the lower body parts to the upper and thinking parts.

The "tale" of the brothers is Horatian—Martin is the existential norm, a sort of golden mean (actually the humanly possible) between Peter and Jack (the original coat, the ideal, now lost, augmented beyond reason or stripped to tatters, impossible of recovery). In the story of the will and coats, the interpretations of the three brothers, Peter, Martin, and Jack, lead to additions or subtractions that distort the original bodies of the coats; and the interpretations have physical effects on others: Peter's on his brothers, Jack's on himself and everyone around him, including the Aeolists and the Banbury Saint. The digressions that interrupt the "tale" are also about bodily-spiritual excess, leading up to the digressions in praise of digressions and on madness: a distortion for purposes of self-assertion, individualism, display, spiritual and secular show, ultimately manifest in the Aeolists with their distended bodies.

The authority for Swift's association of sin with aesthetics as well as (via Hobbes) politics was, of course, Augustine. In the *Confessions* book IV Augustine puts sin in the context of aesthetics: "Do we love anything that is not beautiful?" he asks:

> What is it that inveigles us thus, and that draws our affections
> to the things we love? For unless there were a gracefulness and
> a beauty in them, they could by no means draw us unto them.
> And I marked narrowly and perceived that in the bodies them-
> selves there was one thing as it were the whole, which in that
> respect was beautiful, and another thing that was therefore be-
> coming, because it was aptly fitted to some thing, as some part
> of the body, in respect of the whole body, or a shoe in respect
> of the foot, and the like. (IV.13.183–85)

Referring to a book which he had written "on the Beautiful and the Fitting," set against the analogy with the body of God, he imagines "that
Thou, O Lord God of the Truth, wert nothing but a vast and bright body,
and myself some piece [fragment, *frustum*] of that body? O extreme
perverseness [*perversitas*]!" (IV.16.200–201). Elsewhere he adds, "By my
own swelling I was separated from Thee" (*tumore meo separabar abs te*),
referring to himself as an "abscess," the part that withdraws from the
whole, the sinner who prefers something else to God. The sinner is
the part that withdraws from the whole, preferring something else to
God, politically the traitor, theologically the heretic, and aesthetically the
grotesque.[47]

Augustine's body metaphor followed from Paul's metaphor in Romans and 1 Corinthians of the members of the body of Christ as the
Christian community, individual Christians his "limbs" or "members,"
contrasted with the "limbs of a harlot" who failed to show allegiance to
the community (1 Cor. 6:15, associated with Satan in chapter 7): "For as the
body is one, and hath many members, and all the members that one body,
being many, are one body: so also is Christ" (1 Cor. 12:12); and when the
members rebel: "But I see another law in my members, warring against
the law of my mind, and bringing me into captivity to the law of sin which
is in my members" (Rom. 7:23).

Closer to Swift's own time, the Anglican divine Ralph Cudworth
wrote, in his *True Intellectual System of the Universe* (1678), that the world
"was not properly made for any *Part,* but the *Parts* for the *Whole,* and the
Whole for the *Maker* thereof"; the trouble is that "some sullen and discontented Persons" devoted to "their own *Private, Selfish,* and *Partial Appetites,*"
disturbed by the presence of evils in the world, go about "*Railing* upon

Nature."⁴⁸ Swift may have remembered these passages when he built his *Tale* around his compelling image of the body gone wrong.

Abomination is a mixture of unrelated elements, whose joining is a defilement of one or both; corruption is a degeneration and decline. *Corruption* is the word Swift applies in his "Apology" to explain his intention to satirize only the "Corruptions in Religion," not religion itself (what he calls "the Follies of Fanaticism and Superstition," "Errors, Ignorance, Dullness and Villainy"). This sense of corruption he shares with Juvenal, for whom evil was what had happened to Republican Rome (an ideal in the past) in the Rome of the bad emperors; heresy is religious corruption. The *Tale* evokes John 6:63, "It is the *spirit* that quickeneth; the *flesh* profiteth nothing: the *words* that I *speak* unto you, they are *spirit,* and they are life" (cf. Luke 1:15, John "shall be filled with the Holy Ghost"). The question is, *which* spirit, whether the Holy Spirit, the Word of God, or the fleshly spirit of belching or breaking wind, introduced not by the Holy Spirit but by mechanical means such as a pump. Corruption means (drawing also on Hobbes's materialism) that spirit degenerates into flatulence, enthusiasm into sexual arousal, preachers into seducers, mystic experiences into syphilis and disintegrated nasal cartilage—and the cause: Zeal (for which read: sexual desire).

All of the *Tale*'s terms—masturbation, sodomy, defilement—are, for Swift and the Christian tradition, negations. Evil, wrote Augustine, is one of those things that "are known not by their actuality, but by their want of it," and one example is darkness, which one "nowhere sees . . . but where it begins not to see." Paul Ricoeur points to the Old Testament idea of the "nothingness" of sinful man, come at through the negativity of "failure, deviation, rebellion, going astray. The sinner has 'gone away from' God; he has 'forgotten' God; he is 'foolish,' 'without understanding.'" As Isaiah says, "All nations before him [God] are as nothing; and they are counted to him less than nothing, and vanity" (Isaiah 40:17). But, Ricoeur adds, "there are more striking expressions of this negativity that can be classed with the 'breath of air' that passes and is not retained or with the 'idol' that deceives because it is not the true God."⁴⁹

The Old Testament texts associate sin with the light, empty, unsubstantial: "man is like a breath of air; his days are as the shadow that passes away" and "The sons of Adam are only a breath of air, the sons of man a lie; if they were placed in the balance together, they would be less than a breath of air" (Psalms 144:4, 62:9). And the "idols," which are a form of the absence of God ("For all the gods of the nations are idols, but the Lord made the heavens," Psalms 96:5), are equally "nothing": "You are nothing and your works are nought; to choose you is abominable," says the Second Isaiah. Idols are accordingly another "spectacle of unsubstantial things—vapor, exhalation, mist, wind, dust . . . the spectacle of false sacredness." "All of them together are nothing. Their works are nothing; their statues are wind and void" (41:24, 29, 75).

The two biblical images of breath and nothing serve as the basis for Swift's Aeolists, indeed for all his images of swollen but empty or only flatulent bodies, from the Body Politic down to the preacher whose posteriors are being pumped full of wind.[50] (How much is their shape crime and how much punishment?) Irenaeus called the Gnostic heretics "pneumatics" ("those who are spiritual"—*pneuma*, spirit), and Swift the Hobbesian translates spirit into air, gas, flatulence; breath, air, wind; and the various idols—the tailor-god, the windmill, the preacher-pulpit, and so on, which amount to nothingness and the pseudo.[51]

Transience is, of course, another aspect of the Christian concept of evil as absence of good. In the *Tale* there is the "Piece of Wit" that can only be understood "*today,* or *fasting,* or *in this place,* or *at eight a clock,*" that is, by the moderns, who have "reduced it to the Circumstances of Time, Place and Person. Such a Jest there is, that will not pass out of *Covent-Garden;* and such a one, that is no where intelligible but at *Hide-Park* Corner." As to the reading of his book, the Grub Street author announces: "Now, I do affirm, it will be absolutely impossible for the candid Peruser to go along with me in a great many bright Passages, unless upon the several Difficulties emergent, he will please to capacitate and prepare himself by these Directions. And this I lay down as my principal *Postulatum.*" The "directions" are that the reader go to bed in a garret, "sharpen [his] Invention with Hunger," engage in "a long Course of Physick, and a great want of Money," and, as we learn later, have a case of the pox and spend time in a madhouse: thus the work that can be read only by the reader's replacing the author (43–45).

Then comes the assertion, in the face of such proven impotence, of power (like those references to "the universal benefit of mankind"): "I claim an absolute Authority in Right, as the *freshest Modern,* which gives me a Despotick Power over all Authors before me," and on the other side, the anxiety of ephemerality and transience expressed in the disappearance of the modern works described with such pathos by the author in his "Dedication to Prince Posterity," where he blames it on the prince's tutor, Time, and his monstrous claws as well as scythe.

The Nature of Sin and Evil

A Tale of a Tub is in fact an analysis of sin; it asks and answers the questions: What *is* sin, how can one control sin, and how does sin become evil; the answer being: when, as heresy, it produces civil dissension.

Following Augustine, Swift describes sin as originating in concupiscence; this is Original Sin, present in all of us only awaiting a stimulus. It was commonly asserted, by the orthodox, that the feelings the enthusiast mistook for divine inspiration were in fact erotic in origin, and especially in the case of women. Swift refers to female preachers prophesying, like the ancient sibyls, "through their vaginas."[52] The climactic "Digression on Madness" is based on Augustine's proof for Original Sin in sexual desire. Augustine's imagery, in the *Confessions*, telling how his love was corrupted, anticipates Swift's: "Out of the muddy concupiscence of the flesh, and the bubblings of youth, mists fumed up which beclouded and overcast my heart, that I could not discern the clear brightness of love from the fog of lustfulness" (II.20). And Augustine talks of "that tumult of the senses wherein the world forgetteth Thee its creator, and becometh enamoured of Thy creature, instead of Thyself, through the fumes of that invisible wine of its self-will, turning aside and bowing down to the very basest things" (I.22).

In Swift's version concupiscence creates a vapor in the genital region, its outward manifestation a "protuberance," its inner the vapor's normal outlet through the penis. We can either give it sexual outlet, though this would of course be fornication—and when fornication passes for religious ecstasy it is an abomination; otherwise it would seem preferable to the other alternatives. One is repression, in which case the vapor may rise to the brain and produce new (original, personal) religions, philosophies, or governments, phenomena which can only be accomplished by subjugating the current ones. The consequences are wars and other sorts of violence and destruction: it can overturn the king's brains and result in war—or, in another person, in religious enthusiasm, which leads to the multiplication of sects and the generation of civil chaos. These new religions, etc., if they are not imposed on contemporaries, may simply land the author in Bedlam. Thus the "author's" need for his readers in order to read his book to duplicate his own life and experiences, to become one with the author; another example is Peter's demand, in order to keep pace with the changing London fashions, that his brothers accept *his* interpretation of their father's will—when they will not, he casts them out. Another possibility, in the case of Louis XIV, is for the vapor to travel downward rather than upward, ending in a fistula; yet another is for a surgeon (read: assassin) to release Henry IV's bellicose vapor by an incision. Thus enthusiasts (in *The Mechanical Operation of the Spirit*) wear caps to keep the vapor in, assuring themselves of mystic visions, madness, facilitated by masturbation or, in the case of the Banbury Saint, fornication resulting in syphilis.

And so what is the solution? If Henry IV had fornicated he would not have gone to war (he was fortunately assassinated first), but ideally, if he had practiced the forms of religion, he would presumably have controlled by will the original protuberance. Apparently Swift's solution is to follow the common forms of society and the Church of England.[53] This is Swift's answer to the question of how to deal with our sinning nature. For the Anglican clergyman Swift, sin (disobedience, preferring the part to the whole, oneself to the deity) *was* evil, or rather *produced* the evils of civil disorder, chaos, madness, death, and destruction. For the sinner what was evil or good, right or wrong, depended only on an internal hydraulic mechanism, which Swift knew was self-serving and delusional. The sinner's consciousness of good–evil was radically subjective. However conservative his conclusions, Swift raises an issue that will be questioned in the next two centuries: the analogy between self-sufficiency and Christian salvationism.

CHAPTER THREE

Sin and Evil Redefined: The Enlightenment

1. THE POPULAR STAGE

Marlowe, Doctor Faustus: *Sin or Evil*

Christopher Marlowe, writing in the 1590s, inherited Ovid's humanism, the insurgency that led to his exile. At King's School in Canterbury and Corpus Christi College, Cambridge, he would have had nothing in the curriculum against which to balance the Calvinism of Alexander Nowell's *Catechism, or First Instruction of Christian Religion* except the classical Latin of the pagan poets, in particular Virgil and Ovid. David Riggs's biography of Marlowe shows "how fully his work articulates the contradiction, inherent in the educational system that bred him, between Christian self-abnegation and humanist self-empowerment."[1]

Marlowe's *Doctor Faustus* (1590s, publ. 1604) depends upon the dichotomy of sin and evil, piety and morality, inwardness and outwardness. As the play opens, Dr. Faustus is interrogating the Problem of Evil:

> The reward of sin is death: that's hard. . . . If we say that we
> have no sin, we deceive ourselves, and there's no truth in us.
> Why, then, belike we must sin, and so consequently die:
> Ay, we must die an everlasting death.
> What doctrine call you this, *Che sera, sera,*
> What will be, shall be? Divinity, adieu![2]

Faustus's Calvinist theology (at the time Anglican orthodoxy) is based on the assumption that we cannot avoid sinning and are therefore doomed to God's predestination;[3] a conclusion which, canceling divine studies, leaves Faustus only necromancy and the devil—and so, turning to the Manichaean answer to the Problem of Evil, he can counter natural evil only with moral evil. But since, coming out of "Divinity," he can formulate his problem only in terms of sin, or specifically counter divine with demonic evil, he chooses sin in its most emblematic form, selling his soul to the devil. For what purpose?—so he can "sin," since according to Christian theology he will sin anyway. And so the sins he conceives are only "frivolous demands" (as Mephistophilis puts it), never evils; the best he can do is wish to see the Seven Deadly Sins in person. Faustus is accepting eternal damnation for twenty-four years of mere "voluptuousness" (84a), a state which is summed up when Lucifer himself arises from hell and shows Faustus "some pastime," a performance by the Seven Deadly Sins.

Pride involves only self-sufficiency (Swift's spider) and Wrath ends up wounding himself ("when I had nobody to fight withal"), but Pride "disdain[s] to have any parents," thus in a sense destroying them; Covetousness desires "that this house and all the people in it were turned to gold, that I might lock you up in my good chest," thus killing people; and Envy wishes "that all might die, and I live alone! Then thou shouldst see how fat I would be." Covetousness and Envy do damage others, turning them into objects to be possessed and hoarded; and Wrath, before turning on himself, wounds others. These comprise Marlowe's conception of sins as evils.

But Faustus, as sinner, only creates Old Testament abominations— that is, confusions of God's works: He asks Mephistophilis to "make the moon drop from her spheres, / Or the ocean to overwhelm the world" (83a). The whole transaction is parodied in the subplot by the Clown who is willing to sell himself to Wagner (to become his servant) for a shoulder of mutton (the sin of gluttony). As the chorus concludes, Faustus's sin is to challenge God. His subsequent sins are pointedly victimless, self-destructive (in both the Christian sense and the classical), only in defiance of God. He has performed or effected no evil, and the whole transaction —as critics have noted—is trivial and comic, a parody of the Calvinist doctrine of predestined damnation, though it ends with Faustus for his sin suffering theoretically the greatest of evils.

As he dies and utters the divine (or sacred) parody, "Consummatum est," Faustus's ironic analogy is between his compact and Christ's, the latter for the Atonement of man's Original Sin.[4] One gave his soul to the devil, the other his body to humankind; the continuum, however, is the idea of sacrifice, which recalls Faustus's earlier lines, contemplating the compact, when he first associated himself with the Savior, and like the Savior questioned the Problem of Evil:

> Couldst thou make men to live eternally,
> Or, being dead, raise them to life again,
> Then this profession [of divinity] were to be esteem'd. (80a)

Shakespeare: Revenge/Mercy

The template for the revenge tragedy came from the Roman Seneca. Here is Medea, preparing to avenge herself on her faithless husband, Jason:

> Ye crime-avenging furies, come and loose
> Your horrid locks with serpent coils entwined, and grasp
> With bloody hands the smoking torch; be near as once
> Ye stood in dread array beside my wedding couch.[5]

Seneca's *Thyestes*, which is about one great act of vengeance (no payback here), was the play from which the Elizabethans took off—from Thomas Kyd's *Spanish Tragedy* (1592) to Thomas Middleton's *Revenger's Tragedy* (1607). In *Hamlet* (c. 1600) Claudius murders Hamlet Sr. and marries his widow, and to avenge Hamlet Sr. Hamlet Jr. kills Polonius, Rosencrantz and Guildenstern, indirectly Ophelia and directly Laertes, and finally Claudius, who has accidentally killed his wife (Hamlet's mother) and brought about Hamlet's own death by means of Laertes' poisoned rapier. In *The Revenger's Tragedy* the Duke has poisoned Vindice's sister because she resisted his lust; Vindice kills the Duke and all his sons and is eventually killed himself: revenge, which is after all the subject of the Old Testament *lex talionis* and of the Christian hell, has become the central self-consuming evil. Revenge takes the form of vendetta in which demons and damned are interchangeable, evil is repaid by evil in a domino effect. The Elizabethan-Jacobean revenge tragedies were a phenomenon of England in the years of readjustment from the Calvinist theology of the post-Marian clergy who had taken refuge in Geneva and Amsterdam—a period of belief and secularization of belief. The Calvinist assumptions were being corrected but still, in various ways, remained imaginatively alive in revenge tragedy.

Marlowe's *Jew of Malta* (1590s) was a play about unmitigated evil and damnation. In one speech Barabas claims to have devoted his whole life to punishing Christians for their apostasy, but at the beginning of the play he is provided with an ostensible and plausible motive—revenge: the governor of Venice has confiscated half of his fortune to pay off the Turkish forces. His actions, however, correspond to his later speech and to his stage type: though they begin with the death of the governor's son, they include the death of another nobleman's son, the murder of a whole convent of nuns, as well as the betrayal of Venice to the Turks followed by the betrayal of the Turks to the Venetians. His own end is the plunging through a trapdoor intended for, but sprung by, the governor, the trickster tricked—and into an equivalent of hell, the boiling oil he has prepared for the Venetian nobles. He goes down into the vat of oil as the devil and the damned disappeared into the hell-mouths of the morality plays. The energy and glee with which Barabas carries out his plots connect him to the Vice of the morality plays and the popular contemporary figure of the Machiavel (who in fact introduces the play).

There is no resolution in *The Jew of Malta*, only retribution, sin, and evil followed by damnation; in *Hamlet* the hero, like Oedipus, has his *anagnorisis,* and the state of Denmark recovers political order and stability in the figure of Fortinbras. Evil has run its course, and mere revenge and damnation are replaced by something between the classical resolution of the *Eumenides* and the Christian Redemption.

The Merchant of Venice (c. 1595, publ. 1600) is a comedy, and by its generic nature it humanizes the tragic (or revenge-tragic) stereotype of Marlowe's Barabas. The *Merchant* places revenge in the context of Old Testament justice and New Testament mercy—the former resolved into the latter in a way that again recalls the denouement of the *Oresteia.* The first is embodied in the revenge of Shylock (like Barabas, for slights and injuries by the Christians who persecute Jews, exacerbated by the elopement of his daughter with his ducats), the second in Portia's defense of mercy/forgiveness. When Shylock remains adamant in his demand for Antonio's pound of flesh, Portia turns the letter of the law against him; and then, having brought him to his knees, the court (or rather Shylock's victim, Antonio) forgives him but requires—most significantly—that he convert to Christianity. In short, the Old Testament ethos of strict justice by the law is hoist by its own petard and then, a judgment of *lex talionis* having been passed, corrected with the New Testament ethos of mercy—which fits into the play's larger theme of love and reconciliation (as in the subplot, in which lovers' oaths are broken but the transgression forgiven).

In *Measure for Measure* (1604)—neither tragedy nor comedy—Shakespeare equates sin and law (against fornication), which are represented in counterpoint to evil, the exploitation of one person by another: Angelo hypocritically exploits the sin/law that makes fornication a capital crime in order to rape Isabella; Isabella "virtuously" defends her chastity on the basis of the sin of fornication and a promised reward in heaven, the salvation of her soul at the expense of her brother's body; and so her brother Claudio demands that Isabella save him with the violation of her own body and, as she believes, her soul for the sake of his earthly body; and Lucio urges her on to provoke (seduce) Angelo in order to free Claudio; but ultimately the Duke of Vienna has set up the whole charade partly to test and entrap Angelo, whom he suspects of hypocrisy (and knows treated his mistress Mariana badly), but also evidently out of the sheer pleasure of playing God with people as if they were puppets. Who is worse, we are left asking, the Angelo who cannot control his passions and must betray his beliefs, or the legally guilty and morally innocent Claudio, who is willing to sacrifice his sister's virtue, or the sister who will not give up her virginity to save her brother's life, or the Duke who lets all of these people hang themselves in order to make a point? The Duke, after all, is the deus ex machina (the Marlovian deity whose vicegerent Angelo is) who resolves, passes justice, and redeems, but in Vienna he leaves the question of justice and morality in doubt.

Measure for Measure may question the vexed relationship between sin and evil, or it may be a "juridical argument of treacherous justice and provocative innocence," or more generally a play "about power and control," posing many unanswered and unanswerable questions. It is certainly a play about power.[6] The point is that Shakespeare is not taking sides as one suspects Marlowe does and one knows most of the authors we shall be dealing with do: They are either advocates or critics of the concept of sin, with its inextricable links to law and therefore vengeance and the deity.

As religion was diluted by humanism, writers and artists began to reconceptualize the relations between sin and evil. One way was through the popular stage of the Elizabethans and Jacobeans, which offered a counter discourse to the devotional. These "old" plays, immensely popular in the 1700s (by midcentury bardolatry was a mainstay of English culture), suggest the variations and complications being rung on the orthodox sense of sin and evil. Shakespeare's plays, sometimes bowdlerized by the sensitive, were the silent counterweight to the orthodoxy of the sermons and religious tracts, the sourcebook for interesting models for dealing with, and redefining, the still primary subjects of sin and evil.

Wycherley, The Country Wife: *The Rake and the Cuckold*

The basis of Restoration comedy, coming as a reaction to the Puritan (Calvinist) ethos of the Interregnum, was play upon the relation between the word and the deed, the legal and extralegal, the high and the low, and sin and evil. The hero of this drama was the rake, a sinner who breaks—or, we might say, tests—the laws of society by fornicating, often with married women; the fool or villain was the religious hypocrite who spoke against but secretly practiced concupiscence and who was gulled by the rake.

In *The Country Wife* (1675) William Wycherley presents the sinner Horner, the lawful husband, Pinchwife, who used the legality of marriage to assure himself of the possession of a sexual object all to himself, and Pinchwife's wife, Margery. Horner is not, of course, the only rake of Restoration comedy. George Etherege's Dorimant in *The Man of Mode*, of a year later, is interested primarily in power; he is satisfied not when he has consummated with the lady but when he has made her break her fan in frustration and rage. But Horner's sin—and compared to Dorimant's treatment of women, it is a sin—is simply epicurean; he gives pleasure to women and to himself; his fornications are hardly even seductions with such eager women as Lady Fidget and Margery Pinchwife. In Horner's sexual play no one gets hurt; the women are made happy and the husbands are kept in the dark (or at least partly in the dark; cuckolds, they are dismissable as comic butts). He is a sinner who sins, but he does not prey on innocents; his victims are worse than he, or, like Margery, they are unaware that they have been harmed. To be aware she would have to be informed of the London/Puritan mores.

Pinchwife the lawful husband, on the other hand, as his name suggests, is a nasty character who keeps Margery locked up in the country and threatens her with bodily harm. "Write as I bid you," he orders Margery, "or I will write whore with this Penknive in your face" (54); his metaphors describing his relationship to Margery are military, and on at least one occasion he draws his sword on her. (In fact, he shares the military metaphor with the rakes, but their tenor is seduction, not mutilation.) His marriage to her is, as I have mentioned, strictly for legal possession: "The Jades wou'd jilt me, I cou'd never keep a whore to myself," he explains (15).

When critics have written about Horner they have seen him in terms of sin—as abomination and corruption of ideals such as honor and courtly love. They have noted that while his ruse of impotence suggests the real impotence, psychological and moral, of the men he cuckolds—Sir Jasper Fidget as well as Pinchwife—it also suggests Horner's own state of disease (on the model of Volpone's real moral illness revealed by his feigned illness for profit);[7] there is, in short, a sense in which Horner is in fact impotent—part of him has died and only the animal remains. Few things in his world exist above the beltline, none higher than eye-level.[8] This account, as the vocabulary shows, is of sin, not evil.

On the other hand, as Robert Markley has put it, Horner makes "a devastating assault on patriarchal ideology . . . patrilineal power," given the fact that he appears to father most of the children in the West End of London (his women are married, as opposed to Dorimant's unmarried women).[9] Laura Brown distinguishes the Restoration audience's aesthetic from its moral judgment: we applaud Horner's ingenuity but condemn what he is doing; whereas Markley distinguishes the thematic from the theatrical effect, arguing that "the audience's complicity [with Horner] prevents them from simply imposing inside the theater the values they may hold outside it"[10]—one distinction between reading a novel and watching a play (and, I shall argue, looking at a picture).

Milton's Satan: Sin Up, Evil Down

Milton's Satan, a model for Swift's spider, tries to maintain that he exists "on his own," "self-begot, self-raised by his own quickening power."[11] Parodying God, Satan did not require another for procreation; he produced his daughter Sin out of himself, a child of his own imagination. In *Paradise Lost* (1667) the relation of sin to sexuality is embodied in two women, Eve and Sin: in Satan's "seduction" of Eve (pointing to the "seductive" aspect of sin) and the effect on Adam and Eve's sexual relations consequent on the Fall; and in the relationship between Satan's conception of rebellion, manifested in a woman named Sin, and his sexual union with her. Here is what has been called a genealogical allegory:[12] Sin is rebellion; it is internal, a mental construct; externalized it takes the form of a seductive female and incestuous intercourse with her; followed by her pregnancy and the offspring, a male this time named Death, who rapes her (again incestuously) and produces a litter of monsters (abominations). The actions inside the allegory are seduction, sexual intercourse, and rape; outside the allegory is Satan's arousing the angels to rebel against God. The motivations inside the allegory are the sins—pride, envy, lust, perhaps anger—whose immediate consequences are the actions mentioned in the allegory. All of these involve evils in the sense of pain, but the allegory glosses over these evils, focusing on the sin of rebellion.

Rebellion is characterized as corruption: Satan declines from the shining Lucifer into a cormorant, a toad, and a serpent. Corruption, in Augustine's terms, had close connections to parody and so to satire. Augustine addresses God, "Thus all perversely imitate [*perverse te imitatur omnes*] thee, even they that get themselves far from thee, and who pride themselves against thee; and yet by thus imitating thee, do they declare thee to be the Creator of the whole frame of nature, and consequently, that there is no place whither they can at all retire from thee."[13] In *Paradise Lost* Satan parodies the Trinity with the trio of himself, Sin, and Death, and God's Creation with their bridge connecting Pandemonium and the earth. The whole regalia of Satan's pose among his fallen angels in the first two books is a parody of the God we see in book III. But in one sense the parody is comic: At every step of the way, carrying out his nefarious plan, Satan is in fact merely fulfilling God's plan of *felix culpa;* he is a figure of comic unawareness, of (the negative of God's good creation) stupidity.

The Restoration rake was anticipated by—indeed modeled on—Milton's Satan, who made his appearance a decade before Dorimant took on Satanic trappings, attributed to him by the anxious women of London society ("he is a devil, but he has something of the angel yet undefaced in him"), assumed by himself in his crucial transactions with his Eve, Harriet ("None ever had so strange an art / His passion to convey / Into a list'ning virgin's heart / And steal her *soul* away").[14] The influence went both ways:

Milton constructed his Satan on the evidence of the Cavaliers, who had returned to power in the 1660s—most obviously in the debauching crew of Belial but also in the speeches of Satan and in his main act of aggression—of evil—against mankind, the seduction into sin.[15]

In the figure of Satan Milton posited two distinct senses of sin-evil: First, the equivalent of Dante's Ninth Circle, is betrayal of one's master, Satan's rebellion against God; second is Satan's corruption of God's creation (his seduction of Eve and Adam, and consequently corruption of all their descendants). Both are sin insofar as they involve disobedience to God and one's master; but the first looks upward, the servant betraying his master through pride and envy, a weaker figure challenging a stronger; the second, downward to man from a superior or stronger to a weaker figure—ultimately to a more innocent creature, such as a child (Eve, just born when Satan first met her). The first is seen from the perspective of God, the second from the human perspective, that of Eve and Adam. From this perspective, Satan is a tempter, liar, and corrupter, and so sexually a seducer, though lust is less his vice than the need to persist in his rebellion against God by corrupting his creation; the evil is Satanic seduction, the corruption and injury of one's inferiors, of the powerless by the powerful with the consequent "evils" of pain and suffering. The great acts of evil that everyone agrees upon (torture of children, genocide) are acts of power exerted on the powerless or less powerful. Sin goes in the other direction: a less powerful reacting against the more powerful.

For Swift evil was the usurpation of rightful authority, as treachery, disloyalty, betrayal of a master. In Swift's satire, which in *A Tale of a Tub* is theological, sin, reflecting the Original Sin, is rebellion—of the moderns against their masters the ancients, Whigs against their monarch, enthusiast nonconformists against the Church of England, Latitudinarians against the authority of the Church Fathers, gnostic self-sufficiency against the unity of the Church (in *Gulliver's Travels* a ship's crew mutinying against its captain). Swift's basic metaphor in the *Tale* is summed up in *The Battle of the Books*—the moderns in rebellion, trying to set up a new regime, by overthrowing the ancients.

Pope was concerned with the seduction or persuasion—or usurpation—of the master's authority: the servant's attempt to corrupt and exploit (even to *become*) the master. Seduction and corruption in Pope's satire were of the higher by the lower, as if Satan had corrupted God, not Eve;

as if he had not rebelled against but seduced God. Pope implies a Satanic figure, superficially attractive but impotent—*unless* he can get the ear of his superior, not of an Adam or Eve but God, or rather his surrogate, God's vicegerent, the king or queen. In *The Dunciad* the Dunces do succeed in getting to the ear of kings, as does Sporus in "The Epistle to Dr. Arbuthnot." Pope's satire is about corruption, of the great, of great literature, and of the Great Men of government. Hogarth and Fielding (drawing on the intermediate figure, John Gay) we shall see portraying the betrayal not *of* the master but *by* the master, and *of* the servant.

Milton's Satan stands on the cusp of sin and evil, religion and morality; to the orthodox he was by definition evil—negative, corrupting, and parodic; to the freethinking (to Blake, but already to Dryden) he represented the prototypical sinner, embodying a sort of heroic defiance, the human will attempting to escape (Faust-like) from the legality of the Covenant and the evil of God's wrath.

Gay, The Beggar's Opera: *Low and High; Criminal and Politician*

Gay's *Beggar's Opera* (1728), which maps the liminal area between Restoration and so-called Augustan satire and the more secular humanist satire of Hogarth and Fielding, derives from the tradition of Restoration wit—the finding of similitude between different subjects in order to illuminate one of them. The rake was the chief conveyer of wit, but his analogies were supplemented by those of the honorable lover, a secondary character included in order to establish a norm by which we pass a judgment on the sins of the rake. In *The Country Wife* Horner's metaphors for love emphasize the sexual component: hunger, hunting, military encounters, and other reductive images; the ideal lover, Harcourt, courting the equally ideal Alithea, employs images of heaven and ascent: "with all my soul," "for heaven's sake," "above the world," and "by heavens."[16] Not that Wycherley is not ambivalent: The disguise Harcourt selects to secure Alithea is the costume of a parson.

The many forms taken by Wycherley's wit, as these examples suggest, boil down to burlesque—one subject reduced to a lower equivalent or analogue: Harcourt's heaven to Horner's hell;[17] Dido to a fishwife and (as in Lucian's Underworld) high to low. The gradual narrowing of the subject of wit from Wycherley and Etherege to William Congreve and George Farquhar, and from Richard Steele to Gay, is from a variety of analogues to one: between the respectable ruling class and the criminal lower orders. The Beggar who is the playwright of *The Beggar's Opera* thus concludes, "Through the whole Piece you may observe such a similitude of Manners in high and low Life, that it is difficult to determine whether (in the fashionable Vices) the fine Gentlemen imitate the Gentlemen of the Road, or the gentlemen of the Road the fine Gentlemen.—Had the Play remain'd, as I at first intended, it would have carried a most excellent Moral. 'Twould have shown that the lower Sort of People have their Vices in a degree as well as the Rich: And that they are punish'd for them" (III.xvi). In *The Beggar's Opera* the criminals are low, bad sinners (they break the laws) and are punished, but the respectable folk of the ruling class are worse and go unpunished. Dido has become worse than—the model for and corrupter of—the fishwife, and the reason is that Queen Dido has authority and power, the ability to commit evils with impunity.

The topos had, of course, an existence independent of Restoration wit. In trecento Florence, Matteo Villani wrote, "The powerful citizens who commit the greatest wrongs are never punished, while the small and weak are hanged, broken in pieces and decapitated for every petty misdemeanour."[18] In the eighteenth century, in Defoe's poem of 1702:

> Take Money of the Rich, and hang the Poor,
> And lash the Strumpet he debauch'd before.
> So for small crimes poor Thieves Destruction find,
> And leave the Rogues of Quality behind.[19]

While the poor rogues break the laws, the great rogues *make* the laws: the high against the low, the great against the small (in France, the *menu peuple* or *petits gens* vs. *les gros, les grands*).[20] The respectable folk are the effective evil that is only reflected in the more accessible (punishable) criminals/sinners like the highwayman Macheath and Jonathan Wild: Thus, sin is punished, evil rewarded, in this life at any rate.

Gay makes it clear that the thieves and fences and other criminals follow the example of prime ministers, statesmen, and respectable merchants, who are beyond the reach of the law. In law, however, the distinction was between principal and accessory (Blackstone, 4.3.34–40). The principal is the "absolute perpetrator of the crime," but the accessory can be either *before* or *after* the fact; *after* the fact being one who is "present, aiding, and abetting," while the accessory *before* the fact is the inspirer, one "who being absent at the time of the crime committed [vs. the accessory *after* the fact], doth yet procure, counsel, or command another to commit a crime." He is the one who "let[s] out a wild beast, with an intent to do mischief, or exciting a madman to commit murder" (35–36). "If A then advises B to kill A, and B does it in the absence of A, now B is principal, and A is accessory in the murder," and "if A, the reputed father, advises B the mother of a bastard child, unborn, to strangle it when born, and she does so; A is accessory to this murder" (37). In modern law the advisor is usually regarded as the more heinous criminal. The accessory gets a reduced sentence if he turns state's evidence on the man who employed him. But for Blackstone, "accessories shall suffer the same punishment as their principals" (39).

In the Swiftean sense in *A Tale of a Tub* these are fools to the knaves they imitate and invoke as authority for their crimes; Gay presents the sinners—the whores and highwaymen—who are of the lower orders; by showing them imitating the ruling order—in word and in deed—who do not hang, he implies a higher order that is worse than the lower; one based on the authority of law and the biblical text. The emphasis is on the power of the high/great, which equals evil, as opposed to the down position of the sinner, where low equals helplessness.

There is Macheath, whose sexual power, like that of Dorimant and Horner, is over women; and then there is the Great Man, whose political power, as in the case of Angelo and the Duke of Vienna, is legal: Gay is referring to Sir Robert Walpole, the prime minister, but he includes a whole class of society.[21] They are the implied figures of the Beggar's speech, governing England from beyond the limits of the stage; within the play their imitators are the fathers and jailors, men who have the power to cause sinners to suffer in the name of the law, Peachum by betraying them to the law, Lockit by locking them in his jailhouse.

In 1728 Gay created the significant paradigm by relating the high-low of burlesque to the distinction between respectable and low life, between evils and sins (both doing- and suffering-evils)—legal or scriptural transgressions and those that actually injure or kill; sexual, even romantic peccadilloes, and imprisonment and death.[22]

2. GRAPHIC IMAGERY

Sin

If the popular drama of the English stage was one pivot on which ideas of sin and evil shifted, another was the works of artists who mixed the aim of pious illustration with the artist's agenda of autonomous expression, leading to other ways in which the relation between sin and evil could be conceptualized. Sin was represented in medieval and Renaissance art primarily in scenes of hell, temptation, and the Seven Deadly Sins; evil by scenes of the Passion. The first referred to God, the second to Jesus Christ.

In north Europe representations of hell tended to follow the emblematic mode: Hieronymus Bosch's iconography of hell (taken from the hell of a popular Irish text, *The Vision of Tundal*) included, suggestively but arbitrarily, a huge bird that eats and excretes unchaste nuns and other sinners, a stolen cow, furnaces and ovens, pots and pans that connect the punishment with cooks and bakers, perversions of musical instruments, versions of hell-mouths, and violently misshapen bodies.[23] In *A Tale of a Tub* Swift's imagery recapitulates images of this sort in the Aeolists' and the Moderns' deformed bodies, all posterior or penis—or diseased bodies like the Banbury Saint's, but also the spider, the hollow barrels and guttering lamps and deserted houses, and of course the madhouse, itself a version of hell with its self-sufficient denizens reinfunding their own excrement.[24]

Dante's hell placed the good up in the sky with God, the sinners below the earth, tormented by devils. The topography was of above and below, of effulgent heaven and fiery hell, and artists enjoyed depicting the fall from one to the other, the power of the one and the weakness of the other. Italian artists—as well as some of the north European artists—tended merely to show falling and moiling figures, a subject expanded by baroque artists like Peter Paul Rubens into mighty waterfalls of naked figures.

Luca Signorelli, in his huge frescoes in the Capella Nuova (the San Brizio chapel) in the Orvieto Duomo, shows only nude bodies—of both the damned and the demons mistreating them, dragging them down to hell. The damned are not identified with their sins or evil acts. The saved, in the pendant, are shown in graceful, orderly rows, hands clasped in prayer; the bodies of the damned, in themselves equally beautiful, are contorted, struggling with devils or serpents who claw at their faces, gnaw on their arms, bind them, pull at their hair, and embrace the women. The scene is presided over by a trinity of angels who cast the damned down into the hands of the devils, whose bodies are human except for their wings and the fuchsia, blue, gray, and green coloration of their bodies.

The demons provided artists, largely limited to divine subjects, opportunities to free and exercise the imagination, producing the indecorous mixture (part animal, part human) Horace had warned against in the opening of his *De Arte Poetica*. The grotesque demons in paintings such as the *Last Judgment* in the Florence Baptistry and Fra Angelico's in San Marco set off the realistic agony of their victims.[25] The sinners offered humanist-inclined artists opportunities to explore the nude human body while painting religious subjects—beautiful shapes intermingled with demonic bodies that are prodding and tormenting them—and sometimes female nude bodies in provocative poses.

Some grimmer hells, such as those of Pieter Brueghel, materialized contemporary executions and the tortures imposed on the condemned criminals and wrongdoers, but primarily heretics and traitors: flesh torn with red hot pincers, bodies broken on the wheel, scourged, flayed alive, disemboweled, and burned at the stake (which was regarded as an anticipation of the fires subsequently to be suffered eternally in hell).

In paintings of temptations the sin most often represented was lust. Saint Anthony, as described by Saint Jerome, retreated to the desert, where his only companions were "scorpions and wild beasts," but in his dreams he was "surrounded by dancing girls," which caused "the fires of the passions [to keep] boiling within" him.[26] Matthias Grünewald and Bosch replaced these dancing girls with demons, more threatening than tempting; the latter are abominations or manifestations of the sin's consequences but occasionally are joined by a beautiful woman or a platter of food. By the sixteenth century Tintoretto's Saint Anthony in San Travaso, Venice, is being tempted by three beautiful, partly clothed women.

Other artists domesticated or contextualized the sins—again primarily the sin of lust—in scenes from the Old Testament or the classics. Lust is delineated in the faces and gestures of the old men in paintings of Susannah and the Elders: versions by Tintoretto and Rubens are in the Kunsthistorisches Museum, Vienna; by Rembrandt in the Mauritzhuis, The Hague. There are also classical variants that replace the elders with satyrs peering at sleeping nymphs, that is, beautiful nude women (Annibale Carracci in the Uffizi, Florence; Antoine Watteau in the Louvre, Paris). Rape is implied, voyeurism is shown. In Bronzino's *Allegory of Venus and Cupid* (National Gallery, London), lust is abstracted altogether from Christian sin, though still portrayed in the figure of a beautiful nude woman, set off and defined by the old and young, ugly and beautiful figures surrounding her.

Memento mori paintings dramatized a related situation; simply about dying, their message was that in life you may be rich, happy, and proud but thoughts of death should humble you, thoughts that may evoke hell. Hans Baldung Grien juxtaposed the beautiful young living woman and a corpse, male or female (another example was the *transi* of early Renaissance funerary sculpture—the idealized body juxtaposed with the rotting corpse); so also painters juxtaposed piles of luscious food with signs of decay, books or crowns with skulls.

What most of these images have in common—in the humanist tradition from Signorelli and Michelangelo to Rubens and Watteau—is the beautiful human body, in various ways contrasted with demonic bodies, distinguished either by horns and tails or by grotesque ugliness or decay. This was a way of representing death as one of the evils, the corruption or punishment that follows from the sin of lust or gluttony or vanity (another name for preferring any other thing to God, such as money, food, fleshly love, or self), but in the hands of Tintoretto, Rubens, and Watteau the evils serve predominantly to set off—to emphasize—the beautiful image of human delight.

Evil

Doing-evil emerged primarily, and most meaningfully, in depictions of the Passion. Representations of the Passion were about evil because in them Jesus himself has to suffer the evils consequent upon the Original Sin (death, suffering, etc.) in order to redeem that sin. *This*, the paintings and prints say, is what "absolute evil" really looks like. In practice it tends to follow (visually reproduce) the structure of Juvenalian satire, evils surrounding and overwhelming the single beautiful ideal.[27] With Jesus, who came to earth to redeem Adam's and our sins, evil is what the priests and soldiers do to him; they are evildoers, making *him,* of all people, suffer. He represents the totally innocent human—beyond innocence—punished with the evils of the world. The acts carried out upon him are, of course, technically examples of sin—the very sins of disobedience he is redeeming. But rather than being about sin, the pictorial images are about the evil imposed upon him (in the sense of the suffering he endures) as man-to-man: he is taking our place as sufferer, suffering evil from the doers of evil. Evil, as always, is the consequence of the concept of sin: centered on Jesus and the Passion, on the model of *Ecce Homo,* Flagellation, and Crucifixion scenes (as opposed to Pietàs, Entombments, Resurrections).[28]

Flagellations were painted in the south, by Signorelli, Piero della Francesca, Titian, and Caravaggio; but in Italian Renaissance art the emphasis was less on Jesus' suffering and death than on the Resurrection and the triumph of Redemption. The bloody and ravaged Christ was obsessively treated in northern European religious art, and the faces of the persecutors and mockers become caricatures or grotesques and Jesus is prettified and feminized. In Bosch's and Quentin Massys's *Ecce Homo* and *Christ Mocked* paintings, only Jesus is composed and beautiful, the image of a beautiful face surrounded by hideous persecutors. He replaces, it appears, but with rather different connotations, the beautiful woman of the sin, temptation, and *memento mori* pictures.[29]

The case of the sin of lust in art I cited was Susannah and the Elders, in which Renaissance artists domesticated the sin in the faces and gestures of the old men leering at Susannah. The story in the book of Daniel tells how the elders, usually shown as voyeurs, then threaten her with false witness unless she submits to their lust—a rape prevented when their lies are exposed by the wise judge Daniel. The elders peering at the nude, defenseless Susannah were another version of the mockers around Christ in *Ecce Homo* pictures.

At the center is the one beautiful, totally innocent figure, whether Christ or a saint being martyred, surrounded by figures of evil or lust; the latter serve to define evil as power oppressing the weak (in the extreme case, God-made-human). In rococo paintings the emphasis shifted from the threat of the elders to the beauty of the woman, which is in effect emphasized by the context of the ugly and aged men, titillatingly set off by their impotent voyeurism. The scene of a beautiful figure surrounded by ugly persecutors and mockers was a model first for religious devotion, then for severe satire, and then for a comedy of incongruous contrasts—the old men and the young girl—and finally for an aesthetics in which beauty is defined by contrast with ugliness and the threat of violation.

Sin Punished, Evil Rewarded: Hogarth, A Harlot's Progress

Hogarth's first mature work was the six engravings of *A Harlot's Progress* (1732). In plate 4 (fig. 1), showing the Harlot beating hemp in Bridewell Prison, he evokes the Christian devotional image of Jesus surrounded by mocking and scourging prison warders. In all six plates he shows a sinner and criminal suffering at the hands of the representatives of respectable society. The prurient scene that served as nucleus for the six showed the girl, just out of bed, being seized by a magistrate and his beadles, equivalent to the elders. To make the connection between the law and sin, Hogarth embedded his story of the Harlot's legal crime and punishment in images that allude to Christ's Atonement, scenes based on prints by Albrecht Dürer (fig. 2), ending in plate 6 with her body replacing the Eucharist in a mock Last Supper.

From the religious perspective the Harlot is obviously a sinner. She disobeys God's Commandments *Thou shalt not worship a false god* and *Thou shalt not commit adultery.* To be a prostitute was a sin as well as legally a crime, but the Harlot's sins-crimes are victimless; she hurts no one (she steals a watch; she is shown getting but not transmitting disease), whereas the agents of society punish her with evils (prison, whips, disease, death), in the name of the church, law, and government. (Hogarth had made the equation of sin-evil-law early on in his print of 1725 *Royalty, Episcopacy, and Law.*)[30] Hogarth juxtaposes the concepts of sin-law and evil, showing that sin is simply the name the ruling order gives to pleasure and unsanctioned love.

The punishment is not only for the Harlot's Original Sin of concupiscence; society punishes her for aspiring and attempting to be a "lady," that Levitical *abomination* a harlot-lady. (Jesus' "sin," an equal but opposite abomination, was mingling with harlots and people of the lower orders.) Her aspirations are shown off by the elegant gown she continues to wear after being reduced to prostitution and confined to prison, by the pictures she hangs on her shabby walls in imitation of her former keeper, and by the pretentious funeral escutcheon she has invented for herself in plate 6.

Northern scenes of the Passion had two aspects: One was the mocking and flagellation by the torturers, the other was the apathy of the bystanders.

FIGURE 1   William Hogarth, *A Harlot's Progress* (1732), plate 3. Etching and engraving. Reproduced by courtesy of the Trustees of the British Museum.

W. H. Auden wrote about the latter in his poem "Musée des Beaux Arts," looking at Brueghel's *Fall of Icarus,* where the surrounding figures are farmers continuing to plough—ordinary people carrying on their daily lives unaware of Icarus's fall, as if no tragedy, no miracle, nothing unusual had happened. ("Someone else is eating or opening a window or just walking dully along.") In the Passion paintings the crowd of figures and faces around Christ are not preoccupied; they are cruelly focused on him. In Brueghel's crucifixions the vicious, malicious, and murderous are supplemented by the unaware, ignorant, and stupid as well as by the pragmatists, who just turn their backs.

In the first plate of *A Harlot's Progress* the distraction of the clergyman (who, instead of defending the young girl, is studying the address of the bishop of London, Sir Robert Walpole's chief of ecclesiastical preferment) and the absence of the girl's "lofing Cosen in Tems Stret in London" are set off against the active seduction by the bawd Mother Needham and the rake Colonel Charteris (well known as "Rape-Master of England").

FIGURE 2   Albrecht Dürer, *Flagellation* (detail). Woodcut, from *The Albertina Passion* (ca. 1496). Reproduced by courtesy of the Trustees of the British Museum.

The salvationist Jesus is somewhere up in heaven in the imagination of good Church of Englanders; but Hogarth's Jesus is the Jesus who defended the woman taken in adultery and castigated the scribes and clergymen while keeping company with Mary Magdalen the penitent harlot. In Matthew 23:33 Jesus chose an adulterous woman, not a murderer or thief or rapist, to illustrate his words, "Who is without sin cast the first stone." Sin is what the woman taken in adultery committed; evil is what the Law of Moses demanded: "that such should be stoned" (John 8:5). Jesus consorted, in the eyes of the Pharisees, with harlots, one of whom Hogarth uses as his symbol of sin in *A Harlot's Progress*. Here *sin* refers not only to the Levitical and Pauline Harlot (and the Harlot of Revelation) but to the pharisaic code of sin that (as Blake will point out) in practice replaced Jesus' moral commandments of "Love thy neighbor as thyself" and "Do unto others as you would have done to yourself." The priests ignore the Harlot's plight, evoking in plates 1 and 6 Ezekiel's "Woe to the shepherds who feed themselves, but feed not their flocks" (34:2 and 8).

In *The Beggar's Opera* Gay showed Macheath, in a local piece of wit, betrayed by a Judas kiss, suggesting a witty analogy between Macheath's betrayal and Christ's in the Garden of Gethsemane.[31] The verbal and graphic texts joined in the paintings Hogarth made to illustrate *The Beggar's Opera* (1728–30). He painted the scene in act IV in which Peachum denies his daughter Polly's plea to spare Macheath's life and posed him in a parody of Christ and Mary Magdalen in a *Noli Me Tangere* scene ("Don't touch me, I'm all spirit").

The most famous case of the sort of "sacred parody" suggested by Erasmus's Folly, and now Hogarth's Harlot, was Marlowe's Doctor Faustus signing his compact with the devil as he quotes Christ's words on the cross, "Consummatum est" (John 19:30).[32] He sees himself as a Christ substitute. Marlowe was a subversive Elizabethan, evidently an atheist, whereas Hogarth was a man of the Enlightenment, a Deist (at the least) and Freemason. Like Marlowe's, Hogarth's schooling was classical and Ovidian.[33] But his analogy is more shocking than Marlowe's because it goes far beyond a pair of words to structure the whole six plates of his story as a retelling of the Gospel story.

In his retelling Hogarth conflates Jesus and his mother, Mary: whereas Renaissance artists softened the gentle face of Jesus, Hogarth literally feminizes it. In plate 1 M[ary?] Hackabout (as he names the Harlot) appears as the Virgin Mary in the composition of a Visitation; in 2 the mystery of the conception is revealed (the cuckolding of her keeper with the young lover slipping out of the door behind him), followed in plate 3 by the Annunciation. So far, we have the story of Mary the Mother. Plate 4 shows the Flagellation, but it is *hers*. In plate 5 the soldiers are casting dice for Christ's robe at the foot of the cross, but it is *hers* (the doctors contest her cure, the landlady plunders her clothes)—though she assumes the pose of the grieving Mary the Mother, and the Son now appears, off to the side, picking lice out of his hair, unconnected with the feminine sacrifice that is unfolding. Finally, in plate 6 the Mother's body in her coffin is congruent with the table of the Last Supper and Communion, the Body

next to the Blood (the chalice); she has *become* the Christ figure—Mary
the Mother substituting, in Hogarth's parody of the Incarnation, for the
Son. The son is present, a mute witness (in fact, his back is turned, he is
seated on the wrong side of the table), but it is the mother whose body and
blood figure the most holy of sacraments, the Eucharist. The unmistakable
message is that she, a prostitute and not Jesus, is the person who takes
upon herself the sins and atones for the evils of society in 1730s England
(as Polly Peachum attempted, in the play and in Hogarth's painting, to
redeem Macheath).[34]

Hogarth's Harlot is a descendant of Erasmus's Folly, also female,
also transgressive, who by the illusion she offered "redeemed" unhappy
mankind. Folly, we recall, set up the basic distinction between sin (man's
supposedly original sin based on all the legal structures of church and
state) and the evil that is the consequence of a religion of sin.

Hogarth, Defoe, Richardson, Rousseau

If we glance back at *Robinson Crusoe*, we see that Hogarth's message, while
in the 1730s uniquely subversive, reflected a distinction between sin and
evil that was beginning to be noticeable in the post-soteriological world of
eighteenth-century England.[35] Swift turned Paul's and Augustine's internalizing of sin into the act of sin itself, the heresy of self-enclosure: In this
sense, as an orthodox Anglican, he opened the way to Hogarth's picture of
deeds (evil) as all that matter—perhaps the one bit of anti-Puritan ideology they shared. The next generation, those we associate with the English
Enlightenment, found its evil in the oppression of the ecclesiastical pol-
ity Swift supported. Sin they equated with legal crime (felony, stealing a
pocket watch) as opposed to evil, which designated suffering, punishment
consequent upon Adam's Original Sin, and, in the legal sense, referred
to the "criminal's" death, transportation, flogging, or imprisonment. Hogarth's Harlot is imprisoned, beaten, infected with disease, and killed by
the men who use her, from Colonel Charteris, who may have given her
syphilis and certainly turned her into a whore, to the clergymen, magistrates, and physicians who exploit her. And behind them, the bishop of
London and the prime minister Sir Robert Walpole. Colonel Charteris
and the magistrate Sir John Gonson—whose likenesses appear in plates 1
and 3—were supporters of, surrogates for, and representatives of Walpole.

In Samuel Richardson's *Clarissa*, published fifteen years after the

Harlot and thirty years after *Robinson Crusoe,* the basic situation involves evil:[36] Lovelace is a Satan figure who seduces innocent women; when he cannot seduce Clarissa, he rapes her—indeed does not make her *sin* but commits an act of *evil* upon her, both in the sense of Satan's seduction of Eve and in the literal sense of suffering (primarily to Clarissa but ultimately, in the Augustinian formulation of evil as self-destructive, to himself as well). But there is another story in *Clarissa,* that of the Harlowes, Clarissa's ultrarespectable family, and this, from the theological perspective—which is that of Clarissa herself—involves her *sin* of disobedience to the father (the surrogate of God).

Richardson's audience—and, one must presume, Richardson himself—cannot have read the moral that way: the father himself, insofar as he is imposing on his daughter dreadful but rich husbands, is an evildoer—as evil, in terms of the consequences of his actions, as Lovelace. However complicit Clarissa's actions can be found (a secret love of Lovelace?), her disobedience of her father can no longer be judged solely in religious terms. The sin of Clarissa (disobedience to her parents, Commandment 5, but implicit in Commandments 1–5) is certainly punished but is nothing as compared to what her false suitor-lover Lovelace does to her—or indeed her parents—in a situation that is structurally parallel to that of the Harlot and her male society.

Hogarth stands out in his plain, graphic dissociation of sin from evil, questioning the religious assumption that moral evil (sin, disobedience of God's Ten Commandments) is the explanation for natural evil (suffering, punishment). He anticipates Rousseau's thesis that evil is socially, not theologically, grounded (in his *Second Discourse on Inequality* and *Emile,* of 1755 and 1762, respectively)[37]—though it was not, in Rousseau's case, the fault of a crafty priesthood but man's own once he became part of a social unit. Rousseau argues that *in history* man changes from a life in nature to life in the social contract (civilization), which corrupts his original innocence/simplicity. Rousseau replaces grace and penance with education/knowledge, thereby showing that the situation of evil/misfortune *can* be changed.

Seen from the retrospect of Rousseau and the 1760s, the Harlot is good when she arrives in London from the country and is corrupted by London fashion/society—in the specific sense that she is punished, experiences natural and moral evil, for what society regards as sin by a society that is itself (partly for this reason) morally evil. Colonel Charteris, her first seducer, is only the first in the series of men who represent respectable society—the society of Law (he may be convicted of rape but is pardoned by the king via the prime minister)—which exploits and destroys her. Herein lies Hogarth's sense of evil, related to the one outlined by Rousseau thirty years later, but with a difference: Society for Rousseau is the complex interrelations of people who have contracted to live together—for example, covering possibly earthquake-dangerous hills with rickety dwellings that could collapse and kill people (the Problem of Evil)—whereas for Hogarth it is specific offices and positions, most largely defined by the clergy (Church and Law), and so including English judges, bailiffs, and physicians. Thus, the two views of the Harlot in A Harlot's Progress: as sinner and as victim of society.

But if evil for Rousseau originates in the society constructed by men and women, for Hogarth the ultimate evil is in the power of God, which may manifest itself in Rousseau's society, either by God's presence or absence, in both cases in the law. At first glance, Hogarth's second "Modern Moral Subject," The Rake's Progress (1735), would appear to differ from the Harlot: Tom Rakewell, who (unlike the Harlot) can afford to imitate his betters, is not ruined by the law; he destroys himself—as, we could say, a representative of Christian evil. He has ruined Sarah Young, exploited another woman, and gambled away his money, declining into syphilitic madness. Sarah is, from the religious point of view, another sinner—she fornicates and gets pregnant; but by the evil (or foolish-evil) character, Rakewell, for whom she nevertheless attempts unsuccessfully to be another mediating angel like Polly and the Harlot. She is the Hogarth woman, déclassé, a sinner, but identified with Christ's woman taken in adultery, the Samarian Woman, and Mary Magdalen.

This is, however, to miss the continuity running through Hogarth's sense of what is evil. Evil is the doing-evil and the suffering-evil of Rakewell and, in Marriage A-la-mode (1745), of the Squanders, but the evil agency is assigned not to these weaklings but to the aristocratic order Rakewell imitates in order to be a rake and the ethos of greatness (in the secular and divine images on the walls) that is followed by the Squanders. In the Harlot this was the offstage presence of Sir Robert Walpole. Ultimate responsibility is with the highest authority, the "god" (actually a deus absconditus), who is represented in the paintings on Lord Squander's walls: For example, one is Domenichino's *Martyrdom of St. Agnes,* but in his (and Hogarth's) version her reward in heaven, which filled the upper third of Domenichino's canvas, is missing. Lord Squander, the overweening father, has replaced the spiritual Father.[38]

Evil as power is the way the past in its various forms—as law and religion but, for Hogarth, above all as embodied in art, in paintings of the Old (or, to use Hogarth's word, "dark") Masters—determines and controls our actions, *making* them evil. That is, evil actions *in the past,* when we imitate—or are compelled to imitate—the "heroic" acts of the Old Testament or Greek myths, determine evil acts in the present: as Rakewell imitates a *Judgment of Paris* and a portrait of Nero or old Earl Squander his paintings of Pharaoh, Louis XIV, and various pagan gods. In *Marriage A-la-mode* the paintings and their horrific subjects, demonstrations of divine power and cruelty, in fact exacerbate the wrongs of the actions taking place below them, as well as determining them.

From the point of view of the artist, their baroque forms magnify the actions they portray; this is one of the roles of art to which Hogarth persistently draws attention, going back to his allusions to the Passion in the *Harlot's Progress:* Art adds the capital E to evil; art is therefore, in Hogarth's logic, itself evil, as nature is good—the nature with which in his "modern moral subjects" he was attempting to replace the art of the Old Masters. There is no sign that this burden of past evil represented to Hogarth Original Sin, only the ecclesiastical manipulators of Original Sin, not Adam's eating the apple but imitable actions reproduced in art, to be avoided by basically good (Pelagian) humans.

3. THE AESTHETICS OF SIN

The Rococo
Watteau, founder of the French rococo, was in England in 1719–20 and left paintings behind him—scenes involving figures from the *commedia dell'arte.* A great many of his paintings had been reproduced by etching and engraving and were available by the end of the 1720s when Hogarth began to paint. In particular two prefigured the English rococo developed by Hogarth: One was the *Comédiens Italiens* (National Gallery, Washington) which was in London in Dr. Richard Mead's collection, showing the all-white clown, the figure of innocence, Pierrot, and the Italian comedians

on a stage in an *Ecce Homo* composition; this could have been the model for Hogarth's introduction to his particular version of the rococo in the *Harlot's Progress*.

The rococo was essentially an emphasis on pure play and pleasure, a reduction of the grandiose baroque forms of the seventeenth century to a modest scale; of the baroque subjects (which often meant Counter-Reformation subjects) of crucifixions, martyrdoms, and stories of religio-erotic passion to *fêtes champêtres* and *fêtes gallantes*. Watteau's *Comédiens Italiens* wittily reduces scenes of Christ being mocked by the crowd, surrounded by Pharisees, priests, and Roman centurians, to a scene of actors, and in particular the simple white figure of Pierrot, facing an audience on a stage (again wittily, a dubious, potentially hostile audience). Jesus is replaced by a clown (actors were regarded by the religious as sinners), pain by pleasure. Hogarth then increases the irony by turning the clown Pierrot into a harlot (illicit pleasure) and showing her literally punished and killed by the respectable forces around her. At the same time he turns the purely rococo forms—that he would show in his aesthetic treatise, *The Analysis of Beauty* (1753), operating to lead the spectator's eye a merry chase around and through the composition—into cognitive forms, shifting gestalts and reading structures that vary from the formal to the emblematic and the punningly and literally verbal.

Hogarth is the artist who gave satiric content to the forms of the rococo. From Watteau he takes the subject of love, groups in interpersonal relationships, and (with a few exceptions) moves them indoors. This is where the second Watteau painting, *L'Enseigne de Gersaint* (Charlottenburg, Berlin), comes in: Hogarth's interiors follow from Gersaint's shop, the walls covered with pictures that define the ethos of their collectors. From this work Hogarth takes the contrast of nature and art, life and paintings or sculptures—that reaches its culmination in the two plates that illustrate *The Analysis of Beauty*. Hogarth develops the Watteau themes and forms—the serpentine lines, the miniaturized baroque; he adapts Watteau's witty tone, vastly extending the use of the forms to carry the eye about within the composition, and produces what in his aesthetics he calls "curiosity" and the "love of pursuit."

Disobedience was one element of the rococo, abomination another: As Watteau shows in *L'Enseigne de Gersaint,* his art is *not* going to be baroque —not about the royal figure or about Christian martyrs and saints; it is going to be something less official, more immediate and local. And this is what Hogarth is expressing (for example, in his epigraph from Horace's *De Arte Poetica*, "License is given on condition that you use it with care") in his turn away from religious orthodoxy. He prefers sinning to the evil that follows from its punishment by priests and magistrates; both are hypocrites, as in *Harlot* 1, where the priest is more concerned about his preferment than about the lamb that is being sacrificed under his eyes, and 6, where the priest, instead of officiating, gropes one of the prostitutes. As abomination, we have already noted, the Harlot's real sin in the eyes of society (vs. the legal one of prostitution) is trying to be a lady.

"Rebellious Sexual Fornication": The Comedy of Sin

"Sexually fornicating rebellion" is another way of describing the rococo's reaction against the Counter-Reformation baroque and its elevation of God and the monarch. To employ fornication in a positive light is to satirize the most fundamental of the sins—"rebellious sexual fornication" or "religiously alienating sexual fornication."[39] We recall, contradicting Jesus' defense of the woman taken in adultery, Paul's use of the metaphor of fornication and adultery to describe the evil of rebellion—acts of copulation that worshiped gods other than or in addition to the only God, a doctrine reinforced by Augustine's treatment of lust as the original sin resulting from the uncontrollable male sexual organ. The threat of a religiously mixed marriage was combined with the orgiastic intercourse believed to be part of the fertility rituals of alien gods (that is, "gods to whom they used to direct their energy sexually, reproductively, and in other respects"), thus producing abominations.[40] Such sinners must, according to the Old Testament law, be destroyed as rebels: "Then they shall bring out the damsel to the door of her father's house, and the men of her city shall stone her with stones that she die; because she hath wrought folly in Israel, to play the whore in her father's house" (Deut. 22:21). Sexual intercourse was legitimate only when subordinated to the worship of God and within marriage—anything else gets more attention than God, or than one's husband or father. In all of this the correspondence between "obeisance to a god who requires exclusive worship" and patriarchy is evident.

From the sin of fornication as rebellion follows the seriousness of adultery, and the favorite situation of stage comedy of the old husband and the young wife; the latter loves an "alien" young man and must be locked up—but, because it is comedy, she escapes. From the *commedia dell'arte* through the Restoration comedies of fornication and adultery, the situation primarily involved the old husband cuckolded by his young wife and her young lover. From the perspective of the old man, preferring something to God—focusing attention on the sin of lust, loving a woman more than God—was shown to be primarily self-destructive, as in the case of Molière's old husbands and Wycherley's Pinchwife and Fidget. From the perspective of the woman, virtue was preferring a young man to God or God's surrogate, her father or her husband, the Pantalone of the *commedia*.

Comedy per se, but especially in the England that emerged from the Interregnum, was a release from the Pauline-Augustinian-Puritan condemnation of fornication, harlotry, and adultery, finding its subject in precisely those subjects. It is difficult to find cases in England after 1660, outside devotional literature, in which the Deadly Sins (as opposed to evils such as the rape of Clarissa) are not material for comedy.[41] With the possible exceptions of lust and anger, the Deadly Sins (sloth, gluttony, envy, pride, and greed) were essentially comedic—victimless and object-less human follies, often with Horace's satires as the model, in which excess is on the part of the jealous, possessive husband, set off by the lusty, beautiful young couple.

In the areas of the comic and aesthetic, Hogarth does not regard adultery per se as evil; only when, as in satire, the consequences (as in *Marriage A-la-mode*) entail the ruining of the involved parties does he pass judgment. Comedy, we might say, aestheticizes satire, lifting it into a realm above morality as well as religion.

Aesthetics: Beauty and Adultery

In the late 1720s Hogarth made a series of paintings illustrating Gay's *Beggar's Opera*. The composition with its frontal lineup of figures resembles Watteau's *Comédiens Italiens*. Though fairly androgynous, the Pierrot figure was male, as was his first Hogarthian incarnation—Captain Macheath, at the center of the tableau that includes, symmetrically flanking him, his two lovers, Polly and Lucy, and their respective fathers. Macheath, like the Harlot, was a figure of sin rather than evil—a popular comic character associated with love and multiple love affairs; he was contrasted with the more grasping and "evil" figures of Peachum and Lockit, as Hackabout

FIGURE 3   William Hogarth, *A Harlot's Progress*, plate 2. Etching and engraving. Reproduced by courtesy of the Trustees of the British Museum.

was by Charteris and the bawd Mother Needham. But the spectator could choose, slipping from one gestalt to another: a young man between two lovers, or a young woman between a lover and her possessive father.

Plate 2 of the *Harlot's Progress* (fig. 3), the one plate of the six that was not really concerned with evil (the social-climbing Jew was as much a victim as the Harlot), though not exactly a comedy, posed a comic triangle of the girl Hackabout, her rich Jewish keeper, and her young lover. The Harlot committed adultery in that she took a lover behind the back of her keeper—but the scene is presented as *commedia* farce with the lover slipping out the door behind his back, the Harlot kicking over the tea table to divert his attention. And superimposed on the triangle of *Harlot* 2 (given the sequence of the other five plates and the New Testament allusions, lodged as it is between parodies of the Visitation and the Annunciation) was the freethinker's joke of the young Virgin Mary, the old husband Joseph, and the Roman soldier Mary passes off as the "Holy Ghost."

FIGURE 4   William Hogarth, *The Analysis of Beauty* (1753), plate 2 (detail). Etching and engraving. Reproduced by courtesy of the Trustees of the British Museum.

In *Marriage A-la mode* Hogarth shows a situation in which adultery seems natural, legal marriage unnatural: a passionate young woman is married (contractually) to a husband who only studies his own image in the mirror and has pedophilic preferences. In plate 1 of *The Analysis of Beauty,* a sculpture yard, the Venus de Medici, enlivened, seems to be inclining toward the young, ideally handsome Apollo Belvedere, in the middle of a romantic triangle involving a third party, the huge muscle-bound Farnese Hercules. In plate 2 a young wife agrees to an assignation with a young man while her husband's attention is on other matters, such as getting home to bed (fig. 4). The adultery centers on the woman, the Polly or Lucy rather than Macheath. The reason for this—or the outcome—depends on Hogarth's creation of an aesthetics, for which he requires a woman, not a man.

Hogarth's Harlot *was* a sinner: *they,* the respectable folk, thought so, and Hogarth in the long run agrees; but he revalues sin, preferring it to the evil of the law that exploits and punishes, tortures and kills it, indeed he makes sin the basis of his aesthetics. He defines the beauty as the body of the beautiful woman, but, he specifies, a living and (the same thing?) sinning woman, usually, like Christ's woman taken in adultery, an adulteress. The triangle of the Harlot, the Jew, and the escaping lover in *Harlot* 2 was a first thought for the adulterous triangles of the two *Analysis of Beauty* plates in which Hogarth omitted the evil agents and focused on the sinner, the "silly goose" (in the punning image of *Harlot* 1), a woman associated in the text with Eve and Cleopatra, and in the illustrative plates with Venus and the Woman of Samaria. Hogarth relates his Line of Beauty to the Satanic serpent, confirmed by his epigraph from *Paradise Lost* describing the serpent's approach to Eve at her commission of the Original Sin.

Hogarth, like Watteau, is responding to the allegories with which great houses were decorated, paintings of a beautiful woman, Virtue, and a hideous man, Vice. His association of the beautiful with sin is both subversive and aesthetic—an aesthetic appreciation replacing a moral (or theological) judgment. It is "beauty" as sin that Hogarth opposes to the aesthetics of his chief predecessor, the third earl of Shaftesbury, who simply equated beauty and virtue and embodied them in the antique sculpture of a Hercules.[42] Hogarth, we see, enlivens a sculptured Venus by placing her in a romantic triangle with Hercules and Apollo, inclining toward the handsome young man. "Who but a bigot," Hogarth writes in the *Analysis,* "even to the antiques, will say that he has not seen faces and necks, hands and arms in living women, that even the grecian Venus doth but coarsely imitate?"[43]

Hogarth's relationship to Shaftesbury needs to be more precisely defined: Intermediary as well as opponent, Shaftesbury gave Hogarth the image-of-choice, the Choice of Hercules (employed by Hogarth repeatedly in his works from his *Beggar's Opera* and *Harlot* 1 to *The March to Finchley* of 1750), which consists of a beautiful young male flanked by Virtue and Vice, both female, both beautiful; but the first is statuesque, upstanding, instructing the young man in morals, the second a sprawled, languorous temptress. Hogarth prefers the latter.

Hogarth was, in effect, correcting Shaftesbury when he replaced Hercules with a young woman; when he supplemented and replaced in *Harlot* 1 his classical example of Hercules with the Christian story of the Visitation, and then trumped that with contemporary likenesses of the bawd

Elizabeth Needham, the rake Colonel Charteris, his pimp Jack Gourlay, and presumably (though no portrait has survived) the Harlot's namesake, Kate Hackabout: living Londoners, identified by contemporaries.[44]

What he claims we respond to in this aesthetic situation is the play, ocular and cognitive, the pursuit, of shifting gestalts and overlapping imagery (Choice of Hercules, Visitation, contemporary portraits). The principles he outlines in the *Analysis of Beauty*—curiosity, novelty, surprise, attraction, pursuit, and seduction (though stopping short of consummation)—are all constitutive of the concupiscence behind Augustine's Original Sin.

Curiosity, for Swift a sin that leads to evils, was for Hogarth a virtue. With the idea of curiosity something similar to the revaluation of fornication happened. Curiosity in the Middle Ages was often included in the Seven Deadly Sins, under lust or sloth, pride or greed. Augustine called it *concupiscentia oculorum,* the "lust of the eyes," and Bernard of Clairvaux connected it with sloth and pride. But in the early modern period it, along with its accompanying sins, was elevated into virtues—into natural (experimental) philosophy and the legitimate search for truths obscured by church law. Interestingly for the transformation of fornication and lust, an engraving of 1713 by an Austrian Franciscan shows an allegory: Pilgrim meets two female figures, Devotion and Curiosity, as Hercules met Virtue and Pleasure at the crossroads, and his attention (choice?) turns away from the veiled figure of Devotion and focuses on a sexy Curiosity.[45]

In Hobbes's vocabulary, good and evil equaled peace and war, and in physiological terms desire and aversion. You are drawn toward what you regard as good, away from the bad, and the good is whatever you want or desire. Hogarth's aesthetics of pleasure, curiosity, surprise, and pursuit is Hobbesian insofar as it is based on motion, desire, attraction, and pursuit, seeking and obtaining: "For there is no such thing as perpetual Tranquility of mind, while we live here; because Life itself is but perpetual motion." When Hobbes writes, "The thoughts are to the desires as scouts and spies, to range abroad and find the way to the things desired," we may think we are reading *The Analysis of Beauty*.[46] Something is good because it attracts—draws one to it and into it; evil if one feels aversion; thus Hogarth's aesthetics.

Beauty, then, consists of the Harlot's sins of adultery and harmless affectation (or pride), as evils victimless, but as sin punished by clerics and magistrates, graphic equivalents of Susannah's threatening elders. Evil, as in the *Harlot,* equals the consequences of beauty-sin, which are punishment, disease, and death. This Hogarth takes to be the true story as opposed to the Old Testament story of Eve eating the apple.

Rowlandson

In the next generation Thomas Rowlandson's drawings and prints endlessly elaborate the composition of *Harlot* 2: the lover (Horatio Nelson) hides in an Egyptian sarcophagus, the young wife (Emma, Lady Hamilton) presses herself into the sarcophagus to embrace her young lover, and her old, shriveled husband (the collector of antiquities Lord Hamilton) is engrossed in some art objects (fig. 5). Or art is associated with surgery: a young man poses as a cadaver, a subject for anatomical study, in order to get at the young wife into whose home he has contrived thereby to penetrate, while the old husband, the physician who has bought this body, is in fact getting out his dissecting tools—putting the young lover in imminent danger. Or the lover climbs out of a trunk and is welcomed by the wife as the husband leaves, double- and triple-locking the door (or the lover is climbing in a window). All draw upon the old Shylock, who attempts to lock his daughter Jessica in with several locks, only to have her climb out a window into the arms of her lover with, for extra measure, his ducats. All have in common the handsome young lover, the beautiful young wife, and the old, ugly husband, who is engrossed in one form or other of what Hogarth regards as art (objets d'art, the study of anatomy, or the employment of padlocks on doors). *Art* includes the law that constrains and persecutes the sinner; sin itself is not evil—it is either innocent or (with adultery) comic and liberating; part of Hogarth's comedy is that of liberty trying to find outlets within his closed rooms and systems—within enclosures, closely related to Swift's image of the vapor seeking an exit in "The Digression on Madness."

Rowlandson shows elderly men filling the role of Susannah's elders, mixing lust and curiosity—an impotent curiosity which prefers knowledge to pleasure. He develops the *Ecce Homo* scene through the mediation of Hogarth's *Harlot* 4 and the *Analysis of Beauty* plates into a basic composition: grotesque heads surrounding the body of a beautiful young woman, often nude.[47] But he mediates the *Ecce Homo,* changing cruelty to voyeurism, by way of the tradition of *Susannah and the Elders* paintings (as he shows in

FIGURE 5 Thomas Rowlandson, *Modern Antiques*. Colored Etching. Ca. 1800. Reproduced by courtesy of the Trustees of the British Museum.

various drawings of artists at work, this was his favorite Old Master subject) and Baldung Grien's *memento mori* contrasts of beautiful young women and hideously moribund hags and figures of Death (figs. 6–8). More voyeuristic and less threatening, these men are obviously inadequate, and sometimes the woman appears to be taunting them. When a handsome young man is added, the romantic couple sets off the old men. Rowlandson extends the conceit of the serpent/serpentine line into a drawing of a man and a woman, modern Adam and Eve, in a wild, stormy wood, recoiling (intertwining in serpentine lines) from the serpent, who rears up, making a Line of Beauty (Metropolitan Museum of Art, New York).

Satiric caricature, of which Rowlandson was one of the originators,

FIGURE 6 Thomas Rowlandson, *The Connoisseurs* (1780s). Drawing and watercolor. Yale Center for British Art.

requires the grotesque figure to be complemented by a normal one, in his case a young woman or man. Caricature moves from the merely comic or ugly to satire when it invokes the convention that certain features—an aquiline nose, a candid look, a leonine lock—are noble, while a sheeplike face denotes stupidity, a foxy one slyness ("sly as a fox"). This sense of satire follows from the Shaftesburian aesthetics that equated beauty and virtue, ugliness and evil. The conventions of "the cartoonist's armory" described by Ernst Gombrich also dictate that beauty, harmony, and unity are good, and ugliness, chaos, visual confusion are bad.[48] Obvious graphic equivalents, these were originally part of the hierarchical theory of academic art. In the works of Hogarth and Rowlandson the exemplars of beauty are seductive women, either disobedient daughters or unfaithful wives, in short, what was officially thought of as sinners.

The scenes of dallying, fornication, and adultery in François Boucher and Jean-Honoré Fragonard are similar to Hogarth's and Rowlandson's. Fragonard's clergyman who looks up the swinging lady's skirt (Wallace Collection, London) is another version of Hogarth's clergyman in *Harlot 6*

FIGURE 7   Thomas Rowlandson, *The Coquette*, from *The English Dance of Death* no. 3 (1815–16). Drawing and watercolor. Henry E. Huntington Library and Art Gallery.

groping the nearest whore. Fragonard, however, omits Rowlandson's gross voyeurs and impotent husbands, including only handsome and beautiful people, and produces something that may be aesthetically pleasing but is not an aesthetics.

"Sin Be Thou My Good": Blake, The Marriage of Heaven and Hell
The romantic triangle of Rowlandson's comedy reappears in Blake's satires as the aged Urizen (or Nobodaddy), the beautiful young daughter or wife, and the handsome young lover. Blake begins *America* (1793) with a youth, "fiery Orc," breaking the chains with which the aged Urizen (associated with George III) has bound him and taking Urizen's young daughter: "Soon as she saw the terrible boy then burst the virgin cry," and her joyous cry connects Orc with the spirit of freedom, "who dwells in darkness of Africa" and has succeeded in the revolution "on my American plains."[49]

The romantic triangle fitted into Blake's "Bible of Hell." He begins with the Church's recasting the great sinner Satan, combining him and the pagan Pan into a ram or a goat, a horned devil, connecting (with some help from Augustine) the force of evil with sexuality. Milton, as Dryden noted early on, made Satan in the early books of *Paradise Lost*, before he had completely lost his angelic sheen, a heroic figure of defiance and

FIGURE 8   Thomas Rowlandson, *Serving the Punch* (1780s). Drawing and watercolor.
Henry E. Huntington Library and Art Gallery.

revolt against the established order. At the end of the eighteenth century, in the wake of the American and French Revolutions, Blake recovered this Satan in *The Marriage of Heaven and Hell* (1790). He reverses the value of devils and angels; his hell regenerates, and religious evil (that is, sin) is his good. His personae are "Angels who are all religious" and "Devils who all hate religion" (plate 21).

Devils are now agents of reform, while angels represent the oppressive orthodoxy of church and state that lulls poor chimney sweeps in dreams of a happy afterlife.[50] Evil itself, while clearly associated with torture and suffering, keeps changing places and names with sin, turning from agent to patient and back again; under the irony and play, however, religion is the worst of all evils.

Energy is "call'd evil" by the Church, which says "that God will torment Man in eternity for following his Energies"; but this doctrine is contradicted by the devils' message that "energy is the only life . . . Energy is Eternal Delight" (plate 4), and energy equals "desire," at which point Blake cites Milton's *Paradise Lost*'s true hero as Satan (Milton, "a true Poet of the devil's party without knowing it," plate 5). Energy, in short, indicates sins, which are Blake's natural virtues. "Energy is Eternal Delight" takes on the aesthetic aspect in the "Proverbs of Hell," plate 10: "Exuberance is Beauty." In plates 3 and 4 there are Hogarthian Lines of Beauty, in the former supporting two figures who represent the "marriage" or reconciliation of the words above them, "Love and Hate." We are reminded of Hogarth's logo on the title page of *The Analysis of Beauty,* which combines the serpentine Line of Beauty with Eve's tempter.

To the angels men (excepting Christ) are "fools, sinners, & nothings"; the devil replies that Jesus is in fact in their terms a sinner: "did he not mock at the sabbath, and so mock the sabbath's God? . . . turn away the law from the woman taken in adultery?," etc.—"I tell you, no virtue can exist without breaking these ten commandments" (plate 23).[51]

Thus "the Jehovah of the Bible [is] no other than [the Devil *del.*] he who dwells in flaming fire." Jehovah (the Old Testament God) and Satan are reversed, but then Jesus after his death "became Jehovah," that is, he is made over by priests into the Old Testament God of wrath and evil (suffering). "Know that after Christ's death, he became Jehovah," and the New Testament was recovered by the Old (plate 6). These are the "moral values" that appropriate Jesus' doctrine of forgiveness: Jesus breaks all the Ten Commandments, but his crucifixion, which is intended to indicate forgiveness of sins, is appropriated by the Church and assimilated to the Commandments: revenge and punishment, sacrifice and the Eucharist. Atonement is, or rather historically was, for Blake the institutionalizing of Redemption—of Jesus' crucifixion, his suffering and forgiveness. Blake shows the Old Testament God's Law (given to Moses on Mount Sinai), which required sacrifice and atonement, recovered and worshiped ("on your Altars high") by "religion," the Christian church.

In Blake's poems Mary the Mother is, as Hogarth showed her to be, a harlot, that is, a natural woman, "innocently gay & thoughtless," living "in the midst of a corrupt Age" and therefore to be forgiven.[52] To demonstrate the basic principle of the forgiveness of sins, the true end of Redemption, Blake associates the two Marys (and the woman taken in adultery) with the principle of sexual freedom. The sexual is an urge that "can never be defiled."[53] It is necessary for Blake that Jesus inherit sin, and by sin he means such natural behavior as sexual intercourse, drinking, cursing, and not going to church, which in *The Marriage of Heaven and Hell* he presents as "diabolic," and his contemporaries would have regarded as Antinomian in the sense of "anything is permitted" of the elect (in Blake's sense, we are all the "human divine"). "Sinning" is Blake's irony in that "sins" are only the natural violations of the Old Testament Law; natural behavior is *called* diabolic by the self-styled angels of the Christian religion: the same distinction that Hogarth made in the *Harlot's Progress* between sin and morality. M[ary]. Hackabout "sinned," but the men who debauched her committed moral crimes. Like Hogarth's Mary, Blake's Mary is an ironic conflation of harlot and Savior, mother and son. In terms of his usual "contraries," Blake has a good harlot and a bad; Mary (Virgin and Magdalen) becomes in Revelation the good Mary with her Child *and* the Whore of Babylon. It all depends on what is in a name; sin or evil, Blake says, is in the eye of the beholder.

4. THE AESTHETICS OF EVIL

The "Gratuitous"

> Here last week they found this couple out in California they would
> rent out rooms to old people and then kill em and bury em in the
> yard and cash their social security checks.
>
>   They'd torture em first. I don't know why. Maybe their television
> was broke.
>
> —*Cormac McCarthy*, No Country for Old Men

The case for the gratuitous as the essential of "true evil" was made by Georges Bataille, the French surrealist and Sadean theorist:

> We cannot consider that actions performed for a material
> benefit express Evil. This benefit is, no doubt, selfish [i.e., bad],
> but it loses its importance [its significance as evil] if we expect
> something from it other than evil itself—if, for example, we
> expect some advantage from it. The sadist, on the other hand,
> obtains pleasure from contemplating destruction. . . . If a man
> kills for a material advantage his crime only really becomes
> a purely evil deed if he actually enjoys committing it, indepen-
> dently of the advantage to be obtained from it.[54]

Bataille, though he may not be aware of it, enunciates the other side of the third earl of Shaftesbury's idea, at the end of the seventeenth century, that virtue (a good act) has to be disinterested or it is not virtue (or good); that is, it cannot be virtue within the theological construct of rewards and punishments. According to Shaftesbury, only an action uninfluenced by promises of rewards or threats of punishments can be termed virtuous, and therefore only a man above the pressures of hunger or want (that is, a man of property) is capable of virtue. Shaftesbury's is only a reformulation of the humanist principle, in Kurt Vonnegut's words, "to behave as decently, as fairly and as honorably as we can without any expectation of rewards or punishments in an afterlife."[55] And yet Bataille's gratuitous act of evil was, as much as Augustine's, an act of rebellion against the Christian God. The reason, for example, that he and his surrealist friends advocated sodomy was because it was an abomination—it denied the purpose of sexual intercourse for procreation.[56]

The essence of gratuitous evil in Bataille's hypothesis was cruelty beyond murder, acts of torture, rape, and mutilation. Torture is cruelty employed to get information (perhaps crucial to saving the lives of others), to obtain confessions, to implicate others, but, in a great many documented cases, increasingly so in the twentieth century, torture is cruelty for its own sake. Cruelty is, on the face of it, pain administered in excess, gratuitously. The Third Geneva Convention defined torture as any act that inflicts severe pain or suffering, physical or mental. When the United States ratified the convention in 1990, it defined torture as anything cruel and unusual (recalling the eighth of the Constitution's Bill of Rights, outlawing "cruel and unusual punishments"). By the definition of the U.S. law that incorporated the international Convention against Torture (Section 2340A), for an abuse to be considered torture, the abuse must inflict pain "of such a high degree of intensity that the pain is difficult for the subject to endure."[57]

Torture was associated in the twentieth century with the German Gestapo, the Russian purge trials, the insurgents and counterinsurgents in Algeria, the governments in Chile and Argentina—carried out on the micro and macro levels, by individuals and by groups under orders or by lynch mobs; by ideology or by personal inclination, as in the case of professional torturers, serial killers, and rapists. The torture of children in particular: in Africa the cutting off of their hands, or forcing them to cut off the hands of their parents, or making them sexual slaves—or, in the Western countries, making them the slaves of abusive priests;

at which point cruelty becomes corruption and appropriation of the other.

The criterion of gratuitousness for a sin is difficult to fulfill, as Augustine's self-analysis of his theft of the pears showed. In terms of his pragmatic rationale, in the Catiline sense, the Hutu in Rwanda cut off the children's hands to send a message: Give up, don't resist, don't offend or challenge; *we* have the power.[58] Thus the explanation that in each case the act is not gratuitous but serves an expedient purpose; or that means, however terrible, are justified by the end.

But there is also the hypothesis that cruelty is one way of compensating for the "evils" of the world, as Alford wrote: "Doing evil is an attempt to transform the terrible passivity and helplessness of suffering [evil] into activity," the wish that in compensation for your own pain another might suffer, and suffer *more*.[59]

Cruelty to the Innocent Creature: Hogarth, The Stages of Cruelty
The *Harlot's Progress* involved scenes of cruelty and suffering, but in *The Four Stages of Cruelty* (1751) (figs. 9–12) this is the aspect Hogarth emphasizes: Wrongdoing is raised into something qualitatively different. Tom Nero is a far worse person than the Harlot—replacing her sin with genuine evil. If the *Harlot* polarized cruelty (evil) and sin (wanting to become a "lady"), the *Stages of Cruelty* polarizes cruelty (evil) and innocence—cruelty applied to animals and children. What the boys do to the dogs and cats, what the grown Nero does to his horse is bad enough; what he does to the girl he has seduced, impregnated, and corrupted into stealing from her master is surely *de trop*—he cuts not only her throat but her wrists and a finger, he kills both mother and baby, leaving wounds that appear to be mouths crying for justice.

The second plate shows four lawyers, their prosperity manifest in their bulk, crowding into one carriage to save the shilling fare to the courts at Westminster, thereby collapsing the carriage and causing the driver to beat his innocent horse. Nero's cruelty is not gratuitous but based on self-interest, the fare he is losing. It is nevertheless a case of evil to the nth degree—the more so because of the figures on the right, child and lamb, balancing the horse on the left.

This is a scene comparable in intensity to Raskolnikov's dream of the man beating his horse in *Crime and Punishment*. In his dream, Raskol-

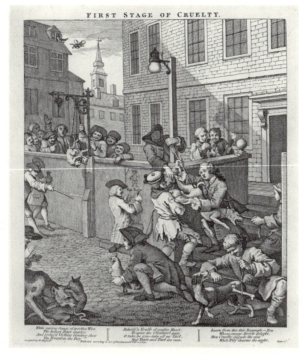

FIGURE 9 William Hogarth, *The Stages of Cruelty* (1751):
First Stage of Cruelty. Etching and engraving. Reproduced by
courtesy of the Trustees of the British Museum.

nikov is a child walking in the country with his father—with thoughts
of his little brother, who died at six months—and he sees a cart: "It was
one of those big carts usually drawn by heavy cart-horses and laden with
casks of wine or other heavy goods. . . . But now, strange to say, in the
shafts of such a cart he saw a thin little sorrel beast, one of those peasants' nags which he had often seen straining their utmost under a heavy
load of wood or hay. . . . And the peasants would be at them so cruelly,
sometimes even about the nose and eyes and he felt so sorry, so sorry for
them that he almost cried."[60] Six men and a fat woman pile on, overloading
the cart; the horse cannot move the cart, and the owner, encouraged by
the drunken young men who accompany him, beats the little horse—"in
the face, in the eyes"—and finally with a crowbar, kills the creature. As
he beats the horse, he keeps repeating, "my property" and one bystander
says of him, "not a Christian." The boy Raskolnikov tries to intervene, gets

FIGURE 10   William Hogarth, *Second Stage of Cruelty*.
Etching and engraving. Reproduced by courtesy of the
Trustees of the British Museum.

a cut of the whip across his face that was aimed at the horse (1.5; 56–60).
The dream foreshadows Raskolnikov's killing of the innocent old woman
Lizavetta Ivanovna.

Dostoevsky's scene shares with Hogarth's the detail of the overloaded
burden that has caused the horse to collapse, and the association of the
animal with the child.[61] The scene returns in *The Brothers Karamazov* in
Ivan's description of a "peasant flogging a horse on its eyes with a knout,
'on its meek eyes'"; it is a little horse, its load "too heavy," and it gets
stuck in the mud and cannot pull the cart: "The peasant beats her, beats
her savagely, beats her finally not knowing what he is doing." The story
of the master flogging his horse leads Ivan into the flogging of children:
"They flog for one minute, they flog for five minutes, they flog for ten
minutes—longer, harder, faster, sharper. The child is crying, the child
finally cannot cry, she has no breath left: 'Pappa, pappa, dear pappa!'"[62]

FIGURE 11 William Hogarth, *Cruelty in Perfection.* Etching and engraving. Reproduced by courtesy of the Trustees of the British Museum.

"They" refers to the child's father and mother, but it is the father to whom she appeals—"a father flogging his daughter," as Ivan puts it. The horse and child lead to Ivan's speech about the Problem of Evil: "It is precisely the defenselessness of these creatures that tempts the torturers, the angelic trustfulness of the child, who has nowhere to turn and no one to turn to—that is what enflames the vile blood of the torturer" (5.4.241): "the whole world of knowledge is not worth the tears of that little child to 'dear God.' I'm not talking about the suffering of grown-ups, they ate the apple and to hell with them, let the devil take them all, but these little ones!" He asks his brother Alyosha to imagine himself God, "building the edifice of human destiny with the object of making people happy in the finale, of giving them peace and rest at last, but for that you must inevitably and unavoidably torture just one tiny creature, that same child

FIGURE 12   William Hogarth, *The Reward of Cruelty*. Etching and engraving. Reproduced by courtesy of the Trustees of the British Museum.

. . . . would you agree to be the architect on such conditions?" Alyosha replies no, but adds that Christ could: "He can forgive everything, forgive all *and for all,* because he himself gave his innocent blood for all and for everything" (5.5.245–46).

The theodicy argued by Alyosha and Ivan, who is about to tell his fable of the "Grand Inquisitor," is the basic one we can infer from Hogarth's *Cruelty* 2. The suffering or death of a child has habitually been taken to be the ultimate *evil;* indeed, the suffering of children is at the root of the sense of evils as what followed from the Fall. Hogarth was careful to evoke the idea by his inclusion of the child and the lamb and by implying something about the care of children (teenage boys) in plate 1.

This will be a strand of evil I follow throughout the remainder of this book —animals associated with innocence and the object of gratuitous cruelty.

Power and Pain: Cruelty Compounded

Nero's evildoing is established by its excess, the movement from motivated evil to the gratuitous (the treatment of the girlfriend). Equally in excess, however, is the angry (or angry-gleeful) crowd cornering and threatening him with pikes and pitchforks, anticipating the dissection of Nero that in the final plate is being carried out by society and the law. Nero's grimace as he lies on the dissecting table makes him appear to be still alive, still suffering what was, incidentally, the punishment for treason—to be hanged, taken down while still alive, and drawn—disemboweled—before being quartered.

In short, still operating within the parameters of the *Harlot's Progress,* Hogarth does not stop with the obvious cruelty of Tom Nero but adds the legal cruelty of "the People of England," aka the ruling orders, upon Nero himself.[63] In the first *Stage of Cruelty* the law is implicit in the absent overseers of the poor, the governors of St. Giles Parish (the representatives of state and church), the only evidence for whom is the armbands worn by the youths who are torturing the cats and dogs. But they are still children, which points to the responsibility of the absent parish officers (as in *Harlot* 1 to the responsibility of the absent cousin and the delinquent clergyman, without whom the girl from the country, herself hardly more than a child, is at the mercy of bawds, rakes, and magistrates). In the second plate, the fat lawyers crowd into one carriage to save the shilling fare (the Thavies Inn sign indicates the farthest shilling fare from Westminster Hall), and capsize the carriage. This is to show the *cause* of the evil (both the doing and the suffering)—for Tom Nero is beating the horse for the sake of his fare, the lawyers.

In the third plate, where the forces of law enforcement, in the form of a posse of property owners and even a churchman (grouped under the tower of a church), bear down on Nero, we are left to decide, in typical Hogarth fashion, whether they are arresting him more for the murder or for the felony. In the final plate the chief surgeon, shown in a magisterial pose, supervises Nero's dissection, adding punishment to punishment (only a year later, dissection-after-hanging became part of the official punishment).[64]

The law represented in the *Stages of Cruelty* is literally the Old Testament "eye for an eye": One of the boys gouges out a bird's eye in plate 1, and then Nero's is gouged out in 4; Nero's torture of the dog in 1 is reprised

FIGURE 13 Sir Anthony Van Dyck, *Christ Taken in the Garden* (c. 1620). Painting. Bristol, City of Bristol Museum and Art Gallery.

by the dog's return in 4 to eat Nero's heart; and the disemboweled cat in 1 is avenged in the disembowelment of Nero in 4. The equation of legal crime and religious sin is underscored, as it was in the *Harlot's Progress,* by allusions to the Passion and Atonement. The posse that apprehends Tom Nero evokes the Roman soldiers and priests of a *Taking of Christ in the Garden of Gethsemane.* Anthony Van Dyck's painting is the closest, and one version was in England by 1747, which Hogarth could have seen in Sir Paul Methuen's collection (fig. 13; cf. Dürer's version, fig. 14).[65] The image recalls Jesus' response, "Are ye come out, as against a thief, with swords and with staves to take me?"—the word "thief" literally rendering the felony aspect of Tom Nero's crime.

The surgeon in *The Reward of Cruelty,* who resembles a magistrate (in a dissecting theater that resembles a court of law) and over whose

FIGURE 14 Albrecht Dürer, *Christ Taken in the Garden* (from the *Great Passion*, 1510). Woodcut. Reproduced by courtesy of the Trustees of the British Museum.

head are suspended the royal arms, evokes images of God the Father in a Last Judgment (in particular Dürer's scene from his *Apocalypse* series in which God sits in a chair not unlike the one in which Hogarth's surgeon sits [fig. 15]): thus, the magistrate's (the royal surrogate's) judgment of a crime equals God's judgment of a sin upon Tom Nero, stretched out in a sacrificial pose (in some *Pietàs* Jesus is stretched out flat in the same manner).[66] The last two, the climactic plates (which Hogarth separately reproduced in the starker form of woodcuts), introduce, once again, a parodic Atonement, the evil Tom Nero at his death turned ironically into an Atoner, a more radical case of the Harlot, by the society that made him evil in the first place. As we recall, in the second plate Hogarth extended

FIGURE 15 Albrecht Dürer, *Apocalypse* (from the *Apocalypse*, 1498). Woodcut. Reproduced by courtesy of the Trustees of the British Museum.

cruelty from the horse being beaten to a small boy being crushed by a wagon carrying casks of spirits and, in the foreground, a lamb, perhaps implying the symbol of child-lamb-Lamb (which Blake would explore in *Songs of Innocence*). Then in the third and fourth plates the hint of the sacrificed Lamb is materialized.

Plate 3, by the allusion to the *Taking of Christ,* introduces the idea of the Jesus ethic (love, etc.), in contrast to the Old Testament allusions of plate 4 (and the child and lamb of 2). But Nero is (as his name suggests) the persecutor of Christians: The imagery reads both ways—as an indication of what has become of Jesus in 1750s London (an abomination, a "Nero") and of what this world does to such people, which puts them in the position of Jesus vis-à-vis the law. In both cases the Jesus reference is positive, the Nero reference negative, and yet Nero becomes both perpetrator and victim.

The image of *The Taking of Christ* and the sacrificial image of the *Reward of Cruelty* are genealogically mock-heroic images, but they do not follow from the mock-heroic satire of Pope and Dryden. The images in *MacFlecknoe* and *The Dunciad* represented an abomination or defilement, saying that these people have fallen short of (are a corruption of) the scriptural story. Hogarth's images say that in this society the only atonement is carried out on (not by) harlots—and on an uninstructed, unsupervised parish boy who accordingly grows up to be a murderer and pays the ransom for ("redeems") the fat lawyers and brutal magistrates who punish him, evil for evil. Hogarth replaces the New Testament story as an ideal against which Hackabout, Rakewell, Nero, and other contemporaries are found wanting with an "ideal" that is now out-of-date, constricting and oppressive to contemporaries.

Cruelty has begotten cruelty: Nero's cruelty begets the cruelty with which the society punishes him; but back in plate 1 the negligent delinquency of society begat his cruelty; and we can infer from plates 3 and 4 that the same society served as model for his cruelty. In each case, most importantly, it is from the position of power that the strong impose cruelty on the weaker—or the weaker on the weakest, Nero on a dog, on a horse, on a woman, until the judicial system imposes it on him. The faint echoes of Christian sin and evil only draw attention to the central fact of the circularity—emphasized by all the circular movements of plate 4—from society to the individual and back to society.[67] The animal's pain is Tom Nero's power; Nero's pain is the judge's power; and in these terms, evil equals pain/power.

The Sublime: Burke, Philosophical Enquiry

The rococo was about sin as seen by the secular, not the religious imagination; what the religious would have called sin, the rococo artist called beauty. In Hogarth's rococo sin is pleasure, the beautiful, the novel, surprising, and momentary (topical, local). But he shows how the artist, familiar with Gay's *Beggar's Opera,* can emphasize either the figures of cruelty and ugliness or the lone beautiful woman, creating in the first case an anatomy of evil, in the second an aesthetics. While his (living) woman is associated with nature, cruelty is associated with the neobaroque subjects and forms of academic art.

In 1757, four years after Hogarth's *Analysis,* Edmund Burke published his far more influential study *A Philosophical Enquiry into the Origin of our Ideas of the Beautiful and Sublime*. If the basis of the beautiful is love, that of the sublime, according to Burke, is fear—fear of a greater power, mixed with awe. Awe because the aesthetic experience holds fear at arm's length, leaving the spectator clear of imminent danger, a spectator at Lord Lovat's execution rather than Lovat himself. Burke's sublime object is what Hogarth would have called evil (oppression, power, cruelty), but Burke associates it with the plot of sin. Perhaps what gives evil its sense of pleasureful transcendence is its association with sin, that is, its raising of wrongdoing from social relationships up to (in Kenneth Burke's words) "the supernaturally tinged realm of relationships between 'God' and man," or at least a tyrant or wicked father and a young girl.[68]

As in Horace Walpole's *Castle of Otranto* (1765), published a year after Hogarth's death, the emphasis on the comic triangle of the *Analysis* has shifted. It is no longer on the beautiful woman as cuckolding the ugly old man with the handsome young man, but now on the old man, the figure of power, authority (legal and paternal), and cruelty, pursuing the helpless maiden and coming close to killing the young man. (Both stories are, of course, based on the ur-romance plot, with its happy ending after all.) If evil is a matter of emphasis and degree, this is the reason tales of terror such as *The Castle of Otranto* and Ann Radcliffe's *Mysteries of Udolpho* (1794) often seem to be about evil when they are in fact about something more trivial, such as the ownership of property, the castle as an item of real estate.

Burke's sublime was, over all, a way of dealing with the evils (suffering-evils) of the world. The evils that were the punishment for Original Sin became sources of pleasure—ambivalent, mixed, but more intense and more "real" than the relatively artificial rococo-beautiful of Hogarth's theory. Burke has aestheticized these evils, distancing them by removing both their sacred and (going a significant step beyond Hogarth) their moral content. The chaos and disorder, obscurity, enthusiasm, and the various sins (abominations) that Swift attacked in the *Tale of a Tub* are by Burke aestheticized and—insofar as he reveals his preference for the sublime over the beautiful—valorized.

Sin, we recall, involves the dread of stain, pollution, or abomination—the uncontained, boundless, overwhelming experience that reemerges in Burke's aesthetics of the sublime: fear of the formless, obscure, and uncertain and of absorption—of power. The sublime, in Burke's terms, is the experience of evil (existential dread). Terror is the incomprehensible, what cannot be understood, either in a theistic or ordered world or in the simple terms of a detective story: How *could* this have happened, and who is really responsible—where does responsibility end? The uncertainty— unformulable, uncanny, ultimately supernatural—is, in aesthetic terms, the "obscurity" of Burke's "sublime": "in nature dark, confused, uncertain images have a greater power on the fancy to form the grander passions than those have which are more clear and determinate."[69]

Hogarth had demystified God in the figure of his surrogates in society, magistrates and priests, and in the religious paintings that hang on the walls of his houses. (Those paintings anticipate the burden of a blood-stained past that weighs like a nightmare on the living in the Gothic novel, which employs the same moldering ruins and religious fanaticism.) We can say that Hogarth offered one answer—that morally the power of God is indeed the source of evil—and Burke offered another—that the power of God is the most terrible, aesthetically speaking sublime (in that sense pleasureful), of subjects, therefore disobedience or offense produces the most terrible or sublime consequences.

Burke's examples are from *Paradise Lost* (Satan and Death) and the passage in Job in which God puts down Job by contrasting him (as one of God's creations) with Behemoth and Leviathan, "which," God says, "I made [along] with thee" (40:15); rather as God is asked by Blake how in fact he could have created both the lamb and the tiger. Making the connection between God and the original evils, Burke writes, "For fear being an apprehension of pain or death, it operates in a manner that resembles actual pain. . . . [T]he idea of pain, in its highest degree, is much stronger than the highest degree of pleasure," and he adds the word "suffering": "And indeed the ideas of pain, and above all of death, are so very affecting, that whilst we remain in the presence of whatever is supposed to have the power of inflicting either, it is impossible to be perfectly free from terror"—and therefore the aesthetic experience of the sublime is based on the dread of evil. The "ideas that rush in upon the mind together" are "strength, violence, pain and terror."[70]

In his list of sublime animals, Burke offers a horse that is quite different from Gay's and Hogarth's: "The horse in the light of an useful beast, fit for the plough, the road, the draft, in every social useful light the horse has nothing of the sublime; but is it thus that we are affected with him, *whose neck is cloathed with thunder, the glory of whose nostrils is terrible, who swalloweth the ground with fierceness and rage, neither believeth that it is the sound of the trumpet?* In his description the useful character of the horse entirely disappears, and the terrible and sublime blaze out together" (66, misquoted). Burke is citing Job 39:19, 20, 24: this horse is either useful to us or it threatens us—the agency shifts from us to the horse, the beater turned into the beaten, at which point the horse, now "terrible," becomes sublime.

Burke cites natural forces, not only storms but "things of great dimensions" (58), such as mountains and the ocean and chaos, natural and social, "a croud of great and confused images . . . dark, confused, uncertain images"—"the ruin of monarchs, and the revolutions of kingdoms"; animals—"serpents and poisonous animals of almost all kinds"—the lion, tiger, panther, rhinoceros; and ultimately "the idea of God himself" (62, 57–58, 67): "Now, though in a just idea of the Deity, perhaps none of his attributes are predominant, yet to our imagination, his power is by far the most striking. Some reflection, some comparing is necessary to satisfy us of his wisdom, his justice, and his goodness; to be struck with his power, it is only necessary that we should open our eyes" (68). We "are, in a manner, annihilated before him." This is, he suggests, an atavism that returns to a time "before the christian religion had, as it were, humanized the idea of the divinity," though he must have been aware of the God of Calvin and others.

Though Burke would not have admitted it, he is making Hogarth's point, that sin is not evil, though it usually gets punished; rather it is evil —even in Burke's aesthetics—that gets rewarded in the sense of being by aestheticians privileged. The Marquis de Sade merely extended the Burkean aesthetics of the sublime into an undisguised aesthetics of evil.[71]

What made the horrible only terrible—and so aesthetic—was distance. The sublime derives from the experience of something we fear: this is terror; but something that is distant enough for the fear to be felt without physical threat, which is horror, as in the character in Matthew Gregory Lewis's *The Monk* (1796) who, crawling through the dark vaults of a convent, touches a soft object that proves to be rotting, wormy human flesh, the corpses of a nun and her baby, the consequence of a sin punished by pious nuns.

While Burke's sublime carried a positive valence in the 1760s, to beauty as tragedy was to comedy, in 1790 the situation changed. The distance Burke posited for the aesthetic experience disappeared, and he was brought into immediate contact with the horrible, the unthinkable phenomenon, the French Revolution, which did not fit into the framework of aesthetic categories he had worked out himself thirty years before.[72] The upstart Jacobins climbing up from below, like rats from the sewer, in order to topple the highest pinnacles of authority and culture, were seen as a terrifying undifferentiated power; in the notorious centerpiece of Burke's *Reflections on the Revolution in France* (1790), the mob—representative of power, fear, cruelty, indeed obscurity—penetrate into the bedchamber of Queen Marie Antoinette—beautiful, aristocratic, defended by cavaliers —and perform a sort of rape, penetrating her recently abandoned bed with their swords. In the process, the lower orders have usurped the rightful place of the king, her husband and their master.

The popularity of Burke's aesthetics of the sublime forced Hogarth to intensify his critique of Shaftesbury's beautiful in light of Burke's sublime. But six years earlier Hogarth had already produced his anticipation of Burke's sublime in *The Stages of Cruelty*. Here was the power exerted on the weak—the frisson of both terror and horror—that Burke calls up, most specifically in his account of the public execution of Lord Lovat, but shown as the evil for which Burke was trying to compensate.

A decade later the beautiful woman whose morality is not as clear-cut as Shaftesbury would have it (beauty does not, Hogarth emphasizes, equal virtue) now becomes something between a madwoman and a witch, on the way to Blake's and Francisco Goya's demonic women. In the lower left corner of *Enthusiasm Delineated* (c. 1760) there is a woman stretched out, fists clasped, in the throws of a religio-sexual seizure (she is being offered smelling salts), a parody of the ecstatic women in Counter-Reformation baroque paintings, in this case Giovanni Lanfranco's *Ecstasy of St. Margaret of Cortona* (Pitti Palace, Florence)—a humanization of the pleasure thermometer on the opposite right, corresponding to "Convulsion Fits." Her face resembles that of Mother Douglas, a notorious London bawd of the time. In the revised and published plate, *Credulity, Superstition, and Fanaticism* (1763), she has been turned into another, rather more beautiful woman, Mary Toft delivering her seventeen rabbits (being offered a jigger of gin)—an example of superstition now (included is a copy of

FIGURE 16   William Hogarth, *Satan, Sin, and Death* (late 1730s). Oil painting. London, Tate Britain.

Joseph Glanvill's *On Witches*), but reproducing the image of *Cunicularii* (1726), in which she was in a composition that parodied a Nativity; and so now, in the context of the religious images surrounding her, she is both an example of popular superstitions such as the Cock Lane Ghost and an abomination—a woman giving birth to rabbits and, if we remember her source in *Cunicularii,* a pseudo–Virgin Mary. As in the case of the Harlot, these are sins against God's laws, not evil(s), but they are moving in the direction of the demonization of evil or, alternatively, the replacement of sin with "evil" in scare quotes.[73]

The pivotal work that connects Hogarth and the nineteenth-century writers we shall examine in chapter 5 was *Satan, Sin, and Death* (fig. 16), a painting based on a scene from *Paradise Lost*, book 2: Sin is intervening between her father-lover Satan and her son-lover Death; she is beautiful from the waist up, but the lower part of her body consists of her snaky offspring by Death. She is plainly an abomination if ever there was one, but she is also a version of Horace's beautiful mermaid in the *De Arte Poetica*. From having been the fornicating Harlot, betraying her keeper with a lover, she has returned to Polly Peachum's role of mediator between her father and her lover. A number of copies were engraved in the later eighteenth century, one by Rowlandson.[74] This painting sums up the figure of Sin as Hogarth formulated her: He shows the other side of the comic figure, not hiding the abominable consequences.

CHAPTER FOUR

Sin/Evil and the Law: The Novel

1. FIELDING

Tom Jones: *Evil Punished, Sin Rewarded*

The place to learn morals in this period, as the last chapter suggested, was not the church but the stage (the sinful stage the Puritans closed during the Civil War), and Hogarth extended the stage to his "modern moral subjects," engravings that were frozen scenes from plays like *The Beggar's Opera* and Nicholas Rowe's *Jane Shore* (1714) and George Lillo's *London Merchant* (1731). In these venues conventional ideas of sin were modified and complicated—and then, above all, rematerialized in the new genre that emerged in the 1720s–40s, the novel.

A primary source for Fielding's, as for Hogarth's, model of sin-evil was *The Beggar's Opera*, in which the criminals are bad and punished but the respectable folk are worse and go unpunished. For Fielding, at the beginning of his career there was the "Great Man," Walpole, and at the end, in *Amelia*, there are all sorts of Great Men,[1] culminating in the Noble Lord and his network of patronage that secures his client rank and a seat in Parliament, as against the repeated image of the aged half-pay lieutenant whose promotion is stymied because he will not give his wife up to the lust of the young, rich, entitled colonel. In *Amelia* (1751) there are only the Great Men themselves (in various degrees) and the Booths;

Fielding, like Hogarth, extends the evil of the Great Man to the ruling class, the governing body of society, indeed to God (at least as represented in baroque paintings)—which in *Amelia* is the law.

In *Tom Jones* (1748) Fielding's protagonist was a sinner in the eyes of respectable folk, including the clergy. He drinks, fights, and fornicates and is ruined, imprisoned, and nearly hanged as a consequence of the interpretation placed upon his actions by the respectable, in particular the malignant Blifil. Tom's lust is explained away or at least mitigated, partly because young women seduce him, partly because his fornication is exploited as sin to discredit him by the Blifils, Parson Thwackums, and schoolmaster Squares (Square turns out to be a fornicator himself), who victimize him—roughly speaking as the clergy and magistrates do the Harlot. Only in *Amelia* does adultery become a serious matter, shifting the blame decidedly onto the seducer—and making both seducer and husband of an age and attractiveness.

In *Tom Jones* "evil" was situated in the negative figure of Blifil (whose name rhymed with *devil*)—a parody of Tom, a negation of Tom's natural vigor and goodness, which is real and substantial; Blifil represents an absence of sexual drive, a libido perverted into sadism as love is perverted into possession and greed, truth into lies. Tom's situation is similar to the Harlot's, but unlike the Harlot, he survives and thrives; Blifil's plots, like Satan's or the flimsy webs of Swift's spider, collapse, and he is exiled to the north, where the Devil is supposed to have resided.

I have said that to believe your good and bad deeds will be rewarded or punished in the afterlife is soteriology, the theology of salvation and sin. To do good out of a sense of what is (or is deemed by custom or conscience) right or wrong is morality. Shaftesbury, arguing that there can be no act of virtue dependent upon hopes and fears of rewards and punishments, believed that an inner, sixth sense directed one toward good acts. Fielding offered a compromise, arguing that doing right makes you *feel* good, doing evil makes you feel bad—unless you are, like Blifil, a "fiend" or a "demon." And Fielding, by way of Tom Jones, included fornication, which makes you feel good partly because it makes your partner feel good; such acts are bad insofar as they hurt a third party, as in Tom's case they hurt his true love, Sophia Western. It is therefore oversimplifying to say that sin is rewarded, but sin, corrected for Tom by the learning process of experience, comes out on top in the struggle with the pharisees who would punish him on the grounds that he is a sinner.[2]

For Fielding a sinning act (fornication, adultery), itself possibly a good, can have evil consequences—can generate harm and suffering; but a greater evil is nonconsensual fornication—the seduction/rape of the weaker by the stronger, the less by the more powerful; this leaves him confronted with the Problem of Evil, which he solves in the Christian way, by showing the evil to be impotent and illusory, even when empowered, and punished as well.

Vs. Hogarth

A decade before Hogarth's image of the horse in *Cruelty* 2, Fielding, in the *Champion* of 22 March 1739/40, had described a similar case.[3] As "Hercules Vinegar," he observed,

> with great Indignation, an ill-look'd Fellow most cruelly lashing a Pair of starved Horses, who labour'd to the utmost of their power to drag on a heavy Burthen. And [Fielding adds, emphasizing the gratuitousness of the cruelty], as they were prevented from making greater Haste, even had they been able, by the Coaches which were before them, this Gentleman must have exercised his Arm thus, for nothing more than his own innocent Diversion, at the Expence of the Skins of these poor unhappy Beasts. (243)

W. B. Coley, in his edition of *The Champion*, has cited the passage as a possible source for Hogarth's print, but in fact both derive from John Gay's lines in *Trivia* (1714):

> The lashing Whip resounds, the Horses strain,
> And Blood in Anguish bursts the swelling Vein.
> O barb'rous Men, your cruel Breasts asswage,
> Why vent ye on the gen'rous steed your Rage?

That Fielding was recalling *Trivia* is confirmed by his invoking one solution to the Problem of Evil, the Pythagorean principle of transmigration of souls, the fantasy of changing places in another life. He supposes that "the Beasts he sees thus abused have formerly been themselves Hackney Coachmen; and that the Soul of the then driver, will in his Turn pass into the horse, and suffer the same Punishment which he so barbarously inflicts on others"; which follows from Gay's lines:

> If, as the *Samian* taught, the Soul revives,
> And shifting Seats, in other Bodies lives;
> Severe shall be the brutal Coachman's Change,
> Doom'd, in a *Hackney* Horse, the Town to range:
> Carmen, transform'd, the groaning Load shall draw,
> Whom other Tyrants, with the Lash, shall awe.
> (II. 230–42, p. 150)

In *Trivia,* in many ways both Hogarth's and Fielding's source, Gay was contrasting the coachman's cruelty to his horse with such legal "crimes" as the youthful pickpocket's withdrawal of a watch from a pompous gentleman's pocket—and this with the brutal punishment that follows—a scene that one may recall seeing the punishment imposed upon the Harlot, who stole a watch from a client in plate 3, and now the beating administered by the driver to his horse in *The Stages of Cruelty.* The metamorphic solution to the driver's evil action is clearly a soteriological fantasy, intended seriously by neither Gay nor Fielding, and of course not even alluded to by Hogarth.

In the beginning of 1751 the two friends collaborated on a "campaign," a visual-verbal collaboration, to reform social and legal "evils" they identified in England. Hogarth produced *The Four Stages of Cruelty* and *Beer Street* and *Gin Lane* in February 1751, a month after Fielding published his *Enquiry into the Late Increase in Robbers,* and a year before he published his last novel, *Amelia* (December 1751). In the legal tracts that appeared with Hogarth's *Cruelty* series, perhaps for pragmatic reasons (he was now a magistrate), Fielding reverses his and Hogarth's old procedure: He goes after the poor and leaves the Great to take care of themselves. He returns to Swift's model of satire on the poor who aspire to the vices of the great; he attacks the very people Hogarth shows suffering the evildoing of the law. In his *Enquiry,* although he expresses skepticism about "the Overseers of the Poor" whom Hogarth blames in *Cruelty* 1, Fielding confines himself "entirely to the lower Order of People" ("the inferiour Part of Mankind")— "the Great therefore [can] answer . . . to their spiritual Governors," that is, ultimately to God's judgment of heaven or hell.[4]

Further, he denies the possibility of official cruelty in England: "the People of *England*" cannot be charged with a "natural inbred Cruelty" when "the Poor are provided for by a tax frequently equal to what is called the Land-Tax, and where there are such numerous Instances of private Donations, such Numbers of Hospitals, Alms-houses, and charitable Provisions of all Kinds?"[5] His comments on mercy for wrongdoers—of whatever rank—are an equally stringent reversal of *Cruelty* 4: "To speak out fairly and honestly, tho' Mercy may appear more amiable in a Magistrate, Severity is a more wholesome virtue; nay severity to an Individual may, perhaps, be in the End the greatest Mercy," a sentence Charles Dickens would have read ironically.[6] We might also note that the *Champion* essay from which I have quoted was not *about* cruelty, though it began with an example, but rather about horses in general.

Amelia: *The Seven Deadly Sins*

In his dedication to *Amelia,* Fielding says his aim is "to expose some of the most glaring Evils, as well public as private, which at present infest the Country" (1.3), and *Amelia* is, as opposed to the picaresque or soteriological drift of his earlier novels, a satiric anatomy of evils. As the novel proceeds, it becomes clear that Fielding means by *evil* as much the suffering- as the doing-evil. It is cruelty, though the term is never used, that makes the treatment of the powerless by the powerful seem more than ordinary wrongdoing, or in fact evil. Fielding, however, focuses his contrast, between those protected and not protected by the law, on the genteel middling sort. While he shows violations of human beings that can only be termed cruel, they are, with a few exceptions, perpetrated on genteel characters—and indeed reflect his comments in the *Covent-Garden Journal* on such misfortunes as befell the genteel daughters of penurious clergymen, whose gentility makes their suffering the more pathetic (the Slipslops of former days, about whom he had joked in *Joseph Andrews*).[7] Cruelty is applied in particular to women, but Amelia includes her children when she cries, "Oh Heavens! What have these poor little Infants done? Why will the barbarous World endeavour to starve them, by depriving us of our only Friend [their father]?" (4.3.166). The emphasis on suffering in *Amelia* takes the form of emotive language—the sentimentality with which the good characters are described and with which they express themselves—not only Amelia, but also Booth when "a Torrent of Tears gushed from his Eyes" (2.1.67). Cruelty, to which these expressions are a response, is the term that by the end is applicable to all—but always aimed downward from the powerful to the weak, so from a magistrate's cruelty (as needless, as gratuitous as that in *Cruelty* 4) to malefactors, Booth's cruelty to Amelia, Colonel James's to the Booths, the Noble Lord's to Mrs. Bennet and the Booths, and so on.

The novel opens with a picture, reminiscent of *The Beggar's Opera* and Fielding's own earlier works, of a law court and prison, where the "poor Wretch [is] . . . charged with a battery by a much stouter Man than himself."[8] The poor are represented by Captain Booth, the discharged or half-pay soldier, vulnerable because he wears "sordid Apparel" (1.4.21, 25, 35). Then once Miss Matthews makes her appearance, Fielding sets in motion a literary analogy, like Hogarth's graphic analogy in the *Harlot* and *Stages of Cruelty*—or his own in *Joseph Andrews* where he framed Joseph's story with Old and New Testament stories (Joseph and Potiphar's wife, the parable of the Good Samaritan). In *Amelia,* however, he selects a classical, not a Christian, analogue. Billy Booth is Aeneas and Miss Matthews is Dido, meeting in the "cave" of Newgate Prison, in a story of a man torn between love and duty. We are asked to contrast Booth's duty to Amelia as his wife and the mother of his children (duty which includes *love*) with his lust for Miss Matthews. But then, still in Newgate, within the story Booth tells Miss Matthews of the past, we are introduced to the six other Deadly Sins—of the Harrises, Booths, Jameses, etc.; and, upon his release, these stories are continued outside the prison in the macrocosm of London. In effect, from the classical story of Dido and Aeneas, Fielding segues into the Christian Seven Deadly Sins, having framed them in prison with the context of Roman civic virtue and law.

Amelia's sister Betty Harris, we are repeatedly told, is directed by envy, which leads her to lie, steal, deceive, perjure, and nearly destroy her own sister (Dante's betrayal of kin, in the ninth circle). Since Betty is the *younger* daughter/sister, her pride and envy could have been interpreted as rebellion against Amelia, but nothing is made of this; she is simply in closer proximity than Amelia to her mother and can therefore forge a will, even though this is because the mother has turned against her and written her out of her most recent will: therefore, with Betty and Amelia the emphasis is on a figure of greater power trying to ruin a lesser. The sin of Mrs. Harris, her mother, is wrath, and it has its destructive effects on others, innocent daughter and son-in-law, but primarily it is exploited by Betty, to the ends of the other sins of greed, perjury, betrayal, and theft, the effect of which upon the Booths is of evils.

Colonel Bath's sin is pride, but accompanied by wrath it leads to duels which affect others and eventually get him killed. His sister (later Mrs. James) shares the sin of pride, though focused in her case on rank. Both characters, in relation to Amelia and Billy Booth, are figures of power and rank who can therefore impose their whims upon their inferiors. All of these sins are directed only downward at the weak and helpless, or innocent or (as may be the case with Mrs. Bennet and certainly was with Mrs. Trent), corruptible (like Trent himself, who easily accepts the role of pimp). The sins of pride and envy (Satan's sins), turned into evil by an evil will, are directed only down to either corruption or punishment of the less powerful, never upward to rebellion against the master.[9]

Lust, however, is the dominant sin in *Amelia*. And lust, unlike envy, is a sin of incontinence and appetite, punished in an upper circle of Hell where the sinners are blown about by the winds of their passions; if not guarded, these sins can descend into the evils (violence, betrayal) of the lower circles. As described by the Church Fathers, the Seven Sins were what we would call vices; these vices became sins when directed against God; what Fielding demonstrates in *Amelia*, as Hogarth does in the *Harlot* and *Cruelty* series, is that when directed against men and women they become evils. Lust is a corruption of love—as a sin it offends God by replacing the love of him with that of another; as an evil, lust in action can affect and injure another human being. Fielding shows sinners who *become* evil when they go beyond lust or lustiness to the need to possess, which entails the injury if not destruction of friends over whom they have power. (If they have no power, as in Beau Didapper's attempts at Fanny's chastity in *Joseph Andrews*, the result is comedy.)

Miss Matthews suffers from the sin of lust (though first, according to James, vanity),[10] which leads to envy and anger, which make her betray and injure the man she loves and his family (the Booths) *because* she can influence a man who loves *her*, Colonel James. Colonel James's vice is also lust—for Miss Matthews—and, based on Booth's primacy in her affections, subsequently envy and anger and pride, and then, once he sees her, lust for Amelia; all of which lead to the betrayal of a friend, the attempted seduction of the friend's wife.[11] In the case of both Matthews and James lust unrequited leads to envy and so to attempted punishment/evil/suffering on the strength of James's rank, wealth, and influence.

Although the reader of *Amelia* ticks off the Deadly Sins one by one, by name, Fielding redefines, or secularizes, them as what Booth calls "predominant passions." Booth cites Colonel James to prove his theory. James's ruling passion is apparently love, or what Fielding in a *Champion* essay had called "good nature." Says Booth: "'For *Bob James* can never be supposed to act from any Motive of *Virtue or Religion;* since he constantly laughs at both; and yet his Conduct towards me . . . demonstrates a Degree of Goodness, which, perhaps, few of the Votaries of either Virtue or Religion can equal'" (3.5.114). Colonel James "loves" Booth and stays with him both day and night until he sees him through his illness, but if anyone shows James a handsome woman he will pursue her and seduce her.[12] Moreover, at this time James has not yet seen Amelia, and so has no ulterior motive for his care of Booth. James is said to be like every one of us who, faced with the beauty of Amelia, would be equally powerless to turn away and leave the room: "To run away is all that is in our Power; and yet in the former Case if it must be allowed we have the Power of running away, it must be allowed also that it requires the strongest Resolution to execute it" (6.2.232). It is difficult to say whether Fielding intends to reflect more the humanity of James or the "Charms" of Amelia, but we can draw the conclusion that "sin" is a passion, one we all share but which left uncontrolled, or supplemented with power, will impose evil in the form of cruelty and suffering on others.[13]

Booth is the victim of his theory. With no copy of the *Aeneid* to hand and no Barrow sermons as yet available, he is guided by purely mechanistic laws, specifically the hydraulic principle, which Swift employed in the *Tale of a Tub,* that if your passion is blocked at one opening it will find a way out another—will be displaced to something else, as lust unrequited leads to the evils of war and madness, and Booth's love in Newgate is displaced from the absent Amelia to the present and tempting Miss Matthews.[14] Booth's error is to believe that we have no control over this process. Amelia is able to control her passions because, presumably acting "from any Motive of *Virtue or Religion,*" she follows Jesus' ideal of love: "This is my commandment, That ye love one another, as I have loved you" (John 15:12). But as Fielding had been writing for years, one *naturally* avoids inflicting pain on another and feels joy at doing good to another person. In *Joseph Andrews* Joseph's actions were taken ostensibly under the influence of Parson Adams's sermons, Pamela's letters, and the Old Testament story of Joseph and Potiphar's wife, but in fact they were replaced by his real love for Fanny Goodwill: the first was bad, the second good. Such love as Joseph's can, momentarily with Booth, totally with James and the Noble Lord, be perverted, but perverted only eventually to be thwarted and punished.

Adultery

If the chief of the Deadly Sins in *Amelia* is lust, the Commandment in question regards adultery: *Thou shalt not commit adultery*—Do not commit adultery because it will break up the family and overthrow the husband (*paterfamilias*). Fielding changes this in *Amelia* by placing the emphasis on the husband and his betrayal of the wife, replacing sin with evil.

In the Old Testament (in the Ten Commandments) adultery is an abomination related to both the worshiping of false idols and the confusion of categories. As Tony Tanner puts it, "According to Old Testament Law, the adulterous man and woman are almost without exception to be excluded from society, canceled even to the point of execution. Christ confronted with the woman taken in adultery makes the would-be lawgivers aware of her problematical reality, calling into question both the impersonal application of the law and the justification and rights of the would-be legislators."[15] Jesus' way is plainly the way Fielding regards adultery. Amelia is on the cusp of seduction (of her) and adultery (her husband's), as adultery is on the cusp of the Old and New Testament treatments of it.

Dr. Harrison, in his admonitory letter on adultery addressed to Colonel James, mixes biblical exhortations with pragmatic suggestions, the idea of the sin (against the Commandments) with the legal precedents of the terrible punishments of the ancients and the pragmatics of property. It follows that adultery, he says, "includes in it almost every Injury and every Mischief which one Man can do to, or can bring on another. It is *robbing him of his Property*" (10.2.414, emphasis added). Only then does Harrison add the humanist aspect (he is referring, of course, to the specific case of the Booths and the Jameses): breaking the ties of friendship and besides, he adds, the impossibility of breaching the virtue of such a woman as Amelia. And then he returns to a pragmatics that recalls Bernard Mandeville's *Modest Defence of Publick Stews:* Use a whore, he advises, or go after an easier mark than the impregnable Amelia.[16]

A year after *Amelia*, Fielding the Westminster magistrate published two essays in the *Covent-Garden Journal*, the first devoted to the horrific punishments inflicted by the ancients on adulterers; this he follows with a second paper on the contemporary need in England for *some* sort of punishment (vs. the prevalent practice of joking about adultery). Fielding's point is that adultery should be a *criminal* as well as a *civil* wrong—a case of "Punishment and Example" rather than merely "Redress of an Injury and Damages," as for the loss of property. He cites a parliamentary bill that would have made adultery a capital offense, putting "the Crime . . . on the Footing of Treason" (which implies *lèse-majesté* to the husband). Adultery, in Blackstone's terms, is a private wrong, treason a public wrong, thus a law biased toward the husband, the property-owner—and the betrayal is either by friend or by wife.[17] But, Fielding notes, the House of Commons merely made a joke of it. Therefore he proposes a popular, a demotic, extralegal punishment—"that same Punishment which the Mob inflict [on a pickpocket], viz. ducking in a Horsepond" (300, 361)—the punishment Gay designated for pickpocketing in *Trivia*. Fielding has remarked, echoing Dr. Harrison, that the adulterer is "as infamous as he who picks his Neighbour's Pocket."

If he himself makes something of a joke of adultery, in *Amelia* he shifts victimhood from the husband to the wife, and the "villain" (Amelia's term) is the seducer, while "villainy" includes his willingness to ruin her husband and children as well as the woman herself. *Amelia* is about adultery, but the adulterers are men, the seducers Colonel James and the Noble Lord. The focus is on violation of the woman—the wife in Amelia's case, and Mrs. Bennet's—and so fits into the larger structure of the powerful and the powerless, the persecutor and the persecuted, the violator and the violated. Blackstone's terms "injury" and "evil" essentially designate the difference between sin (effective only in the jurisdiction of the spiritual courts)[18] and the evil of the adulterer, which is the suffering of the poverty, imprisonment, and potential rape he will inflict—the same evil in the sense of pain, suffering, and death that took the form of the Harlot's punishment.

Ducking, Fielding says, should be primarily reserved for clergymen and magistrates, who add hypocrisy to adultery. Young bucks and soldiers are (as he says of the upper classes in *The Late Increase in Robbers*) beyond the reach of shame and humiliation. The second *Covent-Garden Journal* essay contextualizes the punishments; the proposal of ducking and the despairing of recovering the bucks and soldiers are comical solutions that imply the real one, which is simply shaming people out of committing adultery.[19] Colonel James obviously fits into the category of dishonor and soldiers, but the Noble Lord transcends these—as he does the hypocritical magistrates and clergymen.

The Noble Lord is, by comparison with Booth and James, an allegorical figure, a Satan who seduces downward. Implicitly he enjoys the influence of the king, not in that he has the monarch's ear (like Pope's Sporus and his Dunces) but that he is part of the ruling order: "His lordship was not himself in any Office of State; but his Fortune gave him great Authority with those who were" (4.9.193), thereby dispensing and withholding patronage, the "laudable way of setting ourselves above another Man, and that is by becoming his Benefactor." And by being his benefactor, the Noble Lord acquires the power over him to take his wife (4.4.170). He is closer to Hogarth's representatives of Law than to Richardson's Lovelace, and if we look for an exact precursor it must be in plate 1 of *A Harlot's Progress*—Colonel Charteris with Mother Needham (Mrs. Ellison) and "Trusty Jack" Gourlay (Captain Trent), and implicit behind him the Great Man himself, Sir Robert Walpole.

Evil as Spoiled Good
The Noble Lord is "so passionate an Admirer of Woman" that, as Colonel James says, what sets him off from "the Character of most Men beside him" is his willingness to go to any length: "If he once fixes his Eye upon a Woman, he will stick at nothing to get her" (4.9.193, 5.9.227). Love corrupted into lust, when permitted to go uncontrolled, leads to the evils of seduction, rape, and violence to others. Its corruption corrupts all other virtues. And that explanation applies to the Noble Lord as well who simply uses his power, honor, generosity certainly, even tenderness and good nature (e.g., to children) toward the end of enjoying women (in particular women who resist him). The greater the man, the greater the lust, the greater the power, the greater the evil.

The Noble Lord's evil, in Augustine's formulation, is merely the negative of good, the quality God's enemies have to "oppose His rule," which has "no power to hurt *Him*, but only *themselves*." The Noble Lord is the Christian figure of negation, whose seduction of Amelia inevitably fails and whose final punishment is appropriately to die of syphilis, the result of one of his rapes. (This we must contrast with Hogarth's Harlot, who died of syphilis contracted from one of her male clients, possibly the Noble Lord's equivalent, Colonel Charteris.)

At this stage of his career at least, Fielding still thinks about the nature of evil within the assumptions of the Christian religion, though within also the assumptions of anti-Puritan satire. Sin is initially (rightly) punished but eventually rewarded because it characterizes the good as opposed to the pious man; evil, initially rewarded, is finally punished.

Theodicy

Fielding suggests in *Amelia* two ways that the evil who are above the law will be punished: one, which is in the nature of evil, is by negation and self-destruction; the other will be at the hands of their "spiritual Governors," at the Last Judgment. Whatever else he believed of Christian doctrine, from the later 1730s Fielding appears to have believed in a life after death, a heaven that repays us for those evils such as the Booths suffered, in a happy place where he could anticipate being reunited with his lost loved ones. Fielding's concern for an afterlife in which virtue is rewarded appeared as early as his passionate pleas in the *Champions* of 22 January and 6 March 1739/40—three years before the first of the deaths that he connected with the afterlife in his *Journey from this World to the Next* (1743).[20] For Fielding the real (the original) evil is death. In *Amelia*, however, the hope of an afterlife is expressed only by Dr. Harrison, and on the trivial matter of the Booths' compensation for the news that Betty has made off with Amelia's fortune. The nature of evil in *Amelia* follows Augustine's doctrine of evil as the good spoiled, as self-defeating: not only the Noble Lord but James, Bath, Murphy, and Mrs. Ellison.

Against Fielding's Christian solutions to the Problem of Evil, Hogarth posits the death and dissection of his evildoer here and now, but by greater evildoers, a little fish devoured—to adapt Brueghel's image—by a bigger fish; as if the Noble Lord were in his turn to be devoured by a Walpole rather than by the natural scourge of syphilis. In the "Last Judgment" of *The Reward of Cruelty* one might see an ultimate critique of the theology of rewards and punishments. As if answering those works that had gloried in the anticipation of an afterlife (including Fielding's), Hogarth shows no hint or promise of "rewards" *or* punishments. One recalls his version of Domenichino's *Martyrdom of St. Agnes* in *Marriage A-la-mode* 1, in which he omits her reward in heaven. There is no reference in Hogarth's works to rewards (or punishments) in an afterlife; they simply do not appear, and the image of God is ordinarily elided. Where his painterly or textual source posited God, Hogarth cancels him. But he replaces him, as in *The Reward of Cruelty*, with his representatives, and the law, of English society.

There is, however, a detail in plate 3 (*Cruelty in Perfection* [fig. 11]): On the right side of the composition, balancing the church tower and the posse that is seizing Nero, is a yew tree rising above the head of Nero's murdered lover.[21] It is unnecessary to emphasize the demotic imagery of these prints, the appeal Hogarth made to a broad popular audience;[22] besides the wounds "crying for justice," there tumbles out of the girl's box of possessions a copy of "God's Revenge against Murder," which gives the popular dimension of divine intervention at the same time that it supports the equation of divine and legal justice (revenge) in plate 4. (It offers one example in Hogarth's work in which "God" does make an appearance.) Thus the yew tree (the evergreen, seemingly ageless, symbol of immortality, and so used in many English churchyards) appears to grow out of the dead girl's head, suggesting a kind of rebirth in nature, an implied afterlife that will compensate for this murder—and correspond to the "revenge" carried out in this life on the murderer. But the yew tree has been tailored by a topiary artist ("artist" would have been Hogarth's word) into the shape of a cross, technically an archiepiscopal cross (it could pass for a papal cross, of the sort Hogarth showed held by a religious madman in the eighth plate of *A Rake's Progress*).[23] The image of the afterlife has been pruned into a symbol of the Church of England as he saw it, the sort of appropriation of Christ's Atonement by religion that Blake would attack in his poems.

The pendants to the *Stages of Cruelty* were *Beer Street* and *Gin Lane;* in the latter (fig. 17), the significant feature is the church steeple, as distant from the occupants of Gin Lane as the governors were from the boys in *Cruelty* 1—and on which the cross has been replaced by a statue of the monarch and, not so distant, the sign of a pawnbroker, the only governance in Gin Lane. Hogarth's attack is not on gin (as the *Harlot's Progress* was not an attack on prostitutes) but, especially in the context of the pendant *Cruelty* plates, on the ruling order that makes life so hard (so evil in the sense of suffering) and leaves the only palliative gin—the only way to escape from an intolerable life, precisely of the sort shown in *The Stages of*

FIGURE 17 William Hogarth, *Gin Lane* (1751). Etching and engraving. Reproduced by courtesy of the Trustees of the British Museum.

Cruelty.[24] As Thomas Hardy put it, "Drinking was the regular, stereotyped resource of the despairing worthless."[25] But in gin Hogarth also shows the realistic substitute of the poor and miserable for the idealism and superstition of Fielding's glorious heaven and self-defeating evil. Not heaven will counter evil, but the practice of gin-induced peace and fantasies. As context, we can look back to Swift's credulity and illusion in "The Digression on Madness" and ahead to Blake's chimney sweep's dream of the angel who will waft him off to heaven in order to forget the agony of his daytime labor in the dark and hellish chimneys of London.[26]

In Hogarth's graphic work there is nothing but the world of evils—death, disease, suffering, injured innocence, natural and moral. *Amelia* shares with Hogarth's *Cruelty* prints the primary figure of the young woman who loves and is ruthlessly exploited by her lover (the same figure appears in the *Rake*): Both represent the ideal of love, but it is only threatened in *Amelia;* it is wiped out in *Cruelty* 3 and 4, first by Nero and second (now as charity or mercy) by the legal system that is dissecting Nero. In plate 1 the only sign of *caritas* is the boy intervening between Nero and the dog he is torturing, offering Nero a tart; in 2 it is the young man taking down the number of the cab to report Nero; in 3 it is the girl whose love for Nero led her to steal from her master. But the tart is a ludicrously inadequate palliative; the young man may equally be reporting the accident as Nero's cruelty to his horse; the girl for her pains has been murdered by Nero; and in the final plate, if we look for some indication of the good we can do no better than the ravaged body of Nero himself, formally parallel to that of the girl he murdered in 3, and also to the Harlot's body in *Harlot* 6. This is not, of course, the case in Fielding's novels, with their happy—if sometimes ironical or theatrical—endings. Hogarth was a more radical thinker in religious terms if no other. Fielding was not capable of, or comfortable with, a radical image such as Tom Nero in the pose of Christ taken in the Garden of Gethsemane.

Gin is one compensation for the evils of the world; another is cruelty—we cope with the experience of evil by means of the preemptive strike, becoming the predator we fear.[27] "Is the panic resulting from the consciousness of death the cause of cruelty?" asks Sándor Márai, for whom cruelty may be another consequence of the Problem of Evil, a form of compensation; he noted the relationship between the inevitable Thermidor or day of reckoning and the need to raise the level of cruelty (like doses of morphine or heroin).[28]

2. DICKENS

Oliver Twist: *The Law*

Charles Dickens noticed the church steeple in *Gin Lane:* "Quite passive in the picture, it coldly surveys these things in progress under a shadow of its tower"—although it is too far to throw a shadow.[29] The writer who follows directly from Hogarth in the treatment of cruelty is not Fielding but Dickens. In *Oliver Twist* (1839) Dickens shows evil in the form of masters who have power over any subservient thing, animal or human—villains who occupy positions of at least relative power in relation to Oliver. Mr. Gamfield, the chimney sweep (a prospective master for Oliver), treats his donkey with the same cruelty Tom Nero treated his horse:

[He] bestowed a blow on his head, which would inevitably have
beaten in any skull but a donkey's. Then, catching hold of the
bridle, he gave his jaw a sharp wrench, by way of gentle re-
minder that he was not his own master; and by these means
turned him round. He then gave him another blow on the
head, just to stun him till he came back again. (15)

We learn that Mr. Gamfield has "bruised three or four boys to death already" and that his "villainous countenance was a regular stamped receipt
for cruelty" (17, 20).

In his preface to the 1867 edition of *Oliver Twist* Dickens relates his
novel to its two obvious sources: Gay's *Beggar's Opera* and Hogarth's prints
(primarily, it emerges, *The Four Stages of Cruelty* and *Gin Lane,* but always
in the background is *A Harlot's Progress*). In fact he contrasts them, interpreting Gay's work as a romanticizing of criminals and Hogarth's as
presenting "the miserable reality": that they are "the most criminal and
degraded of London's population . . . the dregs of life," as opposed to
society's "froth and cream." In *Oliver Twist* he claims, like Hogarth, to
"paint them [the dregs] in all their deformity, in all their wretchedness,
in all the squalid misery of their lives." This "miserable reality" is what I
have called suffering-evil, with "the great black ghastly gallows closing up
their prospect." The significant fact, however, is that Dickens also equates
the fate of the horse with that of the apprentice boys.

Arnold Kettle has pointed to the "extraordinary power" of the first
eleven chapters of *Oliver Twist,* the depiction of "a world of the most appalling poverty and ugliness, a world of brutality and violence in which
life is cheap, suffering general and death welcome," which is "unforget-
table."[30] Our response, as Kettle remarked, is based on our "feeling for
any child we see ill treated in the street." From the gruel scene onward,
it is the suffering of innocent children (extended to animals, Gamfield's
donkey and Sikes's dog). The passage Kettle quotes, the symbol of evil, is
topographical, close to an *ecphrasis* of *Gin Lane:*

The houses on either side were high and large, but very old,
and tenanted by people of the poorest class: as their neglected
appearance would have sufficiently denoted, without the con-
current testimony afforded by the squalid looks of the few men
and women who, with folded arms and bodies half doubled,

occasionally skulked along. A great many of the tenements had shop-fronts; but these were fast closed, and mouldering away; only the upper rooms being inhabited. Some houses which had become insecure from age and decay, were prevented from falling into the street, by huge beams of wood reared against the walls, and firmly planted in the road; but even these crazy dens seemed to have been selected as the nightly haunts of some houseless wretches, for many were wrenched from their positions, to afford an aperture wide enough for the passage of a human body. The kennel was stagnant and filthy. The very rats, which here and there lay putrefying in its rottenness, were hideous with famine.[31]

This is the symbol of the oppression and indifference of the parish officers—the ruling order—and the scene is presided over by Mr. Sowerberry the undertaker, as Hogarth's was by a pawnbroker (Fagin as a Jew combines pawnbroker, usurer, and fence).[32]

Mrs. Mann shows Bumble how she quiets the babies by feeding them gin ("I couldn't see 'em suffer before my very eyes, you know, sir"), a method Dickens inherited from *Gin Lane,* where mothers fed their babies gin and gin served in every detail of the scene to keep the poor quiet and in order. Even Bumble appreciates "the temporary blandness which gin-and-water awakens in some bosoms."[33]

Dickens opens *Oliver Twist* with pictures of Bumble and Mrs. Mann, the beadle and the "parochial delegate, and a stipendiary," the "workhouse authorities," the "parish authorities," the board of the parish, and "the gentleman in the white waistcoat" (Bumble is metonymically a cocked hat and a cane),[34] all the figures of legalized authority who reduce Oliver to an "it," as it is implied the governors of St. Giles did the boys in *Cruelty* 1. Oliver is an orphan, as abandoned by mother and family and society as was Hackabout in plate 1 of the *Harlot's Progress* and Tom Nero in the *Stages of Cruelty.* Like another apparent orphan (another of his precursors), Tom Jones, Oliver, it is said by his overseers, was born to be hanged.

If Dickens had read Blake's *Songs of Experience* he would have agreed—for example, with the chimney sweep, whose parents have "clothed me in the clothes of death [the blackened skin of his profession], / And taught me to sing the tones of woe," while they "are gone to praise God & his Priest &

King / Who make up a heaven of our misery." Dickens puts the same emphasis as Blake on the cruelty to innocent children but would have made the boy an orphan and put the blame onto the "Grey-headed beadles [who] walked before [the children] with wands as white as snow"—"the aged men wise guardians of the poor" who drive them to be chimney sweeps ("Holy Thursday" in *Songs of Innocence*). Nor would Dickens have put the blame on religion and its priests as Blake does in "The Garden of Love," in which it is the "Priests in black gowns, [who] were walking their rounds, / And binding with briars, my joys & desires" and in "A Little Boy Lost," in which the little boy (like Oliver Twist asking for another bowl of gruel) tells a priest he loves others as much as he loves God, and the priests "strip'd him to his little shirt, / And bound him in an iron chain. / And burn'd him in a holy place, / Where many had been burn'd before." Dickens, in short, if he does not distinguish sin from law at least distinguishes the legal profession from the religious. There is no religious dimension as such in *Oliver Twist*—only law, justice against mercy in the manner of Shakespeare's *Merchant of Venice*.

The characters Dickens places around Oliver Twist, the grotesque corrupters of children supplemented by the respectable, sin- and law-dependent governors of the poor, are novelistic equivalents of the figures around Christ in the *Ecce Homo* pictures and in *Harlot* 4 and 6. As to the Problem of Evil: Dickens uses Gay's solution, making Mr. Bumble, like the beater of horses who becomes himself a horse, end a pauper in the same workhouse where "he had once lorded it over others."

There are, first, the beadles and parish officers (others, such as Mr. Fang the magistrate, keep appearing), accompanied by the respectable masters like Gamfield the chimney sweep and Sowerberry the undertaker. In the early chapters Dickens establishes the respectable criminals before introducing, by contrast, the nominal, that is, the low criminals, who live miserably and are hanged. His point about the *Beggar's Opera* is that Gay presented the low characters, only implying the great (society's "froth and cream"), but by showing the low imitating the manners of the great, he had romanticized them—associating them with "moonlit heaths" and "merrymaking in the snuggest of all possible caverns," rather than "the haunts of hunger and disease."

Then there is the déclassé Oliver, an orphan like Tom Jones and an apprentice like Tom Idle; and, somewhere in the same area, the harlot

Nancy. Oliver and Nancy are, in their different ways, innocent sinners. Her "atonement"—her suffering and death in order to save Oliver from this world of evil (no Hogarthian parody here)—is appropriate, as is Dickens's imagery of angels and devils (Rose and Monks).[35] "I ask you," Nancy says to the servant at Rose Maylie's house, "to give this message for God Almighty's sake" (40.297), and Dickens, unlike Fielding, seems to believe in the workings of "a stronger hand than chance" (50.373). As Sikes beat her to death, she "drew from her bosom a white handkerchief—Rose Maylie's own—and holding it up, in her folded hands, as high towards Heaven as her feeble strength would allow, breathed one prayer for mercy to her Maker" (48.359)—mercy for the sins of Sikes or her own? In any case, Nancy, like Hogarth's Harlot, by the context of Atonement, joins the concepts of sin-law with the reality of evil (suffering, murder). She becomes, like the Harlot, another redeemer when she gives her life for the salvation of Oliver. Dickens depicts her as a "Soul of goodness in things evil" (16.115) and, in his preface, defends his depiction of her devotion to Sikes but does not mention her self-sacrificing act for Oliver (xxxiii).[36]

Finally, in the lowest depths, Dickens produces the monstrous—the demonic—figures of Fagin and Sikes, Craft and Brutality. Fagin is described with an animal analogy: "As he glided stealthily along, creeping beneath the shelter of the walls and doorways, the hideous old man seemed like some loathsome reptile, engendered in the slime and darkness through which he moved: crawling forth, by night, in search of some rich offal for a meal" (19.135). But when we hear him making a speech very like one of Mr. Peachum's, we recall that he is in fact a fence, and, despite his shabbiness, Dickens constantly refers to him as "an old gentleman" ("pleasant" or "merry" or "good gentleman") and, presumably as ironically, applies "reputable" to his gang.[37] The Artful Dodger, Fagin predicts, will be "a great man"; "being a great man" in this milieu is being a skillful pickpocket.[38] At one point Bumble is referred to as a "great man" (17.118): all of which suggests that Dickens regards Fagin, like Mr. Peachum, on a level of false respectability with Bumble and Fang (in The Beggar's Opera it is Mr. Peachum who sees himself this way). Even Bill Sikes, in the mock heroic diction of Fielding's Jonathan Wild, is "Mr. William Sikes."

Fagin speaks with queasy genteelisms ("my dear"), but Sikes is mere brute. He is a killer, set off by his cruel treatment of Nancy and his dog, the two in the world who love him. The dog is his analogue or emblematically his supporter: "a white-coated, red-eyed dog; who occupied himself, alternately, in winking at his master with both eyes at the same time; and in licking a large, fresh cut on one side of his mouth, which appeared to be the result of some recent conflict," to whom he is as cruel as Mr. Gamfield the chimney sweep is to his donkey. The dog is the animal analogue of Nancy, following him to the rooftop as friend, not as revenger, and falling alongside him.

Monks (his real name, Edward Leeford) is the true, not mock, gentleman-by-blood, the equivalent to Fielding's Noble Lord, who employs these "villains," but as Satan used his tools ("such snares as I'll contrive for my young brother" [40.301]), to totally corrupt and ruin little Oliver, in fact his half-brother, invoking Cain as well as Satan; beyond just obtaining the inheritance, he wants to force Oliver into a life of crime that will end on the gallows (the Evil Dickens describes first in the workhouse and then in the slums of London). The plan, coordinated with Monks, is to have "made a sneaking, snivelling pickpocket of" Oliver, or "got him convicted, and sent safely out of the kingdom; perhaps for life" (27.191), that is, condemning him to the evil world, or the world of evil (both doing- and suffering-), from which Nancy's sacrifice frees him. Beside the banal Bumble and the grotesque Fagin, Monks is a demonic figure who is terrified of (God's?) thunder: "Hear it! Rolling and crashing on as if it echoed through a thousand caverns where the devils were hiding from it," he cries, his face "much distorted, and discoloured" (38.278). His symbol is the infernal abyss that yawns under his feet when he "threw back a large trap-door which opened close at Mr. Bumble's feet," revealing "the turbid water, swollen by the heavy rain, . . . rushing rapidly on below; and all other sounds were lost in the noise of its plashing and eddying against the green and slimy piles" (38.283). In his metonymy Dickens is recalling Isaiah 57:20–21 (which Jonathan Edwards had used to describe sinners): "But the wicked are like the troubled sea, when it cannot rest, whose waters cast up mire and dirt. There is no peace, saith my God, to the wicked."

The significance of evil and sin remained allusive in Hogarth's *Harlot*, indicated by the graphic context of Atonement and Sacrifice. Hogarth in effect secularized sin, and then turned it into a subject for comedy and finally for an aesthetics. In *Oliver Twist* sin is displaced to the harlot Nancy, sentimental now and not comic, and evil resides in the demonic figures of Fagin and Bill Sykes, and behind them, their "principal," Monks; the protagonist Oliver is a suffering innocent *accused* by the Bumbles of being a sinner.

Bleak House: *Court of Chancery*

I have referred to Dickens's notice of the church steeple in *Gin Lane:* "Quite passive in the picture, it coldly surveys these [terrible] things in progress under a shadow of its tower." The language recalls a passage written a few years later in *Bleak House* (1852–53). The Reverend Chadband's sermonizing ends with Jo, the abandoned urchin of Tom-All-Alone's (another Gin Lane), looking "at the great Cross on the summit of St. Paul's Cathedral, glittering above a red and violet-tinted cloud of smoke. From the boy's face one might suppose that sacred emblem to be, in his eyes, the crowning confusion of the great, confused city: so golden, so high up, so far out of his reach."[39] Gin Lane has become Tom-All-Alone's, but this neighborhood has been ruined not by gin but by being overlooked by—being trapped in the coils of—the Court of Chancery (the two areas contrasted in *Bleak House* are Tom-All-Alone's and Lincoln's Inn Fields, where Chancery court was held).

A "red and violet-tinted cloud of smoke" represents the London of Jo—the church is representative of the high, out of reach London of the Dedlocks and Tulkinghorns. In this novel Dickens has turned from the particulars of *Oliver Twist* to symbols and from the villains Fagin and Monks to the general fog of London and the Court of Chancery. In the earlier novel the law was embodied in beadles and governors of poorhouses. The beadle myth remains; in *Bleak House* it is rumored that a beadle has "boiled a boy, . . . that the boy was made into soup for the workhouse" (1:11.175). But the evil now is in the great spiderweb that is Chancery: In Mr. Gridley's words—he is one of the many flies caught in the web:

> The system! I am told, on all hands, it's the system. I must look
> to individuals. It's the system. I mustn't go into Court, and say,
> 'My Lord, I beg to know this from you is this right or wrong?
> Have you the face to tell me I have received justice, and there-
> fore am dismissed?' My Lord knows nothing of it. He sits
> there, to administer the system. (1:15.260)

Dickens's system, though it may originate in *Amelia*'s pervasively powerful law, has become the equivalent of Blake's religion.

Religion and sin now play their equal part: Esther Summerson is an orphan, blighted by the fall of her mother, who had a true love affair with Captain Hawdon resulting in the birth of Esther, the sin that must be shunted off to a foster mother so her mother can become Lady Dedlock; and when her sin is finally being exposed Lady Deadlock goes off to do penance, dying however not in the arms of Sir Leicester, who forgives her, but at the gate of the Potter's Field where her lover (who called himself Nemo) is buried. The ethos of sin has become another aspect of Dickens's picture of the law. The Court of Chancery carries with it the vocabulary of soteriology—especially in the words of Miss Flite (whose case seems terminable only by the Last Judgment) about the Seals of Revelation and the end of all things.

It all goes back to property and money. As Mr. Jarndyce explains "such a state of bedevilment," "It's about a Will, and the trusts under a will—or it was, once. It's about nothing but Costs, now": "A certain Mr. Jarndyce, in an evil hour, made a great fortune, and made a great Will. In the question how the trusts under that Will are to be administered, the fortune left by the Will is squandered away; the legatees under the Will are reduced to such a miserable condition that they would be sufficiently punished, if they had committed an enormous crime in having money left them; and the Will itself is made a dead letter" (1:8.116). Everyone touched by Chancery is corrupted—Richard Carstone touches and is destroyed. As Miss Flite puts it, "But, my dear . . . there's a dreadful attraction in the place. . . . There's a cruel attraction in the place. You *can't* leave it" (2:35:67).

Chancery permeates everything in London society. Krook's rag-and-bone shop is referred to as Chancery and he as the Lord Chancellor; as Krook explains, he has so many things in his shop, "wasting away and going to rack and ruin. . . . And I have so many old parchmentses and papers in my stock. And I have a liking for rust and must and cobwebs. And all's fish that comes to my net. And I can't abear to part with anything I once lay hold of (or so my neighbours think, but what do *they* know?) Or to alter anything, or to have any sweeping, nor scouring, nor cleaning, nor repairing going on about me. That's the way I've got the ill name of Chancery" (1:5.63). Krook is Lord Chancellor of the Rag and Bone Shop; therefore a rag-and-bone shop equals Chancery.

Krook's shop is yet another example of the relation of high (Chancery) to low, the great Lord Chancellor and the poor follower who, unlike

Chancery, eventually (due to the dryness of himself and his work as well as the large amounts of gin he consumes) self-destructs, a victim of spontaneous combustion. Krook "has died the death of all Lord Chancellors in all Courts, and of all authorities in all places under all names soever, where false pretences are made, and where injustice is done . . . it is the same death eternally—inborn, engendered in the corrupted humours of the vicious body itself, and that only—Spontaneous Combustion, and none other of all the deaths that can be died" (2:1.17). When all the money has run out, the case is closed ("the whole estate is found to have been absorbed in costs"): And, as Mr. Kenge says, "Thus the suit lapses and melts away" (2:65.513)—like Mr. Krook.

Karl Marx

Intervening between *Oliver Twist* and *Bleak House* was *The Communist Manifesto* (1848), which defines "civilization" as a "class struggle," between "oppression and oppressed"—defines the state as an instrument of oppression in the hands of the ruling class; not between high thief and low but between Bumble and Oliver, or Monks and Oliver, even between Lady Dedlock ("so high; so very high" [1:23.387]) and Esther Summerson—between "freeman and slave, patrician and plebeian, lord and serf" (1:7.108–09).[40] They are divided into "two great hostile camps, into two great classes directly facing each other," now called "Bourgeoisie and Proletariat."[41]

The evil is therefore not a dictator or king, not a Richard III or an Iago, but capitalism. True, the bourgeoisie "has pitilessly torn asunder the motley feudal ties that bound man to his 'natural superiors,' and has left remaining no other nexus between man and man than naked self-interest, than callous 'cash payment.' It has drowned the most heavenly ecstasies of religious fervour, of chivalrous enthusiasm, of philistine sentimentalism, in the icy water of egotistical calculation . . . In one word, for exploitation, veiled by religious and political illusions, it has substituted naked, shameless, direct, brutal exploitation" (1:111).

But the bourgeoisie is simply living out its role in capitalism—as, Marx suggests, the priests did with the Christian religion—and its expansion in less particular terms involved in the nineteenth century the Opium Wars, genocide in the Belgian Congo, the Great Game in Central Asia, and other forms of what became imperial rivalry. Looking back to the eighteenth century, we recall that Hogarth fitted *Gin Lane* into the capitalism of the gin trade.[42] The dimensions of capitalism—the worldwide expansion, what has come to be called globalization—and the distance between the operator and the consequences of his operation will become part of the twentieth-century evils that include genocide. As Marx and Engels saw it, capitalism as it spread would turn society upside down, destroying entire industries, ways of life, and political regimes. Only to self-destruct, as Augustine predicted of evil and old Krook demonstrated—to be corrected, they believed, by the replacement of the bourgeoisie by the proletariat, by the denizens of Tom-All-Alone's (or Gin Lane, "the social scum, that passively rotting mass thrown off by the lowest layers of old society" [Marx, 1:118]).

3. HAWTHORNE AND MELVILLE

The Scarlet Letter

In the America of Nathaniel Hawthorne's *Scarlet Letter* (1850)—the New England of Puritanism and the witch trials—sin is set up against evil very much as it was in the *Harlot's Progress*. The punishment imposed on Hester Prynne is to wear the letter A as the sign that she has committed the sin of adultery. But contrasted with the sin is the evil of the pain (as humiliation, physical coercion) she suffers at the hands of her community for a natural act and the original wrong she suffered in the seduction by the very clergyman who imposes (has to impose, given his office) the punishment upon her. (Though it may have been to some extent a mutual seduction, her pastor, who now administers the punishment, was the figure of Puritan authority and power who, like the Noble Lord, seduces downward.)

The Scarlet Letter opens with a description of the prison from which Hester emerges to mount the scaffold—the same door, we are told, through which Anne Hutchinson passed. With this detail Hawthorne introduces the idea of persecution and death for heresy (deviant doctrine) in the person of a woman—and memories of Hutchinson's fate back in 1637, trudging through the snow, later scalped by Indians. Hutchinson was an Antinomian—against the Law, legality, works, a believer in universal "sin" erased by Grace alone. A predestinarian, she believed in a small elect that has no need of a church; to her persecutors she was, disregarding the civil-religious authority, potentially an advocate of "anything permitted."

In the context of Hester's crime and punishment, however, she represents a victim, an opponent, of the law that punishes adultery. Hester emerges from the prison, accompanied by the beadle with his staff of office, and ascends the scaffold attended by clergymen, in the town's marketplace: here, we are informed, are punished such types as sluggish servants, undutiful children, Antinomians (like Ann Hutchinson), vagrant Indians made drunk by colonists' alcohol, and witches. In this community Hester is facing, on the scaffold, with the letter A on her breast, "a people amongst whom religion and law were almost identical."[43]

To her the law is "a giant of stern features, but with vigor to support, as well as to annihilate, in his iron arm" (5.91). Later, however, in the forest (where her sin took place), when she let down her hair and "cast away the fragments of a broken chain," she anachronistically sounds the note of the Enlightenment:

> The world's law was no law for her mind. It was an age in
> which the human intellect, newly emancipated, had taken a
> more active and a wider range than for many centuries before.
> Men of the sword had overthrown nobles and kings. Men
> bolder than these had overthrown and rearranged—not actu-
> ally, but within the sphere of theory, which was their most real
> abode—the whole system of ancient prejudice, wherewith was
> linked much of ancient principle. Hester Prynne imbibed this
> spirit. She assumed a freedom of speculation, then common
> enough on the other side of the Atlantic, but which our fore-
> fathers, had they known it, would have held to be a deadlier
> crime than that stigmatized by the scarlet letter. (13.195–96)[44]

This was New England in 1659; *that* ("It was an Age") was England in the 1690s or the 1700s. Hawthorne structures this first scene with a religious iconography that recalls Hogarth's Enlightenment *Harlot* of the 1730s. Hester, a fallen woman considered by her community a harlot, with the letter A on her breast, is "a living sermon against sin" (3.74), but the spectators are "startled to perceive how her beauty shone out, and made a halo of the misfortune and ignominy in which she was enveloped" (2.62). The community sees the scene of Hester's suffering "not without a mixture of awe":

Had there been a papist among the crowd of Puritans, he
might have seen in this beautiful woman, as picturesque in her
attire and mien, and with the infant at her bosom, an object to
remind him of the image of Divine Maternity, which so many
illustrious painters have vied with one another to represent;
something which should remind him, indeed, but only by contrast, of that sacred image of sinless motherhood, whose infant
was to redeem the world. Here, there was the taint of deepest
sin in the most sacred quality of human life, working such
effect, that the world was only the darker for this woman's
beauty, and the more lost for the infant that she had borne.
(2.65)

With the child in her arms Hester is seemingly a Madonna, albeit seen
through idolatrous, "papist" eyes (this being a "crowd of Puritans"), and
the story that is implied with her estranged husband, Chillingworth, "a
man well stricken in years, a pale, thin, scholar-like visage, with eyes
dim and bleared" (2.68), recalls the story of the aged Joseph and, indeed,
the Joseph jest, recounted by Thomas Paine in *The Age of Reason* (1794).
Discussing belief, probably drawing on such works as the *Traité des Trois
Imposteurs*, Paine opened with the story:

When also I am told that a woman called the virgin Mary, said,
or gave out, that she was with child without any cohabitation
with a man, and that her betrothed husband, Joseph, said that
an angel told him so, I have a right to believe them or not; such
a circumstance required a much stronger evidence than their
bare word for it; but we have not even this—for neither Joseph
nor Mary wrote any such matter themselves; it is only reported
by others that *they said so*—it is hearsay upon hearsay, and I do
not choose to rest my belief upon such evidence.[45]

If we follow the jest, it is therefore Parson Dimmesdale, the "Holy Spirit,"
who actually impregnated Mary/Hester.[46] But the sense of sacrificial Atonement is more to the point: "Would," she says of Dimmesdale, "that I might
endure his agony as well as mine!"—her "atonement" for the sin of her
lover/seducer (3.80).

It seems inconceivable that Hawthorne could not have known Hogarth's engraved works, easily available on both sides of the Atlantic, part of the cultural capital of educated Americans as well as Englishmen. In any case, the parallel is worth pursuing. In *A Harlot's Progress* sin (the Harlot) was contrasted with evil (Charteris, Gonson, the Brideswell warder, Walpole, and especially the two clergymen and the bishop), and in *The Scarlet Letter* Sin/Hester is set against Evil/Dimmesdale, the community, and the Puritan religion and ideology. In the *Harlot,* of course, it was not seduction by the clergyman but only indifference (although the clergyman in the final plate is lecherously groping a whore). Indifference is one way of describing Dimmesdale's wrongdoing: neglect of his duty to God (sin), of his duty to his parishioners and to this lone, unprotected woman (parishioner) whose husband was far away. Hester's active gesture of protecting Dimmesdale draws attention to his own passivity. He is not a predator like Charteris and the other figures in the *Harlot* but more like the clergy who should be protecting her as shepherds guard their flocks.

The Harlot begins as Hogarth's Madonna, then Madonna and Christ.[47] The Joseph-Mary-"God" joke was, of course, behind *Harlot* 2 (Mary Hackabout, the Jewish keeper, and the young lover slipping out the door, and in plates 5 and 6 the offspring) and at the bottom of his sin-comedy-aesthetics of sin. D. H. Lawrence recognized Hester's guilt—not only her seduction of Dimmesdale but her pride.[48] Her "transgression" of the Puritan Law is of a different order from the Harlot's "transgression" of being a harlot, but she possesses something like the Harlot's pride, though not its specific form (of wanting to be a lady, pass in society). "Sin" takes the form of Hester's needlework: "Like all other joys, she rejected it as sin" (2.61, 5.98), but it is her assertion of the positive nature of her "sin," the *Letter A:*

> On the breast of her gown, in fine red cloth, surrounded with
> an elaborate embroidery and fantastic flourishes of gold thread,
> appeared the letter A. It was so artistically done, and with so
> much fertility and gorgeous luxuriance of fancy, that it had all
> the effect of a last and fitting decoration to the apparel which
> she wore; and which was of a splendor in accordance with the
> taste of the age, but greatly beyond what was allowed by the
> sumptuary regulations of the colony. (2.61–62)

This embroidered letter, according to Hester's neighbors (the community), is the devil's mark (17.222). But the letter "A" (vs. "AD," the form usually used for adultery) also celebrates (rather than does penance for) her sin and summons up all those other Puritan A's: Adam, Angel, and America. But the A is also for All ("In Adam's fall / We sinnèd all") and Alpha (the beginning of the alphabet) and, as Leslie Fiedler has noted, with its elaborate and beautiful embroidery, Art.[49]

Perhaps the most direct sign of art and its ability to reveal the truth is the damning picture of David and Bathsheba Dimmesdale hangs on his wall: He is David, Hester is Bathsheba—Chillingworth was, like Uriah, out of the country at the time. Only in Hogarth prints does one expect to find symbolic pictures decorating rooms and defining their occupants.[50] And the last sentence of the novel describes Hester's tombstone: the escutcheon of her A, which recalls the Harlot's funeral escutcheon in plate 6, in Georg-Christoph Lichtenberg's words: *"Azure, parti per chevron, sable,* three fossets [faucets], in which three spiggots are inserted, all *proper"*—which recalls also the bawd's sign of the bell and clapper in plate 1.[51]

The embroidered letter A hints at aesthetics as a way of dealing with the evil of moral obtuseness—as a revolt against moralism. Showing her defiance of the punishment, her pride in what she did, it stands out against the tying up of her luxurious hair, which is only recovered in her loosening of it when she meets Dimmesdale once again in the forest where their transgression took place.[52] The hair evokes Milton's description of Eve in *Paradise Lost*—her "wanton ringlets" and the serpent, "curl'd [in] many a wanton wreath, in sight of Eve, / To lure her eye"—lines Hogarth used to illustrate his Line of Beauty, including the epigraph on the title page of *The Analysis of Beauty.*

In *The Scarlet Letter* the embroidered letter is associated with the joy of the forest, of sex, of the Maypole, of transgression against the Puritan ethic. It stands for all those things that were lost with the "Maypole of Merrymount" when it was swept away by Governor Endicott and the Puritans. Merrymount would have been one source for the "papist" reading of Hester's punishment on the scaffold as an analogue to the Madonna and Child, and Merrymount met the same fate at the hands of Governor Endicott as the Tory "Cousin Molineux" at the hands of the American revolutionaries and Hester at the hands of her community.

The purpose of Hester's child, Pearl, is "to connect her parent forever with the race and descent of mortals, and to be finally a blessed soul in heaven!" (6.104)—a Christlike role, reiterating the theme of atonement-redemption; but by the Puritans she, like her mother's A, is associated with witches, elves, and changelings. Neighbors speculate that she's "a demon offspring" (6.116). (Mrs. Hibbens, by contrast, is a real "witch" [8.137], that is, in terms of the sin ethos of her community.) When told by Hester, "Thy Heavenly Father sent thee," little Pearl replies, "I have no heavenly Father," and she means that she wants to know who her *earthly* father was, but she also indicates that she is indeed a child of the Enlightenment. Dimmesdale refers to "this child of its father's guilt and its mother's shame" (8.134). Pearl is the natural symbol, as opposed to the artful symbolism of the letter A, of Hester's sin. She is described as perfect, "an infant worthy to have been brought forth in Eden" (6.105). She has a "circle of radiance around her," Pearl's equivalence to Hester's "halo" ("holiness"); and Hester believes she is endowed with "the power of retribution for my sin" (8.133). Hester "hath an infant immortality, a being capable of eternal joy or sorrow, confided to her care" (8.135), and it is natural to speculate about Incarnation—"was she a human child?" (6.108).

At the same time, however, Pearl is dressed by Hester to resemble the embroidery of her scarlet letter, and we are told that "Pearl's aspect was imbued with a spell of infinite variety. . . . Her nature appeared to possess depth, too, as well as variety" (6.105–06). At the moment when Hawthorne describes her perfect beauty he uses the aesthetic term with which Hogarth described beauty-sin. He could, of course, have gotten "infinite variety" from one of Hogarth's German followers via the Transcendentalists, but the other terms suggest that he knew *The Analysis of Beauty*.[53] Pearl is, significantly, and like her mother, perfectly beautiful but Antinomian: While possessing depth as well as variety, her nature

> lacked reference and adaptation to the world into which she was born. The child could not be made amenable to rules. In giving her existence, a great law had been broken; and the result was a being whose elements were perhaps beautiful and brilliant, but all in disorder; or with an order peculiar to themselves, amidst which the point of variety and arrangement was difficult or impossible to be discovered. (6.106).

And, like Jesus among the moneychangers, she is prone to fits of anger (6.110–11).

The Forest

The forest, where Hester has her crucial meeting with Dimmesdale (where she had her first, her sexual encounter), is the center of both "sin" and "joy"—"sin" for the Puritan community and "joy" (which includes the art of her embroidery as well as her sexual encounter) and liberty (Antinomian liberty) for Hester and, momentarily, for Dimmesdale. The evil is in the Puritan community—they really are of the troop of the Black Man—and in the vengeful old cuckold, Chillingworth, who completes the romantic triangle (Hawthorne's version of Hogarth's Jew who cast out the unfaithful Harlot). He is the Joseph figure of the miraculous conception but also serves as Hawthorne's implication that, as against the Black Man of the forest, there are true devils, for example the demon (as he appears to the community) who takes over Dimmesdale (9.151).

Seen by Hester and Dimmesdale, the forest is joy and liberation, by the community (and again by Dimmesdale) it is Satanic evil, or rather sin in the form of the Black Man and his witches' Sabbath. In the forest, Dimmesdale is beyond "the scope of generally received laws"—"principle" ("fearfully transgressed"), "regulations," "prejudices," and the priest's "framework of his order," all versus "passion," or sin, joy, and the maypole. In the forest he is "breathing the wild, free atmosphere of an unredeemed, unchristianized, lawless region": "his spirit rose, as it were, with a bound, and attained a nearer prospect of the sky." "Do I feel joy again?" he cries. Hester cries, "The past is gone!" and tears off her letter. He joins Hester's Enlightenment stance—about to flee with her, as she tears off the A and loosens her hair (18.243, 246–47). Pearl in this context is "a nymph-child, or an infant dryad, or whatever else was in closest sympathy with the antique wood"—as the Christian imagery is replaced (as in "The Maypole of Merry Mount") by Nature and the Old Gods.

Before she leaves the forest, Hester returns the letter and her hair to their places (making "a face to meet a face"). Dimmesdale also returns to town, but he has given up the momentary pagan joy and, like Young Goodman Brown, sees evil everywhere beneath appearances: "It was the same town as heretofore; but the same minister returned not from the forest" (20.260–61); and his actions, which have to be vigorously suppressed, are of the forest—dirty jokes and the maiden's tender bosom again ("drop into her tender bosom a germ of evil that would be sure to blossom darkly soon, and bear black fruit betimes" [264]). He meets Mrs. Hibbins, who correctly equates the Forest, the Black Man, and Dimmesdale. Once back in his house, he destroys the Election sermon, which must have anticipated his tryst with Hester, and rewrites it in the predestinarian mode.

The celebration joins and embodies the old and the new; and his Election sermon is a repudiation of the Maypole—a return to the ethos of sin; but what he says is not reported, indeed is described as sound only:

> The vocal organ was in itself a rich endowment; insomuch that
> a listener, comprehending nothing of the language in which
> the preacher spoke, might still have been swayed to and fro by
> the mere tone and cadence. . . . These [words], perhaps, if more
> distinctly heard, might have been only a grosser medium, and
> have clogged the spiritual sense. . . . Nor had inspiration ever
> breathed through mortal lips more evidently than it did
> through his. Its influence could be seen, as it were, descending
> upon him, and possessing him, and continually lifting him out
> of the written discourse that lay before him, and filling him
> with ideas that must have been as marvellous to himself as to
> his audience. (13.191–98)

There is another Enlightenment dimension to *The Scarlet Letter*, and that derives from Hawthorne's reading of Swift. In Swift's *Tale of a Tub* evil was associated with the corruptions of religion, which he associated with enthusiast heresy and Calvinist sin. Swift's explanation, for example, for the etiology of the puritan visage was the wind pumped in; Hawthorne's was the Puritan obsession with sin. Swift's explanation for the origin of religious enthusiasm was sexual desire, a diagnosis with which Hawthorne would not have disagreed. It is worth recalling that Hawthorne's model for Hester's community (for the story of Mrs. Hibbins) was the Salem witch trials of the 1690s, over some of which his great-grandfather had presided thirty years after the time of *The Scarlet Letter*. Here there were the innocent victims accused of the gravest sin, of being witches, by the hysterical young females whom Swift interpreted in his *Tale* as sex-mad enthusiasts. Dimmesdale's fame is centered on his "eloquence and religious fervor," and Hawthorne applies this particularly to his women parishioners:

> In their eyes, the very ground on which he trod was sanctified.
> The virgins of his church grew pale around him, victims of a

passion so imbued with religious sentiment that they imagined
it to be all religion, and brought it openly, in their white
bosoms, as their most acceptable sacrifice before the altar.
(11.169)

Again, "the young virgins who so idolized their minister, and had made a
shrine for him in their white bosoms; which now, by the by, in their hurry
and confusion, they would scantily have given themselves time to cover
with their kerchiefs" (12.180): Could he be remembering the girl's bosom
in Hogarth's *Sleeping Congregation* (1738), the focus of the clergyman's
religious devotion?

Finally, the community thinks: "Were there not the brilliant particles
of a halo in the air about his head? So etherealized by spirit was he, and
so apotheosized by worshipping admirers": the "halo" of Hester repeated
on Dimmesdale's brow (23.300) but now recalling a burnt-out lantern like
Swift's image of the Banbury Saint. Hawthorne recalls Swift's explanation
for Puritan eloquence in his *Tale* and especially his *Mechanical Operation
of the Spirit*. Dimmesdale's body, his life rapidly fading, he is like the
Banbury Saint, all spirit:

he saw nothing, heard nothing, knew nothing, of what was
around him; but the spiritual element took up the feeble frame,
and carried it along, unconscious of the burden, and converting it to spirit like itself. Men of uncommon intellect, who had
grown morbid, possess this occasional power of mighty effort,
into which they throw the life of many days, and then are life-
less for as many more. (22.287)

Hawthorne opposes the ethos of sin and the ethos of joy (which is the
ethos of good vs. evil): Mrs. Hibbins for adhering to the latter is hanged;
Dimmesdale dies; Hester repents—she cannot get out from under the
ethos of sin and so must return to New England and resume the letter A.
Perhaps Hawthorne intends to make her a tragic heroine; or perhaps he
implies a sense of Atonement for her community summed up in the effect she and the letter have on her contemporaries—and on Hawthorne's
contemporaries when he discovers the letter in the Custom House in the
1840s.

Young Goodman Brown has been tempted by the devil; he has agreed to visit one of his Black Masses but shows that he is not like the others; or that he is a Gulliver who, returned from Houyhnhnmland, is no longer able to adjust to the domestic reality. As she goes wandering about the community, Hester, like Goodman Brown, believes that the letter "gave her a sympathetic knowledge of the hidden sin in other hearts." She suspects that "the outward guise of purity was but a lie, and that, if truth were everywhere to be shown, a scarlet letter would blaze forth on many a bosom besides Hester Prynne's":

> Sometimes the red infamy upon her breast would give a sym-
> pathetic throb, as she passed near a venerable minister or mag-
> istrate, the model of piety and justice, to whom that age of
> antique reverence looked up, as to a mortal man in fellowship
> with angels. "What evil thing is at hand?" would Hester say to
> herself. Lifting her reluctant eyes, there would be nothing hu-
> man within the scope of view, save the form of this earthly
> saint! Again, a mystic sisterhood would contumaciously assert
> itself, as she met the sanctified frown of some matron, who,
> according to the rumor of all tongues, had kept cold snow
> within her bosom throughout life. That unsunned snow in the
> matron's bosom, and the burning shame on Hester Prynne's,—
> what had the two in common? (5.101–03)

Is this because the Puritan community consists of hypocrites, or because they are all, as Augustine and Calvin believed, sinners unless saved by God's Grace? If the latter, the Black Man's company are simply those (all of them) who are not saved by God's Grace. But then Hawthorne adds:

> O fiend, whose talisman was that fatal symbol, wouldst thou
> leave nothing, whether in youth or age, for this poor sinner to
> revere?—such loss of faith is ever one of the saddest results
> of sin. Be it accepted as a proof that all was not corrupt in this
> poor victim of her own frailty, and man's hard law, that Hester
> Prynne yet struggled to believe that no fellow-mortal was guilty
> like herself.

Does Hawthorne or does he not believe in sin? Presumably Hester does, he does not. In chapter VI she equates her sin with evil (6.105), assuming that it stains her progeny, Pearl; but Hawthorne is contrasting Hester's ac-

tual innocence with her *feeling* of guilt, instilled into her by her community
—yet, at the same time, given her embroidered A and her wonderful child,
he allows her a feeling of superiority to that community.

Does Hawthorne distinguish between sin and evil—or only between
true and false sin?—Dimmesdale the true, Hester only the putative sin-
ner; or sin as the community sees it (from Father Wilson down to Mrs.
Hibbins) as opposed to natural human behavior—or as simply Original
Sin shared by all of these citizens without distinction? Both Hester and
Dimmesdale are technically sinners, but the community and its assumptions are patently evil: either in the sense of all sharing Adam's Sin or in
Hogarth's sense of using sin (law) in evil ways, to persecute the innocent.
We have to believe that Hawthorne, though he never makes the verbal
distinction between sin and evil, does not believe in Original Sin, and yet
seems to accept the fact of evil.

Billy Budd

Melville's Billy Budd—called Baby, Beauty, repeatedly described as being
young, "a child-man" with "a child's utter innocence"—is a blond, ideally
handsome youth ("the Handsome Sailor"), "all but feminine in purity of
natural complexion."[54] He is, among other things, an innocent like Eve or
Adam or like Hogarth's horses and children, confronted by a "depraved"
(Melville's word) man and, recalling both Hogarth and Dickens, the rigid
British law.[55] Impressed by the English navy, he is compared to "a goldfish
popped into a cage" and, a bit later, to another of those innocent animals,
"a dog of Saint Bernard's breed." He is "as Adam presumably might have
been ere the urbane Serpent wriggled himself into his company" (1.293,
2.300). He is attacked by an evil agent, whom he kills, and he is hanged
by the same law that killed Tom Nero. He recalls those graphic images of
the punishment of the Incarnated Christ—ordinarily a thin, effeminate
figure surrounded by gross and ugly men who punish him.

Taken from a merchantman with the significant name *Rights-of-Man*
(after Paine's revolutionary tract), Billy is placed aboard the man-of-war
Bellipotent (again, appropriately named), where he encounters the dark,
depraved man named Claggart, the ship's master-at-arms, Billy's naval
superior.[56] Billy is topman, working in the heights of the mast above
the ship, while Claggart lurks in the lower reaches, the "pit" of the ship
(17.338), its underworld (his pallor is commented on, contrasted with Billy's

ruddy complexion). Claggart is essentially the "maritime chief of police" (8.317), the keeper of law and order on shipboard. He takes a deep dislike to Billy—envy in Melville's definition, probably at bottom sexual, but so unexplained as to suggest an allegory of good and evil. He might be called, given their mutual self-destruction, Billy's evil double. The "subterranean fire" of Claggart's passion applies to not only his physical position on the ship (his "cavernous sphere"), but the diabolic aspect of the figure and the submerged operations of his mind (17.340–41).

Melville devotes a section to a discussion of depravity (L. *de-pravus*, crooked, bad), which he distinguishes from Calvin's generalization of reprobation-to-almost-all. He defines *depravity* as originating in both society and in nature. "Civilization, especially if of the austerer sort, is auspicious to it": "It folds itself in the mantle of respectability. It has certain negative virtues serving as silent auxiliaries. It never allows wine to get within its guard. It is not going too far to say that it is without vices or small sins. There is a phenomenal pride in it that excludes them." By "civilization," in short, Melville means (as his friend Hawthorne did) the civilization of New England, Puritanical and hypocritical, or, in the terms of Fielding and Dickens, the ethos of the Great and the respectable versus sinners like the Harlot and Tom Jones. But he distinguishes the evil man from his fellows: "These men are madmen, and of the most dangerous sort, for their lunacy is not continuous, but occasional, evoked by some special object"—by which he means Claggart's obsession with his opposite, Billy: "Now something such an one was Claggart, in whom was the mania of an evil nature, not engendered by vicious training or corrupting books or licentious living, but born with him and innate, in short 'a depravity according to nature'" (11.325–26)—something like the evil supposed in all men but unexplained by Original Sin.

Claggart reports to the ship's captain, "the Honorable Edward Fairfax Vere," the gratuitous lie that Billy is involved in a mutinous plot (6.309).[57] Melville fills in the historical context of the events, which take place during the Napoleonic war, shortly after the traumatic uprisings at Spithead and at the Nore (known as "the Great Mutiny")—and moreover just after an engagement with a French ship. It is a time of martial law when legality and morality cannot be reconciled, but also in the aftermath of the French Revolution, which put all of these issues in question. Finally, Billy has a speech impediment—a stammer—which is referred to as a "blemish" or flaw (a memory of the Original Sin? or of the Levitical blemish which disqualifies one as both sacrifice and priest?) (2.302).

Captain Vere has Billy summoned, has Claggart repeat the charge to Billy, who, astounded (good-hearted as he is, he has not been able to believe that Claggart is not his friend), cannot get the words out—he stammers—and, unable to express himself in words, launches out a blow that knocks Claggart down and kills him (we have been given an earlier example of Billy's temper when provoked): "The next instant, quick as the flame from a discharged cannon at night, his right arm shot out, and Claggart dropped to the deck." Captain Vere spontaneously cries, "It is the divine judgment on Ananias! Look!" (19.350–51).

Captain Vere from the first has understood that Claggart was lying. Melville tips the scales against Claggart when he says he resembles Titus Oates (8.313), the prototypical liar—and Vere compares him to Ananias; but, according to legal forms, Vere has arranged the confrontation of accuser and accused, which causes the catastrophe. With Claggart's dead body at his feet, he knows that Billy is innocent of the charge of mutiny and Claggart guilty of perjury and defamation, but, according to his logic, which is the logic of the law, in the context of the war and the recent mutinies, in the context of sin (disobedience to the Master), he must hang Billy:

> In the jugglery of circumstances preceding and attending the event on board the *Bellipotent,* and in the light of that martial code whereby it was formally to be judged, innocence and guilt personified in Claggart and Budd in effect changed places. In a legal view the apparent victim of the tragedy was he who had sought to victimize a man blameless; and the indisputable deed of the latter, navally regarded, constituted the most heinous of military crimes. (21.354)

Evil is Claggart's perjury and defamation of Billy, sin is the insubordination, the treason, of Billy Budd vis-à-vis Captain Vere.

Melville shows a case of sin being punished while the evil deed (which has in a Christian sense been punished but still results in Billy's death) has legally no relevance: Claggart dies for his lie, but Billy is hanged from the yardarm for a sin—in the historical context laid out in the narrative, for insubordination. Thus, human morality versus law: As Vere says, it is not "ourselves that would condemn" Billy under these circumstances, "it would be martial law operating through us":

> For that law and the rigor of it, we are not responsible. Our vowed responsibility is in this: That however pitilessly that law may operate in any instances, we nevertheless adhere to it and administer it. . . . But tell me whether or not, occupying the position we do, private conscience should not yield to that *imperial* one formulated in the code under which alone we officially proceed? (21.362).

I emphasize the word *imperial* in order to note the equation of law and state. "But do these buttons that we wear," asks Vere, "attest that our allegiance is to Nature? No, to the King" (361). So justice/law and nature/monarch. The crime—according to the law of England as to the law of sin—is when "in wartime at sea a man-of-war's man strikes his superior in grade, and the blow kills" (363). Indeed, the act of "plain homicide" has to be "committed in a flagrant act of mutiny," which is technically what Billy did. This judgment is contrasted by Captain Vere with a more hopeful judgment in heaven, as it is compared by Melville with the story of Abraham's sacrifice of Isaac (Vere in the Abraham role [22.367]). Presumably things would have been different on the *Rights-of-Man*, whose owner was an admirer of, besides Paine, "Voltaire, Diderot, and so forth." As Billy takes his leave, he salutes the ship: "'And good-bye to you, old *Rights-of-Man*'"—which, we are told, "was a terrible breach of naval decorum" (1.297). There is a kind of dichotomy projected between the British "flag of founded law and freedom" and "the enemy's [the French] red meteor of unbridled and unbounded revolt" (3.303). Claggart, the evil man who avoids sinning, is compared to a Pharisee, and the Pharisee to "the Guy Fawkes prowling in the hid chambers underlying some natures" preparing to blow up the whole constituted church and state (13.330). The irony is that a disobedience to God or the civil law is punished, but an evil to countless other human beings is rewarded or rendered irrelevant (legally, spiritually). Melville's further irony is that among sailors Billy becomes a secular saint; the spar from which he was hanged is turned into a saint's relic: "chip of it was as a piece of the cross" to the sailors, and the story of Billy Budd their promised afterlife (30.383).[58]

CHAPTER FIVE

The Demonizing of Sin

1. "SIN WITH THE CAPITAL LETTER": THE SUPERNATURAL

Sin as Abomination, Evil as Crime

At the end of the nineteenth century, in Arthur Machen's tale of terror and the supernatural "The White People" (1895), a girl is misled by her governess, drawn back into a primitive world of the old gods—back to a powerful atavistic belief in the supernatural, and away, as Machen shows in the introduction to the story, from *A Harlot's Progress* and *Oliver Twist*. The latter are examples of social evil, the former of "sin." "The merely carnal, sensual man," says Machen's spokesman Ambrose,

> can no more be a great sinner than he can be a great saint. Most of us are just indifferent, mixed-up creatures; we muddle through the world without realizing the meaning and the inner sense of things, and, consequently, our wickedness and our goodness are alike second-rate, unimportant. . . . We think that a man who does evil to *us* and to his neighbours must be very evil. So he is, from a social standpoint; but can't you realize that Evil in its essence is a lonely thing, a passion of the solitary, individual soul? Really, the average murderer, *qua* murderer, is not by any means a sinner in the true sense of the word. He is simply a wild beast that we have to get rid of to

save our own necks from his knife. I should class him rather
with tigers than with sinners.[1]

Sin, or, as Ambrose says, "Sin with the capital letter," is thoughts, learning, curiosity, delving into "forbidden" texts. There are, says Ambrose,
"those who have sounded the very depths of sin, who all their lives have
never done an 'ill deed.'"

The examples of the "awfulness of real sin" offered by Ambrose are
Levitical abominations: "What would your feelings be, seriously, if your
cat or your dog began to talk to you, and to dispute with you in human
accents? You would be overwhelmed with horror. I am sure of it. And
if the roses in your garden sang a weird song, you would go mad. And
suppose the stones in the road began to swell and grow before your eyes,
and if the pebble that you noticed at night had shot out stony blossoms
in the morning?" "Well, these examples," says Ambrose, "may give you
some notion of what sin really is" (119).

What Machen is saying is that real evil (not mere murder, even serial
murders or "murder and more") is *sin,* Old Testament sin—disobedience
and transgression: resulting in the abominations of Leviticus, the mutant
mixtures, the deviations, the extent to which the terms of evil have to do
with deformity (as in Aquinas, evil equals the broken leg, a deviation from
the norm); aesthetically, the grotesque, the mermaid of Horace's *De Arte
Poetica;* "morally," incest, homosexuality, onanism, and other perversions;
socially, class transgression; ultimately, same-sex marriage, miscegenation, and abortion.

The distinction Ambrose makes originated in the discourse of witchcraft, from the *Malleus Maleficarum* through the witch trials, between
the two evils confessed to (attributed to the witches): *maleficia,* or acts of
black magic, and demonolatry, attendance at the Sabbat, worship usually
in the form of sexual submission.[2] The first causes harm, the other, a
victimless crime, is to have relations with the devil and knowledge of the
supernatural world. Witches were accused of the evil of harming neighbors or their crops, but they were prosecuted and executed for the sin of
making a pact with the devil.

Machen is returning from a secular to a sacred society. Following the
Christian position on evil, Ambrose says, "The murderer murders not
from positive qualities, but from negative ones; he lacks something which

non-murderers possess," whereas "evil [for which read *sin*], of course, is wholly positive—only it is on the wrong side" (118). It is "simply an attempt to penetrate into another and higher sphere in a forbidden manner"—that is, transgression. "Sin is an effort to gain the ecstasy and the knowledge that pertain alone to angels, and in making this effort man becomes a demon."

Machen's "sin" is based on the assumptions of theology, and so he—like many of his predecessors in the nineteenth century—is recovering biblical senses, especially Old Testament, of sin/evil. He is redefining sin post-Hogarth and -Dickens, carrying it beyond social evil back to Eve and Old Testament blasphemy and the Ten Commandments and the clear assumption that there are demons, and (his point) ergo there is a god. There could be no God without the devil, no Christ without Antichrist.

Corruption: Machen, The Great God Pan

The old gods of polytheism—demons below and angels or saints above—reappeared in Dante's *Inferno:* Charon, along with the Minotaur, was demonized and now in hell helps to punish sinners. Hell was populated with devils named Nimrod, Ephialtes, Briareus, Cerberus, and Antaeus, who help to punish sinners; rivers are named Cocytus and Acheron. Dante tends to identify these figures with parodies of Christian doctrines such as the Trinity: Geryon is a three-bodied giant, Cerberus a three-headed dog, and Satan a monster with three faces.

Milton followed in *Paradise Lost* with Satan, Sin, and Death, his demonic parody of the Trinity. Before this, in "On the Morning of Christ's Nativity," he showed the classical deities fleeing at the birth of Christ. But in *Paradise Lost* he points out that they were not precursors but perversions of the true deity—false gods, abominations, idols whom heretics have tried to pass off as precursors. The classical myths are only corrupted versions of the true story. The corrupted gods who have filled the vacuum after the Fall (and the various other falls) were driven underground by Christ, only to return in the nineteenth century in monstrous forms, as abominations. (In Swift's *Tale of a Tub,* the Moderns, grotesques like Bentley and the Banbury Saint, attempted to replace the Ancients, Homer as well as the Christian God.)

In the Christian adaptation of classical myths and iconography, Satan was given the sexual attributes of Pan and the satyrs who pursue nymphs, returning with the hairy goat's body to reclaim his lost territories. The "unspeakable rites" in which Satan/Pan is worshiped are vague but primarily the Black Mass, *Walspurgisnacht*, a blasphemous parody of the Eucharist and other church sacraments. This was primarily sexual—the body of Christ replaced by a young female virgin; this by way of the old gods Milton had shown fleeing at the coming of Christ. But the sexual, associated with Pan and classical nymphs, also restored a sensuous beauty that had been purged by the rout of the old gods. Aesthetic enjoyment became an alternative, a substitute for religious worship, and a religion in its own right.

Machen's fin de siècle fiction is a British version of Hawthorne's New England: puritan vs. pagan: L. *paganus,* country dwellers—those who clung to the old ways, the rural pre-Christian nature religions; thus stories were laid in remote parts of England or New England or, with Bram Stoker, further afield in Transylvania, recovering the Church's fear of the rural *villes* which were centers of such heretical sects as the Albigensians in southern France (so also *vilain, villager,* villain).

Machen's story "The Great God Pan" (1890, 1894) is about the recovery through brain surgery of the awareness of—an ability to experience—Pan, who then transmits madness and/or evil to everyone who comes in contact with him. Dr. Raymond, the Faustian scientist, raises the orphan Mary Vaughan, the innocent victim, in order to perform (so his friend Mr. Clark can witness) an operation on her—supposedly a simple brain lesion; Dr. Raymond "tampers with certain nerve cells in [the girl's] brain, thereby breaching the solid wall of sense that hides the real world from his patient's sight"—what Dr. Jekyll accomplished with his potion.[3] But when she awakens she screams and goes mad—she has *seen* the Great God Pan, with whom she couples, producing a daughter Helen, an abomination, who becomes the Harlot of Revelation, seducing various men and revealing to them her father, the Great God Pan (unleashing Pan worship, like the worship of the Black Man in Hawthorne's Salem), which drives them to madness and suicide.

In "The Novel of the White Powder" (1896) a young man, Francis Leicester, deep into hermetic studies, becomes depressive. His sister gets Dr. Heberden to prescribe a powder, which at first takes Francis out of his depression, makes him hyperactive, full of joy and sensuous excitement, but then sinks him into corruption, of soul and body, until he ends an oozy substance on the floor of his room, only two blazing eyes discernible in the mass. The powder, an *accident* of temperature and time, is explained by Dr. Chambers, like Francis a dabbler in alchemy, as the powder administered to witches at the Black Mass. In "The Inmost Light" (1894) Mr. Black uses his wife to seek, show transcendence (like Dr. Raymond and Mary), and she transcends but then reverts, corrupts, and dies: He *kills* her, but he does so by *transgressing* the Laws of God.

Sins are victimless crimes: Machen makes evil not the doctor's desire to recover Pan (sin) but doing so by introducing the orphan girl or the pliable wife, female innocents who are persuaded to submit to his experiment, which corrupts them, leading to the abominations of transformation and coupling with Pan, incest leading to the evils of patricide or matricide.

Once again, the undeniable acts of evil (murder of innocents, torture of children) are acts of power exerted on the powerless or less powerful. Sin goes in the other direction, as with Blake: the less powerful reacting against the more powerful, Dr. Raymond challenging and replacing God. With Pan and the other recovered "gods," the story has a scientist, a Faust who summons up Pan—or, later, with H. P. Lovecraft, Yog-Sothoth—in other words, commits a sin, breaking the first two Commandments about worshiping false or graven gods; from this sin the evils (suffering and death) follow as punishments.

What then *is* this sin with a capital S? It is "the taking heaven by storm" and "an attempt to penetrate into another and higher sphere in a forbidden manner" (119). This, offending or challenging God, or internalizing evil acts—imagining the death of the king—to Machen is the interesting part, not the crimes that may follow. In "The White People," in the story the Green Book tells, this takes the form of regression by way of "mysteries" to doors in the hillside, much dancing and "singing and crying" (138), and ancient rituals, more or less on the order of the Merry Mount gatherings in Hawthorne's story; as contrasted with the less interesting part, the girl's death, suicide by poison (it was all too much for her), and the nurse's role, whether we take it to be corruption of an innocent or the unintentional effect this had on one overactive young imagination. The stories her nurse tells her are essentially only fairy tales, with some gory details (which nurses supposedly liked to add to their bedtime tales).

What Machen's sinners amount to is fairies and elves, "not 'ghosts' at all . . . but goblins, elves, imps, demons" who lure "their victims forth to see them dance under the moon," the same scene into which the girl in "The White People" enters.[4] Machen's "fairies" are misbehaving children but with "old men's faces, with bloated faces, with little sunken eyes, with leering eyes. . . . These little people of the earth rise up and rejoice in these times of ours. For they are glad, as the Welshman said, when they know that men follow their ways. . . . There was no infamy . . . that they did not perpetrate; they spared no horror of cruelty. 'I saw blood running in streams, as they shrieked with laughter, but [adds the witness significantly] I could not find the mark of it on the grass afterwards.'"[5] Machen inverts the paradigm of cruelty to innocents, animals, and children, making the child the source of the cruelty—whether in the fairies as a group or in the figure of Wesley, the "bright boy."

Wesley, the little boy of seven or eight in "The Bright Boy" (1897), who does not grow up, is the individual regression (or recovery) of the fairy; he has the traditional appearance of the fairy, "a wonderful little boy" (280), but he is evil. His evil is sexual—fornication with his pseudo-mother, humiliation of his pseudo-father, a perfect Oedipal fantasy; but the one crime that is specified is his rape of a girl of twelve or thirteen. She "had been set upon in the wood and very vilely misused"—"shamefully maltreated"—by which act she was driven out of her mind; all we are given is euphemism and a reference to "nauseous and offensive gossip and conjecture about a horrible and obscene crime" (275, 277). As to his other acts, we are only told of "unpleasant activities in Macao" and doings "of an infamous kind" (281). His "mother" Arabella Mannings' "other occupations" are presumably a euphemism for prostitution.

The sin remains the abomination of the family trio. The initial interpretation of the narrator, Joseph Last, is of "that enchanting child [left] to the evil mercies of his hideous parents. . . . But it was dreadful to think of Wesley slowly or swiftly corrupted by his detestable father and mother, growing up with the fat slime of their abominations upon him" (279). This is one sort of abomination, but the reality turns out to be worse; the "bright boy" is the corrupter and instigator of the "parents," given power by the money he has inherited—not the corrupted but the evil child, the leader of "the horrible trio [who] peregrinated over the earth" (281). Once again, Last places the return of the fairies in the context of the declining world order: "The old world, it has been noted, had crashed down," reflecting the aftermath of World War I as well as the decline of Last himself, already on his way down when he accepted the job of tutoring the "bright boy" Wesley.

As with their later avatars, the protagonists of *The Bad Seed* and *The Omen*, the question is open as to whether the evil is in childhood—a true abomination—or is imposed upon it by evil outsiders. Georges Bataille, for one, connects childhood/innocence/disinterestedness with evil—because the child is "in revolt against the world of Good, against the adult world, and committed, in his revolt, to the side of Evil." "Good," he writes, "is based on common interest which entails consideration of the future. Divine intoxication, to which the instincts of childhood are so closely related, is entirely in the present. In the education of children preference for the present moment is the common definition of Evil."[6] That is, "preference for the present moment" draws attention to the gratuitousness of their actions; condemnation of the present moment is for the sake of the future—adulthood. Swift's view was that evil, in a social, adult world, is childish in the sense of foolish and dedicated to self-interest and womb-like comfort; the Romantic, who idealizes the child, can also imagine the worst evil in the corruption of the child—and so in the consequently possessed child.

Machen's children-fairies are partly his insight (like Bataille's) that children are most capable of true evil; but it is appropriate that they return in times of human, grown-up folly and evil, in particular during the so-called Great War. During these years two things happen in Machen's stories: the old gods return—or are sought out and recovered—and, under special circumstances, Christian spiritualism, a recovery of true Christianity, arises. These are all (to quote the title of one of his stories) "Returns." In Machen's famous hoax, the archers of Agincourt return to save the English soldiers in the trenches at Mons.[7]

If evil is attributed to a grown-up it tends to be sexual. In the late story "The Children of the Pool" (1936), Robert's guilt takes the form of a pool of "black and oily depth"—whereas, "The actual fact had, no doubt, been forgotten or remembered very slightly, rarely, casually, without any sense of grave moment or culpability attached to it; while, all the while, a pageantry of horror was being secretly formed in the hidden places of the man's soul. And at last, after the years of growth and swelling in the darkness, the monster leapt into the light, and with such violence that to the victim it seemed an actual and objective entity" (334). The "monster" is an indiscretion in his past, the seduction of a girl and the jealous re-crimination of a second girl, remorse for which, less the seduction of the girl than the feelings of guilt attached thereto, makes it seem "an actual and objective entity."

Sin is, or eventuates in, corruption and degeneration, summed up in Helen Vaughan's end in "The Great God Pan" (Francis Leicester's similar end in "The Novel of the White Powder" and the wife's, Mrs. Black, in "The Inmost Light"):

> The skin, and the flesh, and the muscles, and the bones, and
> the firm structure of the human body that I had thought to be
> unchangeable, and permanent as adamant, began to melt and
> dissolve. . . . Then I saw the body descend to the beasts whence
> it ascended. . . . I watched, and at last I saw nothing but a sub-
> stance as jelly . . . for one instant I saw a Form, shaped in
> dimness before me, which I will not farther describe. But the
> symbol of this form may be seen in ancient sculptures, and
> in paintings which survived beneath the lava [presumably
> of Pompeii and Herculaneum], too foul to be spoken of (110–11).

The figure into which Helen finally dissolves is, of course, one of those images found in the Naples Archaeological Museum—of copulating sa-tyrs, Priapus and Pan with girls and goats.

They convey that initial sensuous upsurge before revealing the dark side, the consequences of sin—the snakey lower parts of the beautiful Sin. In this fiction the scientist carries out upon the lady a kind of scientific rape, a surgery that, at first liberating, embodied in sexual transgression (with Pan or the devil), leads to her corruption and degeneration, or, in aesthetic terms, the ugly and grotesque, as if reversing the two figures of the Rowlandson comedy—the beautiful girl (no longer a sinner) *became* the hideous old man. Her punishment-consequences (beginning with the Harlot's death from syphilis) implied that evil was either part of the aesthetic compound or that evil(s) must inevitably follow from sin. But the latter evils, most melodramatically in Rowlandson's drawings, amounted to a physical disintegration toward death. What we are seeing is that the subject of sin/evil is now less about good and evil than about beauty, youth, and life versus ugliness, sickness, degeneration, and death. The first has the associations of sin and the Garden of Eden, the second of the evils that followed Eve's fall. (See above, figs. 7, 8.)

Susan J. Navarette relates this degeneration (which can be traced back, in horror terms, to Edgar Allan Poe's "Facts in the Case of M. Valdemar" of 1845) to Emile Zola's naturalist novel *Nana* (1880): The prostitute Nana dies dissolving into a "heap of matter and blood, a shovelful of corrupted flesh," her face a "formless pulp" in which one eye "had completely foundered among bubbling purulence" and the other "remained half open," looking "like a deep black ruinous hole," the nose "suppurating," and the mouth "a large reddish crust . . . peeling from one of the cheeks."[8] What connects Helen and Nana is the role of the young woman who, whether in supernatural or in social terms, becomes a harlot; she "crosses class boundaries, drawing her victims from both the highest and the lowest levels of the society that has corrupted her"; she infects the men and herself succumbs to the ravages of syphilis, which both Zola and Machen paint in their most lurid colors. (Hogarth's Harlot is, in England at any rate, the ultimate prototype; but syphilis was also implicit in the stories of vampires.)

The social sin of marriage between classes underpins the idea of miscegenation between a human and one of the old gods, not only in Mary's case (where her daughter Helen is obviously an abomination) but Jervase Cradock's son—and so on to Lovecraft's Wilbur Whateley, described as "partly human . . . with very manlike hands and head," but the "torso and lower parts of the body were teratologically fabulous"[9]—all resulting from the sin of marrying outside the tribe (fornication), the sin of the Harlot.

Sex is the hidden source for the male sinner as well. Francis Leicester's decline descends from epicureanism to indulgence in secret lusts, and so metaphorically at least syphilis would explain his radical decline into "a dark and putrid mass, seething with corruption and hideous rottenness, neither liquid nor solid, but melting and changing . . . and bubbling with unctuous oily bubbles like boiling pitch" (55).

The Poisonous (Contagious) Text

Ambrose said, "Sin with the capital letter" is thoughts, learning, curiosity, delving into "forbidden" texts. Machen's (and later Lovecraft's) source for the poisonous text was, of course, the medieval works they constantly refer to—books of alchemy, sorcerers' books, even the *Malleus Maleficarum,* a guidebook for Inquisitors, which was intended as a pious work but included much in the way of instruction to witches. In Machen's "Novel of the Black Seal" there is "The Statement of William Gregg"; in "The White People" the Green Book; and in "The Inmost Light" the "little old pocket book." In "N" there is the text of Mr. Hampole, which raises the issue of the restoration of Paradise, and then there is the story of Mr. Glanville and the texts of Behmen and William Law from which he learned how to materialize "paradise" in Stoke Newington. In "The Bright Boy" the book Joseph Last discovers, which gives him a "shock" and makes him "aghast," is "a terrible Renaissance treatise [in Latin], not generally known even to collectors of such things." The few pages at which Last looks "showed him that it thoroughly deserved its very bad character." It is presumably read by the "bright boy" to instruct him in his doings "of an infamous kind" (272, 281). The statement of Henry Jekyll in Stevenson's *Dr. Jekyll and Mr. Hyde* is another of these texts, meant for Utterson's hands "ALONE" and otherwise "to be destroyed unread"; the play *The King in Yellow* in Robert Chambers's "The Yellow Sign" (1895) is yet another: "Oh the wickedness, the hopeless damnation of a soul who could fascinate and paralyze human creatures with such words,—words understood by the ignorant and wise alike, words which are more precious than jewels, more soothing than Heavenly music, more awful than death itself." Ultimately there is Lovecraft's *Necronomicon* by the mad Arab Abdul Alhazred, which has to do with the return of the Ancient Ones to reclaim the earth. These are the "damned" texts that describe an experiment that leads to "unspeakable horror."[10]

The corrupting text is yet another example of the legal concept of principal versus accessory to a crime. The guilt is primarily in the sin-ridden text that the accessories (often blindly) follow, leading them to acts of evil. One of Blackstone's examples was the poisoner, "a principal felon, by preparing and laying the poison, or giving it to another . . . for that purpose; and yet not administer it himself." In a parenthesis Blackstone notes that the administrator need not know it is poison (IV.3.34).

But the tradition has another, a satiric source, returning us to Don Quixote and the romance of chivalry, Swift's Grub Street hack, who pores day and night over the works of his Master the Moderns, which supposedly, from the author's perspective, contains all wisdom; he means all modern follies and sinful teachings, which was embodied in a contaminating document. In his scenario there was the fool who (like Quixote) read the text and then put it into practice, which included passing on the doctrine and the document that transmitted it—evil texts containing doctrines of the Rosicrucians, Gnostics, and other heretical sects with which Swift was concerned, and which in Machen's and Wilde's fin de siècle had become for some artists normative.

The Vampire: Stoker, Dracula

Bridging the gap between believers and humanists was the vampire, the undead, a Levitical abomination in that it is both alive and dead, man and monster, a figure of sin related to the Pan-Satan who replaced God. Satan and the demons were "gods," different from us, impingers from outer space, but the vampire is one of us, an obscene version of Christ's Incarnation—and so of his Passion and Redemption.

In the nineteenth century, in the wake of evangelical movements, there came a refocus on soteriology; in the wake of the Lisbon earthquake and secularizing movements, a focus on the Problem of Evil. Christ and the vampire both spread their stories of an eternal life to the human race, though one, in orthodox Christian terms, was of salvation, the other of damnation; and both were persecuted and ultimately destroyed, and by similar methods: Christ nailed to the cross, the vampire stabbed through the heart. Vampires can be thwarted by Christian weapons and icons such as the cross, holy water, and the consecrated wafer—because they offer an alternative to Christ's Atonement, Redemption, and Grace in eternal life-in-death. The story of death and resurrection becomes the myth of the dead "resurrected" by the bite of a vampire. Above all, vampires drink the blood of others, while Christians drink the blood of Christ in the Eucharist. If, as Stephen King says, the "root source of vampirism" is cannibalism, it is cannibalism of the sort Goya portrayed so often and has its meaningful source in the Roman Catholic Eucharist and the idea of gaining eternal life through eating the body and drinking the blood of Christ.[11]

The vampire's powers are parodic of Christ's: He is, in the words of Bram Stoker's Professor van Helsing (in *Dracula*, 1897), "an arrow in the side of Him who died for man," but like Christ, the vampire can raise the dead—"and all the dead that he can come nigh to are for him at command"; "he can, within his range, direct the elements: the storm, the fog, and thunder; he can command all the meaner things: the rat, and the owl, and the bat—the moth, and the fox, and the wolf; he can grow and become small"—and so on into the range of Milton's Satan.[12]

In van Helsing's terms, the vampires represent the "evils of the world": "they cannot die, but must go on age after age adding new victims and multiplying the evils of the world; for all that die from the preying of the Un-Dead become themselves Un-Dead, and prey on their kind. And so the circle goes on ever widening, like the ripples from a stone thrown in the water" (16.229). Everlasting life is, after all, the Christian solution to the Problem of Evil, and the vampire's coven is an alternative to Christ's Elect: Either you drink his blood or he drinks yours—in either case the ultimate end is everlasting life, so long as you keep drinking another's blood and, in the case of the vampire, avoid daylight, crosses, and holy water. The vampire possesses and destroys another human creature in the particular demonic sense of giving him/her everlasting life-in-death rather than eternal life in paradise. The undead have found a way to circumvent death, as well as the eternal life promised in heaven, by remaining alive, or partly alive, eternally *on earth*. This is presumably the ultimate sin—to pervert the role and mission of Christ and so parody the symbolism of Christ's body and blood ("Blood is the life"). One of Dracula's male servants, Renfield, speaks of himself as, like Enoch, walking with God (20.287).

On the other hand, Stoker makes explicit the presence and ultimate dominance of God. Always in the background, God appears in the invocations of Mina Harker and others and, ultimately, in the expression of relief and peace that returns to the face of the destroyed vampires, whether Lucy Westerna or Dracula himself.[13] In a sense, vampires are the damned, condemned (who have condemned themselves) to eternal life-in-death, who, like Satan, try to seduce/rape humans into joining them as their lovers. An example of the recovery of God through demonology: If vampires exist, then the efficacy of crosses and holy water against them proves the existence of God.

The female vampire conflates the associations of Christ with the beauty of the two Marys, extending the aesthetics of beauty-sin into Burke's aesthetics of the sublime. In Stoker's *Dracula* van Helsing describes what it is like to come upon a female vampire in her coffin with the intention of driving the stake into her heart, "so full of life and voluptuous beauty that I shudder as though I have come to do murder" (27.393). But a perversion of God's creation, the vampire is, as Dr. Seward notes, no longer Lucy but "the foul Thing which ha[s] taken Lucy's shape without her soul"—"a nightmare of Lucy as she lay there; the pointed teeth, the bloodstained, voluptuous mouth" (16.228).

In Samuel Taylor Coleridge's *Rime of the Ancient Mariner* (1798) the lady Life-in-Death (or the Undead) is set off against the Virgin Mary of line 294 ("To Mary Queen the praise be given"), who causes the albatross to fall from the Mariner's neck:

> *Her* lips were red, *her* looks were free,
> Her locks were yellow as gold:
> Her skin was as white as leprosy,
> The Night-mare LIFE-IN-DEATH was she,
> Who thicks man's blood with cold. (ll. 190–94)

In the sister poem, *Christabel,* the vampire Geraldine, appearing suddenly in the darkened wood to Christabel, is "Beautiful exceedingly," "most beautiful to see, / Like a lady of a far countrée" (ll. 224–25); J. Sheridan Le Fanu's vampire Carmilla of the 1860s is also "absolutely beautiful," "the prettiest creature I ever saw," an alluring creature. Geraldine is also a "lady strange," her voice is "faint and sweet" ("languid" is the word used by Le Fanu and Bram Stoker), and the attraction of her eye is always noticed.[14] She appears to Christabel on a night when the "toothless mastiff bitch" is howling, and Christabel herself is thinking of and praying for the safety of her "own bethrothèd Knight" who is off at the wars. In short, Geraldine's seduction of Christabel is same-sex, an abominable intrusion between a heterosexual couple. In "Carmilla" Le Fanu follows Coleridge (who only this once mentions the betrothed) in making the significant couple in fact father and daughter, something roughly like Satan's temptation of Eve, except that having had Christabel, Geraldine turns her attention to Sir Leoline, who by the end of the fragment is also in her power. At the end of the second part Christabel and the Bard Bracy have both come to recognize the evil of Geraldine, but at just this moment Sir Leoline has accepted her—inviting her in as Christabel had in part 1—and he has chosen Geraldine over his daughter. Geraldine is balanced against the guardian spirit of Christabel's mother—who is also on the mastiff bitch's mind ("she sees my lady's shroud," the ghost of Christabel's mother) and on Sir Leoline's; so the fragment ends on the threshold of a second betrayal.

Why did Christabel invite Geraldine into her house and her bed? Like all subsequent vampires, Geraldine has to be invited into the castle she is to corrupt. She simulates weakness, and Christabel "with might and main / Lifted her up, a weary weight, / Over the threshold of the gate" (ll. 130–32), and then she asks Geraldine "to share" her couch (l. 122).[15] W. J. Bate's comment on these lines is interesting: "The character of Geraldine coalesces several things, for the interest there is in the elusiveness and ambiguities of evil, its varied and quickly shifting nature, and above all its need for human welcome and embrace if it is to become completely alive and fulfill itself." The vampire herself is, as he says, "a creature partly living through or by means of human beings, and to that extent dependent on them, like evil itself, for what she can be or do." She is "a phantasm . . . able to attain concrete existence only through the mind of a human being." Sir Leoline's ostensible reason for inviting Geraldine into his quarters is a slight years ago to his old friend, supposedly her father: "Here again," Bate writes, "the thought is that through our virtues—in the case of Christabel's father, the impulse for forgiveness—we become vulnerable."[16]

As a figure of sin, Geraldine is an abomination and a challenge to the story of God's grace in the Atonement and Redemption; as a figure of evil, she seduces Christabel from faithfulness to her betrothed, Sir Leoline to his daughter and the memory of his wife—a form of corruption. Le Fanu's Carmilla embodies the same equivalence of love, cruelty, and death in both its senses, but she makes explicit what Coleridge only implies. "In the rapture of my enormous humiliation," Carmilla tells the protagonist she is seducing and whose blood she is sucking, "I live in your warm life, and you shall die—die, sweetly die—into mine. I cannot help it; as I draw near to you, you, in your turn, will draw near to others, and learn the rapture of that cruelty, which is love."[17]

Vampires, male and female, are sinners because they are perversions of the figure of God; evil because they inflict possession and death on humans, analogous to Satan's corruption of those humans. This is a sin that also involves an evil—Satanic in that it repeats what he did to Eve, seducing (she must first invite him across the threshold) and possessing primarily women, who become his servants. The evil is possession and exploitation of a human—by a living-dead or by just another human.

2. THE SUPERNATURAL AND MORAL VALUES: HENRY JAMES

The Turn of the Screw: *Transgression and Predation*

At the end of the Salem witch trials it was Increase Mather's conclusion that "it was the false accusers, not the convicted witches, who were the true 'Daemoniacks' and servants of the 'Father of Lyes.'"[18] If the witch trials remained a basis for the fictions of Hawthorne, we might detect something similar at the bottom of Henry James's *The Turn of the Screw* (1898): specifically the situation in which the accuser (a neurotic young woman) is the guilty party rather than the accused "witch."

To set the context of the 1890s—the effect of the "suffering of children" (by this time James could have read Ivan's meditation in *The Brothers Karamazov* [1880]) reflected the sentimental view of children "trailing clouds of glory" and (in Sigmund Freud's words) "the belief, which was only destroyed by psycho-analysis, that children are creatures without sexuality"; as well as the more immediate memory of Machen's "Bright Boy" and the violated young boys who emerged into the limelight in the wake of the Oscar Wilde trial.[19] This, and the corruption of youths carried on by Dorian Gray, was the context for Miles's expulsion from school and his relationship with Peter Quint. Miles's dismissal was supposedly, according to the Governess, for acts "revoltingly, against nature"—presumably euphemisms for sodomy or masturbation, as opposed to Mrs. Grose's banal explanation that he "stole." Most likely it was for things *said*—for dirty stories, jokes, locker room talk, or blasphemy rather than propositions.[20] In short, for sins rather than evil acts, unnameable and protected behind the screen of euphemisms.

The explanation is left indeterminate—the Burkean belief in the power of the vague and undefined, of terror rather than horror. Miss Jessel's death may have been due to a pregnancy, childbirth, and suicide in the lake; impregnation presumably by Peter Quint. Thus when the Governess uses the word "infamous" she is referring to sex and to Miss Jessel's pregnancy (7.48–49).

The second aspect of sin/evil is social class. The Master has sometimes been proposed as an alternative to Quint as Miss Jessel's impregnator, but the point is precisely that it is not the Master, that the evil does not rise that high. Quint is of the lower orders: he has a "bold hard stare," is guilty of "indiscretion," was "never a gentleman" (4.27, 5.35, 6.39).

But most significant is the class slippage: he wears his master's cast-off clothes but no hat (as a gentleman would); he looks like "an actor"; and he, a valet with ambitions to pass as a master, sleeps with the gentlewoman, the Governess Miss Jessel. The same applies to the children: Miles's and Miss Jessel's association with Quint, the contamination of the higher by the lower orders (9.60–61); implicit also is the Master's absenting himself, which (originating with his favoring of Quint) permitted such disorder. The evil, which is once again in fact within the parameters of sin, is an "abomination," the "love between classes" and between adult and child—both "against nature," both erotic and social violations.

This "evil" is trivial and snobbish, a queasiness at, a repugnance to, vulgarity, which we have to attribute either to James or to the Governess. The idea of vulgarity, lowness, class violation, which we would see as snobbery, is said by her to be evil. In James's words, recalling the original source of the tale, the "servants, wicked and depraved, corrupt and deprave the children: [Thus] the children are bad, full of evil to a sinister degree." But that, of course, was only the point of origin. What he adds is a point of view distinguished from his own, and the idea of two people who seek or contest power over a third.

Lurking beneath the Governess's theory and the ghost story's "obscurity" is the situation of the innocent children. The children are both the innocent sufferers of the cruelest evil (inherent in the Problem of Evil) and the worst evildoers, original sinners. Miles stands outside looking up at where Quint may be standing; why, the Governess asks him, did he do this: Just in order that you will "think me—for a change—*bad*"—words he brings out with "sweetness and gaiety," as he bends forward and kisses the Governess. "Then you didn't undress at all? . . . And when did you go down?" "At midnight. When I'm bad I *am* bad," replies Miles, and when she expostulates that he could have caught his death of cold in the night air: "He literally bloomed so from this exploit that he could afford radiantly to assent. 'How otherwise should I have been bad enough?' he asked" (11.70–71). He seems to be merely showing off for the Governess; "bad" means simply the sin of disobedience.

This view of sin and evil is, of course, from the Governess's perspective, and she is unreliable if not deranged. She is a more sophisticated version of Poe's unreliable, indeed mad, narrator (as in "The Telltale Heart" or "The Black Cat"), which also recalls, looking back, Hogg's Justified Sinner and, further back, Swift's Grub Street hack, who was a satiric device that also supplied a psychological dimension to an abstraction. On the level of fact, the Governess is the only one who sees the ghosts; Mrs. Grose never sees Quint or Jessel (20.110); though scholars have had a hard time explaining how the Governess's ghosts can accurately correspond to the couple she has never seen.

The true evil, as opposed to the Governess's sense of sin, is internalized in her curiosity and her own, supplementing Quint's and Jessel's, need to possess the children. By the end the children regard her as their jailer. Miles wants to get out of the house and back to school or *somewhere*—"I want to see more life," he says, at just the moment when he and the Governess arrive "within sight of the church" (14.83–84). On the other side, with the church (which he enters to escape the Governess's questions), is the school administration that has expelled him, the Puritan community, which at home is embodied by the Governess. Miles's attempt to escape, to return to school, the Governess uses as an opportunity to force him to tell her *why* he was expelled, ending in the ambiguity of the final page: Miles's final words—"Peter Quint—you devil!"—can refer either to Quint or, regarding the dash, to the Governess. His last word, "*Where?*"—because he has lost Quint, or because Quint now *has* him?— can refer either to the ghost Quint or to the real Governess as murderer-possessor. Caught between the ethos of Quint and that of the Governess, Miles dies—that is, he goes either to Quint or to the Governess. In *her* final words ("*I* have you"), she *has* him, but he's dead—has to be dead to be possessed, by either Quint or Governess. (Apparently Flora, via Mrs. Grose, escapes; while the Governess goes on to charm Douglas.)

In any case, the Governess is a young woman, herself hardly twenty years old, the inexperienced child of a country parsonage, of great sensitivity (1.13–14), clearly in love with the Master—reflecting another forbidden desire, a governess's need to unite with her employer, which seems to recall the happier example of an earlier governess, Jane Eyre, and Mr. Rochester. Indeed, her first sight of Quint comes when she is daydreaming about a visit from the Master (3.23): Quint then becomes an objectification of the Master as a source of fear—wearing his "better's" clothes. As her own reference suggests, she is another Catherine Morland transformed by her reading of Radcliffe's *Mysteries of Udolpho* (4.26). Further, she has had some trouble at home and now, with the children, is "dazzled by their loveliness" (4.29); in fact she seems to regard herself as an agent of Atonement for the children ("I should serve as an expiatory victim and guard the tranquility of my companions," she says [6.38]).

The frame narrative of the ghost story and the MS is employed, as in so many ghost stories, for purposes of authenticity, but it incriminates the readers of the ghost story as analogues to the Governess based on a similar curiosity, prurience, willingness to pay the "utmost price" for titillation (2); and Douglas is passing on the story at least partly because he has himself fallen for the Governess.[21] The MS titled "The Turn of the Screw" is another of those poisonous texts that have a dangerous effect upon its readers. The party of ladies and gentlemen has been listening to ghost stories, in particular a "gruesome case" in which "such a visitation had fallen on a child." But the story Douglas has to tell is about not one but *two* children; it is "beyond everything. Nothing at all that I know touches it," says Douglas—"for dreadful—dreadfulness!"; "for general uncanny ugliness and horror and pain." It cannot be told because "the story's written. It's in a locked drawer—it has not been out for years" and must be sent for. It was written down by the Governess herself. The ladies are "in a rage of curiosity" to hear the story but, Griffin (the frame narrator) says, "They didn't, of course, thank heaven, stay" for the reading, which had "immense effect" (1–5), not least on the readers of the published *Turn of the Screw.*

James's ghost story represents two things for us: the suffering of children and the evil of the vampire's desire to possess a child, which in one way or another (whether the vampire is Quint or the Governess) makes the child attempt to imitate (sin). Second, it juxtaposes the demonic and banal—Quint and Miss Jessel and the Governess (which is the true evil?) and her transforming imagination of sin (social offense) into evil; thus, the struggle for the children's souls by the ghosts and by the real, banal young woman. In *The Turn of the Screw* we have the unreliable narrator; the opposition of sin and evil, abomination and wrongdoing; and the first, the Governess as unreliable narrator, mystifies the evil by interpreting it as sin/abomination—in effect, demonizing it. The Governess's idea of "evil" is sin, like the one attacked by the citizens of Salem—a mixture of sex and class, abomination as miscegenation or social solecism.

Possession

James probably regarded Machen's stories as examples of the modern version of that "beautiful lost form" of the ghost story that he himself still practiced. A ghost story, he argued, "must be connected at a hundred points with the common objects of life," must derive "from its prosaic, commonplace, daylight accessories. Less delicately terrible, perhaps, than the vagaries of departed spirits, but to the full as *interesting*, as the modern novel reader understands the word, are the numberless possible forms of human malignity."[22] This is, among other things, James's way of describing the difference between the two plot levels in *The Turn of the Screw,* the plot of the "ghosts" and that of the Governess, which is from the "prosaic, commonplace, daylight" world; but both represent degrees and forms of "human malignity," which for the novelists I shall discuss in the next chapter will become demonic and banal.

In *The Turn of the Screw* Quint and Jessel appear to be evil ghosts, and in a sense are (insofar as they do want to possess, for evil purposes, the children), but it is primarily to the Governess—the *living* person—that they appear, by whom they are interpreted as sinners, sexual and social predators. James's unambiguous ghost stories are not ordinarily stories of evil; his ghosts are merely revenants, usually good or at worst retributive, an avenger like the ghost of Sir Edmund Orme. That is, the evil (or merely wrongdoing) is located in the living person (the woman who jilted Orme) and not in the ghost who pursues her and disappears when he has made his point, having reordered her sin in her daughter's "redemption"—at which point *she* dies, apparently *joining* him if James believed in the religious aspect of ghosts as harbingers of an afterlife. There is no sign, however, that he did. His ghosts are simply projections of the living or the lately living, demonic echoes of a banal reality.

The Jamesian ghost is a force of nature, a residue of human dignity, contra a living man who wants to possess the spirit—the remains—of the deceased. The ghosts defend themselves from predatory biographers, the exploitation of their manuscripts and other property. One of James's ghost stories, "The Real Right Thing" (1899), has the biographer protagonist appropriate a dead person—the private papers of a dead poet; he undertakes a biography, reads the poet's most personal papers, interferes with the life of the surviving wife: "We lay him bare. We serve him up. What is it called? We give him to the world"—and he is warned off such a project by an emanation of the dead victim. The ghost returns to protect his integrity or identity. "He strains forward out of his darkness, he reaches toward us out of his mystery, he makes us dim signs out of his horror," the biographer realizes—"At what we're doing," he says, including the wife who asked him to write the biography. "But he's there as a protest" (564). Again, in "Sir Dominick Ferrand" (1892), in which the appropriation is of a politician, his personal letters, and a love affair, the plot is analogous to the story of ghosts in *The Turn of the Screw* and the non–ghost stories of evil-as-appropriation in the novels of the 1900s, beginning with *The Sacred Fount*.

In *The Sacred Fount* (1901), the work that bridges *The Turn of the Screw* and the major novels of 1902–04, the first-person narrator tells a story— we see him creating it as he participates in a weekend at the country house of Newsome—of a middle-aged woman who marries a young man and exchanges with him his youth for her age; a process the narrator sees as either on her part taking or on his part giving. He detects another pair of lovers, unmarried, in which the man has seemingly (as he interprets it) absorbed the intelligence of the woman, leaving her confused and inane; in order to conceal her inanity she flirts with all the men in the party. The narrator uses the eponymous metaphor of drinking at the "sacred fount," but he shows the process to be one of appropriation. You present your receptacle at the "sacred fount" of the other person and imbibe, becoming younger or more intelligent as the other becomes less, and so in effect (as one of the characters suggests) serving the function of a vampire. Here is the narrator's description of the seemingly youthful Mrs. Brissenden: "Mrs. Briss had to get her new blood, her extra allowance of time and bloom, somewhere; and from whom could she so conveniently extract them as from Guy [her husband] himself? She *has*, by an extraordinary feat of legerdemain, extracted them; and, on his side, to supply her, has had to tap the sacred fount." However, as he adds, the sacred fount "may be sometimes too much for a single share, but it's not enough to go round," thus the depletion and aging of Guy Brissenden, who can ultimately "only die of the business."[23]

As in *The Turn of the Screw* the story he tells is questionable—the other people cannot see it except when he has imposed his vision upon them, and eventually the woman "shrunken" to "inanity" or "idiocy," May Server (whose name seems to support his hypothesis), tells him he is making it all up—is, in fact, out of his mind. As in the case of the Governess, the appropriation of one person by another (his word is "possession") that he identifies in the people around him at Newsome is in fact his own.[24] We have the fictionalized vampiric possession and that of the narrator himself who may be imagining it all (comically in this case) and is thereby attempting to possess and use these perhaps innocent characters as part of *his* story. By himself absorbing the vitality of these people, making them his own—one of James's senses of authorship[25]—he is creating an illusory reality, what Mrs. Brissenden calls his "house of cards."

The basic situation, however comic, is of possession.[26] One sense of evil to James is the vampire story; and so his stories descend in a way from John Polidori's account of Lord Ruthven (Lord Byron) and Le Fanu's description of Carmilla, which could describe Fielding's Noble Lord, George Eliot's Grandcourt, and James's Gilbert Osmond:

> The vampire is prone to be fascinated with an engrossing vehemence, resembling the passion of love, by particular persons. In pursuit of these it will exercise inexhaustible patience and stratagem, for access to a particular object may be obstructed in a hundred ways. It will never desist until it has satiated its passion, and drained the very life of its coveted victim. But it will, in these cases, husband and protract its murderous enjoyment with the refinement of an epicure, and heighten it by the gradual approaches of an artful courtship. In these cases it seems to yearn for something like sympathy and consent. In ordinary ones it goes direct to its object, overpowers with violence, and strangles and exhausts often at a single feast. ("Carmilla," 136)

The vampire's seduction is of one special person, though while she is being slowly and carefully pursued it is supplemented by the killing of neighboring peasants and their animals, who are dispatched to satisfy the vampire's immediate needs.

Thus Quint passes on to Miles "an infernal message," which will "spoil," that is corrupt, him; while Miss Jessel's description as a "pale and ravenous demon" supports her role as a vampirish spirit (16.93, 20.108).[27] More generally, vampires find their equivalent in James's money-hungry characters: not everlasting life but money and power (or the "power" of the writer, trying to live off another writer, or another's experience, making it his own), at the expense of another; not sucking out the life but using the victim to get money—and, as it happens, love; but the Christian telos remains, submerged, for the plan is no more successful than Satan's, and the crime has its built-in punishment along with its failure.

Aestheticism

Vampirism and aestheticism are closely related. Gilbert Osmond happens to be an aesthete, in the sense of Shaftesburian detachment as well as connoisseurship; which seems to be part of the baggage of the Satan-Lucifer who is vaguely reflected in figures from Richardson's Lovelace to Fielding's Blifil and from the Noble Lord to George Eliot's Grandcourt.[28] You begin by collecting art and end with people, often lovers. Osmond seduces Isabel because he needs money to launch his daughter Pansy properly, but he also sees her as a trophy; Isabel, it is implied, is another of those objets with which he fills his villa. Osmond embodies a kind of acedia, owed perhaps to his derivation from Eliot's Grandcourt, in whose cold heart the only passion is to control and own something that has resisted his power, poor Gwendolyn Harleth *because* she at first rejected him. The objectification and possession of the woman makes Osmond a figure closer to Fielding's Noble Lord—than to Merton Densher or Prince Amerigo.

What James rightly questions is the amorality or immorality of aestheticism: plain in Osmond, a figure who judges by aesthetic rather than moral criteria. As Ralph Touchett, who sees through Osmond, puts it, "'He's the incarnation of taste,' Ralph went on. . . . 'He judges and measures, approves and condemns, altogether by taste.'" When he gradually learns that Isabel's opinion does not agree with his, he "despises" her.[29]

The Wings of the Dove: *Betrayal and Atonement*

In *The Wings of the Dove* (1902) the American Milly Theale, orphaned and immeasurably rich, meets Merton Densher, a journalist temporarily working in New York, and falls in love with him. Back in London he is already in love with, and deeply involved with, a lively, beautiful but (like him) penniless young woman named Kate Croy, whose rich Aunt Maude has her eye set on an appropriately splendid marriage to someone like Lord Mark, a dim but nasty scion of a great family. Milly comes to London and meets Kate, who becomes her friend and confidante; she has also just received notice that she has not long to live (in effect given a death sentence). The clever Kate connects the dots and conceives a plan that will give her both Merton and a fortune: He will go along with Milly's love of him, marry her, and keep Kate on the side until Milly dies and he and Kate have Milly's fortune to themselves.

So rich and yet so aware of her mortality, Milly Theale is pondering the abyss from the summit of an Alp. In this scene she recalls (or is made by James to recall) the devil's temptation of Jesus with unparalleled wealth and power: "She was looking down on the kingdoms of the earth, and though indeed that of itself might well go to the brain, it wouldn't be with a view of renouncing them. Was she choosing among them, or did she want them all?"[30] Christ immediately after his baptism by John the Baptist was carried by the devil ("the tempter") to the summit "of an exceeding high mountain, and show[n] all the kingdoms of the world, and the glory of them," and told, "All these things will I give thee, if thou wilt fall down and worship me" (Matt. 4:8–9). He was tempted by the desire to possess the fullest human satisfactions, but his mission, which he chooses, is to save the souls of humankind.

Traces of divinity inform *The Wings of the Dove* in allusions not un-like those employed by Hogarth, Dickens, and Hawthorne. Hackabout, Nancy, Hester, and Milly make a series, but James displaces the harlotry (the sexuality) from Milly to Kate Croy, who secures the agreement of the reluctant and guilt-influenced Densher to go through with her plot vis-à-vis Milly by giving him her body. ("Come to me in my room." . . . "You'll come?" "I'll come.") The religious references (as Millicent Bell puts it, the images "connected with Milly suggest that religious tradition is be-ing invoked—but there is no need to see allegory in the novel") remain as a value metaphor, or (as in the *Harlot*) an enhancement of the human situation, of both good and evil action, without directly evoking God.[31] In Milly's case, unlike the Harlot's, the biblical parallel is not undermined but fulfilled: Like Jesus, she triumphs over temptation and atones for (in a sense saves) the souls of the wrongdoers.

It is Kate who, as the Governess demonized Quint and Jessel, angel-izes Milly by associating her, as in the book's title, with the dove. The dove evokes the dove of Noah's covenant with God and the dove of Psalms 55:6: "And I said, Oh that I had wings like a dove! For then would I fly away, and be at rest" and 68:13: "Though ye have lain among the pots, yet shall ye be as the wings of a dove covered with silver, and her feathers with yellow gold." But the Old Testament dove only anticipates the New Testament dove of the Holy Spirit, the mediator between God and Christ, which descended upon him from heaven at his baptism (just prior to the three temptations of the devil) with a voice declaring him the "beloved son."

The implication for James's novel (or is it only Kate's assertions?) is that Milly in a sense dies—by her final act of unselfishly bequeathing her fortune—for the sins of Kate Croy and Merton Densher; that Milly serves as a "sacrifice," is betrayed by her dearest friends, and at the end Kate, who has called Milly a dove, tells Merton, "She died for you then that you might understand her" (2:10.8.438).[32] As the Holy Spirit and Christ Milly, according to Kate, attempts to redeem Densher by her death—literally, in the monetary sense of ransom from which "redemption" derives.

But she "redeemed" Merton as Harriet Hearty redeemed Mr. Wilson from Debtors' Prison in Fielding's *Joseph Andrews.* Milly notes the analogy with the temptation of Christ; Kate makes the connection with the dove. "I used to call her, in my stupidity—for want of anything better—a dove. Well," Kate now adds, "she stretched out her wings, and it was to *that* they reached. They cover us" (2:10.38.438). "That" has to refer to the plot of Kate and Merton. "They cover us" is ambiguous, suggesting as well as Atonement (to protect, to make provision for), to maintain a check on, to envelop and wrap around, even to sit on and incubate, or to play a higher-ranking card on a previously played card.

As in *The Scarlet Letter,* and indeed Hogarth's *Harlot,* the religious figuration appears most prominently in the form of art, art objects interpreted by other characters. Susan Stringham sees Milly's great party in her palazzo in Venice as "a Veronese picture, as near as can be—with me as the inevitable dwarf, the small blackamoor, put into a corner of the foreground for effect" (2:8.28.225). When Milly joins the party Sir Luke Strett, her physician, feels "her as diffusing, in wide warm waves, the spell of a general, a kind of beatific mildness."[33] The implication is that if Mrs. Stringham is the dwarf, Milly is the Christ, the remote but luminous central figure who diffuses beatific mildness—and that she is thinking of Veronese's *Christ at the Marriage of Cana* in the Louvre (rather than the *Christ in the House of Levi* in the Academia, in Venice itself). The Marriage at Cana was Jesus' first miracle, where he turned water into superior wine, which "manifested his glory" (John 2:11).[34]

It seems appropriate that Milly accidentally, but significantly, encounters Kate and Densher in the National Gallery—then in Venice, where the Veronese allusion becomes apposite. (It is possible that in Milly's evocation of the temptation of Christ she was also recalling Venice, in this case Tintoretto's painting in the Scuola di San Rocco.) Art-replacing-religion served this purpose in the pictures on the walls of Hogarth's prints, but also in the pictures on the walls of Dickens's rooms and occasionally Hawthorne's (as well, of course, in the letter A and elsewhere).

At Matcham, the great English country house (which reappears in *The Golden Bowl*), she is compared by Lord Mark to a Bronzino portrait, and as she looks at her double in the portrait, she can only think "she was dead, dead, dead" here and now or about to be (1:5.11.242), yet continuing to live in the artist's paint.[35] In *The Sacred Fount* the work of art was subordinated to the relativity of perception: In Newsome's gallery, in the pastel of a man holding a mask, the narrator and the other characters see what they want to see. "It's the picture, of all pictures," the narrator says, "that most needs an interpreter."[36] To one the mask is the mask of life, to another the mask of death, and so on. In the Matcham gallery it means one thing to Lord Mark, another to Milly, and a third to the reader, but the important interpretation is Milly's. The Bronzino portrait resembles Milly, who knows she will die, and represents to her death, but death immortalized by art. One sense of immortality reflected Milly's original, Minny Temple, and James's claim that with Milly he sought "to lay the ghost [of Milly] by wrapping it in the beauty and dignity of art." But another connects the transfiguration by art in the Bronzino portrait with Milly's bequest to Merton Densher.

With Mrs. Lowder, after Milly's death but before he knows of her bequest, Densher has this epiphany:

> The essence was that something had happened to him too
> beautiful and too sacred to describe. He had been, to his recov-
> ered sense, forgiven, dedicated, blessed; but this he couldn't
> coherently express. It would have required an explanation—
> fatal to Mrs. Lowder's faith in him—of the nature of Milly's
> wrong [his wrong to Milly]. So, as to the wonderful scene, they
> just stood at the door. They had the sense of the presence
> within—they felt the charred stillness; after which, with their

association deepened by it, they turned together away.
(2:10.34.372)

The time, appropriately, is Christmas. The sacred overtones are in the minds and the words of the characters. The religious allusions by themselves have the effect of making Kate and Merton's plot seem a sin; and so Milly's death is their redemption, which, however, fails in the literal sense that it destroys their love; but in a spiritual sense it does redeem Merton, in that he can refuse both the money and Kate.

Milly inevitably recalls the Governess, who thought of herself as an agent of Atonement for the children ("I should serve as an expiatory victim") and also failed in the sense that she destroyed Miles, if not Flora. A more positive sense of redemption appears in the contemporary ghost story "The Third Person" (publ. 1900), which tells the story of two elderly cousins who inherit a house in a coastal town like James's own Rye. They find some eighteenth-century letters and clippings, at which time a ghost begins to appear around the house—his head twisted to one side; it emerges that he was hanged for smuggling. The ghost, needless to say, was both "bad" and, as the cousins note, "handsome."[37] The two women want to put him to rest—and they also want to get rid of him. Using a hint from the clergyman who had deciphered the letters for them, they think in terms of redemption and atonement: For the "wrong—as it *was* wrong—he did" they could, the parson suggests, "vicariously repent" or "atone"—and in their own terms, "make a sacrifice" (648–49, 661). One sister attempts to redeem him by paying twenty pounds ("conscience-money," "atonement by deputy" [662]) to the customs service, but this fails, the ghost remains; the other sister goes to Paris, buys a Tauschnitz book (not under copyright in England) and sneaks it through customs ("get through the Customs—under their nose"), thus recommitting the ghost's crime—and he now, "redeemed" (or at least "appeased" [665]), disappears.

From one perspective James retains the Christian interpretation of an essentially good divine creation in relation to which evil is self-thwarting, and the actors' guilt is complicated and to some extent mitigated—the *what*, the evil act, being plainer and less ambiguous than the *who*. As he shows, the punishment of evil is an inherent component of the evil—is defined by the appropriate punishment. The evil act is complicit in its punishment: Kate Croy has, at the end, no Densher and no money; is stuck with her father and sister. At the end of *The Portrait of a Lady* Mme. Merle's daughter, for whom she has committed her betrayal of Isabel, dislikes her, and although Isabel returns to Osmond it is only to save Pansy from him. Isabel is rejecting the alternative of adultery and returning, yet not to Osmond but to Pansy.

There are, however, two possible interpretations of Milly's will, as atonement or as punishment. There are, in James's intricate morality, two forms of evil (doing- and suffering-): Kate's betrayal of her friend Milly, and Milly's atonement, judgment, and yet perhaps at bottom punishment of Kate and Densher (their suffering-evil) by leaving Densher the estate for which he and Kate had betrayed her. I suggest that the allusions to Christ's Atonement, especially as it is embodied in art of the Venetian Renaissance, as opposed to Merton's natural epiphany (though at Christmas), force a deep ambiguity on the matter of atonement. Who is finally worse, Kate or Milly? What constitutes an evil act is rather clear—what was done to Milly—but less so what was done to Kate and to Merton; and what defines the evil agent? Is the first possible without the second?—because the second requires intention, an evil will and malice? What of *mixed* intentions or a discrepancy between intention and act? From Kate's perspective at least Milly has "covered" her and Merton in the sense of smothering their love, making it impossible—"We shall never be again as we were!" are the words with which the novel ends.

Both acts as evil are compromised by the less-than- or more-than-evil motives of the actors. Kate's motive is money *and* love, love of Densher; Densher's motive, only Kate (sexual desire for). Milly's motive is love of Densher *and* Kate—but seen, presumably by her, in the context of the New Testament Atonement.

The Golden Bowl: *Evil Down and Evil Up*

Until now we have noted that evil essentially follows from power inflicted downward, from a position of power to that of powerlessness. Elizabethan revenge tragedy dealt with the victim returning his pain in spades, with appalling consequences to all. James picked up the subject in his earliest novels. *The American* (1876) depicts the betrayal of an innocent American by old world aristocracy, the "inferior" by the "superior." Newman makes explicit what remains implicit in later novels: "This is my revenge, you know," he tells the Bellegardes, flourishing the document that will disgrace the family: "I mean to show the world that, however bad I may be, you are not quite the people to say it."[38] We may tend to read the story of Milly in the context of both *The Golden Bowl* and *The American*, both stories of evil perpetrated on a person who then replies with an act of revenge. In the context of *The American* the act is revenge, and in the context of *Washington Square* (1881)—as in Isabel's return to Pansy and Osmond—it is simply a form of giving up, of existential withdrawal.

Prince Amerigo and Charlotte are deeply in love, but with no money; he marries Maggie Verver, who loves him, for her money, and she marries Maggie's father, the American millionaire Adam Verver, giving each access to the other. When Maggie learns that Charlotte and Amerigo were involved prior to her marriage, and the punishment is separation—midwest America and Italy—Maggie's act is at least partly one of revenge, destroying the relationship of Charlotte and Amerigo as effectively as Milly's bequest destroyed the relationship of Merton and Kate, but also sacrificing the thing that is apparently most precious to her, her close relationship with her father.[39]

Maggie carries out her revenge on Charlotte, who had betrayed her, by leaving her in the dark—suspended and never knowing, the same "doom" (the word she uses repeatedly about Charlotte's fate) that Newman imposed on the Bellegardes in *The American;* second, she exiles her to darkest middle America, which Charlotte hates most. But to do this, to establish the proper equilibrium as she sees it, she must "sacrifice" (her word) her relationship with Adam. She "sacrifices" him in order to be avenged on Charlotte and Amerigo, but also to make sure with their permanent separation that the right equilibrium (wife, husband, and child) can no longer be disturbed.

If revenge was ambiguous in *Wings*—Milly can be acting only out of love for Merton, or she can be destroying his relationship with Kate—in *The Golden Bowl* it cuts both ways: It punishes the betrayers, but it separates the victims, making their future as bleak as that of their (in this case no longer betrayers but) victims. It is hard to determine at the end which situation is the less happy. As in Dante's hell, the punishers and the punished are equally damned and equally therefore suffering: Satan chews on Judas, Brutus, and Caesar but is himself submerged in the ice of the ninth circle and, of course, as far removed as possible from the presence of God.

Though both Milly and the Ververs have all the money and the caché, the fact that they are, or at least appear to be, in every other way innocents without (sexual) power gives those who prey on them the onus of blame. On the other hand, their almost regal status does seem to balance the evil and the sin of their betrayal—as if betraying them combines the downward with the upward movement. James gave an almost theological dimension to the example of Milly, reinforced by the references that associated her with the Atonement and implied something like an *Ecce Homo* composition. Adam Verver's grandiloquence, his regal diction—his discourse of Stout Cortez on a peak in Darien, his great museum in American City—makes him a figure it seems a sin to betray. Besides, both Milly and the Ververs do ultimately have the power: She can leave or not leave her millions to Merton; Adam and Maggie can take and lodge Charlotte and Amerigo anywhere they wish—the two miscreants are totally at their mercy.

What distinguishes James is that he shows in *Wings* and *Golden Bowl* a situation in which the power may lie with the betrayed—and the betrayer, while in some ways stronger (with more knowledge of the past), is in the long run weaker, ending up, like Charlotte, "in the dark"; the betrayed has ultimately all the cards. The figures endowed with power—Isabel, Milly, and Maggie—are nevertheless vulnerable, their responses ambiguous. Isabel chooses to return to Italy and Osmond, with a commitment she cannot shirk to Osmond's daughter Pansy and the decision *not* to commit adultery—as with Maggie, the solution, however unsatisfactory, has to be worked out within the marriage contract. Milly's act may have been intended to redeem Kate and Merton, though it has the opposite effect; and Maggie's leaves nobody happy. At the end Amerigo tries to reassure her and look into her eyes; she cannot look into his. The embrace is formal rather than felt.[40]

The Turn of the Screw is a talismanic work, a watershed and introduction to the works of James's major phase. Some of the early novels could almost have been written by Jane Austen; and yet why does one think of evil as a subject of James's novels and not Austen's? In *The American* the Bellegardes do Newman a wrong little different from those done by characters in Austen's novels. What makes *The American* seem to be within the evil range is the melodramatic trappings—the old French aristocracy, the dark family secret, a probable murder, not to mention the family château—most of the conventions that jazzed up the wrongdoings of *The Mysteries of Udolpho* into gothic extravagance. In *Washington Square* the hardly Mephistophelian Morris Townsend would not attract our attention did his matrimonial plot not have the effect it has on the almost Dickensian innocent Catherine: the wrongdoing is evil if not "Evil."

The ending of *The Wings of the Dove* with Kate Croy forced to live with her sister's dreadful family in Chelsea, which now includes her egregious father, is very Austenian. The difference is that in Austen's novels it is the heroine who is forced at the end to continue living in a family or society that includes people who have proved themselves to be little or no worse than Kate or Charlotte Stant, Gilbert Osmond, or Morris Townsend. Kate is very different from Elizabeth Bennet, first in that she is the wrongdoer who is punished by ending up this way (evil compounded), without either the money or the love she plotted for. Second, partly because, while she shares Elizabeth's intelligence and social poise, she is driven by a passion, an obsessive love for one man that drives her to betray her best friend. She has a demonic dimension altogether lacking in Austen's bad characters. Finally, Austen is writing in a comic mode, and so wrongdoers like Wickham are reabsorbed into the good society, at however much discomfort to either him or the heroine, whereas no one would want to argue that *Wings of the Dove* is a comedy.

Graham Greene commented on "supernatural evil" (vs. "supernatural good") in Henry James, specifically in *The Wings of the Dove* (though his words may tell us more about himself than about James): "Milly Theale is all human; her courage has not the supernatural support which holds Kate Croy . . . in a strong coil. The rage of personality is all the devil's. The *good and the beautiful* meet betrayal with patience and forgiveness, but without *sublimity*" (emphasis added): In short, the key is aesthetics, Burkean aesthetics of the sublime that Greene, invoking James, gets by citing damnation—suffering, pain, etc., via the demonic (with the occasional echo of Machen & Co.) as against "the dogmatically 'pure' [aesthetic in that other sense] novel" of Flaubert and his tradition.[41] Greene's essay brought James's study of evil to the forefront—"the incomparable figures of evil, Kate Croy and Charlotte Stant" (112); "his main study of corruption in *The Wings of the Dove*" (115); and "James' main fantasy, the idea of treachery which was always attached to his sense of evil" (118). He is, of course, describing *his* James, but it is the James seen from the perspective of *The Turn of the Screw* and the stories of his father's and brother's experiences of "evil."

Greene would also have been aware that James endows evil with Christian (if not biblical) proportions: As Mrs. Assingham in *The Golden Bowl* says, this is "what's called Evil with a very big E"—"the very, *very* wrong."[42] He does this by locating it in various familiar Christian ways: as allusions to the Christian story; as possession (evoking demonic, Satanic possession, vampirism) or a form of betrayal (evoking Dante's ninth circle) or simply the intermediate term "usage" (Maggie Verver's word).[43] Not necessarily corruption, though one might argue that Merton Densher and Prince Amerigo are in a way corrupted by, respectively, Kate and Charlotte; and, in turn, argue that love corrupts Kate and Charlotte—only to suggest how complex James's moral landscape is; how genuinely he explores what has been called moral values on a spectrum that weighs heavily toward the negative. But what bears the capital E, as Greene has noted, always is betrayal of one's closest friend—Kate Croy's of Milly Theale, Charlotte Stant's of Maggie Verver, and Mme. Merle's of Isabel Archer.[44] Even in *The Ambassadors* (1903), the major James novel least concerned with evil, Lambert Strether is to some extent betrayed by Chad and Mme. de Vionnet—but this is subordinated to the other Jamesian evil of the possession of others: Strether, by his attempts to understand Chad Newsome, is in James's terms trying to possess him. Possession is part of Strether's story, of the changing scenarios of understanding he imposes on Chad. *Is* Chad good or bad, vulgar or gentleman, improved or corrupted? But Strether himself has been coerced by, and is trying to get out from under, Mrs. Newsome, Mrs. Pocock, and Woollette, Massachusetts. "Sin" to Strether is an ethical failure, a loss of independence, being Mrs. Newsome's factotum and editing her *Review.* He is trying "again to find himself young," and he echoes Miles's cry, "I want to see more life" when he says to Little Bilham, "Live all you can; it's a mistake not to . . . Live!"[45]

CHAPTER SIX

Demonic and Banal Evil

1. DEMONIC DOUBLES

Robert Wringhim and Gil-Martin (and George Colwan)
How do possession, demonism, and vampires relate to haunting? Le
Fanu's characteristic plot, as in "Green Tea" or even "Carmilla," is "one
in which the protagonist, whether deliberately or otherwise, opens his
mind in such a way as to become subject to haunting by a figure which
is unmistakably part of his own self."[1] In contemporary terms, Stephen
King's *The Shining* (1977) tells the story of Jack Torrance, whose "beast
within," in the setting of the Overlook Hotel, breaks out and turns him
into the croquet mallet–wielding monster in lethal pursuit of his own
son. Again, King's good-natured dog Cujo (1981) is bitten by a rabid bat,
which either releases the buried evil in the dog's nature—or, vampirelike,
possesses the good dog. The two models, then, are of the buried beast
(with its roots in Original Sin) and the vampire; one producing fictions
of doubling—the evil double, the return of the repressed shadow—and
the other of demonic possession. Cujo literally, perhaps Jack Torrance
also, goes mad. Poe's characters internalize demons and can be regarded
as mad, preparing us for James's Governess and, in the case of "William
Wilson," specifically for doubling (although this happens to be a good
double correcting the bad narrator). In King's *Pet Sematary* (1983) we

192

can say that death releases "the deep part of us" that hates and envies the survivors, the living whom they haunt.[2] The classic cases of doubling are James Hogg's *Confessions of a Justified Sinner,* in which Robert Wringhim's repressed demon is released in the figure of Gil-Martin, and Robert Louis Stevenson's *Dr. Jekyll and Mr. Hyde* in which Jekyll's potion releases the repressed demon of "evil," Mr. Hyde.[3]

The Private Memoirs and Confessions of a Justified Sinner (1824) demonizes sin by introducing the devil himself as the double of the so-called "justified sinner"; he is hardly an evil double, since Robert Wringhim was from the start evil, or at least nasty. At his best Robert can be said to have inherited and been instructed in evil by his mother and her lover (Robert's father) the Rev. Mr. Wringhim. The principle Robert learns from old Wringhim is sin punished/evil rewarded; with the introduction of Gil-Martin this becomes: Kill the sinner and expect a reward in heaven as one of the justified.

Robert's half brother George Colwan is, like Tom Jones, the sinner because he frequents taverns, plays games, and is interested in women ("in what a sink of sin was he wallowing").[4] Sinning is concupiscence; evil is telling lies about the sinners, getting them mercilessly beaten, and eventually killing them. It is "against the carnal portion of mankind" that, Robert says, "I set my face continually, . . . and the preachers up of good works I abhorred, and to this hour I account them the worst and most heinous of all transgressors" (108).

Evil, then, is the murder of Blanchard (by "upholders of pure morality and a blameless life"), and the innocent man Gil-Martin contrives to have convicted and hanged for the murder—the "reprobates, cast-aways, beings devoted to the wicked one," that is, the sinners, the destruction of whom is "our great work" (143–45). Robert says, "My vengeance has been wreaked on [religious] adversaries," by which he means "the wicked of this world," and by "wicked" he means "man all over spotted with the leprosy of sin" (97); this turns out to mean someone like his father's servant John Barton or his smarter schoolmate M'Gill, both of whom he perjures into suffering evils. Barton "discovered some notorious lies that I had framed," as Robert tells the story, and so he tells his father lies about Barton.[5] In M'Gill's case the evils perpetrated by Robert are both perjury and cruelty, "getting him severely beaten for faults of which he was innocent. I can hardly describe the joy that it gave to my heart to see a wicked creature suffering, for though he deserved it not for one thing, he richly deserved it for others [i.e., making better grades than Robert]"—beatings that Robert observes with the pleasure of one who loves cruelty, anticipating the cruelties that will be administered to his enemies in hell (109).

The dichotomy of "purity and corruption" figures Robert's account of his putative parents: His mother is the first, and her husband, old Colwan, the second ("her upright heart," "his iniquities"); in Hogg's story, however, they represent once again evil and sin—she selfish, withholding, corrupting her son, destroying the Colwan family; he a drinker and, when she withdraws from any sexual conduct, an adulterer (she of course, with the elder Wringhim, is covertly an adulteress).

As a story of doubling, the *Confessions* tells of two half brothers, one a sinner and the other, who calls himself a "justified sinner" and one of the saved, evil.[6] But justification means making a compact—not with God but with the devil; thus enters the supernatural, or only the allegorical. The devil Gil-Martin is initially Robert's double in the sense that he instructs him and directs him in evil. He is primarily Robert's tempter and instructor—though in fact only a second manifestation of Robert's first instructor, the Rev. Mr. Wringhim, whose conversations "with the Almighty" over Robert's "justification" can be interpreted, in the context of subsequent events, as dealings with Gil-Martin.

When old Wringhim gets "the Almighty" to agree to Robert's justification, immediately thereafter Gil-Martin appears to Robert: "What was my astonishment, on perceiving that he was the same being as myself! The clothes were the same to the smallest item. The form was the same; the apparent age; the colour of the hair; the eyes; and, as far as recollection could serve me from viewing my own features in a glass, the features too were the very same" (116–17). In one sense, the devil can assume the shape of anyone with whom he engages—his ability, noted by Augustine, to imitate and parody; in another, Robert (through his father) has asked to merge with the devil, and, as his father notes when he next sees him, "You are quite changed; your very voice and manner are changed," for he has taken on the form of Gil-Martin.

So although there is doubling (George and Robert, Robert and Gil-Martin, even Robert and old Wringhim, and Gil-Martin and an angel or "the Almighty"), the central event of the *Confessions* is Faustian. Old Wringhim works out a contract with "the Almighty" aka Gil-Martin for the soul of his son Robert, and Robert eagerly accepts it, and in this case Faust's subsequent actions are not trivial sins; they are a string of murders—the evils of death and suffering imposed, as they were at the Original Sin, on sinners. The contract, the "attainment of your services" (144), involves the commitment to "slay" the "reprobates." In this version of the Faust story, the devil's contract corresponds to the ideology of predestination. What Gil-Martin gets Robert to do in "cutting off" these sinners is to commit acts of evil. Punish sin and reward evil (the reward being election to heaven) is Gil-Martin's and Robert's motto.

When Gil-Martin "dwell[s] much on the theme of the impossibility of those ever falling away, who were once accepted and received into covenant with God," he means with the devil; and when Robert takes him to be an angel, not a devil, like Blake's devil he carries his own Bible of Hell and fulfills the underlying Blakean irony that extends from the reversal of angel-devil to morality-immorality, good-bad, righteousness-unrighteousness. But Hogg goes off into variations on this basic reversal: Robert kills Blanchard, the most popular of Glasgow's "preachers of morality" (142–47), which means "becoming an assassin in the cause of Christ and his Church"—a double irony in that the words say, "cause of the *devil* and his Church," but also "'Christ' and the Presbyterians of Scotland" (if not indeed the plain "Christ and his Church"). Again, when Gil-Martin refers to "the pleasure the Lord took in such as executed his vengeance on the wicked," his words can be taken as "the devil quoting Scripture" or as the Enlightenment Hogg's opinion of Old Testament morality. Gil-Martin's discourse is precisely that of a Presbyterian divine quoting scripture. But to dispense with any doubt that he is Satan, he remarks, "I have no parents save one, whom I do not acknowledge" (129).

The only concern of Robert Wringhim is "the salvation and condemnation of all mankind" (118). Hogg employs the Swiftean fiction in the *Tale of a Tub* of student and instructor. Old Wringhim is "my mother's early instructor" (98), and Robert acknowledges him as his own: "To him am I indebted, under Heaven, for the high conceptions and glorious discernment between good and evil, right and wrong, which I attained even at an early age. It was he who directed my studies aright, both in the learning of the ancient fathers, and the doctrines of the reformed church, and designed me for his assistant and successor in the holy office" (98). And, of course, Robert follows the instructions of Gil-Martin. His references to "my master here" echo the Grub Street hack's "my Masters the Moderns": When he perjures himself in court, he admits it "was not the truth; but as it was by the advice of my reverend father, and that of my illustrious friend, both of whom I knew to be sincere Christians and true believers, that I gave it, I conceived myself completely justified on that score" (160, 163).

In many ways, the *Confessions of a Justified Sinner* is a Swiftean satire, even to the utilization of a spokesman for the normative view of Scottish Presbyterianism, Mr. Blanchard, who accepts John Knox's doctrines but argues that Gil-Martin and Robert "are carrying these points to a dangerous extremity . . . forcing them beyond their due bounds" (131). And, of course, this brief indication of a norm has to be murdered (as in *An Argument against Abolishing Christianity* the ideal is thrust into the distant past, the age of the Apostles). Robert himself gradually—as Gil-Martin pushes the envelope—begins faintly to perceive the evil of their actions, eventually realizing that he is the devil, "the great enemy of man's salvation"—not the Prince of Russia but the Prince of Darkness (182). In any case, Hogg presents the mean and petty Robert (and his mother and father) and adds the demonic, rather romantic figure of Gil-Martin.

Robert is related to the ironic Swiftean narrator rather than to the Poe madman, though he sometimes sounds like the latter (and, like Faust himself or Milton's Satan, he has his moments of doubt and conscience [157–61]). But this is not the MS of a madman: we have the substantiation of the editor's narrative that introduces Robert's; we are evidently dealing with demons rather than with credulity, superstition, and fanaticism. Like Swift's Aeolists, Robert is "moved by the spirit within me" to attack "the dens of voluptuousness and sin" (149).

Mr. Hyde and Dr. Jekyll: Respectability

"We are all subjected to two distinct natures in the same person," Gil-Martin said (192), anticipating Dr. Jekyll in Robert Louis Stevenson's *The Strange Case of Dr. Jekyll and Mr. Hyde* (1886), who says, "My devil had been long caged," and with the taking of the potion, he "comes out roaring."[7] The evil Mr. Hyde contained in Dr. Jekyll is released and materialized. The ethical question is: at whose desire? In Wringhim's case, the conditioning of his mother and the elder Wringhim; in Dr. Jekyll's case, the doctor himself.

Mr. Hyde—the demonic aspect of Dr. Jekyll—permits Jekyll to live the wild life, which then takes over, overwhelming the respectable, socially acceptable Dr. Jekyll. Demonic and banal evil are examples of doubling—Dr. Jekyll is enabled by his evil double to satisfy his deeper desires without putting in question his social mask, but then Mr. Hyde gets out of control, can no longer be suppressed, takes over (possesses) Dr. Jekyll, perhaps showing that he had all along been the stronger of the two.[8]

The more interesting question is of what does Mr. Hyde's evil consist? Is it clearly "Evil" over evil: "There is something more," says Mr. Utterson, "if I could find a name for it. God bless me, the man seems hardly human!" Utterson calls him a sinner (6.29), and there is certainly the sin aspect, vaguely designated: Hyde lives on a shabby street in Soho with a "gin palace, a low French eating house, . . . and many women of different nationalities passing out, key in hand, to have a morning glass" (5.21). This is the only reference to concupiscence and women. He says he "laid aside restraint and plunged in shame," giving release to the "lower elements in my soul"; all he tells us is that his "pleasures were (to say the least) undignified" (10.55, 56).

We can only guess at the actions that preceded the accidental collision with the child or the outburst of anger that caused the death of the MP. But, as we have seen, Mr. Hyde does not need to perform actions; one has only to look at him: deformity—of size, of face (abomination)—is the equivalent of "evil." In Jekyll's words, "Evil (which I must still believe to be the lethal side of man) had left on that body [of Hyde] an imprint of deformity and decay . . . because all human beings, as we meet them, are commingled out of good and evil: and Edward Hyde, alone in the ranks of mankind, was pure evil" (10.54).

Utterson says that "tales came out of the man's cruelty, at once so callous and violent; of his vile life, of his strange associates, of the hatred that seemed to have surrounded his career" (6.27). Of the only two direct manifestations of Mr. Hyde's actions the first is the image of a "human juggernaut" that is seen to "crush a child and leave her screaming" (2.11), and the second is of the frenzied, wrathful beating and murder of an innocent old man, who happens to be an MP. Among the words used to describe the latter action are "ape-like fury" and "insensate cruelty" (3.20), and the account, with the repetition of the word "cruelty," recalls such cases as those of Hogarth's Tom Nero and Dickens's Mr. Gamfield.

Hyde's size is made much of: He is smaller than Jekyll, shrunken, indeed "dwarfish," because, Jekyll speculates, he is younger, that is, he has not had a chance to grow as old as Jekyll, or grow up. Utterson remarks, "The man seems hardly human!" He contains "the haunting sense of unexpressed deformity"—references that work upon the indeterminacy Burke associated with terror and the sublime;[9] but then, Utterson adds, "Something troglodytic, shall we say?" (2.14, 4.22). To say he "seems hardly human," is "troglodytic" and "ape-like," is to say he is regressive. His short temper can be attributed to his yet uncivilized state. He is smaller in the sense of younger, also "less robust, less developed," an earlier stage of growth or of humanity, on the one hand youthful, and on the other "primitive"; and so the comic-grotesque effect of his wearing Dr. Jekyll's clothes—"enormously too large for him in every measurement—the trousers hanging on his legs and rolled up to keep them from the ground, the waist of the coat below his haunches, and the collar sprawling wide upon his shoulders"—though, "strange to relate, this ludicrous accouterment was far from moving me to laughter" (9.47), again suggests degeneration as regression and atavism, the reversal of Darwinian genealogy.

It is the more positive, childish aspect that is developed by Dr. Jekyll in his final confession. He characterizes his evil side as "a certain impatient gaiety of disposition" and "irregularities"; the immediate result of taking his potion—perhaps the initial youthfulness—was to discover (anticipating young Miles's desire "to see more life") "something indescribably new and, from its very novelty, incredibly sweet. I felt younger, lighter, happier in body; within I was conscious of a heady recklessness, a current of disordered sensual images running like a mill race in my fancy, a solution of the bonds of obligation, an unknown but not an innocent freedom of the soul." Then, what appears to be a non sequitur: "I knew myself, at the first breath of this new life, to be more wicked, tenfold more wicked, sold a slave to my original evil; and the thought, in that moment, braced and delighted me like wine. I stretched out my hands, exulting in the freshness of these sensations; and in the act, I was suddenly aware that I had lost in stature" (10.51–53). Jekyll is talking the discourse of sin as seen by a Scottish Presbyterian, not too distant from Robert Wringhim's views of the Colwans; but the word "wicked," which seems out of place in the talk of "freshness" and "delight," is the discourse of childhood and parental disapproval. Only the last phrase, "I had lost in stature," warns us that these sins will lead to, and freedom will degenerate into, acts of violence and cruelty; childhood unchecked, again as in the case of Tom Nero and Machen's Wesley, will lead in time to adult violence. The transitional terms are "drinking pleasure with bestial avidity" and "torture to another"—such as, he confesses, "an act of cruelty to a child" (10.56).

And ultimately he prefers the social, the mature solution—"the elderly and discontented doctor, surrounded by friends and cherishing honest hopes"—to "the liberty, the comparative youth, the light step, leaping pulses and secret pleasures" of Mr. Hyde. The division is between not good and evil but "a fellow that nobody could have to do with, a really damnable man" and a person who "is the very pink of the proprieties" (1.6). Utterson considers Jekyll's past life—"the many ill things he had done, and . . . the many that he had come so near to doing, yet avoided" (2.15). Dr. Jekyll himself tells how "it came about that I concealed my pleasures; and that when I reached years of reflection, and began to look round me and take stock of my progress and position in the world, I stood already committed to a profound duplicity of life . . . hid them with an almost morbid sense of shame"—and so seeks a release of "those provinces of good and ill which divide and compound man's dual nature" (10.51). What he refers to as the "vicarious" nature hints at a more sophisticated kind of "depravity": He gets pleasure out of being able, as the straightlaced Dr. Jekyll, to watch Mr. Hyde do his deeds—perhaps vicariously as Rowlandson and his voyeurs did.

The Picture and Dorian Gray: The Ugly and the Beautiful

Oscar Wilde's *The Picture of Dorian Gray* (1890) is another novel of doubling, with its two Dorian Grays, one the man and the other the painting, but the doubling takes off from another contract like the one Wringhim made with the devil. Dorian wishes it and it happens—we are not told why.

Wilde, who called Arthur Machen the "author of our sacraments of evil, just as there is that of the sacraments of goodness," uses the words *sin* and *evil* interchangeably, the reference being to East End London, aristocratic slumming, opium, and, though unnamed, sodomy. Dorian takes a "sordid room of the little ill-famed tavern near the Docks . . . under an assumed name, and in disguise." All we are told is that "he had mad hungers that grew more ravenous as he fed them." The consequence is the same evil described by Machen—Dorian's body, "withered, wrinkled, and loathsome of visage" (the portrait, "in all the wonder of his exquisite youth and beauty").[10]

Except for the sodomy this is pretty much the same vague lifestyle Stevenson attributes to Mr. Hyde. In fact, the words and the examples designate Wilde's own ambivalent feelings about society's laws and their relationship to personal guilt, or at least his need to cover his steps in a hostile society; thus making himself another Dr. Jekyll. Lord Henry Wotton refers to "the terror of society, which is the basis of morals, the terror of God, which is the secret of religion—these are the two things that govern us. And yet—"; "—" presumably referring to the criminal excitement of Dorian's secret escapades (2.20).

To attach Dorian's sin/evil only to sodomy must have seemed an acceptance of society's laws, and so Wilde supplements this sin/evil with the more conventional acts of murder, both intentional and accidental. As in Hogg's *Confessions* and in Stevenson's *Dr. Jekyll* murder is the final evil that validates what society calls sin.

The initiating act—which sets the portrait of Dorian Gray on its decline—is the sin of Faust, in this case wishing for eternal life (a memory also on Wilde's part, perhaps, of Swift's Struldbrugs); but the evil of the brutal and, as it happens, fatal treatment of Sibyl Vane is the point at which lines begin to appear on the face of the portrait ("a touch of cruelty in the mouth," "the burden of his passions and his sins" [7.87–88]). On the surface the dismissal of Sibyl is merely a matter of style—she fails at a role, she embarrasses Dorian in front of his male friends—and below the surface it is a reflection of his choice of men over women; for, of course, his abandonment of Sibyl is based on the mediated desire of his friend and model (his Gil-Martin), Lord Henry Wotton.[11]

So there is Dorian's sin—his Faustian pact on one level, his preference for men on another—and then there is the evil of what he does to Sibyl, to Basil Hallward, to the various named and unnamed young men he corrupts, and indirectly to Sibyl's brother. The sin goes back (behind the Victorian law and public opinion) to the Levitical abomination; the evil is the same old cruelty, exploitation, and corruption we saw in the vampire narratives. Corruption is primary, sin in that it affects only himself, but evil in that corruption expresses an action which passes over to an object, reflected in both the degeneration of Dorian's portrait and the active corruption of innocents. Dorian's destruction of Sibyl is also presumably the sort of thing Lord Henry referred to when he remarked earlier, echoing Fielding's Noble Lord, that "beautiful sins, like beautiful things, are the privilege of the rich" (6.76).

Both *Dr. Jekyll* and *Dorian Gray* show a man keeping his respectable social mask while displacing his antisocial behavior—equally vaguely described—onto a double, a portrait, or a chemically induced second self; both reflections of those Victorian phenomena of the closeted gay lifestyle and the marriage that compartmentalizes the idealized wife/mother and the courtesan who is the outlet for concupiscence, by tacit agreement unacknowledged, kept in St. John's Wood in a detached villa.

The latter is the world of Lord Henry Wotton. Lord Henry says that "one charm of marriage is that it makes a life of deception absolutely necessary for both parties" (1.8). From our meeting with Lady Henry it is clear that his is the Victorian *mariage de convenance,* though we are given no substantial evidence that Lord Henry is more than vaguely bisexual. Wilde gives Dorian an explanatory genealogy in his mother's "sin" against society—she was a romantic, married beneath her—and the evil of his grandfather, who has the unacceptable son-in-law murdered: "A beautiful woman risking everything for a mad passion. A few wild weeks of happiness cut short by a hideous, treacherous crime. Months of voiceless agony, and then a child born in pain. The mother snatched away by death, the boy left to solitude and the tyranny of an old and loveless man. Yes; it was an interesting background" (3.37). This was also the plot of Hogarth's *Harlot* and all its progeny, and later the assumption underlying the melodramatic plots of Wilde's stage comedies—which beneath the witty chatter were problem plays treating the case of the fallen woman who tries to regain a respectable position in society (*Lady Windermere's Fan*).[12]

As with Jekyll and Robert Wringhim, the seed or inclination is already in place and only needs a Lord Henry to free it (Dorian's name, of course, already designates his sexual tendency). As Hallward says of the young Dorian, not yet acquainted with Wotton, "Now and then, however, he is horribly thoughtless, and seems to take a real delight in giving me pain" (1.14).[13] Lord Henry merely adds, as if speaking for Dr. Jekyll, "I believe that if one man were to live out his life fully and completely, were to give form to every feeling, expression to every thought, reality to every dream—I believe that the world would gain such a fresh impulse of joy that we would forget all the maladies of mediaevalism, and return to the Hellenic ideal—to something finer, richer, than the Hellenic ideal, it may be" (2.21).

At this point what he refers to is Greek sexuality; to "give form to every feeling" is a beautiful, therefore noble desire. Blake could be speaking when he adds, "Every impulse that we strive to strangle broods in the mind, and poisons us." And introducing the discourse of sin: "The body sins once, and has done with its sin, for action is a mode of purification. Nothing remains then but the recollection of a pleasure, or the luxury of a regret"—and the well-known aphorism follows, "The only way to get rid of a temptation is to yield to it." Dorian is pointedly a sinner, whom Wilde has to conceal as evil by making him into, in addition, a murderer. Wilde, like Marcel Proust, feels he has to officially accept society's judgment of homosexuality and condemn it.

Demonic Aesthetics

In the words of Dorian's wish, expressed at the time, "If it were I who was to be always *young*, and the picture that was to grow *old!* . . . I would give my soul for that" (2.28). But in retrospect, after his life of depravity, it has changed: "He had uttered a mad wish that he himself might remain *young*, and the face on the canvas bear the burden of his *passions and sins;* that the painted image might be seared with the lines of *suffering and thought*" (emphasis added). It is telling that Dorian's contract is originally for youth and beauty, not for pleasure or vice or sin; and yet when the portrait changes, the process of aging, or the loss of beauty, corresponds to the consequence of sinning: "For every sin that he committed, a stain would fleck and wreck its fairness" (7.89).

Wilde opposes the respectable and unrespectable—the young Dorian Gray, whose evil is covert, and the hideous portrait; but the terms are first aesthetic and then social. Conventional aesthetics in England was based on Shaftesbury's assumptions that virtue is beautiful and vice ugly, that the sculptured Venus de Medici is more beautiful than any mere human. In *Dr. Jekyll and Mr. Hyde* the evil was therefore displaced to the grotesquely ugly Mr. Hyde; in *Dorian Gray* Wilde gives the beautiful unchanging body to the evil man, displacing the hideous corruption to a work of art. Wilde's aesthetic, insofar as it is anti-Shaftesburian, goes back to Hogarth's association of beauty and sin, those qualities of social transgression, curiosity, and playfulness condemned by conventional eighteenth-century art and society. The most beautiful object was the living woman: "Who but a bigot, even to the antiques, will say that he has not seen faces and necks, hands and arms in living women, that even the grecian Venus doth but coarsely imitate?"[14]—who is also a temptress, an Eve or Cleopatra, a Samarian woman or a Magdalen. Beauty was for Hogarth the most human of situations, a sexual encounter of seduction or adultery. Wilde follows Hogarth in equating beauty and sociosexual transgression—so regarded in Victorian England, as it was in Hogarth's time.

But to sin Wilde adds evil. He conflates the demonic glosses of sinning (disobedience/abomination and sodomy) with acts of evil (cruelty, possession, corruption, and murder of innocents), simply extending the rococo sense of sin to include what Hogarth would have regarded as evil. And, most significant for his sense of the transgressive, he replaces—returning to Shaftesbury's original aesthetics—the beautiful female body with the male.

Hogarth used the art object (the Venus) to set off, in effect define by contrast, his living women—death against life, as in Wilde's living Dorian and dead portrait. This as opposed to Shaftesbury's ideal of male beauty *in the antique sculpture*, perpetuated by the copying procedures of the art academy and contrasted with the ugliness and contingency—or the lesser beauty—of live human beings. (Rowlandson, we recall, built his drawings around the same contrast between living women and the distanced copies of artists; women observed, not slept with, by aged voyeurs.) Dorian's homoerotic aesthetics applies to projected acts of real, live people; Shaftesbury's to meditation on or worship of idealized sculptures like the Antinous—which in the first plate of *The Analysis of Beauty* Hogarth introduced as a joke, tempting both sexes, an effeminate dancing master *and* the Venus de Medici.

Wilde's aestheticism draws him from the heterosexual to the homosexual, from homosexuality to opium addiction, and from the aesthetics of Hogarth back to that of Shaftesbury, presented (flaunting social pretensions) as a perversion. Hogarth's famous Line of Beauty, though associated with sin (Cleopatra and the others), was not a perversion but an ideal; the perversions were deviations from the Line, whether in the excesses of Rubensian form or the works of "dark painters," but primarily in the interference of connoisseurs and aristocratic amateurs, that is,

Lord Henry Wotton. Like Gilbert Osmond's, Lord Henry's aestheticism perverts moral principles. Depending on how we read Wilde's ironies, Lord Henry is either a spokesman or a Mephistophelian tempter and Dorian another Faust.

When Lord Henry calls the qualities of living, experience, and freedom ("the impulse of joy") "evil," he is only describing sin, validating sin with some acts of obvious doing-evil (murder) and attaching it, as cause and effect, to the evils of disease, degeneration, and death. Wilde and James meant the same thing by "I want to see more life" and "live while you can," but, in supernatural fictions, they had to call it evil and show terrible punishment/consequences. (In novels, as in *The Ambassadors*, this could be immensely complicated.) Stevenson suggested much the same, as did Machen: that first (after a pact or a potion) comes youthful freedom and joy, a recovery of infantile pleasures, but then, like the obligatory rewards and punishments at the end of old Hollywood movies, punishment and death. The model was Lucifer, a figure of beauty, glamor ("bright star"), and then corruption, reduced to a vulture, a toad, and a crawling, hissing snake. The form these moral evils take is aesthetic, reminiscent of the contrast Hogarth and Rowlandson made between "sin" and evils—sexual joys and threatening but impotent old age, disease and death, dying men who end looking as Dorian Gray must have looked and not unlike Mr. Hyde, certainly like Francis Leicester. Rowlandson's old men, looking as if they are in the process of degenerating from human into animal and plant shapes, appear to "melt and dissolve. . . . Then I saw the body descend to the beasts whence it ascended" (see fig. 8).[15]

Principal and Accessory
"Don't spoil him," says Hallward to Lord Henry. "Don't try to influence him. Your influence would be bad"—but this also means, as he adds, "Don't take away from me the one person who gives to my art whatever charm it possesses" (1.16). As Lord Henry sees, for both of them art is a way of possessing or altering. But Lord Henry is not an artist, like Hallward—from whom he steals Dorian—but an aesthete.

Lord Henry is the advocate of the separation of beauty and morality, beauty remaining in the figure of Dorian, evil detached to the degenerating portrait—art as mere style. Recalling Rochester's remark on Charles II, that he never said a foolish thing nor ever did a wise one, Basil Hallward says to Wotton, "You never say a moral thing, and you never do a wrong thing. Your cynicism is simply a pose" (8)—which sets him up as the instigator; it is Dorian who, following his instructions as Robert Wringhim followed Gil-Martin's, does the wrong things. Hallward also equates saying with art, doing with immorality. *Art* in Wotton's discourse is evident in its formalism—its chiasmic contrasts, for example, of *soul/senses* and *senses/soul:* "Nothing can cure the soul but the senses, just as nothing can cure the senses but the soul" (23); "When we are happy we are always good, but when we are good we are not always happy" (6.76)—where, although he is parodying forms of Christian paradox, the terms, always reversals, cancel each other, implying the primacy of form over content and, beyond that, the nihilism that follows when Dorian puts Wotton's words into actions; for form remains beautiful while content rots.

It is Lord Henry who turns Jesus' commandments on their head. It is Lord Henry who plants the wish for eternal youth as well as its association with beauty and evil. "When your youth goes, your beauty will go with it, and then you will suddenly discover that there are no triumphs left for you. . . . Every month as it wanes brings you nearer to something dreadful" (2.24). Then Dorian's echo, as he looks at the portrait: "'How sad it is! I shall grow old, and horrible, and dreadful. It will never be older than this particular day of June,'" and what follows is his fatal wish ("'If it were I who was to be always young, and the picture that was to grow old!'" (2.28). There is no clap of thunder, no Mephistopheles who appears, but—as elsewhere in *The Picture of Dorian Gray*—Lord Henry's words and art manifest themselves in reality, in the world of evil(s). Dorian has, like Faust, sold his soul for a wish. And like the vampire, as Lord Henry reminds Hallward, the devil only stayed on to tempt Dorian because he was invited: "I stayed when you asked me" (2.29).

In the morality play that is at the bottom (or on the surface) of *The Picture of Dorian Gray*, Dorian is the fin-de-siècle Faustus and Lord Henry is Mephistopheles—but does Wilde mean it? Or is it his aesthetics that needs this story to safely moralize it—as he also needs murder to complement sin? Lord Henry is anticipating Machen's Ambrose when he goes on to say, "It is in the brain, and the brain only, that the great sins of the world take place"; words that apply to him, as to Ambrose, but not to Dorian, whom he is instructing in modes of action—of art turned from theory into practice.

One of the elements, introduced by Lord Henry Wotton, that affected Dorian was his reading the so-called "yellow book." When he read it, "It seemed to him that in exquisite raiment, and to the delicate sound of flutes, the sins of the world were passing in dumb show before him. Things that he had dimly dreamed of were suddenly made real to him" (11.20). Wilde is recalling Doctor Faustus's pageant of the sins—and perhaps his immersion in such damned books; and the suggestion is that the book opens to Dorian possibilities he had not entertained before. The book is not identified, though it is generally accepted that Wilde intended at least in part Huysman's *À Rebours* (1884); it probably was no more than that, a work expressing decadence and, within contemporary social limits, depravity; for Wilde the "yellow book" must have preached homosexuality, pederasty, and such forbidden practices. In any case, it embodied sin with a capital S, and also "evil" in that it corrupts whoever reads it.[16]

Professor Moriarty and Mr. Sherlock Holmes

Holmes and Watson are, of course, the significant pairing in Arthur Conan Doyle's Sherlock Holmes stories: they are Don Quixote and Sancho Panza, or, in Michael Chambon's words, "wildly limited men who find in each other, and only in each other, the stuff, sense, and passion of one whole man."[17] But Holmes and Professor Moriarty are demonic doubles and antagonists, good and evil. Holmes is the great detective, and Moriarty's "genius" "puts him on a pinnacle in the records of crime."[18] They share the power of ratiocination and deduction, though Holmes's is pursuit and Moriarty's concealment: "He is a genius, a philosopher, an abstract thinker. He has a brain of the first order." He is, like Holmes, brilliant, but unlike Holmes, he has "a criminal strain [that] ran in his blood" (544).

Holmes is first described by Watson:

His very person and appearance were such as to strike the attention of the most casual observer. In height he was rather over six feet, and so excessive lean that he seemed to be considerably taller. His eyes were sharp and piercing, save during those intervals of torpor to which I have alluded; and his thin, hawk-like nose gave his whole expression an air of alertness and decision. His chin, too, had the prominence and squareness which mark the man of determination.[19]

Moriarty's height is stressed ("a tall man," "that tall Englishman" [549, 553]): "He is clean-shaven, pale, and ascetic-looking, retaining something of the professor in his features. His shoulders are rounded from much study, and his face protrudes forward and is forever slowly oscillating from side to side in a curiously reptilian fashion. He peered at me with great curiosity in his puckered eyes," Holmes concludes, describing an evil version of himself (545).

Holmes claims that "if he could be assured that society was freed from Professor Moriarty he would cheerfully bring his own career to a conclusion," which he does (apparently) at the Reichenbach Falls—the two of them falling "locked in each other's arms . . . the most dangerous criminal and the foremost champion of the law of their generation" ("The Final Problem," 552, 555).

In *The Valley of Fear* (1914) Holmes compares Moriarty to Jonathan Wild, which invokes Gay as well as Defoe: "Jonathan Wild was the hidden force of the London criminals, to whom he sold his brains and his organization on a fifteen per cent. commission. The old wheel turns, and the same spoke comes up" (912). Moriarty is a "power behind the malefactor, some deep organizing power which forever stands in the way of the law, and throws its shield over the wrong-doer. Again and again in cases of the most varying sorts—forgery cases, robberies, murders—I have felt the presence of this force." He is Conan Doyle's version of the evil power-figures of Swift, Pope, Gay, Fielding, and Hogarth. "He is the Napoleon of crime," as Holmes tells Watson, rather than the Walpole, another "great man." "He is the *organizer* of half that is evil and of nearly all that is undetected in this great city." "The agent may be caught. In that case money is found for his bail or his defence. But the central power which uses the agent is never caught—never so much as suspected. This was the *organization* which I deduced, Watson, and which I devoted my whole energy to exposing and breaking up" (emphases added). Moriarty transmits his plans through others, his followers who hang while he remains above it all, "invisible." He evokes the Swiftean villain, the spider: "He sits motionless, like a spider in the centre of its web, but that web has a thousand radiations, and he knows well every quiver of each of them. He does little himself. He only plans." He is a descendant of Swift's moderns, gnostics, and Pope's forces of darkness, but then so is Sherlock Holmes.

Holmes describes his own method as "an exact science," in which "detection" "should be treated in the same cold and unemotional manner. You," he tells Dr. Watson, "have attempted to tinge it with romanticism, which produces much the same effect as if you worked a love-story or an elopement into the fifth proposition of Euclid" (*The Sign of Four*, 92).

Both Holmes and Moriarty are characterized as being distanced and detached from the crime they respectively analyze and perpetrate.[20] Holmes obviously acquires more detail than Moriarty and is from the first characterized as a Wildean aesthete. Holmes works, says Watson, "rather for the love of his art than for the acquirement of wealth" (292). In Holmes's own words, he is "the man who loves art for its own sake" (361). He has habits usually attributed to the underside of Victorian society and celebrated by Wilde and others: his drug habit, his vampirish schedule, his focus on only the facts that interest him, not "useless facts" such as the order of the solar system or contemporary politics. His métier, in short, he treats as an art, while Watson's versions of his adventures are put into stories that shamefully "pander to popular taste." His vocabulary recalls Hogarth's aesthetics, and his methodology is essentially (though he sometimes introduces the vocabulary of the moral and, indeed, the demonic) the love of pursuit, the aesthetics Hogarth derived from Addison, which defined a middle area between Shaftesbury's ugly and beautiful, an area of the commonplace designated the "novel" or the "new" and, at its extreme, the "strange." In "The Adventure of the Copper Beeches," Holmes could be expressing the Hogarthian aesthetic of the commonplace when he says to Watson, "To the man who loves art for its own sake . . . it is frequently in its least important and lowliest manifestations that the keenest pleasure is to be derived." This means giving prominence "not so much to the many *causes célèbres* and sensational trials in which I have figured [for which read: baroque history paintings of cruelty and murder] but rather to those incidents which may have been trivial in themselves, but which have given room for those faculties of deduction and of logical synthesis which I have made my special province" (361–62).[21] And further, "'If I claim full justice for my art, it is because it is an impersonal thing—a thing beyond myself. Crime is common. Logic is rare. Therefore it is upon the logic rather than upon the crime that you should dwell,'" and he refers to "the finer shades of analysis and deduction." Holmes is outlining an aesthetics to Watson, and in *The Valley of Fear* he refers to himself as "a mere connoisseur of crime" and an "artist" (362–63, 948, 951).

But Holmes's aesthetic does not eschew the strange or demonic, in fact, invokes it. In *The Hound of the Baskervilles* (1902), Conan Doyle has already set up the demonic dimension in the eighteenth-century document that retails the tradition of the hound; Hugo Baskerville "became as one that hath a devil," and he tells his drinking companions that "he would that very night render his body and soul to the Powers of Evil if he might but overtake the wench," the innocent girl who is trying to escape his embraces. He puts the hounds upon her, but one of his followers sees pursuing him "'such a hound of hell as God forbid should ever be at my heels,'" and it is this "great, black beast, shaped like a hound, yet larger than any hound that ever mortal eye has rested upon" that overtakes him and tears out his throat (789–90).

Holmes, confronted with a large hound footprint, "shrugged his shoulders": "'I have hitherto confined my investigations to this world,' said he. 'In a modest way I have combated evil, but to take on the Father of Evil himself would, perhaps, be too ambitious a task. Yet you must admit that the footmark is material'" (796). His problem is to ascertain whether there is "a diabolical agency," as appears to be the case; nevertheless he describes this as one of the most evil cases he can remember, "an ugly business, Watson, an ugly, dangerous business, and the more I see of it the less I like it" (816). The setting, he remarks, "is a worthy one. If the devil did desire to have a hand in the affairs of man—"; and he adds that the "devil's agents may be of flesh and blood, may they not?"—which could describe the plot of Rodger Baskerville (799). It is, after all, fear that caused Sir Charles Baskerville's death—a form of murder of which Conan Doyle was fond.

The imagined scene of the "desolate plain," on it "lurking this fiendish man, hiding in a burrow like a wild beast, his heart full of malignancy against the whole race which had cast him out," in fact describes only an "ordinary convict," cold and hungry. And yet, his sister explains, when he was young he "met wicked companions, and the devil entered into him" (846). In fact, the devil is only a large hound dabbed with phosphorous. A metaphysical reality is replaced by a verbal, a lurid metaphor. The supernatural and demonic are explained away by Holmes's ratiocination and the solidity of the real world. It is a way for Conan Doyle to portray evil with the capital E, deck it with Gothic trappings. As in the Gothic of Horace Walpole and Ann Radcliffe, possession of the Baskerville property is the mundane motive, resulting in two killings, one accidental, and a third intended but prevented; evil is demonized by the story of the hound, the Devonshire moors, the phosphorous paint, and the language of Dr. Watson, but mediated by the ratiocination of Holmes, who can say this is the most diabolical murderer in his experience—presumably because the killer scares his victims to death, going to the trouble of getting a large dog, hiding in the Grimpen Mere, and so on, rendering a crime evil.

The banal subject of "The Adventure of the Copper Beeches" is given Gothic emphasis by allusions to the story of the curiosity of Bluebeard's last wife and by the strange "disposition of the child" of the family: "The child's disposition is abnormally cruel, merely for cruelty's sake, and whether he derives this from his smiling father, as I should suspect, or from his mother, it bodes evil for the poor girl who is in their power" (377). The "poor creature" has been locked up by her father simply because she inherits the property and is in love with a man who will carry away girl and property. The evil child mystifies the simple story.

Conan Doyle likes to acompany a case of simple murder and ratiocination with religion—the devil and demonic possibilities, as with Moriarty himself, but more particularly in *The Hound of the Baskervilles,* and in *The Sign of Four* Hindu and in *Study in Scarlet* Mormon beliefs, even the Masonic fraternity of *The Valley of Fear.* There is no supernatural, but religious belief of various sorts—unsubstantiated—takes its place. The ratiocination ends with a letdown as to what actually happened. In *A Study in Scarlet* (1887) all the blood comes down to Hope's (the killer's) nose bleed. The solution to the puzzle is followed (especially in the novels, on a smaller scale in the tales) by a long narrative explaining the motive of the crime—in effect, internalizing the evildoing. The internalizing further takes the form of a distancing into exotic and mysterious places, whether India (back to the Sepoy Mutiny) or America (Utah or California) and the idea of a secret society or group—the Mormons or Freemasons.

As in the novels and stories of James, betrayal and revenge are the two chief motives with which Holmes deals. A paradigmatic story is "The Adventure of the Crooked Man." A man is in love with a woman; his rival betrays him to the Indians, who imprison and torture him (making him the "crooked man"), a situation compared to David's treatment of Uriah the Hittite; the betrayed man returns to and by his mere presence terrifies the David figure to death. Beneath the mystification of crookedness, India, the Indians' unnamed tortures, and the idea of frightening a person to death is the actual crime, no less an evil—betrayal of a rival for love.

The end, as Conan Doyle originally planned it, is apocalyptic, full of terror, horror, and the evil destroying itself along with the good. The Falls is indeed

> a fearful place. The torrent, swollen by the melting snow, plunges into a tremendous abyss, from which the spray rolls up like the smoke from a burning house. The shaft into which the river hurls itself is an immense chasm, lined by glistening coal-black rock and narrowing into a creaming, boiling pit of incalculable depth, which brims over and shoots the stream onward over its jagged lip. (552)

This is apocalypse in an aesthetic of the sublime, but popular protest made Conan Doyle correct the ending, ostensibly so that good vanquished evil but in fact in order to leave the Holmes stories open-ended. The original ending corresponded to the end of "The Adventure of the Cardboard Box," in which, after a particularly savage act of vengeance, Holmes introduces the Problem of Evil:

> "What is the meaning of it, Watson?" said Holmes, solemnly, as he laid down the paper. "What object is served by this circle of misery and violence and fear? It must tend to some end, or else our universe is ruled by chance, which is unthinkable. But what end? There is the great standing perennial problem to which human reason is as far from an answer as ever." (1059)

In *The Hound of the Baskervilles* Watson expresses a similar view: "Life has become like that great Grimpen Mire, with little green patches everywhere into which one may sink and with no guide to point the track" (832).[22]

2. THOSE WHO BURN AND THOSE WHO ROT: CONRAD

The Heart of Darkness: *Kurtz and the Congo Company*
F. R. Leavis's criticism of Joseph Conrad's *Heart of Darkness* (1902) was that it was damaged by an "adjectival and worse than supererogatory insistence

upon 'unspeakable rites,' 'monstrous passions,' 'inconceivable mystery' and so on"—which became for Albert Guerard, "unspeakable lusts." Conrad's own words, or rather Marlow's referring to Kurtz, were "gratification of his various lusts" and his "gratified and monstrous passions."[23]

The distinction between evil acts and demonolatry serves as the model for Conrad's *Heart of Darkness*. The "unspeakable rites" must, of course, remain unspecified, as in James's silence as to the misdemeanors of Miles, of Quint and Jessel, and in *Wings of the Dove* of Lionel Croy. In this respect Conrad is drawing upon the notion of terror as obscurity, but, in the second place, we notice that the words are Marlow's and (like the Governess's) conditioned by his community of ideas. Kurtz's unspeakable rites/lusts are on a level with the "evil" of Quint and Miss Jessel—they are sins in the sense of the breaking of religio-social laws.

It is important to see *The Heart of Darkness* in its relationship to the tales of terror and the supernatural of Machen and the others: What Marlow describes with his paraphrases and euphemisms—his hyped-up but vague vocabulary of horror—is essentially "Evil." To begin with the title, *Heart of Darkness*: Evil presumably equals Burkean darkness and obscurity, but in particular savagery, atavism, or (in the soul) Original Sin. The "heart" of the "dark continent" (into which the man-of-war is hopelessly firing [1.17]) is equated with the "hearts" of men. Atavism is simply going native, a form of regression and corruption not unrelated to the fate of Dr. Jekyll: "Going up that river was like traveling back to the earliest beginnings of the world, when vegetation rioted on the earth and the big trees were kings. . . . And this stillness of life did not in the least resemble a peace. It was the stillness of an implacable force brooding over an inscrutable intention. The steamer toiled along slowly on the edge of a black and incomprehensible frenzy. The prehistoric man was cursing us, praying to us, welcoming us . . . we glided past like phantoms, wondering and secretly appalled, as sane men would be before an enthusiastic outbreak in a madhouse" (2.35–36). Back, back, *eugenically*—from white Caucasian descending to African blacks, to apes, and so on—the order followed in the New York Natural History Museum before the revisions of Franz Boas and Margaret Mead. Marlow: "Measure my head . . . [with] callipers" (1.15). And so "Evil" in fact equals sin as "unspeakable lusts"—Kurtz is given (or takes) a native mistress, materializing lust and implying or projecting the abomination of miscegenation.

Kurtz's degeneration, deterioration, and corruption are due to solitude and the worship of the natives. We remember the case of Marlow's predecessor, Fresleven, "the gentlest, quietest" creature—"but he had been a couple of years already out there engaged in the noble cause, you know, and he probably felt the need at last of asserting his self-respect in some way. Therefore he whacked the old nigger mercilessly" (1.12), producing another of those scenes of merciless beating that we have seen connecting Tom Nero with Mr. Hyde.[24] Alternatively, to "go up country" leads to the case of the stolid Swede who hanged himself—too much sun (1.18).

Kurtz's final words, "the horror, the horror," refer, we might ask, how much merely to his sexual behavior? and how much to Kurtz trying to act according to Enlightenment morality, without Faith and without Christianity and so suffering his Christian fate? The latter would be the implication of a Machen story. If so, then he has proved himself an Original Sinner, showing once again that man, in common with the "savages," is naturally flawed—once he is free of the Congo Company, of society, and free to be, to do anything, whether good or evil; in short to become his own god (which *is* of course a redaction of the Fall).

Evil with the capital E is attached to the discourse of sin and abominations, what Marlow calls the "fascination of the abomination":

> The utter savagery had closed round him—all that mysterious
> life of the wilderness that stirs in the forest, in the jungles, in
> the hearts of wild men. . . . He has to live in the midst of the
> incomprehensible which is also detestable. (1.10)
>   . . . all along the formless coast bordered by dangerous surf,
> as if Nature herself had tried to ward off intruders; in and out
> of rivers, streams of death in life, whose banks were rotting
> into mud, whose waters, thickened into slime, invaded the con-
> torted mangroves that seemed to writhe at us in the extremity
> of an impotent despair. (1.17)

Marlow is describing the grotesque, the transgressive railway trucks that look like animals, in passages that sound as if they could have been written by Machen. And Kurtz, who is said to "preside at certain midnight dances ending with unspeakable rites, which . . . were offered up to him" (2.50), is the figure who, in the Hawthorne context, was the Black Man, in Machen's the person who, shown the Great God Pan, goes mad and/or commits suicide.

Conrad undergirds the Christian story with echoes of Dante's *Inferno:* "Black shapes crouched, lay, sat between the trees, leaning against the trunks, clinging to the earth, half coming out half effaced within the dim light, in all the attitudes of pain, abandonment, and despair" (1.19–20). Such passages specifically recall the Gustave Doré illustrations to the *Inferno,* as do the tortures of the stinging flies, the man who is forever making bricks without straw, the "objectless blasting," and the chain gang.[25]

But in this atmosphere of sin, set against it, is the banal evil of the "flabby, pretending, weak eyed devil of a rapacious and pitiless folly" (1.20)—the actions of the Congo Company men—beginning back in Brussels, a "whited sepulchre," a door to the Dantesque underworld, but also Jesus' term for the scribes (Matt. 23:27), which applies to the Company manager and accountants. Quite different, Kurtz is searching for the "idea"—he wants to apply "moral ideas of some sort" to the natives. He is opposed to the demoralized greed and total cynicism of the Central Station, let alone the Company in Brussels: the manager, says Marlow, is a "papier-maché Mephistopheles, and it seemed to me that if I tried I could poke my forefinger through him and would find nothing inside but a little loose dirt, maybe" one of what he calls "the hollow men" (1.29).

There are those who rot (the Company) and those who burn (Kurtz), and the latter is the Renaissance-Enlightenment Man, with moral ideas, and also a painter (of moral allegory: Marlow sees his painting of "a woman draped and blindfolded carrying a lighted torch" [1.27]), a musician, orator, and secular hero. Kurtz's "idea" is summed up in his motto: "I had a heavenly mission to civilise you" (1.11)—"the idea—something you can set up, and bow down before, and offer a sacrifice to"; and in his report (his "poisonous text") to the International Society for the Suppression of Savage Customs, which degenerates into, "Exterminate the brutes" (2.50–51). He has tried to civilize them—instead they worship him, and he becomes one of them—and has given up on them; he has found their darkness in his own heart and can only scribble his lesson to "exterminate *them.*"[26] He himself, like the Company's chief accountant, is still talking about his ivory hauls. If "evil" is being opposed to sin, then we see the natives as being exploited—by the Company, which is certainly evil, but by Kurtz as well.

It is the case of Kurtz who tries to introduce the "idea," but it is only a "civilizing" that leads to his own corruption and that reflects the hollowness of the whole business enterprise of colonialism. For he becomes, like the managers, "a hollow man": The wilderness "echoed loudly within him because he was hollow at the core" (3.57–58); when he is dying, "the shade of the original [uncorrupted] Kurtz frequented the bedside of the hollow sham whose fate it was to be buried presently in the mould of primeval earth. But both the diabolic love and the unearthly hate of the mysteries it had penetrated fought for the possession of that soul satiated with primitive emotions, avid of lying fame, of sham distinction of all the appearances of success and power" (3.67).

A problem of contradiction? Conrad, as Guerard puts it, "suggests and dramatizes evil as an active energy (Kurtz and his unspeakable lusts) but defines evil as vacancy."[27] Clearly the Company men are worse. Why colonialism? "To make money, of course" (1.23); and, as in the "lusts" of Kurtz, because there are "no external checks"—the situation that will lead to Kurtz's downfall (1.25). And Conrad contextualizes colonialism by equating the African "savages" of the present with the English them-selves in the past. The point of the opening in the yacht on the Thames is to juxtapose Roman Britain then—and memories of Dryden's "Essay of Dramatic Poesie" (1665), which foreshadowed the situation of Marlow and his friends, in Dryden's case during the Dutch war for naval (colo-nial) supremacy—with the Congo now, the literal darkness of the night in 1900: "This also has been one of the dark places of the earth. . . . The conquest of the earth, which mostly means the taking it away from those who have a different complexion or slightly flatter noses than ourselves, is not a pretty thing when you look into it too much. What redeems it is the idea only. An idea at the back of it, not a sentimental pretence but an idea; and an unselfish *belief in the idea*—something you can set up, and *bow down before, and offer a sacrifice to*" (1.9–10). The passage is recalled when we hear of "the tremor of far-off drums . . . as profound a meaning as the sound of bells in a Christian country" (1.23). Marlow's audience, after all, consists of company director, accountant, and lawyer.

We can conclude that sin (God-Devil[s]) is the bogus evil of Kurtz's native rites (Christian sins and abominations) as opposed to the real, social evil of the Company and what it (and Kurtz) is doing to the Africans—even for Kurtz, "civilize" means getting more ivory.

Where does Marlow fit in? There is respect as well as irony in Mar-low's admiring account of the Company's chief accountant and his respect for discipline, routine, and keeping up appearances: "When one has got to make correct entries one comes to hate those savages—hate them to the death" (1.22). But his immaculate appearance is preceded by the blacks' hell and the sick person's groans—"The groans of this sick person . . . distract my attention"; and yet the accountant's efficient account-keeping is also related to the artist's solution to the Problem of Evil: to Marlow's sense of duty, his skillful work, the fireman's expertise (he, we learn, is a cannibal), and the reason why the cannibals don't eat the whites (2.36–39, 42–43).

Marlow and Kurtz are doubles (3.68). Marlow by his trip up the Congo repeats Kurtz's idealistic beginnings and, traveling deeper, deeper up the Congo, his pilgrimage to the "heart of darkness"—to discover the potential "hell" in the heart of every man and so, replicating Machen, the Christian context. As opposed to the Company agents, Kurtz has faced the hell within himself; they turn away from it. So Marlow learns about his own capacity for evil and his capacity to resist it; they have learned nothing.[28]

Victory: *Mr. Jones and Schomberg*

The evil of *Victory* (1915) is foregrounded—at the outset—by Schomberg, who is pointedly described as German, with emphasis on "Teutonic"; he is a "Lieutenant of the Reserve," "manly"; the date is 1914, at the height of German imperialism, on the verge of World War I. Schomberg is a commercial figure, like the Congo Company managers, a hotel keeper primarily interested in money. He is a "tame, respectable gin-slinger" as opposed to the "desperadoes"—as Schomberg calls Mr. Jones and his friends who invade his hotel.[29] His sins, or rather vices, are unbridled anger and perjury (lies, calumny), and his motivation for his act of evil is simple: first, irrational (gratuitous) hatred of Axel Heyst, perhaps because Heyst does not frequent his hotel; second, more specifically because Heyst rescued the girl Lena from Schomberg's lustful attentions; and, finally, his anxiety to get the plainly criminal trio (Jones, Ricardo, Pedro) out of his hotel. Schomberg's vices are themselves affectless, subject perhaps for laughter—except in two instances when his perjured story is believed: When he tells Lena, her innocence causes the lie to be lodged in her memory, and when he tells Ricardo, the latter's greed for the supposed hoard of gold (and lust aroused by the story of the girl Lena) lead to action and so consequences—five deaths. The trio's motive is rationalized by

Schomberg's calumny/perjury, the wrong he tells them Heyst had done his friend Morrison; in fact it is greed—the alleged fortune Heyst has stolen from Morrison and supposedly secreted on the island of Samburan. Heyst's alleged evil act justifies Jones's fascination with Heyst. (We might contrast Mrs. Schomberg, whose motive for telling Davidson was fear that Lena would return to occupy her husband.)

Schomberg *needs,* in an almost schematic way, the uncanny, allegorical "Evil" of the trio he sends to Samburan to destroy Heyst. The trio, as Schomberg calls them—the spectre gentleman Mr. Jones, the feline-feral Ricardo, and the ape Pedro—are an allegorical "trio of fitting envoys" dispatched by Schomberg, "envoys of the outer world. Here they are before you—evil intelligence, instinctive savagery, arm in arm. The brute force [Pedro] is at the back" (4.5.329). They are on the one hand an almost Miltonic parody of the Trinity: The Father, Son, and Holy Ghost created the world, Satan, Sin, and Death create an alternative, negative version—the bridge connecting hell with earth. And on the other, they are part of a spectrum of evil which corresponds roughly to the spectrum in *Heart of Darkness* from the company men to the natives whose rites Kurtz joins, with their associations of demonolatry.

In Schomberg Mr. Jones inspires "not a frank physical fear . . . but a superstitious shrinking awe, something like an invincible repugnance to seek speech with a wicked ghost." "Daylight only made him a more weird, a more disturbing and unlawful apparition" (2.6.121). Of the three, "Pedro, at any rate, was just a simple, straightforward brute, if a murderous one. There was no mystery about him, nothing uncanny, no suggestion of a stealthy, deliberate wild-cat turned into a man, or of an insolent spectre on leave from Hades, endowed with skin and bones and a subtle power of terror" (2.5.115–16). So we have the trio: grotesque man-animal creatures, abominations.

Their uncanny evil is contrasted with the banal, mundane, stupid malice of Schomberg, who thinks of himself: "He wasn't capable of murder. He was certain of that. And, remembering suddenly the plain speeches of Mr. Jones, he would think: 'I suppose I *am* too tame for that'—quite unaware that he had murdered the poor woman [his wife] morally years ago. He was too unintelligent to have the notion of such a crime" (2.6.120). But his stupid malice has *effect.*

The trio, unlike Schomberg, actually have very little effect: Half their water supply is left behind (very possibly another treachery of Schomberg's); when they reach the island, aside from the fear they instill in Heyst, they have no effect—Pedro and Mr. Jones are killed by Wang, Ricardo by Mr. Jones, and Lena's death is the result of Mr. Jones's first bullet missing Ricardo, his real object—they more or less kill each other. Heyst's death is by suicide, but it's the consequence of Lena's death (and her heroism).

The trio is a parody of the Trinity but all male, decidedly so since there is a strong homosexual strain in Mr. Jones, who is an image of Death, in the description of him and in his hatred of the female, that is, of the reproductive function. Mr. Jones is skeletal, a "gentleman," "ailing" (4.5.316–17), where ailing seems to be part of being a gentleman. Like homosexuality, sickness, and deformity, debility seems to be an aspect of evil—sin defined as the negative aspect of good (Dryden's Achitophel—the body a wreck or paralyzed; only the scheming, destructive brain is active). Homosexuality is apparently for Conrad sin disguised as evil.

Jones's motive is resentment against society (the other gentlemen who cast him out) more than money, which gives his motivation a gratuitous—aesthetic—quality that evokes Dorian Gray. Speaking of Heyst, he says to Ricardo, "You, of course, would shoot him at once, but I shall enjoy the refinement and the jest of it. He's a man of the best society. I've been hounded out of my sphere by people very much like that fellow. How enraged and humiliated he will be [to be fleeced by Jones at cards]! I promise myself some exquisite moments while watching his play" (4.6.337).

Jones's oracular "I am he that is" (4.5.317, 4.11.376) invokes Exodus 3:14: "And God said unto Moses, I AM THAT I AM: And he said, Thus shalt thou say unto the children of Israel, I AM hath sent me unto you." When Heyst asks Jones to explicate his gnomic words, he replies, "'It means that I am a person to be reckoned with.'" Jones, like Kurtz, plays God.

Mr. Jones, the false god, specter, gentleman, and sick man sums up the "evil" evil—or, in Machen's terms, sin—of Kurtz's rites and abominations: He is grotesque, if not spectral, then skeletal; sounds in fact physically like Kurtz, with Ricardo filling to some extent the role of Kurtz's worshipful Russian acolyte. The description of Jones associates him with Kurtz's abominations, in particular the heads he sticks on posts: "He resembled a painted pole leaning against the edge of the desk, with a dried head of dubious distinction stuck on the top of it" (4.11.376).

One suspects that Conrad is drawing for Mr. Jones upon the seedy devil of Dostoyevsky's *Brothers Karamazov*, who combines the shabby and the demonic: Like Mr. Jones he is a gentleman down at heel, with expensive clothes but soiled and threadbare—"a style no one wore any more." Ivan Karamazov points out to him, "'You just pick out all my bad thoughts, and above all the stupid ones. You are stupid and banal. You are terribly stupid. No, I can't endure you! What am I to do, what am I to do!" To which the devil answers, "My friend, I still want to be a gentleman, and to be accepted as such": "I am poor, but . . . I won't say very honest, but . . . in society it is generally accepted as an axiom that I am a fallen angel. . . . [N]ow I only value my reputation as a decent man and get along as best I can, trying to be agreeable." The devil is now stupid, banal, living according to contemporary mores at their lowest—but trying not to forget that he was once an angel.[30]

Jones and Heyst are, like Kurtz and Marlow, doubles: First Jones sees Heyst as one of the people who drove him (Lionel Croy–like) from society; then he associates himself with Heyst as two gentlemen who were forced out of society—outsiders both, as Jones draws the analogy (4.5.319, again 4.11.378 and 380–83). While Pedro represents the simple slave/master relation, Ricardo is attached to Jones because he is a gentleman; he regards himself as his "secretary" and his "chum"; like Quint in *Turn of the Screw*, he is a valet, Jones's valet. Heyst's supposed crime, to Ricardo, is that he "violated in cold blood" "the elementary principle of loyalty to a chum" (3.10.269)—which suggests the homosocial and/or homoerotic link between the two and anticipates the motive for Jones's murder of Ricardo at the end. Ricardo is heterosexual, highly sexed, and it is he who initiates the plot. Ricardo in fact gets more emphasis—more time and space—than Jones: Jones's "secretary," spokesman, admirer, he is again Swift's middleman. His heterosexuality causes him first to conceal the fact of Lena from the woman-hating Jones and then to pursue her (Ricardo sees Lena as *his* double [4.6.336]), thereby prompting her to action—and so precipitating the ruin of the trio, but her own death as well, followed by Heyst's suicide.

These negative figures are posed against Heyst and Lena, the good man and the innocent whore (sin as beautiful): he the man of detachment and thought without action, she the woman of love plus action. Lena was originally called Alma (soul) and Magdalen, alluding to the myth of the prostitute reclaimed by Jesus, becoming his follower and the first to see him upon his resurrection—a vague but apposite naming for a girl who begins as a musician and part-time prostitute.

Victory could be described as a love story, the story of Heyst and Lena; or as Heyst's learning to act in the world—or his failure to act without the love of Lena, who acts for him; but one cannot escape the world of Schomberg and the satanic/infernal trio. The typical Conrad plot is about initiation—the *Lord Jim* story of Jim (an inch or two under six feet tall) and the tests of the *Patna* and *Patisan:* a test failed, disgrace, ending with another test which is also failed (ending in the hero's death). In "The Secret Sharer" the test is passed with the help of the dark double, who has failed his. In *Heart of Darkness* Marlow goes on a quest to find his dark double Kurtz, who has failed his test and dies; Marlow learns from this and, coming to terms with the task of passing on his knowledge to Kurtz's "Intended," survives in the world of lies. (Kurtz's Intended is opposed to the splendid native woman he takes up with in Africa.)

The allegorical evil of Jones, the vile rituals of Kurtz, ask to be compared with (in a way they parallel) the activities of Quint and the governess in *Turn of the Screw,* as also the ambiguous ending: who is responsible for Miles's death, Quint or the governess? In *Heart of Darkness* evil is what the men of the Congo Company have done—are doing—in Africa. The sin lies in (is displaced to) the abominations such as sex, pagan rituals, the cross-social and cultural "fornication" that take place when a Belgian Renaissance Man encounters his savage past. Evil is, in short, reality—the evils of suffering-evil—in fact the consequences of sin-directed morality—custom, illusion, ignorance, and prejudice.

The Banal: Eliot and Yeats

The post–World War I sense of evil was embodied for the generation of the twenties and thirties in the poetry of Yeats and Eliot; and Eliot's formulation found one of its chief images in Conrad's *Heart of Darkness*. His "Hollow Men" (1925) opens with the epigraph "Mr. Kurtz—he dead." Mr. Kurtz at least had a crazy faith, misdirected from God to strange atavisms. Evil in Eliot's "waste land" is a secularism which he figures as hollowness, the opposite of (or the reality at the bottom of) the demonic Kurtz. In another epigraph for "The Hollow Men" it is Guy Fawkes ("A penny for the Old Guy") now reduced (Eliot's version of Pope's mock-epic) to a children's ritual—or, in other poems, to the banal modern equivalent of

John the Baptist, Barabas, or Hamlet. Augustine is quoted: "To Carthage then I came. . . . Burning burning burning burning," where "burning" is the important word, preferable to a "handful of dust." It is the burning and even damned who are preferable to the spiritually dead-in-life and neither damned nor saved. In *The Waste Land* (1922) Eliot invoked the first circle of Dante's *Inferno,* where those reside who refused to make a choice, who "lived [a life] with no blame and with no praise":—"so many that I wondered / how death could have undone so great a number" (ll. 90–91). Evil, as opposed to sin, is trivial, valueless, inane—other words that describe it are dreadful, mean, grim, vile, nasty, horrid, creepy-crawly. It is these qualities Eliot treats as the great threat to modern living, which for him should be of the spirit. His poems fall like a shadow across the novels I shall be discussing in the following sections.

In Yeats's poetic world it is the worst who "are full of passionate intensity," while "the best lack all conviction." In "Meditations in Time of Civil War" (1923) the Renaissance Man ("some violent bitter man, some powerful man") called in architect and artist to make an art object of a "sweetness" and "gentleness none there had ever known." This was essentially (to take a subtitle from "Meditations") the "ancestral house" (containing "portraits of our ancestors") and its grounds with the "great rooted blossomers" of Burke, who, with his organic metaphors, "proved the State a tree."

A matching act of "passionate intensity" has the demonic man possessing a woman—the sexual act between agents of difference, the woman and gods, demons, or stable boys; in the microcosm this is lust and abomination, the traditional locus for sin and the biblical Fall; in the macrocosm, civil war—the chaos whose model is the final stage of the Trojan War. The assumption is of the raging sexuality buried in a respectable lady and unearthed by the god, demon, or stable boy. There is the "serving man" of the "ancestral house" who divines Mrs. French's desires and brings her an insolent tenant's ears "in a little covered dish" (195); he carries out her half-conscious desires—as Herod did Salome's, as some invisible demon did Dorian Gray's. Then there is "that insolent fiend Robert Artisson," who possesses Lady Kyteler, becoming her familiar. There is the passionate sexual encounter of Helen and Paris (to her a "fool") and the rape of Leda by Zeus-as-swan or Mary by the Holy Spirit—acts that have dire consequences: "mere anarchy," the Trojan War, all the wars in which the falcon can no longer hear the falconer, and the Antichrist slouches "toward Bethlehem to be born." In the present of the Irish "troubles," the situation involves not a lecherous god and a human woman, as with the swan and Leda, but a highborn lady, owner of the ancestral home, possessed by a groom or a servant or a local demon, the result being the end of the old order and generational murder.

As the rapist swan is beautiful (recall the swans at Coole Park), the "violent bitter man" builds beautiful houses, and we are asked to "take" his greatness along with his violence (200–01). This then is followed by decline, as the violent bitter man's descendant degenerates into "but a mouse."[31] "I see," the poet sums up in the title of the final section of the "Meditations," "Phantoms [by which he means his poetic images] of Hatred and of the Heart's Fullness and of the Coming Emptiness." *Hatred* produces the art object, which educes the *heart's fullness,* or our sublime experience of art; but this is followed by *emptiness*—and these *phantoms* are the subject of poetry, the "Monstrous familiar images" such as the murder of Jacques Molay and the subsequent vengeance by his followers: the "rage-driven, rage-tormented, and rage-hungry troop, / Trooper belabouring trooper, biting at arm or at face"—an image that evokes both the chaos of the Greeks and Trojans on the last night of the war and the ninth circle of hell (Ugolino devouring Ruggieri). They are plunging "towards nothing," embracing "nothing," that is, the "Coming Emptiness" of the title.

The next poem in the sequence, "Nineteen Hundred and Nineteen," refers to the year after World War I ended, when the civil war in Ireland resumed. It had appeared "that the worst rogues and rascals had died out . . . All teeth were drawn, all ancient tricks unlearned, / And a great army but a showy thing," whereas a year later the demons arrive:

> Now days are dragon-ridden, the nightmare
> Rides upon sleep: a drunken soldiery
> Can leave the mother, murdered at her door,
> To crawl in her own blood, and go scot-free.

As "some violent bitter man, some powerful man" is succeeded by his mousy descendant, the Great War is succeeded not by peace but by "weasels fighting in a hole," the hole being Ireland. The imagery now is of dragons and Salome's desire for John the Baptist ("with amorous cries, or angry cries," the two stages of her passion, lust and revenge), and Lady

Kyteler's passion for "that insolent fiend Robert Artisson," who "lurches past, his great eyes without thought." (It is Wilde's Salome Yeats evokes.) The "love-lorn" Lady Kyteler has offered Robert Artisson the sort of artifacts that the "violent bitter man" has caused to be made—not the pitiful "ix red cockes, & ix peacocks eies" of the historical Lady Kyteler but the "bronzed peacock feathers" Yeats had envisioned as the subject of his redemptive art in "Sailing to Byzantium," which projected one escape route from the "mere anarchy" of contemporary Ireland.[32]

Another way of expressing the Yeats plot, this time the plot of the poet himself, is to say that the demons, fiends, and dragons ("frenzies," "monstrous familiar images") are among the fictions that he keeps reminding himself of (others involve his friends, John M. Synge and Lady Gregory, Maude Gonne and Lionel Johnson, Burke and Grattan, and the fictional Cathleen ni Houlihan and Cuchulain, and so on). These, like the other "masterful images," and like the slumming loves-lusts of Lady Kyteler and the other women, originate in a "mound of refuse or the sweepings of a street"; they all "start / In the foul rag and bone shop of the heart." To Lady Kyteler and the other stories we could apply Crazy Jane's words to the Bishop, echoing Augustine: "But *Love* has pitched his *mansion* in / The *place of excrement*" (emphasis added).[33] These are the elements of Yeats's poetics.

The summation is the one-act play *Purgatory* (1938), in which the lady's obsession with "a groom in a training stable," a drunk and rowdy (read *demonic*) man, leads to copulation and thus to the birth of a social abomination; to her death and his drunken burning down of the great house (the "mansion"); on the anniversary of the fire to the son's murder of the father; and, years later, to his murder of his own son in order to bring an end to the vicious cycle that would lead, he believes, only to other monsters slouching toward Bethlehem to be born.[34]

As the Old Man (the boy's father) tells it, his mother resembled Mrs. French and Lady Kyteler: "This night she is no better than her man / And does not mind that he is half drunk, / She is mad about him."[35] The "house" is reduced by this stable hand to "a pig-stye." He cuts down the trees to pay for his losses at cards, horses, drink, and women, and burns the house. To kill a house, says the Old Man, "Where great men grew up, married, died, / I here declare a capital offence" (193)—as if to justify his killing of his father. When his mother took up with the groom, he tells us, his mother's mother never spoke to her again—"And she did right," says the Old Man. But the Boy (his son, the next generation) responds pragmatically, "What's right and wrong? / My grand-dad got the girl and the money." The son represents those who lack all conviction; the father and grandfather at least acted out of passionate intensity.

The image of the burnt great house, narrowed down in *Purgatory* to the interloper who destroys it, is the microcosm of the civil war poems, in which "A man is killed, or a house burned" (205). Yeats's image of stable hands replacing the master (Burke's image of the plebeian Parisians replacing Louis XVI, in bed with his queen), of masters reduced in their descendants to mice, great houses reduced to "pig styes" and charred ruins, houses and the great trees reduced to a tree stump ("to burn that stump on the Acropolis") harks back to Juvenal's portraits of Romans of the Republic juxtaposed with present decadence. Virgil's Trojan War becomes the Irish Civil War and, contemporaneously, World War I—and, when it is over, what remains is the Peace Conference at Versailles; "weasels fighting in a hole" applies to both war and peace. He is invoking Gresham's Law when he writes,

> I lived among great houses,
> Riches drove out rank,
> Base drove out the better blood,
> And mind and body shrank.[36]

Yeats's country house with its portraits of the great of the past does not draw upon Hogarth's sense of the oppression of the portraits and historical-mythological-religious models: "But take our greatness with our violence" is Yeats's more ambivalent motto. They remain, as for Juvenal, a standard against which the mice and weasels of the present are judged; as works of art they are recovered in Yeats's poetry as a buttress—or an escape—from the evils of his world, if no more than ceremony and song, or only the clapping of hands.

3. POPEYE AND GOWAN STEVENS: FAULKNER

Sanctuary: *The Rape of Temple Drake*

In William Faulkner's *Sanctuary* (1932) any study of evil must begin with the action of Popeye, his spectacular violation of Temple Drake. It is a shocking act, raping a virgin of eighteen with a corncob. But is this an act of sadism, or of malice with any intention to hurt or enjoy her pain? We do not, of course, witness the scene—and only the foreplay is described by Temple in retrospect. Faulkner gives no indication of anything except Popeye's need to *have* her, parallel with the desires of all the other men on the Old Frenchman's Place. It is an act of total unfeelingness, another version of his killing, as a child, a pair of lovebirds and a cat. There is no indication that he enjoyed their pain. Killing them showed his lack of regard for them as anything more than objects. Or perhaps it was, as when at the Old Frenchman's Place a dog surprised him and he shot it, an automatic response to fear and the unknown—anything outside himself.

His rape of Temple is to prove that he is a man, or at least a being; the rape of the girl Temple is related to his annual return to see his half-crazed mother in Florida, the only living proof of his own existence. So the rape can be interpreted as a horrifying but futile protest against both his impotence and his isolation, the child's response to evils in the world. Without Temple, taunted and betrayed by her, he chooses death. The lovebirds he cut up as a child were, in the same way, living things by whose death he could in some sense affirm his own livingness. Having killed Tommy and Red, repudiated by Temple, he makes no attempt to kill her: he just drives to Florida.

Perhaps we need to recall Popeye the impotent voyeur, with his black rubber eyes (in a novel obsessed with voyeurism, all the eyes are described in detail), and relate him to the town boys who watch the college girls and their college boyfriends and, out of a kind of frustration, scrawl lewd remarks on lavatory walls and break bottles, scattering the fragments on the street to puncture the tires of the college boys' cars. This desecration parallels, as it anticipates, the gangster Popeye's treatment of Temple—and suggests that part of Popeye's rape is determined to some extent by the social status of Temple, which he violates in a way comparable to the town boys' breaking and scattering fragments of glass in the roadway.

He presumably does desire Temple—possibly, as I've said, because the other men do, possibly because she is simply desirable as she flaunts her charms (which are particularly boyish, described as those of neither girl nor woman), running in and out of the rooms where the men are drinking, a constant advance and retreat, showing herself in varying degrees of undress. The corncob, the aggravated—the monstrous (or demonic)—aspect of the rape, is the result of Popeye's inability to perform while she taunts him with the words "Coward! Coward!" He could presumably have used his finger, but the corncob is a better simulation of his inoperative manhood and was perhaps provoked, as the nearest available object of aggression, by her taunt, "Coward!" Certainly it implies a violence and infliction of pain and indignity that is not called for; but that is also more monstrous to Faulkner and his readers than, in all probability, to Popeye. All it verifies about Popeye is the sociopath's inability to empathize.

One suspects, especially when the violence is perpetuated in Miss Reba's brothel in Memphis—refined into Popeye's watching Temple and Red as they make love—that Faulkner is recalling that prototypical scene in Richardson's *Clarissa* in which the virgin Clarissa is locked in Mrs. Sinclair's brothel, drugged, and raped by the rake Lovelace as the whores pass by the open door—sadism, violation, and voyeurism, the latter Popeye's but also the reader's; in both cases the scene is left to the imagination, the more powerful for being itself omitted from the narrative.[37]

The act is, of course, an abomination, a corruption of the normal sexual act, drawing upon fantasies of mutilation and contamination, the anxieties of which tend to be focused on genital injuries, indeed the conflation of the fears of rape and castration in Popeye and his corncob (violation and impotence) fulfilled in the second rape, the more terrible replay of Temple's in the fate of Lee Goodwin at the hands of the Jefferson lynch mob.[38]

We know that Faulkner set out to write a potboiler and that part of his intention was to shock; and it is obvious that so sophisticated an author as Faulkner carries the outrage perpetrated on Temple just to the point where the horrible borders the grotesque. Voyeurism is a form of evil teetering on the grotesque and the comic: First, Clarissa's rape witnessed by the whores who are passing by the open door; second, Rowlandson's ancient, impotent voyeurs; third, Faulkner's Popeye watching as Red makes love to Temple Drake.

The grotesque-to-slapstick appears most plainly in the scene that—without informing us of particulars—proves to be the funeral of Red, the lover Temple prefers to Popeye, whom Popeye has killed. The funeral turns into a free-for-all:

The bouncer whirled again and met the rush of the four men.
They mingled a second and flew out and skittered along the

floor on his back; the bouncer sprang free. Then he whirled and rushed them and in a whirling plunge they bore down upon the bier and crashed into it. The orchestra had ceased and were now climbing onto their chairs, with their instruments. The floral offerings flew; the coffin teetered. "Catch it!" a voice shouted. They sprang forward, but the coffin crashed heavily to the floor, coming open. The corpse tumbled slowly and sedately out and came to rest with its face in the center of a wreath.

"Play something!" the proprietor bawled, waving his arms; "play! Play!"

When they raised the corpse the wreath came too, attached to him by a hidden end of a wire driven into his cheek. He had worn a cap which, tumbling off, exposed a small blue hole in the center of his forehead. It had been neatly plugged with wax and was painted, but the wax had been jarred out and lost. They couldn't find it, but by unfastening the snap in the peak, they could draw the cap down to his eyes.[39]

The scene replays, in a comic register, the central action of penetration and withdrawal associated with Popeye and both Temple and Lee Goodwin; and the whole world of the brothel is, of course, highlighted by the respectable conversation of the whores, a burlesque of the genteel society of Jefferson, Mississippi ("I been running a house for twenty years but this is the first time I ever had anything like this goin on in it" [25.311]).

Popeye himself is a grotesque in a novel in which horror is played off against the interludes of comedy-burlesque, slapstick and buffoonery, with the sardonic and excruciating denouement in which Popeye, guilty of at least two murders, for one of which another man is punished, is hanged for a crime he did not commit, and Temple Drake ends sitting in the Luxembourg Gardens with her awful father. (From later evidence, we learn that she marries Gowan, the man who abandoned her to rape.)

The name Popeye, in 1931, evoked only one figure, the comic strip hero invented in 1929 by Ellie Segar—the Sailor Man. The resemblance ends with the name; the comic strip hero was a figure of strength, gained by eating spinach, faithful to his girlfriend, Olive Oyl, and in no way resembling Faulkner's character. The association with a popular comic strip character may have come from the gangster habit of picking up nursery names ("Baby Face" Nelson, "Legs" Diamond), but more likely simply makes the reader see him as something of a comic strip character—and so relates his action with the corncob, in its horrible way, to the comically brutal actions found in comic strips like "Popeye." Presumably it was Faulkner's private joke that the logo of Segar's Popeye was the corncob pipe he perpetually smoked.[40]

Popeye, then, is a grotesque, a character out of Dickens—a Fagin or Quilp but, significantly, without an Oliver or Little Nell. Temple Drake is not a Dickensian innocent, and Popeye is by no means the only guilty party in the rape. He is only the symbolic center, the instrument, or rather literally the holder of the instrument that is the symbolic center. When we examine the intention and the responsibility, the *who* is distanced from the *what*, the brutal act.

The most obviously guilty party is Gowan Stevens, the callow youth (unlike Temple, he is out of college) who places Temple in the lair of "evil," or rather of sex-hungry bootleggers, and leaves her to her fate. Gowan's problem is that he has accepted the belief, absorbed from his years at U. Virginia, that one proves he is a gentleman by how much drink he can hold. Because his proposal of marriage is rejected by the proper widow Narcissa Benbow Sartoris, he takes Temple out to a baseball game; but first he sees that the town boys have written Temple's name on the wall of a public lavatory, implying that she dates townies and provoking a need to prove himself superior to them in the only way he knows. He starts to drink, is drunk when he picks Temple up, and, in order to get more liquor, goes to the Old Frenchman's Place, continues to drink to prove himself, now to the moonshiners, eventually passes out, and in the morning leaves without seeing what has happened to his date. When he gets back to Jefferson he is penitent, but his guilt is felt not for leaving Temple to the lecherous moonshiners but only for his failure to hold his liquor (what he calls "unforgivable"); he has no feelings about Temple or what may have happened to her.

Gowan and Temple have intruded themselves upon the ordered—we should say, in Faulkner's terms, codified—community at the Old Frenchman's Place, disrupting it, putting honey before the bears, and the result is, expectably, rape and murder.

Temple is herself both victim and cause of her victimization, nearly as responsible as Popeye for the rape and Tommy's murder and the lynching of Goodwin—as she is, even more, responsible for Popeye's murder of Red when they have moved to Memphis. Like Gowan, she is unable to think outside the established ways of her group. Part of the code for the southern female was, Faulkner shows, to be provocative and flirtatious while fearing (or subconsciously desiring) contact with the lower orders, these gangsters. By not following Ruby's advice to get out and by running from room to room and displaying herself to the men, she is demonstrating ambivalence and in effect provoking the rape. When Popeye approaches her in the corn crib, as she relates the story to Horace Benbow, she fantasizes that she has changed into a boy, that she is wearing a medieval chastity belt, that she is dead, that she is a matronly (unattractive) schoolteacher, and then an old man with a long white beard: itself a comic series. And yet at the same time she is taunting Popeye, "Come on. Touch me. Touch me! You're a coward if you don't. Coward! Coward!" And, excitedly, "Something is happening to me." Hearing her story, Horace concludes that the self-confessed "victim" is "recounting the experience with actual pride, a sort of naive and impersonal vanity."

One effect the rape has on her is suggested by her eating habits once she is lodged in Miss Reba's brothel: "When she looked at the food [that is brought her] she found that she is not hungry at all, didn't even want to look at it," but soon she "took up a strip of potato gingerly in her fingers and ate it. She ate another, the unlighted cigarette in her other hand. Then she put the cigarette down and took up the knife and fork and began to eat, pausing from time to time to draw the gown up onto her shoulder" (18.187–88). In short, once started she eats and eats, and so it is once she experiences sex, to which she has been so brutally introduced.

The result of her ambivalence is that Temple contributes to the death of Tommy, causes Red to be killed (as she contributed to the death of her lover Frank earlier), kills Goodwin by giving false testimony at his trial (it is the rape, not the murder that causes the mob to lynch him), crushes the lawyer who tries to help her, and indirectly kills Popeye by her taunts and rejection, her attachment to the virile Red. Why in the courtroom does she not identify Popeye instead of the innocent Lee Goodwin? She sees her father at the back of the courtroom, and Popeye was, in relation to Red, her "daddy," as her real father the judge was to her earlier love Frank. And it is her father who claims her when she has finished her testimony and carries her away with him.

The stain of guilt does not end with Gowan and Temple (and Temple's father). Lee Goodwin can be blamed for failing to prevent the rape and, indeed, for (the indirect evidence suggests) contemplating his own ravishing of Temple. He has set down the rule (part of the Frenchman's Place code) that there can be no women besides his wife, Ruby, and he makes gestures of complaint when Temple appears, but he does not carry through on them, perhaps because of his own intentions—which Temple may have reflected when, in court, she lies and points the finger at Lee and not Popeye. It can be argued that if Popeye had not preempted the opportunity that morning, Lee might have carried out his plan, understood by his complaisant wife, who anticipates the rape, advises Temple to get out, offers her ways, but then simply walks away. Indeed, she seems to be preparing Temple for the onset of Lee when she tells her, "Lee says hit wont hurt you none. All you got to do is lay down" (13.118). Only Tommy, the retarded black, knows enough to see what may happen and has enough moral sense to protect Temple by following her and standing guard over her until Popeye kills him.

Faulkner gives us an action—brutal, symbolic, grotesque—and the actors who (the *who* to the *what*) are almost all in one way or another, in one degree or another, guilty or responsible for its happening—supplementing the Gothic melodrama, the all-too-ostensible guilt of the demonic Popeye. Intention as well as responsibility is obscured, as we have seen. The only "evil" intention, as opposed to preventive intention, is on the part of Popeye—and perhaps, though not fulfilled, of Lee Goodwin. Certainly a deliberate, conscious, intended evil is countered at the Old Frenchman's Place by mere animal lust—and, in Jefferson, by the self-interest and respectability of Narcissa and, when she finally returns to the courthouse, Temple and her father the judge, who has already been demonstrated to share the code of Gowan Stevens: he has killed Temple's first love, Frank—or rather, Temple, understanding her father's code, and Frank's observance of the code, has brought them together in much the way she later brings together at the dance hall, with equally fatal consequences, Popeye and Red.

Popeye's demonism is further compromised by what the reader suspects throughout and, in the last chapter, learns about his hereditary syphilis and insanity (father and grandmother), which prevents him from making any sort of meaningful contact, either physical or social, with other people. The doctor says of Popeye the child, "He will never be a man, properly speaking. With care he will live some time longer" (31.369). In the original sense of evil, the evil of *Sanctuary* is impotence, the genetic and social harm, injury, misfortune, disease, etc. of the Problem of Evil. Popeye was a monster but, in an endnote, Faulkner attributes it to nature and nurture, genes and society, responsible for his birth defects and his subsequent aberrant behavior. Popeye was a monster, and Faulkner, at the very end of the novel, demystifies him: takes up the subject of how he was made (a Frankenstein monster): by society, which convicts him for a crime he didn't do while killing the wrong man for his own crime, but which, together with his parents, was responsible for his birth defects and his subsequent aberrant behavior; and by his own twisted psychopathology. By adding this endnote, Faulkner was writing and righting his novel in the age of Marx and Freud: though we may suspect that Popeye's congenital syphilis and madness are less a social explanation than a stain extending and enlarging the grotesque idea of evil that is Popeye; or it is a displacement of the mystery of evil onto an understandable explanation.

Popeye's responsibility—his centrality—is notably compromised by the parallels Faulkner suggests with Horace Benbow, the true southern gentleman, who does his best to uphold the code; who, consequently, and unlike the isolated figure of Popeye, wills his own isolation. When he appears, the first respectable visitor to the Old Frenchman's Place, he is disillusioned with his marriage: What determined him to leave home, he claims, was his weekly chore picking up and carrying home a dripping package of smelly shrimp (presumably Faulkner's sly allusion to the odor demotically associated with women); but in fact it is his jealousy of his stepdaughter Little Belle and his obsession with the grape arbor where she carries on flirtations with the local men. Sitting on opposite sides of the spring near the Old Frenchman's Place, Horace and Popeye, one with his book and the other with his gun, are both men fixated (before and prospectively) on young pubescent girls, in particular voyeuristically fixated; and Horace, when he hears Temple tell her story of Popeye's first touching her body, associates the two in a way that implicates him in Popeye's voyeuristic fantasy—the rape of a composite Temple-Little Belle:

Then he knew what that sensation in his stomach meant. He put the photograph [of Little Belle] down hurriedly and went to

the bathroom. He opened the door running and fumbled at
the light. But he had not time to find it and he gave over and
plunged forward and struck the lavatory and leaned upon his
braced arms while the shucks set up a terrific uproar beneath
her thighs [Temple's]. Lying with her head lifted slightly, her
chin depressed like a figure lifted down from a crucifix, she
watched something black and furious go roaring out of her
pale body. She was bound naked on her back on a flat car [the
train in which Little Belle had met the one of her men friends
Horace was chiding her for before he left Kinston] moving at
speed through a black tunnel, the blackness streaming in rigid
threads overhead, a roar of iron wheels in her ears. The car
shot bodily from the tunnel in a long upward slant, the darkness overhead now shredded with parallel attenuations of living fire, toward a crescendo like a held breath, an interval in
which she would swing faintly and lazily in nothingness filled
with pale, myriad points of light. Far beneath her she could
hear the faint, furious uproar of the shucks. (23.268)

Finally, Benbow's sister Narcissa, who opposes Horace's marrying a
married/divorced woman with child, and then, even worse, leaving her,
represents female respectability, the code of social decorum. She has set
her cap for Gowan, the "gentleman," but he is too young. Her "moral
values" are opposed to the "sin" of the other characters, to the drink (Prohibition, the Volstead Act), prostitution, sex, rape, and murder that are
embodied in the Old Frenchman's Place (associated with Grant, Vicksberg,
and the great antebellum plantations [1.6–7]) and Miss Reba's brothel; both
of which have a vitality and integrity that in fact she, and her degeneration
of the code, lacks. Narcissa is summed up in her assertion to her brother
Horace: "I don't see that it makes any difference who did it. The question
is, are you going to stay mixed up with it?" But, like Jason Compson and
the Snopses, Narcissa acts while Horace, the truer embodiment of the
code, only talks.

So there is the monster Popeye and then there is the society, which
convicts him for a crime he didn't do, the wrong crime, and kills the wrong
man for this crime (the innocent man lynched for Popeye's crime). Then
there is Temple Drake, who accuses the same man wrongly of the rape

she knows Popeye committed on her; and her boyfriend, whose carelessness (he gets drunk and leaves his girlfriend in the lion's cage) permitted
her rape and so all the subsequent evils. Thus, first the psycho-sociopath
Popeye, the ostensible center of evil, and then the "respectable" southern
gentleman and belle, and the society they represent, which includes the
Narcissa Benbows. Popeye *is* evil—as opposed to the Harlot, who was not,
whose crimes were victimless sins, in Faulkner's scheme a role assumed
by the innocent bootlegger and womanizer "criminal," who suffers for
Popeye's crimes.

Sin is no longer an issue. The word appears only in the context of
religiosity: The preacher, denouncing Ruby and Lee Goodwin, preaches
"that Goodwin and the woman should both be burned as a sole example to
that child [their unborn baby]; the child to be reared and taught the English
language for the sole need of being taught that it was begot in sin by two
people who suffered by fire for having begot it" (17.151). Benbow attaches
the word *sin* to the Little Belle of his imagination ("face suddenly older in
sin than he would ever be," 19.200), and God appears only when Benbow
says he believes God to be a gentleman, as presumably Gowan also does.
But the word *evil* is applied to Popeye by Benbow, who says, "Dammit, say
what you want to, but there's a corruption about even looking upon evil,
even by accident; you cannot haggle, traffic, with putrefaction—" (17.152),
and earlier, though he does not use the word, he is describing something
more than wrongdoing when he refers to "Popeye's black presence lying
upon the house like the shadow of something no larger than a match falling monstrous and portentous upon something else otherwise familiar
and everyday and twenty times its size . . . and Popeye somewhere in the
outer darkness peaceful with insects and frogs yet filled too with Popeye's
presence in black and nameless threat" (16.143).

The descriptions are portentous, vague, and reminiscent of Conrad's
discourse of evil in *Heart of Darkness*. The words describe the sort of
atavism Kurtz found and became part of, and corruption is the form evil
takes in *Sanctuary*, symbolized by the congenital syphilitic Popeye and
by the title itself, as "sanctuary" is in every case a degeneracy of the concept, most obviously in the Old Frenchman's Place, but also Miss Reba's
brothel, Horace Benbow's home in Kinston, to which he returns at the
end—the jails in which Lee and Popeye end their days—and even the
Luxembourg Gardens where we last see Temple guarded by her father (her

other Popeye, "daddy"), as unhappy a situation as Horace's back "home" with Belle and Little Belle.

The Compsons and the Snopses

Faulkner wrote that Jason Compson, of *The Sound and the Fury* (1929), was the person "who to me represented complete evil. He's the most vicious character in my opinion I ever thought of."[41] In terms of doing-evil, Jason's acts are merely mean and nasty—"vicious"—and in varying degrees cruel. The black boy Luster, who cares for Benjy, wants to see a show; Jason taunts him with the tickets and finally throws them in the fire; he cheats his niece Quentin of the money her mother sends her for her maintenance; he even, in his extreme meanness, takes fifty dollars from her mother, his sister Caddy, to let her see Quentin (her illegitimate daughter) and then reneges.

His worst, most violent (Popeye-like) actions are directed at his brother Benjy. When Benjy, the idiot youngest Compson, becomes a burden, Jason first has him castrated and then, when Mrs. Compson has died, packs him off to the insane asylum. I suppose we have to see the castration of Benjy in terms of its motive, which is simply selfishness and lack of feeling—compared to the castration of Joe Christmas in *Light in August,* which is based on racial hatred. But Benjy is the ultimate innocent—and we might note that *The Sound and the Fury* ends with Jason beating the horse that is carrying Benjy around the town square (the tortured animal topos); the driver, Luster, has directed the horse the wrong way around the square, thus causing the idiot Benjy to howl—his "sound and fury signifying nothing"—and Jason to translate his anger to the innocent animal.

Popeye's was an unambiguously cruel, indeed monstrous act, but Faulkner showed how diffused was the responsibility for the act, how dependent on the eye of the beholder. Jason's acts are unambiguously nasty, petty, and, in the innocent Benjy's case, cruel. But Faulkner (in this respect close behind James in *The Turn of the Screw*) is defining evil as ungentlemanly behavior, the violation of a postbellum southern code of honor. Jason represents the corruption of the Compson family and what it originally stood for—which was the Scottish clan, the lost battle of Culloden, Sir Walter Scott, the southern code of honor, the Civil War (also lost), the building of Jefferson, Mississippi, etc.—what Faulkner correctly regards as a largely fatal illusion but at any rate a sort of ideal that is corrupted by the influx and rise of the Snopses and by the Snopsifying of Jason, whose name misleadingly associates him with the Argonauts and the quest for the Golden Fleece.

Jason is worse than the Snopses because he inherited the code of the ante- and postbellum Compsons, even perpetuated by his brother and sister in their way (even his other, idiot brother Benjy), but degenerates into a Snopes. That is, he is the only Compson who can compete with the Snopses on their own terms, down to the pettiest (of a letter, "Send it collect"); which in other terms means with the practical world, to which their code has closed them off.

Finally, Jason sells the Compsons' "ancestral house" and turns out the faithful old retainer Dilsey. But when he speaks to young Quentin, "I don't care what you do, myself. . . . But I've got a position in this town, and I'm not going to have any member of my family going on like a nigger wench" (207), he sounds like Narcissa Benbow Sartoris telling Horace that the family name is more important than whether the guilty party hangs for the death of a black.

George Marion O'Donnell, in his seminal essay "Faulkner's Mythology" of 1939, first noted the connection between the Old South tradition of chivalry with orthodox religious belief—and the losing battle being waged between this (the Narcissa aspect of *Sanctuary*) and the amoral world of the Snopes family. The orthodox religious belief in sin is embodied in *The Sound and the Fury* in Quentin Compson:

> The rest of his family have either succumbed entirely to the Snopes world, like Jason Compson, or else have drugs to isolate them from it—Mr. Compson his fragments of philosophy, uncle Maury his liquor, Mrs. Compson her religion and her invalidism, Benjy his idiocy. . . . When he [Quentin] discovers that his sister Candace has been giving herself to the town boys of Jefferson, Mississippi [as Gowan discovers that Temple has], and is pregnant, he attempts to change her situation by telling their father that he has committed incest with her. It is a key incident. Quentin is attempting to transform Candace's yielding to the amorality of the Snopes world into a sin, within the Sartoris [and Compson] morality; but the means he employs

are more nearly pseudo-traditional and romantic than traditional; and he fails.[42]

As O'Donnell notes, Quentin tells his father the lie that he has committed
incest with his sister Caddie in order to protect the appearance of sin—and
the Christian old chivalric ideal as against the reality of the local men with
whom she has slept—the amoral Snopes ethos in which she has lost her
Compson self. So, the Compsons are saying, it is better to be damned than
to just fornicate with the lower orders: a class transgression, but at bottom
deeply Augustinian (and Pascalian), the idea that the City of God (soul,
interior, salvation) is all that matters, not the City of man or morality. But
the old southern ethos of the Compsons also equals the Christian sense
of sin as drinking, gaming, idiocy, suicide, chivalry—vs. the evil of the
local poor white trash, the carpetbaggers from the North.

In short, in the Faulkner chivalric world sin is sex, evil is rape, betrayal, torture, and killing. But the important term is abomination—the
perversion and corruption of the ethos of the Old South in *Sanctuary* by
the Stevenses, the Snopses, Temple Drake, and her father; in *Sound and the
Fury* by Jason Compson.[43] The sin is corruption, decline, and perversion of
an ideal (though a questionable one) in the past. The elaborate diffusion
of guilt in *Sanctuary* amounts to the Compsons against the Snopses, the
Old South against the New, as laid out in *The Sound and the Fury.*

4. PINKIE BROWN AND IDA ARNOLD: GRAHAM GREENE

Brighton Rock: *Sin Romanticized*

> While there is something humdrum about being bad, and an irritat-
> ing banality in the act of doing wrong, high drama can be achieved
> with the words "sinning" and "evil." Greene indulged himself by
> casting his actions in these terms. Right and wrong did not much
> interest him, but good and evil did. He was a sucker for diablerie.
>
> —*Paul Theroux,* New York Times Book Review

The ending of *Brighton Rock* (1938) takes and, with a turn of the screw,
rewrites the ending of *The Heart of Darkness,* a work Graham Greene regarded with reverence.[44] Marlow calls upon Kurtz's Intended back in Brussels, and she asks for Kurtz's last words—"'Repeat them,' she murmured

in a heart-broken tone. 'I want—I want—something—something—to—live with'"; he does not tell her that his last words were, "The horror, the horror." He lies to her: "'The last word he pronounced was—your name.'" Her response to the lie is a "cry of inconceivable triumph and of unspeakable pain. 'I knew it—I was sure!' . . . She knew. She was sure."[45]

At the end of *Brighton Rock* Rose, still devoted to Pinkie after his death, believing she is at least carrying his child, goes to play the message he recorded for her at her insistence on the gramophone, which the reader knows was, "God damn you, you little bitch, why can't you go back home for ever and let me be?" (6.1.236):

> She turned out on to the front opposite the Palace Pier and began to walk firmly away from the direction of her home toward Frank's. There was something to be salvaged from that house and room, something else they wouldn't be able to get over—his voice speaking a message to her: if there was a child, speaking to the child. 'If he loved you,' the priest had said, 'that shows . . .' She walked rapidly in the thin June sunlight towards the worst horror of all. (7.11.333)

Greene is also remembering Faulkner's *Sanctuary* of half a dozen years earlier. Pinkie is another Popeye, the same stunted shape, infantile, called throughout "the Boy"; he doesn't drink and is a crack shot—though he smokes and toward the end is induced to drink. But unlike Popeye he is a sadist: "He sat there, anger like a live coal in his belly, as the music came on again: all the good times he'd had in the old days with nails and splinters: the tricks he'd learnt later with a razor blade: what would be the fun if people didn't squeal?" (2.1.65). For Pinkie "the finest of all sensations [is], the infliction of pain" (4.1.134). When he sees the strip of sticking-plaster on Spicer's cheek, "he watched it from the doorway with rising cruelty: he wanted to tear it away and see the skin break" (5.1.159). Unlike Pinkie and Rose, Popeye had, after all, some sort of a relationship with, some feelings for, Temple. In Pinkie's pocket is not a gun (as with Popeye) but a bottle of vitriol with its associations of pain and disfigurement. He recalls the anarchist is Conrad's *Secret Agent* (another of Greene's favorite novels), who always carries a bomb attached to his person ready to be detonated, to blow up himself and all around. It is the vitriol bottle Pinkie "caressed"—a substitute for a woman (2.1.63).

From Mr. Jones in *Victory* Pinkie gets his hatred of women and of sex and marriage (the two-backed beast [2.1.58, 62]), but the difference lies, aside from Mr. Jones being a gentleman, in the fact that Pinkie is one of two main centers of consciousness in *Brighton Rock,* and so we know what we never knew about either Popeye or Mr. Jones. His hatred/fear of sex comes from the "frightening weekly exercise of his parents which he watched from his single bed . . . the Saturday night movements from the other bed . . . the horrifying sound of *pleasurable pain.* He was filled with hatred, disgust, loneliness: he was completely abandoned: he had no share in their thoughts—for the space of a few minutes he was dead, he was like a soul in purgatory watching the shameless act of a beloved person" (3.3.117, 121, and 4.1.132).

In the long run his problem turns out to be lack of experience ("a horrifying ignorance. . . . He'd never yet kissed a girl" [121]), and the same is true of Rose: He is consistently "the Boy" and Rose is "the girl" (lowercase), and opposite them—the other center of consciousness—is "the woman," Ida Arnold, who is experience personified. In *Sanctuary* Temple was "the child," while Ruby Goodwin was always "the woman," the generic designation; Temple is not quite girl, not quite woman, and she and Gowan are, by the best interpretation, children; and indeed, Popeye, we learn at the end, was never more than a child. And yet Tommy, also in his way childlike, was the one person who nevertheless behaved in a moral way.

In *Brighton Rock* there is sin and wrongdoing. Pinkie Brown is the sinner—and Rose Wilson, who loves him, accepts him and joins him in prospective damnation. Both are Roman Catholic, and their discourse is of heaven and hell, good and evil; their imaginations are primitive Catholic, based on the most popular elements—images, incense, and the rest (the "plastic statues with the swords in the bleeding heart"). On the other side is Ida Arnold, who believes not in good and evil but in right and wrong—actions, not sin, faith, or predestination.

Ordinary expectations would require Pinkie to represent Satanic negation (Christian evil), with hatred of sex and love of cruelty (however explained) set against the ideal of Ida's life force; but in *Brighton Rock* Greene simply opposes them, leading us to expect a middle term but none appears; and he tends to denigrate Ida.

His tone whenever he refers to Ida is acrid: When she says, "I want justice," Greene adds, "the woman cheerfully remarked, as if she were ordering a pound of tea. Her big prosperous carnal face hung itself with smiles." Her campaign to indict Pinkie is compared to "warships cleared for action and bombing fleets [that take] flight between the set eyes and the stubborn mouth. It was like the map of a campaign marked with flags" (7.1.263, 267). If Pinkie's imagery is theological, of salvation and damnation, Ida's is of an extreme banality: right and wrong are, for her, fun ("you're only doing it because it's fun" [7.6.299]), exciting, close to what Pinkie refers to as a game. "You're a terrible woman, Ida," her friend Clarence says at the end (7.10.328).

Ida's god is very different from Pinkie's: "God didn't mind a bit of human nature—what he minded—and her brain switched away from Phil [Corkery] in pants to her mission, to doing good, to seeing that the evil suffered" (5.6.201). She says to Rose, who shares Pinkie's beliefs, "Now let's talk sensible, dear. I'm here for your own good. You got to be saved. Why—" (7.1.264). What Ida means by "saved" emerges when she tells us whom she has saved—"a man she had once pulled out of the sea when she was a young woman," and there is "the money to a blind beggar, and the kind word in season to the despairing schoolgirl in the Strand" (7.7.300). She is associated with (as Pinkie is alienated from) the secular world of Brighton—luxury hotels, fortune-telling machines, popular fiction (which she keeps in her flat), and the two-valve receiving sets. She is all nature, defined by her big breasts: she is, or at least tries to be, a mother, a sanctuary, a Mae West.[46] Her favorite song, a music hall ballad, is, "One night in an alley Lord Rothschild said to me," and her lusty vulgarity is summed up for Greene in images of digestion. Indigestion is one of Greene's symbols; Ida's belching, the result of her beer-drinking, is contrasted with the guilty indigestion of the lawyer Prewitt—and Pinkie's unsettled stomach whenever he thinks of sex.

Sin for Pinkie is having sex with a woman you haven't married in a church (with the sacrament)—a mortal sin; while murdering several people is something else—of less concern to this particular Roman Catholic, a wrong vs. a right. Pinkie's assumptions are simply based on the Catholic religion and Ida's on ideas of social morality—in fact Pinkie's are based more on the Old than the New Testament: there is no Christ and Jesus here, but only the church and the priests. Pinkie's hell is "the slash of razor blades infinitely prolonged" (4.1.144).

But Ida's God is related to Pinkie's in this one respect: "An eye for an eye, Phil," she tells Corkery (3.1.99). The vestiges of her religious life remain as demotic superstition. She believes in ghosts and employs ouija boards.[47] She believes in racing tips and fortune machines, and what funds her detective activities is the winning of the horse Black Boy on the tip of Hale, the murdered man.

Her persistence and pursuit of Pinkie (presumably based on her vestiges of *lex talionis*), coming close to obsession, recall Schomberg's pursuit of Heyst, with consequences as deadly as Schomberg's. As Greene and the people around her see her, she is a busybody, and the final consequence of her busybodying is that Rose goes back to her "mother and dad" (as Temple Drake went back to her father and brothers)—and to the gramophone record: *would* she have been better dead?

Pinkie is without empathy except in matters of religion: "The word murder conveyed no more to him than the word 'box,' 'collar,' 'giraffe'": "The imagination hadn't awoken. That was his strength. He couldn't see through other people's eyes, or feel with their nerves. Only the [church] music made him uneasy, the catgut vibrating in the heart" (2.1.56). It is church music that touches him, memories from his childhood: "'Why I was in a choir once,' the Boy confided and suddenly he began to sing softly in his spoilt boy's voice: 'Agnus dei qui tollis peccata mundi, dona nobis pacem.' In his voice a whole lost world moved—the lighted corner below the organ, the smell of incense and laundered surplices, and the music"; though, he adds, "any music moved him, speaking of things he didn't understand"—but this refers to the Latin ritual of the Roman church (2.1.66).

Unlike Popeye or Mr. Jones, Pinkie is obsessed with salvation-damnation and therefore with sin. Greene associates him (as he did at the beginning with Hale, Pinkie's first victim) with the Seven Deadly Sins, in particular with the sin of pride, but also envy and anger. Pinkie's chief motivation is pride and ambition—his "scared pride. He knew what he was good at: he was the top: there was no limit to his ambition." Even his lust is "scared lust" (with which he watches Rose) because lust is one of the Seven Deadly Sins. But his pride and envy center on the Cosmopolitan Hotel, where the gang chief Colleoni lives, and when he seeks a room there for his honeymoon night he is turned down: "He had an insane impulse to shout out to them all that they couldn't treat him like that, that he was a killer, he could kill men and not be caught. He wanted to boast. He could afford that place as well as anyone: he had a car, a lawyer, two hundred pounds in the bank" (6.2.232). When the sleek, expensive cars "rolled smoothly past them" in his old Morris, on his way to fulfill the suicide pact with Rose, he is outraged: "They were upper-class, they'd learned that tankard trick in class hotels: he watched their gambits with hatred" as they compare speeds—"I think we touched eighty." "I made it eighty-two" (7.6.305, 7.9.319).

Pinkie recalls more and more church/liturgical phrases as his crimes spiral downward from killing Hale (a stoolie, who caused Kite's death) to his friend Spicer, and to Rose, who loves him—the Dantean vortex leading down to the ninth circle. At the end Pinkie, who contemplates burning in hell and has told his old schoolmate Piker, "I'm not afraid . . . of burning" (6.2.231), does indeed "burn," by way of his vitriol bottle intended for the faces of others. He goes over the cliff and falls: "They couldn't even hear a splash. It was as if he'd been withdrawn suddenly by a hand out of any existence—past or present, whipped way into zero—nothing," as if he were one of those Faust figures, perhaps Don Giovanni, who has sold his soul and his time is up.

Seen from one angle, he descends into Dantean evil and Dantean hell; from another he, in fact the "Boy," cannot get at the real, strong evil. Colleoni killed Pinkie's boss, mentor, and substitute father, the gang leader Kite, but Pinkie goes after neither Colleoni nor any of his gang, but only poor Hale (an easy scapegoat), whom he stalks, taunts, tortures, and kills. The Dantean echoes seem mock-heroic (as they often did in Eliot), and appropriately the weapon he uses to kill Hale, a stick of Brighton Rock, is the "sweet" of a seventeen-year-old "Boy." He kills Hale "by turning a child's sweet into a murder weapon"[48]—which hardly lives up to the razor that killed Kite. He carries a razor himself but, when he is attacked by Colleoni's men at the race track, cannot make efficient use of it. After Hale he makes no further attempts at the Colleoni mob, turning instead against his own men (one by one) in order to cover for the murder of Hale, and this comes to include Rose, who knows that Spicer was only posing as Hale at the table in Snow's. The formidable opponent, Ida Arnold, he never touches.

What is "evil" about Pinkie is his sin (religion and thoughts of damnation), not his actions, which are all expedient, following from the death of Kite—revenge and then to cover his steps; what is in the ordinary sense evil is his relationship with Rose, and this comes down to his/their lack of knowledge and experience except in the narrowest sense. Ignorance, lack of experience, not stupidity; rather, in the Roman Catholic context, asceticism and a literal understanding of the Seven Deadly Sins—religious nostalgia—these are the sources of Pinkie's evil. For example, he has not had the experience to know that love is not the two-backed beast he overheard every weekend of his childhood, and so when Rose says she has been in love, his response is, "'You're green. You don't know what people do. . . . You're innocent. . . . You don't know anything'" (2.1.64–65). It is, of course, Pinkie who knows nothing.

Ida Arnold, "the woman," on the other hand, knows everything; she bases her conclusions on evidence: "'You're young. You don't know things like I do,'" she tells Rose, who replies,

> "There's things *you* don't know." She brooded darkly by the bed, while the woman argued on: a god wept in a garden and cried out upon a cross. . . . "I know one thing you don't. I know the difference between Right and Wrong. They didn't teach you *that* at school."
>
> Rose didn't answer; the woman was quite right; the two words meant nothing to her. Their taste was extinguished by stronger foods—Good and Evil. The woman could tell her nothing she didn't know about these—she knew by tests as clear as mathematics that Pinkie was evil—what did it matter in that case whether he was right or wrong?
>
> "You're crazy," the woman said. "I don't believe you'd lift a finger if he was killing you."
>
> Rose came slowly back to the outer world—"greater love hath no man than this." She said: "Perhaps I wouldn't. I don't know. But perhaps. . . ." (7.1.267–68)

The Roman Catholic theology represents the "things *you* don't know"—Rose's innocence and ignorance but also her total love for Pinkie even if, or because, he is damned, are set against Ida's knowledge, evidence, common sense, and belief in right and wrong and a kind of justice.

Pinkie hasn't had, experienced, or known sex or drink or love. When he says he is "haunted by his ignorance" (7.1.272) he means ignorance of the practical world—the world of Colleoni as well as of Dallow and Spicer: "Other people's feelings bored at his brain: he had never before felt this desire to understand" (272). In the terms of such knowledge, Spicer "*knew too much*" and had to be killed. Dallow too: "Like Spicer he knew too much: but what he knew was far more deadly than what Spicer had known. Spicer had known only the kind of thing which brought you to the dock, but Dallow knew what your mirror and your bed sheets knew: the secret fear and the humiliation" (5.4.197–98). This is also the knowledge of Ida Arnold.

Greene internalizes sin—it is something inside one—or Pinkie externalizes it in the candles and statues: He associates Pinkie with a sense of sin but also with acts of evil, and these he opposes to the banal goodness, the good deeds of Ida. Greene is clearly interested in sin; whereas good works, he believes, do more harm—leading ultimately to the catastrophic "good works" of the liberal American in *The Quiet American* (1955), Greene's version of James's *The American*.

Innocence and Depravity

In 1979 Greene wrote to Marie-Francoise Allain, "I don't think that Pinkie was guilty of mortal sin because his actions were not committed *in defiance of God,* but *arose out of the conditions to which he had been born*"—that is, because of his social background (like Popeye); by inference, by his Roman Catholic upbringing.

Pinkie parodies the lines on childhood from Wordsworth's "Ode on Intimations of Immortality" when he says that "Hell lay about him in his infancy" (2.2.88):

> But trailing clouds of glory do we come
> From God, who is our home;
> Heaven lies about us in our infancy!

Pinkie's sadism is compensation for the suffering of an abandoned child; for the death of his father/hero Kite (possibly a homosexual attachment).[49] But compare Rose, who is unaffected by her similar environment. Rose says, "Life's not so bad," but the Boy answers, "Don't you believe it . . . I'll tell you what it is. It's gaol; it's not knowing where to get some money. Worms and cataract, cancer. You hear 'em shrieking from the upper windows—children being born. It's dying slowly" (7.7.304). Pinkie returns to Nelson Place, near where he was born: He sees "a child with a leg in an iron brace limp[ing] blindly into him; he pushed it off; someone said in a high treble, 'Stick 'em up.'"

Pinkie is rehearsing the Problem of Evil in the world, which we may be led to believe drives him, as it did Augustine, to Manichaeism. He does not believe in a hell after death but here and now as a condition of human life. "Why, this is Hell, nor are we out of it," the shabby lawyer Prewitt says, quoting Marlowe's Mephistophilis' words to Faustus (7.3.281). Life is "horror without end," "Saturday nights: and then the birth, the child, habit and hate." And then: "He looked across the tables: the woman's *laughter* [i.e., Ida's] was like defeat." For Rose, life is hell and damnation, having her cake in *this* world, not the next (7.7.301; 7.1.254, 262).

Greene is making a statement about children, for his story is essentially that of two teenagers; theologically he is demonstrating with the example of Pinkie that "evil is not necessarily something which comes with age and experiences: It exists, it is there at any age"[50]—even in children (both are "children"). Speaking of children, the evil of vs. the suffering done to, Greene wrote in a movie review of a film called *These Three*, 1 May 1936,

> These three [adult characters] represent innocence in an evil world—the world of childhood, the world of moral chaos, lies, brutality, complete inhumanity. Never before has childhood been represented so convincingly on the screen, with an authenticity guaranteed by one's own memories. *The more than human evil* of the lying sadistic child is suggested with quite shocking mastery. . . . It has enough truth and intensity to stand for the whole of the dark side of childhood.[51] (emphasis added)

Like Bataille, Greene connects childhood/innocence/disinterestedness with *evil*—with Bataille's locus for evil, because the child is "in revolt against the world of Good, against the adult world, and committed, in his revolt, to the side of Evil."[52] Greene's children, Pinkie and Rose, and his overgrown boy Harry Lime, are forces of Bataille's childish evil.

Greene was looking for evil where he could find it. In his interpretation of Henry James, he exposes the Jamesian evil of exploitation, engrossment, and betrayal. His notorious essay on Beatrix Potter attempts to turn her children's books into Jamesian novels whose subject is evil. It is hard to say to what extent this was a Rochesterian send-up and to what extent an insight into what is rather sinister about her stories, what to him made them important. In Potter's *The Tale of Mr. Tod* there is, of course, Mr. Tod, the gentleman fox, and Tommy Brock, the dirty, vulgar badger, who steals Flopsy's baby rabbits; Brock puts them in the oven while he takes a nap, intending to bake them; the ending, Tod and Brock fighting, shows how the evil fall out among themselves and the innocent escape.

Mr. Tod (both the Lake District name for a fox and the German, *Todt*, for death) is the grotesque-human animal, who would not feel out of place in the company of Mr. Jones, Ricardo, and Pedro, let alone Pinkie. There are also, like the baby rabbits, the innocents, Heyst and Lena and Rose, but in the children's story a happy ending. In *Jemima Puddle-Duck*, there is Mr. Tod again, Jemima's eggs, her folly, the collie, and the foxhounds to the rescue. But, as in one of Greene's plots, the latter, after chasing away Mr. Tod, eat the eggs; Jemima has another batch, though most don't survive —she's not a good sitter. The damage is collateral and marginalized but taken note of. In fairy-tales evil takes the obvious Mr. Tod-Jones form of a giant, dragon, or witch, with often a wicked stepmother who serves the role of Schomberg vis-à-vis the evil trio in *Victory*.

Greene and Eliot

Greene wrote of W. Somerset Maugham, a novelist who in some ways covered the same territory, "Creative art seems to remain a function of the religious mind. Maugham the agnostic is forced to minimize—pain, vice, the importance of his fellowmen. He cannot believe in a god who punishes and he cannot *therefore* believe in the importance of a human action. . . . Rob human beings of their infernal importance, and you rob your characters of their individuality" (emphasis added).[53] He refers to Maugham's "indifference to the gravest of human matters"—by which he means "mortal sin," as opposed to good or harmful acts, right or wrong (the world of Ida).

Is Greene expressing Roman Catholic theology or (as Swift did in his *Tale of a Tub*) Pinkie's perversion of it? The dichotomy on which Greene builds *Brighton Rock* is religious discourse against secular; or the religious mind, centered on God, against the secular, concerned with life only; or religion with the fear that faith is being reduced to morality; or the relations exclusively between God and man against those between man and man. The former terms are associated with Pinkie, the latter with Ida. The first are, to focus on Greene's vocabulary and his borrowings from T. S.

Eliot, essentially Jansenist; the second roughly Pelagian, or the orthodoxy of the common Roman Catholic, Anglican, and many others. The first is condemned by the Roman Church and by most of the Protestant churches, though Jansenism emerged originally as a Counter-Reformation response to Calvinism. Ida is the Pelagian do-gooder. Pelagius denied original sin, arguing that we are capable of striving for perfection by our own unaided efforts—for Pelagius this meant a life of renunciation and asceticism, but for more moderate Pelagians like Ida this meant the ability to make choices between good and evil.

The Waste Land is about what Eliot refers to as internal evil, or sin— and the sin of acedia (sloth) or even the worst sin, despair: and the fragments shored up are all concerned with religious belief now lost. The worst the Waste Landers do is have joyless sex and fall far short of Tristan and Isolde's love, which was suicidal but at least based on passion (though, of course, the result of a drug). Greene's subject is evil, and he continues to use the basic model of The Waste Land with its juxtaposition of aridity with damnation and salvation—Conrad's rotting and burning. Behind this is Eliot's insistence that the writer needs a belief, a myth, something commonly held (unlike the private myth of Blake), and Greene chooses the same myth Eliot adopted, going Eliot one better, converting not just to the Church of England but to Roman Catholicism.

Greene was also aware that Eliot had made clear in the late twenties in book reviews in The Criterion that he was addicted to murder mysteries—and the potential of the conflation was obvious to him. Before Pinkie there was the Paddington killer in It's a Battlefield (1934). Called the Salvationist, he keeps saying to himself—or to some unseen audience, "'Come to Jesus. . . . Oh, I've sinned too, friends, believe me, I've sinned too. . . . I've been as big a sinner as any of you. But I've come to Jesus and I've been forgiven. . . . Oh, if you only knew, my friends, the sweetness of forgiveness, the balm, the peace.'"[54] Then he kills.

The Jansenist of the seventeenth century, like the Lutheran and Calvinist of the same period, believed that grace is a gift of God, unaffected by the individual's actions. "Dilige et quod vult fac," "Love [God] and do what you will"; "good works" will necessarily follow from true faith. Luther: "Esto peccator et pecca fortiter"—"Be a sinner and sin strongly, . . . but more strongly have faith and rejoice in Christ."[55] This, in Greene's time, was quite different from the orthodox Catholic view that good acts, including taking the sacraments, confession, etc., whatever their motivation (Augustine's distrust of), can contribute to the individual's salvation.

Greene's source, as he showed by the epigraph for *The Heart of the Matter* (1948), was Charles Péguy, a radical Catholic killed in the First World War and much admired by Eliot: "Le pécheur est au coeur même de chrétienté," "The sinner is at the very heart of Christianity." Greene is drawing on Eliot's essay of 1930 on Charles Baudelaire:

> So far as we are human, what we do must be either evil or good; so far as we do evil or good, we are human; and it is better, in a paradoxical way, to do evil than to do nothing: at least, we exist. It is true to say that the glory of man is his capacity for salvation; it is also true to say that his glory is his capacity for damnation. The worst that can be said of most of our malefactors, from statesmen to thieves, is that they are not men enough to be damned.[56]

Both Eliot and Greene have in mind (as Eliot shows by his epigraph to "The Hollow Men") the company directors versus Kurtz; Greene has Ida versus Pinkie and Rose—rotting or burning. Greene quoted Eliot again at the end of his third essay on Frederick Rolfe, that great sinner, on sin as a conduit to salvation: "Most people are only a very little alive; and to awaken them to the spiritual is a very great responsibility: it is only when they are so awakened that they are capable of real Good, but that at the same time they become first capable of evil."[57]

Greene, however, raises the question: How much is Jansenist belief and how much mock-heroic jest? It is notable, for example, that Pinkie's telephone number is 666, the Number of the Beast in Revelation (60). Was Greene a believer or a total skeptic who never believed in God, converted to get Vivien to marry him, and was only playing the same sort of games he played with MI5?[58]

As satire/parody (essentially Michael Shelden's thesis) Greene was, in *Brighton Rock* at least, producing something that was in the tradition of sacred parody or, in Greene's own phrase, "tender blasphemy."[59] First there is his use of objects that have lost their symbolic significance and are now essentially lurid parodies: "the plaster statues, the candle flames, the Communion wafers, the wine in the chalice, the rosary beads, the Latin phrases, the stuffy confessionals, the figure of Christ hanging above the altar with his painted wounds" (107).

Take the case of Raven in *A Gun for Sale* (1936), the novel published just before *Brighton Rock*. As James had set Merton Densher's pilgrimage back to London, Raven's pilgrimage of revenge to Nottwich (Nottingham/Norwich) is at Christmas. As Shelden says, recalling (probably with Greene) Yeats's "Second Coming," "The modern world has given birth to a predator, not a savior ['slouching toward Bethlehem to be born'], but there is no longer anything worth saving. . . . The Jewish child came with a message of peace, but the ultimate purpose of Raven's mission is to murder the Jewish Sir Marcus," who is, I might add, a warmongering steel manufacturer, the equivalent of Conrad's Ambassador Vladimir in *The Secret Agent*: he had hired Raven to kill a war minister in a Balkan state in order to start a war so his steel sales would go up.[60]

This might explain why he gives Pinkie the phone number 666. He names the gang boss Colleoni after the great *condottiere* Bartolomeo Colleoni, whose equestrian statue by Andrea del Verrocchio is one of the sights of Venice—another mock-heroic gesture. But there is another aspect to Greene's echoes: Ida's other name, we are told, is Lily, and she evokes more than once the pub scene in *The Waste Land,* in which the woman is named Lil and we hear "Good night." Ida-Lil's flat is behind Russell Square station; her old beau is Tom—Tom Eliot of Faber in Russell Square. As Shelden has shown, Greene does this sort of thing. In *A Gun for Sale* the girl who is about to be shot by Raven is saved by the providential intervention of a Mr. Green (Greene). Shelden has drawn attention to many details of Greene's biography, for example, his confessional game. "'Let's find a little church with some awful little priest,' he said. 'I'll go in and confess some ghastly crime. Let's cheer ourselves up.' . . . 'Father, I've fucked an Alsatian this afternoon. How many Hail Marys?'"[61] In other words, do we take seriously his use of Eliot—or find it a parody of, satire on, his Jansenist religion?

The strongest evidence for the view of *Brighton Rock* as play is Greene's early and only "scholarly" book—on John Wilmot, earl of Rochester, the great Restoration travestier of the court and the royal figure himself; a rake and an atheist who played with blasphemy and may or may not have converted on his deathbed.

Or is Greene, as a *novelist* (versus a satirist), "interested in delineating the terrific impact of theology on human souls."[62] This requires a primary belief in salvation and damnation (vs. right and wrong) on the part of some characters (Pinkie and Rose vs. Ida), if not of the author himself, who demonstrates the intensity of his feelings with what are referred to as his heightened "Greeneane" similes. Or, put differently, Greene's basic questions are, What is the attractiveness and fascination of evil to X, Y, Z? What is the price that must be paid for this attraction, for *being* evil?[63]

Or does Greene use Péguyean religion as his aesthetics of the sublime? The religious context creates "a heightened awareness of evil"—as, for example, Machen saw in his tales of terror and the supernatural. I have already quoted Greene on "supernatural evil" in James's *Wings of the Dove*. The key may be aesthetics, Burkean aesthetics of the sublime that Greene gets by invoking damnation—suffering, pain, etc.—through the demonic echoes of Machen.

While still at Oxford Greene published a story called "The Trial of Pan," which sounds like his version of Machen's "Great God Pan." He presents the tyrant God, senile, no longer able to remember why he created the world, now mechanically passing judgment on souls. Pan is brought before him; God banishes him to hell, but Pan sings a song that draws all God's followers away.[64] Machen, like James, stigmatized "children of the lowest type," or what the governess detected in Quint and feared in Miles; their words—"every foulness, every filthy abomination of speech; blasphemies that struck like blows at the sky [i.e., at God]"—recall Mrs. Grose's attribution of Miles's dismissal from school to his language. And Machen's fairies pass for misbehaving children but have "old men's faces, with bloated faces, with little sunken eyes, with leering eyes." "There was no infamy," we are told, "that they did not perpetrate; they spared no horror of cruelty."[65] They are the fairies—the real fairies, not those represented by Henry Fuseli, Richard Dadd, and the photographers' images of fairies that convinced Conan Doyle. Machen's description of the truth of fairies, and James's Governess's sense of Miles, may explain the process by which Greene arrived at Pinkie Brown.

Greene was certainly thinking of Dante's categorization when he justified his claim that James's real subject was evil by identifying this evil as the betrayal of a best friend; it also substantiates his rather strange leap to identifying these characters (Quint, Densher, and Croy) as the "damned." The two Greene sins are betrayal and suicide—but the first is an evil, the second a sin (the ultimate denial of God's creation in self-destruction), which under mitigating circumstances is acceptable, or at least makes damnation worthwhile (as with Scobie in *The Heart of the Matter*).[66]

The Power and the Glory: *Sin and Evil*

The novel that followed *Brighton Rock* was *The Power and the Glory* (1940): The whisky priest and the lieutenant are extensions, respectively, of Pinkie and Ida Arnold, the first as the "glory," the second as the "power." Like Ida, the lieutenant is a pursuer of the (in Péguy's sense) damned/saint, then Pinkie, now the priest who is a drunkard and fornicator; he is her reason and obsession turned against the irrational, but his actions are now evil in the conventional sense—he executes priests and hostages in the name of order and reason. He is Greene's version of Dostoevsky's Grand Inquisitor in *The Brothers Karamazov*, who is willing to kill Christ again in order to feed the poor; he has taken up the position of the devil in his temptation of Christ—bread is worth more than sanctity—"give people food instead" of God, until "everybody has got enough to eat."[67] This is either a commentary on or an extension of the logic of *Brighton Rock*.

Greene materializes and emblematizes sin: The whisky priest's first sin seems to have been "despair, the unforgivable sin"; sin in fact does not matter—drink, fornicate, and so long as you perform the Eucharist, you are a priest. But the sin that is materialized, his fornication with Maria, takes the sinister form of their offspring, an equivalent of little Pearl in *The Scarlet Letter* as if seen from the perspective of the clergy; though Greene qualifies the genetic symbol by prefacing it: "one who had been sharpened by hunger into an appearance of devilry and malice beyond her age. A young woman stared out of the child's eyes." This "small malicious child" laughs at the priest's discomfort, watches him "with acuteness and contempt." "They had spent no love in her conception: just fear and despair and half bottle of brandy and the sense of loneliness had driven him to an act which horrified him—and this scared shame-faced overpowering love was the result . . . it was like seeing his own mortal sin look back at him, without contrition" (2.1.77–83). When he tries to make some contact with the girl, she "sniggered": "The child's snigger and the first mortal sin lay together more closely than two blinks of the eye." She sticks her tongue out at him, and her mother says, "You little devil you" (2.1.83). The girl, with the traits of Satan, *is* the image of Sin, a proto-Pinkie, at the same time that she is the evil that is seemingly the consequence of the sin of a priest's fornication.

To the lieutenant the priest is "a danger. That's why we kill you"— Why? Because "It's God [the lieutenant is] against" (see 3.3.250–51). Thus he can be, as the priest says, "a good man," because his quarrel is on the level of holiness and sin, not morality. In the same way, the mestizo's betrayal of the priest is plainly evil, but to the priest only original sin ("he expected nothing else of anything human" [3.3.250]). It is as if Hogarth or Blake or Voltaire had been given the power (in Greene's terms, vs. the glory) to implement their convictions.

The Power and the Glory was followed by *The Heart of the Matter* (1948). The whisky priest and Henry Scobie are officially, and in their own eyes, sinners: the first drinks, the second breaks the seventh commandment, indeed contributes to both theft and murder; but what convinces him that he is damned is his taking communion when in a state of sin and committing suicide—that is, succumbing to despair, officially the worst sin. Whereas Scobie in fact commits suicide in order (he believes) to make the lives of various other people "happier," the act of suicide is in moral terms a virtuous one, though a folly since in the event it helps no one.

Scobie is a good man in that he does all he can to prevent others' suffering; yet in Catholic doctrine (and to his own mind) he is damned. In *The Heart of the Matter* sin is made to seem more than evil—internal to external wrong—if only to one good man, a Job who will not curse God; though it turns out, after he is dead, that God has pretty much given him the Job treatment. Damnation, Roman Catholicism, and sin are what he shares with Pinkie. But, like Pinkie, he needs his Ida Arnold. The world around both of them is the fallen world of the Jansenists and Calvinists, but opposite Pinkie is Ida Arnold, on the side of the law, representative of the everyday undamned world. So in *Heart of the Matter* there is Wilson, another investigator and pursuer, technically on the side of the law but driven by adolescent passions that help to destroy the people around him, in particular Scobie, whose wife he covets. While Ida was a lusty, healthy nature goddess, Wilson is a neurotic incompetent, the young, naive meddler who brings chaos with him, a prototype for the naive American do-gooder-murderer Pyle in *The Quiet American*.

We have seen Machen's demonizing of paganism—then Conrad's demonizing of Kurtz and the natives of the Congo, or James's (the governess's) of Quint and Jessel—or of Miles and Flora—or Greene of the idea of Pinkie: all are a matter of degree and opinion. But opposite these stands the reality of what the mad scientist does to his innocent victims, the oppression of the Congo Company, what the governess does to Miles: essentially two supplementary worlds, one Gothic and demonized, the other a banal everyday evil.

However we interpret Greene's intentions, demonic and banal evil have been transmuted into sin and evil, Machen's "evil" and crime. The first is fiction, the second reality in the sense of those basic undeniable evils, death and pain, murder and rape. Greene, like Eliot, puts his emphasis on the first—not on those existential facts intensified ("murder and more") but sin distinguished from evil as something different, more melodramatic and "sublime," namely, the greatest of all issues, salvation/damnation. He comes to see sin as preferable to evil, or at least more interesting. The final chapters of this book will return to the other, more secular strain that retains the social realist assumptions of Hogarth and Dickens, and so casts a cold eye on the romantic drama enjoyed by Eliot and Greene. Chapter 7 will look at the analysis of sin by the sufferers of evil in the nineteenth and twentieth centuries, and chapter 8 will pursue the same tradition of fiction, now impelled by the grim facts of the two World Wars, after which sin seems trivial against the real horrors of genocide—but finally returns, once again a way, however deluded and self-serving, of coping with such unimaginable phenomena.

CHAPTER SEVEN

The Original Evil and the Original Sin

1. DOING-EVIL

Sin Without Evil: Jonathan Edwards's Hell

Hell posed problems that remained to worry the Enlightenment. It was a place where sin was punished with evils, and the evils were imposed by sinners whose punishment included imposing these evils. Post-Reformation hell posed a second problem: punishment that was essentially sinless, or that rested only on the Original Sin. When everyone sinned, there was no sin-directed punishment in hell. Hell was essentially punishment, imposed on those designated sinners who had been denied grace. It was not, however, merely the absence of God; it was vividly burning forever in a fiery furnace.

This was, of course, the Calvinist hell, not the Church of England hell, which was more along the lines of Dante's Purgatory. But the Calvinist hell survived into the modern period; an idea of this hell can be drawn from Jonathan Edwards's notorious sermon "Sinners in the Hands of an Angry God," preached in Enfield, Connecticut, in 1741 as part of his Great Awakening. Sin is identified not by its nature (Edwards refers to it as "wickedness" and defines it as without-Jesus) so much as by its punishment, which is the ultimate reach of the evils following upon Adam's sin.[1] You in the congregation, he says, can look to right and left and see two out of three who are damned. It is the damnation that is important for Edwards, or rather the fear of damnation—distinct from the sense of sin—that may lead to rebirth and so (perhaps) salvation.

It is the suffering of the damned that matters—and the evils of hell—not the sin, the action which is secret and unknowable because it is essentially a psychological state, the rejection of Christ (or being unconverted). This is the belief that real evil, by which he means sin, is in our hearts, not out there in society with betrayal and murder. The best that can be said for Edwards's sense of sin (as opposed to evil) is that he presents it as—or rather tries to make it—its own punishment: "There are in the souls of wicked men those hellish *principles* reigning, that would presently kindle and flame out into hell fire, if it were not for God's restraints."[2] Sin is internal, pushing to get out and manifest itself (presumably in an act of some sort), restrained only by God—but, apparently for this reason, by an incredibly angry God, who at the same time is dangling the sinner over the pit of hell with its everlasting burning torments. In fact, Edwards suggests that if sin *were* permitted to get out, it would have no effect on fellow humans: "The corruption of the heart of man is immoderate and boundless in its fury; and while wicked men live here, it is like fire pent up by God's restraints, whereas if it were let loose, it would set on fire the course of nature; and as the heart is now a sink of sin, so if sin was not restrained, it would immediately turn the soul into a fiery oven, or a furnace of fire and brimstone" (154). This means, I take it, that hell would immediately manifest itself, and God is only restraining (until the moment of his own decision) the state of damnation, the suffering-evil which is all that matters.

The image Edwards uses to describe "wickedness" is the suffering of evil (Isaiah 57:20): "But the wicked are like the troubled sea, when it cannot rest, whose waters cast up mire and dirt. There is no peace, saith my God, to the wicked"—a powerful metaphor for the feeling of the sinner (which Dickens attached to Monks), the state of mind or inner workings of his mind, but strangely indeterminate. There is nothing specific, only something frightening, as in the description of hell itself (a "furnace," a gaping mouth, as of the "old serpent")—obscure, and so all the more terrifying and (in Burke's terminology) sublime. And where part of the evil is in the obscurity, the imagination is left free to imagine the horrors of "darkness visible" and eternal fires forever and ever. But nothing is said of the sin, let alone an evil act, because they are essentially irrelevant.

Edwards, describing hell, did not mention evil acts; only sin matters, and sin is only whether or not Christ is in you, the lack of which will result in the evil of hellfire. He shares Calvin's view that acts are corrupt (man's will is corrupt), but he is looking at sins, which are largely internal, unverifiable, not to be judged in terms of acts and consequences. In short, sin is subjective, evil objective; the first treated by theology, the second by the law courts; and the first is what interested Edwards.

In Hawthorne's story "The Minister's Black Veil" sin is not an act but a sign of something invisible and internal. When the minister delivers his sermon on secret sin he wears the veil covering his face as a sign and yet will not reveal the signified to anyone, including his fiancée; this would appear to be his way of indicating that he, the minister, is representative of all, not just himself but his Edwardsian congregation. Edwards would have assumed that those of his congregation who had Jesus in their hearts were, though not without sin, at least saved. And yet the minister's gesture fails because his congregation and everyone else reads it as personal to him, his private, secret sin. And whether personal or not, he takes the veil with him to his grave, and the sin it betokens remains either undisclosed or as general as the sin in Hester Prynne's village. The veil is the sign of our universal sin, which the minister takes on himself as Atonement for the congregation. He is, in this respect, the equivalent of Hester, who bore the specific sign of her sin in the letter A on her breast until her death, except for the fact that she revealed and in a sense exulted in her particular sexual act, which her society called sin.

The Innocent Creature: Coleridge, Wordsworth, and R. P. Warren
Between the late 1790s and 1800 Coleridge produced two major poems, *The Rime of the Ancient Mariner* and *Christabel,* developments of his plans for writing "The Origin of Evil, an Epic Poem."[3] The first is about the original act, about Original Sin, Fall, and redemption; the second, though it introduces the evil of the vampire, is at bottom another version of the Fall.

Coleridge's albatross can be added to the list of innocent and (in Burke's terms) "useful" beasts who are wantonly killed by men. But the critics (from Anna Laetitia Barbauld to John Livingston Lowes and Irving

Babbitt) who complained about *The Ancient Mariner*'s lack of moral emphasis felt the killing of the albatross was too trivial an act for such harsh punishment. They were judging the act in moral terms—it is merely a bird (only an apple). As Robert Penn Warren recognized, Coleridge's point is that it is not a moral lapse but a sin—symbolically *the* sin.[4] If Coleridge had used a man rather than a bird "the secular nature of the crime—a crime then against man—would have overshadowed the ultimate religious significance involved." Moreover, the bird is made to carry the associations of a man—the creature is humanized: "As if it had been a Christian soul, / We hailed it in God's name"; the bird becomes part of the ship's company, even attending "vespers nine." In Warren's words, "It partakes of the human food and pleasure and devotions. To make matters more explicit, Coleridge adds in the Gloss the statement that the bird was received with 'hospitality' and adds, after the crime, that the Mariner 'inhospitably killeth the pious bird of good omen'" (361–62).

Coleridge got close to the Problem of Evil in *The Rime of the Ancient Mariner* when he remarked, answering (as recorded in *Table Talk*) Barbauld's criticism that the poem lacked a moral, that, on the contrary, he thought "the poem had too much": "It ought to have had no more moral than the Arabian Nights' tale of the merchant's sitting down to eat dates by the side of a well, and throwing the shells inside, and lo! A genie starts up, and says he must kill the aforesaid merchant, because one of the date shells had, it seems, put out the eye of the genie's son."[5] These words tell more about the nature of the Mariner's act—*as* sin—than about the absence of a moral. Whether it was Coleridge or Henry Nelson Coleridge, the recorder of Coleridge's *Table Talk*, who misremembered the Arabian Nights story, in fact the date shell had killed, not blinded, the genie's son, and when the merchant begs for mercy, the genie replies, "No mercy! Is it not just to kill him that has killed another?" Warren comments, "What is important here may be that the story referred to from *The Arabian Nights* is not merely a tale of the miraculous, but is one dealing with a random act and its apparently incommensurable punishment, much on the order of that in *The Ancient Mariner*. The mystery of sin and punishment is again before us. There is even a faint hint of a theological parallel with Christianity, the avenging Father and the Son who suffers at the hand of man" (414).

The Ancient Mariner shows the Mariner committing what is essentially an *acte gratuit* that represents both evil (killing another creature, more-over one that has been friendly and helpful) and sin. The arbitrariness of the Mariner's act is simply another aspect of the mystery of Original Sin. Coleridge wrote his brother George upon finishing the poem, "I believe most steadfastly in original Sin; that from our mothers' wombs our understandings are darkened; and even when our understandings are in the Light, that our organization is depraved, and our volitions imperfect." Evil is caused by our innate sin, which is one of the evils that originated in and followed from Adam's Original Sin ("In Adam's fall / We sinnèd all"). According to Coleridge, in W. J. Bate's words, "'Original sin' is not something 'inherited,' as the 'Bibliolators' maintained. It is something built into the very nature of 'individuality'"[6]—that is, Eve's eating the apple is a declaration of her "independence" from God or from Adam (when in Milton's version she goes her separate way).

The Mariner's act as sin, of course, reflects the sixth Commandment (thou shalt not kill), which is punished with the evils the Mariner and his crew suffer subsequently. But it is also sin because by killing the bird he is violating the "moral order in the universe," "the bond of communion between man and the natural world," which can also be stated as the relationship between the part and the whole[7]—what Coleridge sums up in the lines, "For the dear God who loveth us, / He made and loveth all"; and in the words, "But in its utmost abstraction and consequent state of reprobation, the will becomes Satan's pride and rebellious self-idolatry in the relations of the spirit to itself, and remorseless despotism relatively to others . . . by the fearful resolve to find in itself alone the one absolute motive of action."[8] Self-idolatry, preferring oneself to God, nature, or any whole (or any other), is the Mariner's sin; as Warren notes, Coleridge fits the punishment to the crime "with Dantesque precision": "It is loneliness. And when the Mariner bites his own arm for the blood to drink, we have the last logical extension of 'self-idolatry' converted to its own punishment" (414). The motive of the killing of the albatross is as mysterious as Augustine's for stealing the pear.

It is in fact, like Eve's and Augustine's, a perverse and trivial corruption of the will—a careless act with unexpectedly grave consequences, like the merchant's dropping of the date shell in the well. In short, Original Sin could perhaps be called an evil in itself, and so explain how doing-evil comes about. While we have equated sin with violation of the law (disobedience) and evils with the external consequences, there is another equation, of sin with an inner flaw imposed by the Original Sin, so to speak transmitted in the genes, whose consequences are inner disquiet and dread.[9]

Coleridge also wrote, in an autobiographical note of 11 January 1805, "It is a most instructive part of my Life the fact, that I have been always preyed on by some dread, and perhaps all my faulty actions have been the consequences of some dread or other in my mind from fear of Pain, or Shame, not from prospect of pleasure."[10] That is, the evil that follows from Original Sin is inflicted on us by our dread of the evils of the world, or in fact is the faculty that makes them seem evil. Coleridge's "dread" is not, as he seems to suggest, an original sin but a consequence of the original evils—the "fear of Pain" and presumably death—which caused him to create an original sin and consequent "Shame" to explain and understand it.

With the Ancient Mariner's haranguing the guest on his way to the wedding feast, Coleridge adds to the story of the origin of evil a story of personal redemption, but he does so by conflating the Ancient Mariner's sin against nature (inhospitality, etc.) with fallen humankind's evil treatment of Christ.

Warren noted the "symbolic transference" from "Christ to the Albatross, from the slain Son of God to the slain creature of God," the "pious bird" that cares for the icebound sailors: a mission of mercy, of salvation, a typical Romantic rewriting of the story.[11] The albatross has come to guide the ship and its crew and the Mariner wantonly kills it, and so, "Instead of the cross, the albatross / About my neck was hung." He must wear it until he has again become one (in sympathy) with his natural surroundings ("A spring of love gushed from my heart"—looking at the slimy creatures of the sea), at which point it falls away, as the burden fell from the back of Bunyan's Christian—the burden in his case of Original Sin.[12]

In Warren's dramatic poem *Brother to Dragons* (1953; rev. 1979) it is Thomas Jefferson who must carry around his neck the burden of guilt for an original sin he has denied the existence of. Warren's essay on *The Ancient Mariner* (1946) reverberates in the poem he wrote at the end of the 1940s, a study in the nature of evil. The evil act is the murder and dismemberment of a completely innocent slave by Lilburne Lewis, a nephew of Jefferson. (How could a nephew of Thomas Jefferson do such a thing?)

The act is, in the same sense as the murder of the albatross, inexplicable and attributed by Warren to the evil that lurks at the heart of every man, even the Enlightenment ideal humanist, Jefferson himself, believer in progress, author of the Declaration of Independence, and founder of the University of Virginia. The act is attributed to the original sin in all of us—not the Original Sin of the theologians but the Hobbesian evil that contradicts the hopeful Pelagianism of the Enlightenment philosophers, the deep flaw that contradicts the idea of progress; not just in the murder of the slave John but in Jefferson's Louisiana Purchase and the dispatch of Meriwether Lewis (his relative) and William Clark to map the area, a project that ends with Lewis's suicide and curse on Jefferson for the evil entailed in the building of the western empire.

Lewis tells Jefferson that the revelation of evil taught him "that you were human. Human, too," but "unprepared for the nature of the world," and Jefferson concludes, "Reason? That's the world / I sought to live by—but, oh, / We have been lost in the dark."[13] The poem teaches Jefferson the "truth" about men and himself, as the consequences of killing the albatross did the Mariner, but Warren gives us enough information about Lilburne to enable us to see that he is a particular case of an Oedipal son, bereft of his mother, who kills John the slave for having broken his mother's favorite crockery. What Warren attempts to pass off as a theory of evil, an equivalent of the poem Coleridge intended to write called "The Origin of Evil," is in fact a shocking case history based on the popular (Eliot, Yeats, Tate, Faulkner) idea of the time that progress is an illusion concealing our basically evil nature. The Mariner's "incommensurable punishment" becomes in *Brother to Dragons* incommensurable guilt.

Wordsworth rewrote and corrected his friend's *Ancient Mariner* with *Peter Bell,* begun immediately after reading Coleridge's poem.[14] He replaced the rather neutral figure of the albatross with the stoic, suffering "solitary Ass," who recalls the servant of Isaiah, prototype of the Jesus of the Gospels. More specifically than the albatross, the "solitary Ass" is in the tradition of those animals in Gay's *Trivia,* Fielding's *Champion* essay, Hogarth's *Stages of Cruelty,* and Dickens's *Oliver Twist*—examples of cruelty to innocent creatures. Wordsworth's ass reflects the story of Balaam's—how he "smote the ass with a staff" and threatened to kill him if he would not move; the ass, unknown to Balaam, is a holy creature acting under instructions from God (Numbers 22:27, 29).[15]

Peter Bell, coming upon an unattended ass in the woods, attempts to steal him—the animal, like Balaam's ass, is following a higher calling: he is guarding his dead master, who lies at the bottom of the pond. When the ass will not budge, Peter mercilessly beats him:

> Dropped gently down upon his knees
> The patient beast on Peter turned
> His shining hazel eye.
>
> 'Twas but one mild, reproachful look,
> A look more tender than severe. (ll. 430–37)

This poor creature leads Peter to the body of his dead master, to various emblematic spots (a chapel, a tavern, a Methodist revival meeting), causing Peter to remember one of his many transgressions—his betrayal of the "Highland girl," his sixth (polygamous) wife, a young girl pregnant and dead of heartbreak over his sinful ways. The memory causes Peter to repent, roughly as the Mariner repents, and to make explicit Wordsworth's intention of replacing the Mariner's albatross with the ass:

> 'Tis said, meek Beast! That, through Heaven's grace,
> He not unmoved did notice now
> The cross upon thy shoulder scored,
> For lasting impress, by the Lord
> To whom all human-kind shall bow;
>
> Memorial of his touch—that day
> When Jesus humbly deigned to ride,
> Entering the proud Jerusalem
> By an immeasurable stream
> Of shouting people deified! (ll. 970–80)

The ass directs Peter to his master's home and Peter's redemption. Wordsworth has replaced Coleridge's archaic ballad with his own peculiarly elevated diction ("Once more the Ass, with motion dull, / Upon the pivot of his skull / Turned round his long left ear"); he drops Coleridge's Roman Catholic penance and priest, writing a Protestant story of conversion, self-redemption, and salvation. But his Protestant perspective is in its way more conservative than Coleridge's mock-archaism, for he looks all the way back to Bunyan—back to the sexual sin of the Puritans (indeed, of *The Prelude,* where his own betrayal of Annette Vallon is the private face of the public Fall of the French Revolution).[16] There is no complex issue of sin and evil here: Peter Bell commits acts of gratuitous cruelty, presumably out of his own fallen nature, and the Christlike figure he ravages brings him to conversion and a happy ending. The ass in *Peter Bell* may have been at the back of Warren's mind when he replaced Coleridge's Mariner with Lilburne Lewis, the albatross with the slave John, and the story of the Fall with the nightmare of the Enlightenment (what Francisco Goya called "The Dream of Reason breeds Monsters" in the frontispiece to his *Caprichos*).

Poe, "The Black Cat"

Poe did write a few stories of evil in the sense of murder—"The Tell-Tale Heart," "The Black Cat," "The Imp of the Perverse," "The Cask of Amontillado"—but his interest was not in the nature of the crime or of evil itself so much as in the point of view, madness, motivation, or lack of motivation, whether in the sense of Jonathan Edwards's sermon or of Coleridge's Mariner: what he calls the perverse, or the gratuitous, which may be called the sin that by its inexplicability transcends mere murder, and so in that sense is Evil.

Poe's "spirit of the perverse" is his version of Original Sin—of the act of the Mariner, again as mysterious, or as transparent, as Augustine's theft of the pears. And, like the Mariner, the Poe narrator has to unburden his soul. In "The Black Cat," once again in relation to an animal like the horse, ass, or albatross, Poe attempts to define "the spirit of Perverseness":

> Of this spirit philosophy takes no account. Yet I am not more sure that my soul lives, than I am that perverseness is one of the primitive impulses of the human heart—one of the indivisible primary faculties, or sentiments, which give direction to the character of man. Who has *not,* a hundred times, found himself committing a vile or stupid action, for no other reason than because he knows he should not? Have we not a perpetual inclination, in the teeth of our best judgment, to violate that which is *Law,* merely because we understand it to be such?
> This spirit of perverseness, I say, came to my final overthrow.

It was this unfathomable longing of the soul *to vex itself*—to offer violence to its own nature—to do wrong for the wrong's sake only—that urged me to continue and finally to consummate the injury I had inflicted upon the unoffending brute. One morning, in cold blood, I slipped a noose about its neck and hung it to the limb of a tree—hung it with the tears streaming from my eyes, and with the bitterest remorse at my heart—hung it *because* I knew that it had loved me, and *because* I felt it had given me no reason of offense—hung it *because* I knew that in so doing I was committing a sin—a deadly sin that would so jeopardize my immortal soul as to place it—if such a thing were possible—even beyond the reach of the infinite mercy of the Most Merciful and Most Terrible God.[17]

Warren, who cites the passage in relation to the shooting of the albatross, points out how when the narrator aims a blow with an axe at the ghostly second cat, his wife intercedes and takes the blow herself—thus symbolically identifying the animal and the human (as Tom Nero did by progressing from the horse to the lamb, boy, and girl; as Lilburne does by leading up to his blow of "the axe" on the slave John with wanton cruelty to his "favorite hound").[18]

The narrator is even, he tells us, a man "especially fond of animals . . . never so happy as when feeding and caressing them"—he contrasts "the unselfish and self-sacrificing love" of the animal with "the paltry friendship and gossamer fidelity of mere *Man*" (550–52). Despite his wife's story that "all black cats [are] witches in disguise"—and this cat is named Pluto, after the god of the underworld—the narrator does not, as we might expect, demonize the cat but demonizes his own drinking problem, which he attributes to "the Fiend Intemperance": "The fury of a demon possessed me. . . . My original soul seemed, at once, to take its flight from my body; and a more than fiendish malevolence, gin-nurtured, thrilled every fibre of my frame"—when he cuts out the cat's eye. It is "the Fiend Intemperance" that changes his personality. However, what the narrator explains as perversity and possession he reveals as in fact due to alcohol.

In "The Imp of the Perverse" Poe comes closer to a crime of pure perversity, "a *mobile* without motive, a motive not *motiviert*. Through its promptings we act without comprehensible object; or, if this shall be understood as a contradiction in terms, we may so far modify the proposition as to say, that through its promptings we act, for the reason that we should not"—in other words, Augustine's motive—"the overwhelming tendency to do wrong for the wrong's sake" (438–39).

As in all Poe's stories, however, what he represents is what it feels like, in this case to be perverse. "The Gold Bug," "Murders in the Rue Morgue" (though there is a throat cutting, of a human by an orangutan), "The Mystery of Marie Roget," and "The Purloined Letter," are merely forerunners of the Sherlock Holmes stories. Puzzles are solved: Not only how to break a code or explain a crime, but how to escape a descending razor-sharp pendulum; how to measure the size of a pitch-dark room in which you are imprisoned; how to hide a letter; how to survive a whirlpool. "MS. Found in a Bottle" and "Descent into the Maelstrom" show what it feels like to have extraordinary experiences. They describe psychological states. "Ligeia," "The Premature Burial," and "Berenice" show how it feels to be buried alive or how it feels to imagine this—all responses to terror (Burke's sublime) and, to some extent, not always defined, guilt.

The way it feels to commit a murder is described in "The Imp of the Perverse" as standing "upon the brink of a precipice. We peer into the abyss —we grow sick and dizzy. Our first impulse is to shrink from the danger. Unaccountably we remain. By slow degrees our sickness and dizziness and horror become merged in a cloud of unnamable feeling." Gradually, as the thought of falling "chills the very marrow of our bones with the fierceness of the delight of its horror," one wants to leap:

> It is merely the idea of what would be our sensations during
> the sweeping precipitancy of a fall from such a height. And
> this fall—this rushing annihilation—for the very reason that
> it involves that one most ghastly and loathsome of all the
> most ghastly and loathsome images of death and suffering
> which have ever presented themselves to our imagination—
> for this very cause do we now most vividly desire it" (440–41).

The metaphor of Adam's Fall is materialized in Poe's metaphor. Augustine's description of his temptation to sin is ratcheted up by Poe into the sublime, but Poe designates death as the consequence and, here, the desired end—in this case, first murder and then, giving oneself to the police, one's own death.

I have been exploring the relationship between original sin and original evil in writings of the nineteenth century. Original Sin applies of course to the Fall, original evil(s) to the consequences of the Fall: two actions, defy God or injure another human; in fact, eat an apple or kill an innocent creature—an animal or a child; the latter is an act of evil necessarily taking place in the postlapsarian world, and it is followed, not by expulsion from Eden but by the torture in turn of the guilty torturer (Tom Nero in chap. 3). The two converge in the examples of albatross, ass, and cat—and other Tom Neros, whether representatives of Original Sin or of original evil? The question is significant because the discourse of sin is being preempted by the discourse of evils; and any story that evokes the Fall (Coleridge's *Ancient Mariner* is the prime example) takes place now in the fallen world we encountered in the works of Dickens, Hawthorne, and Melville in chapter 4, which is the world not of Adam and Eve but of Cain.

And yet when we search into motives we recover Augustine's explanation for his theft of the pears. The more apparently gratuitous the acts, the more they are explained by the sin of disobedience and defiance of God or, in any case, of the part denying its subordination to the whole. Even an original (inexplicable, gratuitous) sin is now in the realm of human reactions. With whom then do we associate—the Mariner who, as Eve ate the apple, kills the bird; or the bird whose death is his Original Sin? the man who demonizes, disfigures, and kills the cat or the poor cat itself?

2. SUFFERING-EVIL

When Doing-Evil Becomes Suffering-Evil: Little Father Time

> There drove up at this moment with a belated Doctor [an Oxford don], robed and panting, a cab whose horse failed to stop at the exact point required for setting down the hirer, who jumped out and entered the door. The driver, alighting, began to kick the animal in the belly.

This image, toward the end of Thomas Hardy's *Jude the Obscure* (1895), is the next stage in the sequence of cruelties to innocent creatures.[19] It is climactic in that it is the only one, in a novel permeated by cruelty, in which a human's malice is permitted to intrude. The slow, agonizing death of a pig is presented not as an act of wanton cruelty, as it was in the other examples from Gay's *Trivia* onward, but as part of nature, the country way of life, what has to be done in order to get the most flavor out of the pork and the most monetary return. Only Jude's pity—and enforced involvement in the act—makes the act seem cruel. Arabella regards this as indicating no more than Jude's aspiring "ardour for Christminster" (Oxford) and upward mobility.

A second example is a rabbit caught in a trap, which Jude kills in order to cut short its suffering. Rabbits are caught in traps and may suffer all through the night until put out of their misery by the gamekeeper in the morning. It is only part of the hard cycle of country life. But the horse is mistreated in Christminster, Jude's heart of civilized life, and by a callous driver, because the academic (equivalent to Hogarth's lawyers) he was conveying was late for the Remembrance Day parade. "'If that can be done,' said Jude, 'at college gates in the most religious and educational city in the world, what shall we say as to how far we've got?'" A policeman replies, "Keep yer tongue quiet, my man, while the procession passes" (6.1.367), indicating the power of "Oxford" and "dons."

Once again, the culprit of such acts of cruelty is the law (the novel's subtitle is "'The Letter Killeth'"), but in the works of Gay, Hogarth, Fielding, and Dickens the law was perverted and exploited by evil men—the "great"—while in *Jude* it is the law itself, specifically the marriage contract, but also the "insentient, complacent institutions" of the university and the church, the establishment that carry the onus—and the way ordinary people are prone to carry out their mandate to the letter.[20] There is no malice—even in the horse-beater—only the following of ordnances, which is in fact more a way of dealing with suffering-evil than doing-evil. Hogarth, we saw, extended the evil of the Great Man to the ruling class, the governing body of society, indeed to God (at least as represented in baroque paintings). Hardy includes the gamekeepers and the dons of Oxford, but they are only other representatives of God.

Little Father Time's act of hanging himself and his two little siblings appears to be an act of evil with a capital E; the three children he hangs up in the closet like clothes drying on a line present an image horrible yet grotesque, almost comic in its sheer insanity:

> At the back of the door were fixed two hooks for hanging garments, and from these the forms of the two youngest children

were suspended, by a piece of box-cord round each of their necks, while from a nail a few yards off the body of little Jude [Father Time] was hanging in a similar manner. An overturned chair was near the elder boy, and his glazed eyes were slanted into the room; but those of the girl and the baby boy were closed (6.2.375).

If this "strange and consummate horror"—"Done because we are too menny" (376)—is to be regarded as evildoing, we would have to attribute it to deep, pathological stupidity (as Sue says, "He took it literally" [378])—or to innocence. The little boy has heard his mother say they are being put out because there are too many children. He is literally correct, but his solution is out of the apocalyptic books of the Bible (or an apocalyptic reading of Thomas Malthus), with which he seems to be familiar. The family's entrance into Christminster, which echoes in some ways Christ's into Jerusalem, appears to Father Time as "the Judgment Day," and he adds "mournfully," "I don't think I like Christminster!" (6.1.364–65). (Father Time thinks the Oxford colleges are jails.) His name suggests not only his weird appearance of age but evocation of the Grim Reaper he turns out to be. "Cruelty," says Richard Phillotson, "is the law pervading all nature and society; and we can't get out of it if we would!" (5.8.359).

Father Time's experience has been strange (two mothers, two fathers) and is Darwinian, but at a remove. He listens carefully to what his parents say; when Sue exclaims, "O why should Nature's law be mutual butchery!" he replies, "Is it so, mother?" and absorbs this "truth" as he later does the arithmetic of living conditions in inns. "'I ought not to be born, ought I?' said the boy with misgiving." "Can I do anything?" he asks his mother. "No!" answers Sue. "All is trouble, adversity and suffering"—which we may regard either as Hardy's truth or Sue's melodramatization along the lines of classical tragedy (her address to Melpomene). "It would be better to be out o' the world than in it, wouldn't it?" says Father Time, unconsciously echoing his father's conclusion that he was not up to suicide, only drinking himself into oblivion. "It would almost, dear," says Sue, and Father Time goes on: "I think that whenever children be born that are not wanted they should be killed directly, before their souls come to 'em, and not allowed to grow big and walk about!" To this "Sue did not reply. She was doubtfully pondering how to treat this too reflective child"—until she adds, fatally perhaps, "There is going to be another in our family soon." "How ever could you, mother, be so wicked and cruel as this, when you needn't have done it till we was better off, and father well!" (6.2.373).

Father Time's problem derives from his creation, the accidental offspring of Jude and Arabella, rather like the monstrous offspring of Dryden's Achitophel, whose thoughts were plotting rebellion when they should have been on conceiving the child. He has "the habit of sitting silent, his quaint and weird face set, and his eyes resting on things they did not see in the substantial world" (5.4.320). Sue characteristically sees in his face "the tragic mask of Melpomene," the muse of tragedy. Running in his blood is the memory of Jude's and Sue's ancestor who killed his wife and was hanged for burglary—the "tragic doom [that] overhung our family, as it did the house of Atreus," the pagan Sue again notes. The "quondam theologian" Jude adds, "Or the house of Jeroboam." As a result of all this, Father Time is "singularly deficient in all the usual hopes of childhood" (6.5.323, 329, 333).

As in so much of Hardy's poetry, the first evil is in creation, the second in the way people cope with the evils of the world. Evildoing is not Hardy's subject, but rather the suffering and coping with evil. His image of God is not the malicious "vengeful god" of the Old Testament, who says, "Know that thy sorrow is my ecstasy," but rather "Crass Casualty," "purblind Doomsters [who] had as readily strown / Blisses about my pilgrimage as pain." Implicitly, one way of dealing with evil, this by the powerful, is to make laws and establish institutions, which are therefore part of the evil. The two chief ways the ordinary characters of Hardy's novel deal with evil is by getting drunk and by going to chapel.

The first, as I noted earlier, is the same as Hogarth's in *Gin Lane;* the second could reflect the chapel-goers in his *Sleeping Congregation* and *Credulity, Superstition, and Fanaticism.*[21] "I felt a need for some sort of support under my loss," Arabella tells Sue Bridehead, "and, as 'twas righter than gin, I took to going [to the chapel] regular, and found it a great comfort" (5.7.354). Sue's solution is to give up her pagan rebellion and submit to the ethos of the chapel; she now believes in rewards and punishments: "My babies have been taken from me," she tells Jude, to punish her for living with Arabella's "husband" Jude: "Arabella's child killing mine was a judgment—the right slaying the wrong" (6.4.390). "'We must conform!' she said mournfully. 'All the ancient wrath of the Power above us has been

vented upon us, His poor creatures, and we must submit. There is no
choice. We must. It is no use fighting against God!'" (6.2.382). Jude, totally
disillusioned with the religious belief that at first sustained him, recovers
Sue's pagan freedom, returning to the Arabella who first introduced him
to that world when she threw pigs' testicles in his face.

But toward the end of the novel, neither drink nor chapel seeming
sufficient, what remains is a fatal third alternative, Little Father Time's:
death, whether murder-suicide or Jude's fading away in illness. Jude's earlier meditation on life led him to conclude that unfortunately "he was not
a sufficiently dignified person for suicide": "What could he do of a lower
kind than self-extermination; what was there less noble, more in keeping
with his present degraded position? He could get drunk. Of course that
was it; he had forgotten. Drinking was the regular, stereotyped resource
of the despairing worthless" (1.11.114). Arabella's response to Jude's talk of
suicide is mundane: "Lord, you do talk lofty! Won't you hae something
warm to drink?" (6.8.432).

Hardy starts, like Dickens, on the level of society. As Jude says, "There
is something wrong somewhere in our social formulas," that is, of contemporary England (6.1.367). But according to Sue, "The social moulds
civilization fits us into" do not conform to human fact (4.1.247), and Phillotson believes that an "instinctive . . . sense of justice" is not "permitted
with impunity in an old civilization like ours" (6.4.397). "Civilization"
carries "society" back into the distant past as "the source of evil," and to
the "indifference and cruelty of 'Nature'" and the Problem of Evil.[22]

When Sue leaves her husband, Phillotson, she says (as she often repeats) it is "wrong and wicked of me," yet adds, "But it is not I altogether
that am to blame?" "Who is then?" asks Phillotson. "Am I?" "No—I don't
know!" Sue replies. "The universe, I suppose things in general, because
they are so horrid and cruel!" Either she is reflecting what seems to be the
case in *Jude the Obscure* or Hardy intends her words to be self-justification
—perhaps something of both, but the latter is also part of "things in general." Phillotson continues, referring to "domestic laws":

> "But we married———"
> "What is the use of thinking of laws and ordinances," she
> burst out, "if they make you miserable when you know you are
> committing no sin?"

"But you are committing a sin in not liking me."
(4.3.263–64)

Botched Creation ("Did He Who Made the Lamb Make Thee?"):
Mary Shelley and H. G. Wells

Coleridge's *Ancient Mariner* falls into line with a sequence of stories of the origin and problem of evil, beginning with Blake's "Poison Tree," in which God plants a poison tree in his garden in order to tempt his neighbor into stealing an apple, and so, having introduced "evil" into the world, elicits the sin that explains and justifies the punishment of evil-death. In *Frankenstein, or the Modern Prometheus* (1818) Mary Shelley creates a fiction in which a scientist, analogous to the deity-as-creator, creates a "creature" and then, dissatisfied with the result, repudiates it and thereby releases into the world the "evils" of suffering and death. Victor Frankenstein's project relates to the Problem of Evil in that one motive that leads him to create his man is the desire to "renew life where death had apparently devoted the body to corruption," that is, find a substitute for the promised afterlife in heaven.[23] In that sense, Victor's rejection of his creature explains in Blakean terms the Fall. But from Frankenstein's point of view, the Original Sin was the creature's ugliness, which caused the doctor to recoil and disown him. But the ugliness was, after all, the way Frankenstein created his monster, the responsibility of the maker. There is nothing inherently evil in his creation, only his grotesque appearance; technically he is an abomination (clumsily made up by the doctor from the parts of different corpses) and a "horror" (5.57–58): for Victor, the problem of coming to terms with his creation is not moral but aesthetic. Possibly, Shelley suggests, one explanation for our "evils" is as the consequence of the maker's dissatisfaction with his creation.

The other original sinner is the Enlightenment scientist who (in Frankenstein's words) seeks "the acquirement of knowledge . . . for the dominion I should acquire and transmit over the elemental foes of our race," who may think of himself as a parallel figure to the Creator. The human agency comes from a scientist who commits the sin (blasphemy) of usurping God's function but then adds evil to sin by repudiating his own creation—as, of course, in one sense, God did at the Fall; but he also refuses to give it a mate with which (Adam-like) to reproduce its kind, thereby unleashing its vengeful evils on the world. The parallel with

Coleridge's *Ancient Mariner* is noted (Letter 2.21, 5.59). The Mariner committed an original sin; Victor Frankenstein also does so in the sense that he, like Eve, is violating the Tree of Knowledge. Both are turned upon—by nature, by Frankenstein's "creature"—and pursued relentlessly.

The creature's every crime is motivated by his treatment at the hands of other living creatures: When the village becomes aware of him, women faint—"some fled, some attacked me, until, grievously bruised by stones and many other kinds of missile weapons, I escaped to the open country" (11.106). In fact, Shelley presents the creature's crimes so that they appear to be malign—in particular making him plant the picture on the innocent Justine, thus killing her as well as William (8.85). But as he tells his story, in each case he is responding to an evil in the world. Having educated himself by reading *Paradise Lost,* he confronts Frankenstein with Milton's story: "Remember, that I am thy creature; I ought to be thy Adam; but I am rather the fallen angel, whom thou drivest from joy for no misdeed. Everywhere I see bliss, from which I alone am irrevocably excluded. I was benevolent and good; misery made me a fiend" (10.100). Adam "had come forth from the hands of God a perfect creature, happy and prosperous, guarded by the especial care of his Creator; he was allowed to converse with, and acquire knowledge from, beings of a superior nature: but I was wretched, helpless, and alone" (15.129).[24] "I am malicious because I am miserable," he says, suggesting one of the explanations for cruelty and doing-evil: evil is compensation for evils. Indeed, the creature describes the other, more civilized way of coping with this situation: a hut. He is "enchanted by" its appearance, tapers, and other devices invented by man to deal with darkness, cold, and misery; but he is driven out (11.105, 109).

At the far end of the century, in H. G. Wells's *The Island of Dr. Moreau* (1896), another scientist attempts to create men, or rather (in the age of Darwin) hurry animals up the evolutionary scale. Darwin's *Descent of Man* (1871)—that is, from the apes—most likely set Wells onto this particular line of satire.

The frame story tells of Prendick, a biologist who is shipwrecked and rescued by a ship bound for a remote island, where he is unceremoniously dropped off. Prendick's story is, in one sense, an updating of *Gulliver's Travels,* in particular the fourth voyage, to Houyhnhnmland, where the clean horses are in charge of the more humanoid creatures, the foul, filthy, sexually incontinent Yahoos; the horses are *animal rationale,* the two-footed Yahoos are apparently closer to the ape than the human, and, though Gulliver sides with his masters the horses, implied between these alternatives is an *animal rationis capax,* the actual Englishman like Gulliver before he becomes deranged, going off in one direction or the other.

Like Gulliver, when he returns to England, Wells's protagonist Prendick notes, "I could not persuade myself that the men and women I met were not also another, still passably human, Beast People, animals half-wrought into the outward image of human souls; and that they would presently begin to revert, to show first this bestial mark and then that."[25] The equivalent of Gulliver abandoning his family for the barn and the company of horses, Prendick, when he goes out, thinks that "prowling women . . . mew after me," and his clergyman appears to him another Ape Man (22.138).

Here Gulliver/Prendick encounters a mad biologist who wants to raise animals into men—or elide the stages of descent Darwin outlined—and so in one sense he imitates God, but in another shows how God must have, given the human evidence, operated, how the evils in the world actually came about, and how men dealt with them. Evil in this case is primarily pain; sin is the making of abominations. God is responsible for both.

Dr. Moreau's story, which encompasses Prendick's, is first about the mad doctor (the Dr. Frankenstein, Dr. Jekyll—as opposed to Machen's Dr. Raymond, whose aim is to *recover* the Great God Pan) who wants to create a new, improved species, in Moreau's case by performing surgery on animals. His experiment, of course, fails, and he is killed by the puma on which he has been working from the time of Prendick's arrival on the island (the puma was the cargo of the ship that picked him up). It is his surgery ("vivisection") that inflicts the pain on the animals—on the puma, whose cries for Prendick punctuate the unfolding story. We are told again and again that Moreau's experiments, which are exclusively on animals, "were wantonly cruel" (7.32).

Prendick's response begins by reflecting the Gulliverian detachment of Montgomery, Moreau's assistant, who is in "a state of ill-concealed irritation at the noise of the vivisected puma." He admits that

I found myself that the cries were singularly irritating, and they grew in depth and intensity as the afternoon wore on. They were painful at first, but their constant resurgence at last altogether upset my balance. I flung aside a crib of Horace I had been reading, and began to clench my fists, to bite my lips, and pace the room. . . . The emotional appeal of those yells grew upon me steadily, grew at last to such an exquisite expression of suffering that I could stand it in that confined room no longer. . . . It was as if all the pain in the world had found a voice. (8.37)

The vivisection that transforms the animals into animal-humans recalls the cruelty and pain of Darwin's "survival of the fittest." The cruelty of Gulliver's fourth voyage, which is imposed on the Yahoos (their skins, for example, were made into gloves), is reversed and returned on the animals—and to the paradigm we have followed of evil as cruelty to the innocent, ultimately animals and children.

Pain is used by Wells in his Darwinian fable to introduce the subject that is at the heart of his story, the Problem of Evil, how evil came into the world and how humankind deals with it. One of the creatures, echoing the old ethos of rewards and punishments, says, "Evil are the punishments of those who break the Law. None escape" (12.62). The evils of the world are interpreted by the "half-bestial creatures" who suffer under Moreau's scalpel as "the punishments of those who break the Law." The official (Moreau) way one deals with pain is through the Law:

"Not to go on all-fours; that is the Law. Are we not Men?"
"Not to suck up Drink; that is the Law. Are we not Men?"
"Not to eat Flesh or Fish; that is the Law. Are we not Men?"
(12.61)

And so on, down a list of commandments to "'Not to chase other Men; that is the Law. Are we not Men?'" These are followed by the god-directed theodicy, taught the animal-men as a litany:

"His is the House of Pain.
"His is the Hand that makes.
"His is the Hand that wounds.
"His is the Hand that heals."

To the Law has been added a theodicy based on guilt and pain, similar to the Christian. But Wells gives alternative etiologies of how these came about: on the one hand, that Dr. Moreau had "infected [the animals'] dwarfed brains with a kind of deification of himself" (12.61); on the other, that the animals themselves (albeit with their partially human consciousness) created the Law, God, and guilt-punishment as a way of explaining to themselves their pain. In Dr. Moreau's words, "There's something they call the Law. Sing hymns about 'all thine.' They build themselves their dens, gather fruit and pull herbs—marry even." Moreau suggests that they made these up themselves, although he is only rationalizing his own procedures.

His conclusion about his creation is both Frankenstinian ("They only sicken me with a sense of failure. I take no interest in them") and Swiftean: "But I can see through it all [that is, the laws and hymns], see into their very souls, and see there nothing but the souls of beasts, beasts that perish—anger, and the lusts to live and gratify themselves. . . . Yet they're odd. Complex, like everything else alive. There is a kind of upward striving in them, part vanity, part waste sexual emotion, part waste curiosity." "It only mocks me," he concludes, meaning that it mocks him as their disappointed creator, just as his creature disappointed Victor Frankenstein (14.82).

To complete the satiric genealogy, Prendick's description of mankind recalls Rochester's theriophily in his "Satyr against Mankind": "Before they had been beasts, . . . their instincts fitly adapted to their surroundings, and happy as living things may be. Now they stumbled in the shackles of humanity, lived in a fear that never died, fretted by a law they could not understand; their mock-human existence began in an agony, was one long internal struggle, one long dread of Moreau—and for what?" For mere "wantonness," Prendick concludes of the First Mover: "I could have forgiven him a little even had his motive been hate. But he was so irresponsible, so utterly careless. His curiosity, his mad, aimless investigations, drove him on, and the things were thrown out to live a year or so, to struggle and blunder and suffer; at last to die painfully." Like Gulliver, Prendick suffers disillusionment: "I must confess I lost faith in the sanity of the world when I saw it suffering the painful disorder of this island" (16.99–100).

The sin of Dr. Moreau is the creation of abominations—the "half-bestial creatures" and, clothed in bluish cloth, "grotesque human figures" (9.40–41); the evil is the pain and cruelty—and Moreau's power, which creates the abomination and inflicts the cruelty; then it is the guilt and category confusion that are for the animals the consequences of the pain and the abomination.

When Moreau is killed, Prendick steps into the breach—attempts to insert himself into Moreau's fiction of creation and damnation with the Christian Atonement, though its motivation, to save his own hide in the moment of crisis, is dubious. Thinking quickly, he tells the man-beasts, "'Children of the Law,' I said, 'he is not dead. . . . He has changed his shape—he has changed his body,' I went on. 'For a time you will not see him. He is . . . there'—I pointed upward—'where he can watch you. You cannot see him. But he can see you. Fear the Law'" (18.108–09).[26]

Moreau's assistant, Montgomery, presents his life as a microcosm, a comic reduction, of the world of evil: "'This silly ass of a world,' he said. 'What a muddle it all is! I haven't had any life. I wonder when it's going to begin. Sixteen years being bullied by nurses and schoolmasters at their own sweet will, five in London grinding hard at medicine—bad food, shabby lodgings, shabby clothes, shabby vice—a blunder—I didn't know any better—and hustled off to this beastly island. Ten years here! What's it all for, Prendick? Are we bubbles blown by a baby?'" (19.111).

Montgomery, Prendick concludes, "was in truth half akin to these Beast Folk, unfitted for human kindred" (19.114). What had Montgomery, in fact, done? He had "lost [his] head for ten minutes on a foggy night" (4.17)—the result, presumably of a sexual peccadillo, a "sin," is disgrace and exile. So Dr. Moreau's experiment becomes not the raising of the beasts but imposing "the human taint" on animals (21.133). The one faithful, trustworthy beast is the Dog Man—an equivalent of the Sorrel Nag, the one horse, mentally challenged, who remained faithful to Gulliver.

In *The War of the Worlds* (1898) Dr. Moreau's creatures are replaced by the Martians, who are, however strange, parallel to earthlings in that they too inhabit a fallen world; they live on a dying planet and must colonize another in order to survive; their choice of Earth is purely pragmatic, and at the end, having failed, they may move on to Venus. In other words, Wells is again dealing with the Problem of Evil, looking at both the Martians' situation and, in many ways the same, ours. They share "an incessant struggle for existence," and now, Mars "far gone in its cooling," "their only escape from the destruction that, generation after generation, creeps upon them" is to destroy and take over another planet. But, writes the author, "before we judge of them too harshly we must remember what ruthless and utter destruction our own species has wrought"—not only on animals but on "inferior races. . . . Are we such apostles of mercy as to complain if the Martians warred in the same spirit?"[27] One recalls the similar passage in which Conrad characterizes European colonization of the Congo.

On the one hand, Wells relates the Martians to ourselves, the frailty and flaws of humanity; on the other he compares their catastrophe to "the earthquake that destroyed Lisbon a century ago" (13.95), the standard example, from Voltaire onward, of the Problem of Evil. The problem of evil (the cooling of Mars) produces the problem of evil (their colonizing of our planet). Against the protagonist's Defoe-like concentration on facts and the real (Wells often sounds like the Defoe of *Journal of the Plague Year*) is posed the curate who, like the trained animal-men of Dr. Moreau, gives the traditional interpretation based on rewards and punishments: "Why are these things permitted? What sins have we done? . . . What have we done—what has Weybridge done?" (13.99). "Did you think God had exempted Weybridge?" says the protagonist. "He is not an insurance agent" (101). The curate reads the Martians' invasion as "the great and terrible day of the Lord"; but Wells's protagonist remarks, "What good is religion if it collapses under calamity?" At the end, when the Martians have been dispatched by human disease, he believes for a moment that "the destruction of Sennacherib had been repeated, that God had repented, that the Angel of Death had slain them in the night" (8.236); but of course what finally kills the Martians is their immune system, which is vulnerable to the tiniest microbe: one of the suffering-evils.

The bathos of their end is anticipated in the form of the Martians and their machines, which are compared to a dish cover, a milking stool, a fisherman's basket, boilers on stilts, vast spiders, even cowled human figures. At the least these mitigate "the huge unknown and hidden forces" that would have constituted a stronger version of terror. There is an element of the comic grotesque in the situation: The Martians are being driven off their planet by "natural evils" and in order to survive they have to occupy another planet—which happens to be ours. *Lebensraum*, of course, will be Adolf Hitler's motive for eastern conquest: a view Wells anticipates and ridicules, parodying G. T. Chesney's "The Battle of Dorking" (vs. his Woking), published in the *Spectator* of May 1871, which imagined an invasion of England on the model of the recent German invasion of France. The effect on the English had been similar to that of Orson Welles's radio production of *The War of the Worlds* on American listeners in the 1930s.[28] The subject is the Problem of Evil, which means simply suffering and death, war being one venue—from the 1900s the most compellingly problematic.

The Problem of the Anthropomorphic God: Twain, The Mysterious Stranger

> The vilest thing must be less vile than Thou
> > From whom it had its being, God and Lord!
> > Creator of all woe and sin! Abhorred,
> Malignant and implacable! I vow
>
> That not for all thy power furled and unfurled,
> > For all the temples to Thy glory built,
> > Would I assume the ignominious guilt
> Of having made such men in such a world.
>
> —*James Thomson,* The City of Dreadful Night *(1874), ll. 445–52*

At the beginning of the twentieth century, in *The Mysterious Stranger* (post-humously published, 1916), Mark Twain takes his model for God from Samuel Johnson's review of Soame Jenyns's *Free Enquiry into the Nature and Origin of Evil* (1757) and turns it on its head.

Jenyns's solution to the Problem of Evil was: Evil is part of God's plan (all good), of which we can see only a part, not the whole; evils may perhaps serve to entertain superior beings on the Great Chain of Being. Jenyns argued that "evil may be said to be our good . . . that there is some inconceivable benefit in pain abstractedly considered; that pain however inflicted, or wherever felt, communicates some good to the general system of being, and that every animal is some way or other the better for the pain of every other animal."

Johnson's was the solution of Job, accepting the absolute unknowableness of God. The Christian resolution, which Johnson accepted, was the Redemption by Christ's sacrifice—and so by the promise of compensatory rewards in the hereafter. But in the central part of his essay Johnson treats Jenyns as Swift had treated the Moderns and Iranaeus had treated the gnostics, by expanding upon their own writings, developing the fictions they have unconsciously (but revealingly) generated:

> He imagines that as we have not only animals for food, but choose some for our diversion, the same privilege may be allowed to some beings above us, who may deceive, torment, or destroy us for the ends only of their own pleasure or utility. . . . I cannot resist the temptation of contemplating this analogy, which I think he might have carried further very much to the advantage of his argument. He might have shewn that these hunters whose game is man have many sports analogous to our own. As we drown whelps and kittens, they amuse themselves now and then with sinking a ship, and stand round the field of Blenheim or the walls of Prague, as we encircle a cockpit. As we shoot a bird flying, they take a man in the midst of his business or pleasure, and knock him down with an apoplexy. Some of them, perhaps, are virtuosi, and delight in the operations of an asthma, as a human philosopher in the effects of the air pump. To swell a man with a tympany is as good a sport as to blow a frog. Many a merry bout have these frolic beings at the vicissitudes of an ague, and good sport it is to see man tumble with an epilepsy, and revive and tumble again, and all this he knows not why.[29]

And so on. Johnson's orthodox Christian satire of Jenyns laid the groundwork for Romantic satires on the deity himself.

Twain takes Johnson's satire not as a foil to the truth, which is God's unknowability, but as the truth itself. His fiction is Manichaean—creation is the work of a bad or merely indifferent god. The stranger who calls himself Satan entertains a group of boys by creating for their amusement a little world of animals and humans; first by frightening his tiny squirrels and then by arbitrarily killing his little humans:

> Two of the little workmen were quarreling, and in buzzing little bumblebee voices they were cursing and swearing at each other; now came blows and blood; then they locked themselves

together in a life-and-death struggle. Satan reached out his hand and crushed the life out of them with his fingers, threw them away, wiped the red from his fingers on his handkerchief, and went on talking where he had left off: "We cannot do wrong; neither have we any disposition to do it, for we do not know what it is."[30]

The scene of destruction is followed by the expression of human suffering —by the "crowds of pitying friends" who "with their bare heads bowed and many with the tears running down—a scene which Satan paid no attention to until the small noise of the weeping and praying began to annoy them [*sic*], then he reached out and took the heavy board seat out of our swing and brought it down and mashed all those people into the earth just as if they had been flies, and went on talking just the same" (2.643).

Again, with the irony of a Huck Finn, Theodor writes, "It made us miserable, for we loved him, and had thought him so noble and so beautiful and gracious and had honestly believed he was an angel, and to have him do this cruel thing—ah, it lowered him so, and we had had such pride in him" (642). Detachment has become an explanation for evil in the world, its focus always on cruelty: the girl burned at the stake, the cruelty to the so-called witch.

Appropriately, Twain's most striking example of evil as cruelty is, once again, an animal: Hans Oppert's torture of his dog is described with Swiftean vividness: "'Well, [says Satan] he is always clubbing his dog, which is a good dog and his only friend, and is faithful and loves him, and does no one any harm; and two days ago he was at it again, just for nothing—just for pleasure—and the dog was howling and begging, and Theodor and I begged too, but he threatened us and struck the dog again with all his might and knocked one of his eyes out.'" This is followed by Satan's conversation with the dog, who has forgiven his master and is urgently trying to lead the men to his body so that extreme unction can be administered before he dies; but, because he arrives too late, the priest condemns him to burn in hell—this contrasted with the poor dog's forgiveness (6.672). In Satan's attack on man's "moral sense," where animals are held up for comparison ("No brute ever does a cruel thing—that is the monopoly of those with the Moral sense" [5.669]). One of the idealized figures, Father Peter, comes as close as Twain permits to the truth when he defines the moral sense as "the faculty which enables us to distinguish good from evil" (4.655). But in fact Twain means by the moral sense what people mean by sin; like the priest who condemns the man to hell because he did not get there in time to shrive him, they are sinless but do evil.

In Twain's satire God is not God but a demiurge who, having demonstrated the utter amorality of creation and its creator, becomes a figure closer to Blake's devils in *The Marriage of Heaven and Hell*. He describes Satan upon first appearance as a youth, apparently about the age of the naive first-person narrator Theodor, with "new and good clothes on, and [he] was handsome and had a winning face and a pleasant voice, and was easy and graceful and unembarrassed, not slouchy and awkward and diffident, like other boys"; "he was so beautiful, you know—stunning, in fact" (2.637, 9.731). He recalls not only the unfallen Lucifer but Pan ("fresh and cheery and beautiful, and brought that winy atmosphere of his and changed the whole thing" [7.690]). There is even a parody of Blake's source, *Paradise Lost,* in Satan's offering Theodor a Pisgah vision of the future (as in Milton's books XI and XII), in which Satan describes Christianity and civilization marching hand in hand, "leaving famine and death and desolation in their wake, and other signs of the progress of the human race," and always "wars, and more wars, and still other wars" (9.718). Satan starts as a sort of magician; then we are asked to focus on his extreme disinterestedness—and its manifestation not just in amorality but in acts of cruelty such as the smashing of the little people, whom he compares to bricks and manure piles.

Twain is demonstrating one of the characteristics of satire—the use of a single figure in different ways; for example, like Blake's devil his detachment permits him to utter wisdom, act as a corrective force, even as a satirist—but the satire works both ways, for Satan is only amused and interested, "as a naturalist might be amused and interested by a collection of ants" (10.741). In the manner of Erasmus's Folly and Swift's Grub Street hack, Satan's detachment also permits him to utter truths, but his peroration evokes both Erasmus's *Praise* and Swift's "Digression on Madness":[31] The good Father Peter, as close as Twain comes to an ideal in the novel, has been driven mad by the machinations of Traum, and Traum explains in Jenyns fashion the justice of his act: "I said he would be happy the rest of his days and he will, for he will always think he is the Emperor and his pride in it and his joy in it will endure to the end. He is now, and will remain, the one utterly happy person in this empire." But, Theodor responds, "Couldn't you have done it without depriving him of his reason?" "Are you so unobservant," replies Traum-Satan, "as not to have found out that sanity and happiness are an impossible combination? No sane man can be happy, for to him life is real and he sees what a fearful thing it is. Only the mad can be happy, and not many of those." Turning on Theodor, he concludes, in the voice of Erasmus's Folly and Swift's Hack: "I have made him happy by the only means possible to his race—and you are not satisfied!" (735). Thus the credulous and the curious cooperate in the "perpetual Possession of being well Deceived."[32]

Ultimately, in the final pages, Satan is summed up in the name he has assumed, Philip Traum: "Life itself is only a vision, a dream" (11.742). "I myself have no existence; I am but a dream—your dream, creature of your imagination." The preference of "dreams, visions, fiction" over reality (which recalls Swift's "Those Entertainments and Pleasures we most value in life, are such as Dupe and play the Wag with the Senses" [*Tale*, 171]) is the summation of the novel, "the deluded dream of a God who could make good children as easily as bad, yet preferred to make bad ones; who could have made every one of them happy, yet never made a single happy one; who made them prize their bitter life, yet stingily cut it short . . . who mouths justice and invented hell—mouths mercy and invented hell—mouths Golden Rules, and forgiveness multiplied by seventy times seven, and invented hell; who mouths morals to other people and has none himself; who frowns upon crimes, yet commits them all; [etc., etc.]" (11.743).

In an autobiographical dictation made on 19 June 1906, Twain discarded the guise of a demiurge for a direct portrait of God:

> The portrait is substantially that of a man—if one can imagine a man charged and overcharged with evil impulses far beyond the human limit; a personage whom no one, perhaps, would desire to associate with now that Nero and Caligula are dead. In the Old Testament His acts expose His vindictive, unjust, ungenerous, pitiless and vengeful nature constantly. He is always punishing—punishing trifling misdeeds with thousandfold severity; punishing innocent children for the misdeeds of their parents; punishing unoffending populations for the misdeeds

of their rulers; even descending to wreak bloody vengeance upon harmless calves and lambs and sheep and bullocks as punishment for inconsequential trespasses committed by their proprietors. It is perhaps the most damnatory biography that exists in print anywhere.[33]

Note that God is now the one blamed for the death of the innocent animals and children, their deaths being traced back to the sacrifices of the Old Testament. Once again sin and evil are conflated in the creator or demiurge; from mistreatment of *one* innocent, as if anticipating World War I, the act has been extended to *all* creatures; from the mangled animals of Dr. Moreau to the terribly vulnerable Martian invaders on another (created but fallen) planet, and to the tiny helpless citizens of Satan-Traum.

We have looked at a series of creation myths—the creation of creatures (all children) ranging from Jude Frawley's Little Father Time, from the newly born Frankenstein monster to the animals mutated toward the human by Dr. Moreau, and finally to the tiny creatures, human and animal, a whole world created by the demiurge Satan-Philip Traum. (Jude himself, Hardy makes clear, is the creature of *some* malign "creator.") And suffering-evil introduces the question of how these creatures cope with the evils of the world, which are seen as the work of a malign creator.

3. COPING WITH EVIL

I and the public know
What all schoolchildren learn,
Those to whom evil is done
Do evil in return.

—W. H. Auden, "September 1, 1939"

Child and Parent: Folktales

What the majority of folktales do is introduce children to evils of the world they are entering—suffering-evil and, consequent upon this, in return doing-evil. The mother dies, and the father replaces her with a wicked stepmother. The family becomes so poor it cannot feed the children and survive; the parents abandon the children in the deepest part of the forest. The forest is occupied in these stories by wolves and witches: Hunger leads to the children's eating the gingerbread off the witch's house, and she—not apparently out of hunger—plans to devour the children either for their transgression or for sheer evil-doing; but she is herself made a meal of when the boy pushes her into the oven she has prepared for the children. The implication, though not in the gentler versions of the story, is that they will now eat her. In other stories a little girl ventures into—or must pass through—the forest and is approached by a wolf, who is charming at first but when the opportunity arises is intent on eating both the girl and her grandmother.

The moral in the Grimm brothers' "Little Red Riding Hood" is plain enough: she is instructed not to loiter but to go straight to grandmother's house; the consequence is that the wolf gets there first and devours grandmother and then Riding Hood; but the woodsman arrives and, in one version at least, cuts open the wolf's stomach to extract both grandmother and Riding Hood; in other versions the woodsman merely cuts off the wolf's head. The moral, according to Bruno Bettelheim, is the choice between the pleasure principle and the reality principle; as it is again in "The Three Little Pigs," in which the wolf devours the two lazy pigs and is defeated and himself cooked by the prudent third pig.[34]

The imagery of devourment, however, indicates (as Robert Darnton has shown) real physical hunger as a motive for the tales and the ways they show of dealing with evil.[35] The French and German tales, supported by the association of hunger with the Eucharist, project a particularly strong image of evil—the giant who "eats the blood of an Englishman," the wolf who eats both the little girl and her old grandmother, and the witch who would bake and eat children.

The devouring wolf relates to the vampire, both representing for the child the difference between eating and devouring: "The child subconsciously understands it as the difference between the pleasure principle uncontrolled, when one wants to devour all at once, ignoring the consequences, and the reality principle, in line with which one goes about intelligently foraging for food [mere nourishment]."[36] It is devouring that characterized James's characters, who must "possess" this or that cathected person. But for writers who were James's contemporaries, as for the children who read the tales, the wolf represented the world of death and suffering—evils that had to be explained and dealt with. To deal with meant to combine intelligent planning and foresight in order to cope with the wolf or witch—not, with the first two little pigs, lazy epicurean living. These tales taught the child that "a struggle against severe difficulties in life is unavoidable, is an intrinsic part of human existence—but if one does not shy away, but steadfastly meets unexpected and often unjust hardships, one masters all obstacles and at the end emerges victorious." The powerlessness of the child puts it into a proper position—with the innocent animal—to have a unique understanding of the dread of evil in the world. As Bettelheim puts it, in the case of fairy-tales and folktales, the aim is to come to terms with both inner demons and the outer world—not only actual death and suffering but "narcissistic disappointments, oedipal dilemmas, sibling rivalries," all of "the existential predicament" (6). A ghost story like W. W. Jacobs's "Monkey's Paw" is based on the old folk-tale of "The Ridiculous [or Three] Wishes," which was about hunger and the need for food; Jacobs replaces the hunger with that original evil, death—the parent's desire to recover a dead son.

The picaresque novel—a secular spiritual autobiography—was, among other things, a phenomenon parallel to the folktales. The anonymous *Lazarillo de Tormes* (1554) consists of a series of episodes that are based on folktales.[37] A poor boy, Lázaro, without parents or sustenance, avoids starvation and death by attaching himself (or allowing himself to be attached) to a master who both starves and mistreats him, and so he retaliates with tricks and subterfuges; he repays the cruelty and stinginess of the blind beggar by directing him to leap into a stone post. In the second episode he encounters a priest—even worse than the blind beggar, "a living portrait of the utmost niggardliness" (41), who virtually starves Lázaro to death. The only "food" in the priest's house is "a string of onions locked away upstairs," and the stingy priest keeps the loaves of holy bread for Mass locked in a chest. Lázaro gets into the chest; mixing the discourses of the spirit and the flesh, he says, "I opened my bread-filled paradise and took up in my hands and teeth a loaf of holy bread and in the time you could say two credos I had made it invisible" (45). Lázaro opens the chest and, "seeing the bread, began to worship it, but did not dare kiss it, even"; all he can do is "contemplate there the blessed face of God (as children are wont to call bread)" (46). He uses the bread as, it is suggested, it should be used, as a last resort to the hungry—preferable to its spiritualization by the hypocritical priest, who eats the bread himself. Hunger was what the Spanish picaresque was about. Lázaro ends his story married off to a canon's mistress and surviving as a contented cuckold.

Fratricide: Byron, Cain

The "evils" that entered the world with Adam's Fall were death, strife, and labor—disease, pain, and natural disaster, and all those effects people have found inexplicable given the belief in an all-powerful and benevolent deity. But these evils were initiated with death—the first death being the murder of Abel by his brother Cain. Cain represents the second Fall: "The act of eating the Forbidden Fruit was a crime only because God prohibited it. The murder of Abel, on the other hand, strikes us as an inherently criminal act."[38] The first is sin, the second is evil, illustrating the suffering-evil that is God's punishment for the Fall, and it is a case of doing-evil. From it descend, more directly and understandably than from the first Fall (the sin-Fall), all the evils with which we are concerned. And yet, as Byron notes in his drama *Cain* (1821), Cain does so because God preferred the animal sacrifice of his younger brother Abel: his act is a rebellion against God's choice of Abel and (Byron at least claims) of blood sacrifice, and so God punishes him with crop failure and vagabondage—hunger and homelessness.

Byron's *Cain* is about the Problem of Evil—"expulsion from our home, / And dread, and toil, and sweat, and heaviness; / Remorse of that which was," but primarily death—

LUCIFER. Dar'st thou to look on death?
CAIN. He has not yet
Been seen.
LUCIFER. But must be undergone.[39]

—which Cain resolves (solves) by killing Abel. Byron was to interpret the story not as the birth of evil (the first appearance of the consequence of Adam's sin) but as the birth of humanism with Cain's overthrowing the altar of blood sacrifice and killing the sacrificer, which in effect repudiate the God who demands it and lives through such blood sacrifices. Abel's sacrifice was acceptable to God, a blood sacrifice; Cain's, the fruits of the field, was unacceptable, and Cain committed high treason by killing God's surrogate. (A second transgressive subject—Byron's private subtext—was sexual; it appears to have been, in the central story of Cain and Adah, justification for the sin-transgression of sibling incest. The love is mutual. Lucifer asks Adah if she loves Cain "more than thy mother and thy sire?" "I do," she replies. "Is that a sin, too?")[40]

Cain raises once again the issue of cruelty to animals, which is the point of origin for his questioning of theodicy: "But animals— / Did they too eat of it [the apple], that they must die? . . . Alas! The hopeless wretches! / They too must share my sire's fate, like his sons; / Like them, too, without having shared the apple" (2.2.153–54, 158–60, p. 264). And when he overturns the altar it is the innocent animals he includes in his condemnation of Abel, "the sad ignorant victims underneath / Thy pious knife," sacrificed to "thy God [who] loves blood!" (3.1.302–03, p. 310).

Cain becomes aware of the consequent evils of his mother's sin—its implications: "Knowledge is good, / And life is good; and how can both be evil?" he wants to know (1.1. 37–38, p. 233), and what he learns is the distinction between sin and evil. The first is to do what God has "forbidden," the second is the consequence of doing so, and blood sacrifice of animals is man's way of seeking God's forgiveness.

Abel's response is the religious one: "I love God far more / Than life" (3.1. 315–16, p. 287), by which he means than living, than the living creatures, than the world of evils that Cain cannot comprehend; in terms of which Abel's altar is "yon vile flatt'rer of the clouds" (l. 290, p. 286).

The perplexed Cain gets his advice through the figure called Lucifer, who, related to the devils of Blake's *Marriage of Heaven and Hell*, proffers Cain reasonable information and sensible advice. Given the basic assumption of blood sacrifice, Lucifer imagines God:

> So wretched in his height,
> So restless in his wretchedness, must still
> Create and re-create—perhaps he'll make
> One day a Son unto himself—as he
> Gave you a father—and if he so doth
> Mark me!—the Son will be a Sacrifice. (1.1.161–66, p. 237)

As if recalling Blake's "Poison Tree," he asks,

> The tree was planted, and why not for him [Adam]?
> If not, why place him near it, where it grew,

> The fairest in the centre? They have but
> One answer to all questions,—''twas his will,
> And he *is* good.' How know I that? Because
> He is all-powerful must all-good, too, follow?
> I judge but by the fruits—and they are bitter—
> Which I must feed on for a fault not mine. (1.1.72–79, p. 234)[41]

Lucifer's embodiment of the Christian religion in blood sacrifice corresponds to Blake's, though Blake focused on the Atonement for sin, the forgiveness of sin which renders blood sacrifice irrelevant—and yet the blood sacrifice is recovered by the priests. Lucifer is Manichaean in the sense that he is God's opponent—a representative of morality versus religion, not of evil versus sin. When Cain says he will worship neither Lucifer nor God, Lucifer replies, "Not worshiping / Him makes thee mine the same" (1.1.318–19, p. 243).

Parents get rid of their children because they cannot feed them; the children have to eat or be eaten (the witch intends to cook them, they cook the witch); Cain's problem is concerned with the question of whether meat or vegetables, whether edibles or sacrifice, based on the criterion of which are the more acceptable to God. In *Moby-Dick,* the hunted whale's response to the whalers pursuing him to the death is to devour their captain piecemeal.

Revenge: Melville, Moby-Dick

Moby-Dick, or, The Whale was published in 1851 but achieved its classic status only in the 1920s (which then led to the publication of *Billy Budd*). At the heart of the story is Captain Ahab's pursuit of the whale. Ahab is pursuing evil—"evil," by his definition—or evil in the world, more precisely in nature; this happens to be the animal who devoured his leg: "All evils, to crazy Ahab, were visibly personified, and made practically assailable in Moby-Dick. He piled upon the whale's white hump the sum of all the general rage and hate felt by his whole race from dam down." That is, he is trying to destroy natural evil, or the cause of suffering-evil in the Problem of Evil; and in the process he comes to represent doing-evil because he destroys himself and his ship and its crew—all except Ishmael, whose last words ("I alone survive to tell thee") evoke Job and the Problem of Evil out of which his actions have emerged.[42] These were the words addressed to

Job, reporting the loss of his fortune and family; and in these terms, Ahab is a Job who does curse God, going so far as attempting to avenge himself on God's Leviathan itself—the animal God held up to him in his effort to humble his pride. (Melville quotes the passage in the encyclopedic series of epigraphs at the beginning of *Moby-Dick*.)[43]

In this story, from the years of Melville's prime, no sin is involved— unless we are to take Ahab's act against God as the ultimate "sin," which might be the case if we read *Moby-Dick* in terms of the Job story only. But the man who tells Ishmael of Ahab and prophesies the dire end of the voyage calls himself Elijah, the name of the prophet who warned and prophesied the end of the biblical Ahab, who was punished for killing Naboth in order to obtain his vineyard—possibly a reference to Ahab's original economic motives for attempting to kill Moby-Dick. Of course, Elijah may call himself that because he is talking about Ahab, and Ahab himself acquired his name through apparently irrelevant circumstances.

Why then is Father Mapple's sermon on Jonah? In his telling, the whale is both God and separate from God. God enters the whale in order to swallow Jonah, but then when Jonah repents he instructs the whale to rise from the bottom of the sea, whence he has conveyed Jonah, to the surface and "all the pleasant delights of air and earth" in order to vomit Jonah onto dry land—so he can do "the Almighty's bidding" (10.79). God-One has been defied by and so punishes Jonah. God-Two recovers him, sets him on dry land, and sends him on his mission to condemn the Ninevites (about Jonah's problems in Ninevah Father Mapple is silent). So Jonah-One can be read as Captain Ahab and Jonah-Two as Ishmael, who introduces with the prophet Jonah the Ishmael who was cast out by Abraham to become a wanderer but also was progenitor of a vast nation (Gen. 25.12–17).

There are different responses to—different readings of—Ahab. According to Captain Peleg he is an anticipation of Conrad's Mr. Kurtz: "He's a grand, ungodly, god-like man. . . . Ahab's above the common; Ahab's been in colleges, as well as 'mong the cannibals; been used to deeper wonders than the waves" (16.119–20). We also learn from Peleg of Ahab's wife and child, whom he abandons to go on his mad quest; which may align him with Bunyan's Christian or Defoe's and Swift's avatars of Christian: This would make Ahab's quest parallel—or parody—the salvationist story. On the other hand, according to the man named Elijah, Ahab is "Old

Thunder," and he tells the story of his lying "like dead for three days and nights," Christlike; which is supported by chapter 28, "Ahab," in which his cabin is described as the Holy of Holies, where the ship's "supreme lord and dictator" resides, "unseen by any eyes not permitted to penetrate into the now sacred retreat of his cabin" (167). In Ahab's own words, "I am demoniac; I'm madness maddened" (37.226).

Job's whale, the Leviathan described in Job 41, "a king over all the children of pride," is also Burke's whale (41.251), which Melville connects with the "magnificent milk-white charger, large-eyed, small-headed, bluff-chested, and with the dignity of a thousand monarchs in his lofty, over-weening carriage"—Burke's sublime horse. Ahab applies Burke's nonsublime animals—the dog, donkey, and mule—to Stubb (who replies, "I will not tamely be called a dog, sir"), himself assuming the sublime aspect, advancing upon Stubb "with such overbearing terrors in his aspect, that Stubb involuntarily retreated" (29.173).

The idea of the whale's—and the horse's—whiteness has brought to Melville's mind Coleridge's albatross, "whence come those clouds of spiritual wonderment and pale dread, in which that white phantom sails in all imaginations"—a bird not invented by Coleridge but by "God's great, unflattering laureate, Nature," to which Melville adds a long footnote concerning his own first contact with an albatross, "a regal, feathery thing of unspotted whiteness, and with a hooked, Roman bill sublime," which, in a tame version of the Mariner's act, is "caught . . . with a treacherous hook and line," labeled "with the ship's time and place" and let go again (24.155–56).

The sublime horse returns in the "strong young colt," a "dumb brute" in which one beholds "the instinct of the knowledge of the demonism of the world," and again he is white: "It is at once the most meaning symbol of spiritual things, nay, the very veil of the Christian's Deity": "Is it that by its indefiniteness it shadows forth the heartless voids and immensities of the universe, and thus stabs us from behind with the thought of annihilation, when beholding the white depths of the milky way?" (42.263). It is Burke's aesthetics of evil Melville is invoking (though he shows knowledge of Hogarth's beautiful as well).[44] Burke's sublime sea, "panting and snorting like a mad battle steed that has lost its rider, the masterless ocean" in which the whale lives is the world of evil(s)—insubstantial, unpredictable, different from the world of the land, which by comparison is unfallen, or civilized (see 23.148). This "everlasting terra incognita" dwarfs mankind: "Columbus sailed over numberless unknown worlds to discover his one superficial western one"; "however baby man may brag of his science and skill, and however much, in a flattering future, that science and skill may augment; yet for ever and for ever, to the crack of doom, the sea will insult and murder him, and pulverize the stateliest, stiffest frigate he can make"; and God too is evoked, the God who punished Korah and his family for rising against Moses by having the ground open up and "swallow them up for ever" (58.362–63; Numbers 16:29–34).

Chapter 99, called "The Doubloon," figures the significance of the white whale in this coin, which means inherently nothing in itself, but one thing to the crew, something else to Ahab, and something else to Ishmael, who tries to reconcile all of these: "And some certain significance lurks in all things, else all things are little worth, and the round world itself but an empty cipher."[45] Besides Ahab's response to the whale there are Starbuck's, Flask's, and Stubb's: Starbuck, the practical man ("I came here to hunt whales, not my commander's vengeance. How many barrels will thy vengeance yield thee even if thou gettist it, Captain Ahab?"); most significantly, Starbuck and Ahab disagree on "the dumb brute," the animal being attacked, with Ahab's blasphemy at stake: "'Vengeance on a dumb brute!' cries Starbuck, 'that simply smote thee from blindest instinct! Madness! To be enraged with a dumb thing, Captain Ahab, seems blasphemous'" (36.220). But in this one instance, this is a dumb animal that strikes back. Putting the whale in a larger context, Flask says "that in his poor opinion, the wondrous whale was but a species of magnified mouse, or at least water-rat," easily caught, killed, and boiled; an opinion, however, which Ishmael calls "ignorant, unconscious fearlessness" (27.163). Melville's whale can be called "evil" by Ahab, something else by his crew.

Atonement: Nathanael West, Miss Lonelyhearts
The first letter Miss Lonelyhearts reads is from the mother of seven children who, despite the suffering of seven pregnancies, is again pregnant. The Catholic church will not let her use contraceptives, and her husband ("so religious," she says) keeps demanding sex of her: "I cry all the time it hurts so much and I don't know what to do"—a setting for the next letter, which is from a noseless girl. She has, she writes, only "a big hole in the middle of my face that scares people, even myself."[46] Then there is

the little deaf and dumb girl who is raped and beaten up and locked by her mother in a closet.

The girl born without a nose asks why this happened to her?—because she was wicked at two years old? But she had no nose from birth. Because she committed a sin in a former life? Because her father was wicked? But he was wise, etc. Or take Fay Doyle—is it her own fault? Or the Dago's? Or the cripple's? Or God's? With Broad Shoulders is it her husband (is he sane?), the boarder, or the war (his VD)?

The question West asks about the Problem of Evil is to what extent it is God's fault and to what extent our own—or do we carry any responsibility for all these evils? Fay Doyle's problem is that she has needs way beyond what her crippled husband can satisfy, and Miss Lonelyhearts regards her need as love. She does not attract him, and indeed, in an oceanic metaphor, engulfs him, but he submits because he sees one of his Christ roles as that of love.

Noselessness, being deaf, dumb, and crippled, are natural evils, but in *Miss Lonelyhearts* (1933) West shows them specific to 1930s America, which meant the Depression, the aftermath of World War I, and in literary terms the Waste Land. Evoking "April is the cruelest month" and the "handful of dust," Miss Lonelyhearts detects "no signs of spring. The decay that covered the surface of the mottled ground was not the kind in which life generates. Last year, he remembered, May had failed to quicken these soiled fields. It had taken all the brutality of July to torture a few green spikes through the exhausted dirt" (70).

Who is responsible for these evils? God—society—Rousseau, Marx, the Communists, etc.? What are the human remedies for such as the noseless girl? There are illusions—the illusion of the Lonelyhearts column: "Life is worthwhile, for it is full of dreams and peace, gentleness and ecstasy, and faith that burns like a clear white flame on a grim dark altar" (66); the illusion of Christ and, if that fails, of art: "Forget the crucifixion, remember the renaissance" and become an artist or writer—or, "For those who have not the talent to create, there is appreciation" (71, 69); the illusion of retirement to the country, a return to nature and primitivism, of escape to the South Seas and the pursuit of pleasure; but then what? Perhaps the church. But all are illusions (107–10).

Christianity is Miss Lonelyhearts's nightmare of the sacrifice of the lamb, the bungled sacrifice—"he brought the knife down hard. The blow was inaccurate and made a flesh wound. He raised the knife again and this time the lamb's violent struggles made him miss altogether. The knife broke on the altar. . . . Their hands were covered with slimy blood and the lamb slipped free. It crawled off into the underbrush." He is left by his friends to put the lamb out of its misery: "He crushed its head with a stone and left the carcass to the flies that swarmed around the bloody altar flowers" (77–78). The passage needs to be read in the context not only of Genesis 22 but of Twain's portrait of a God who even "wreak[s] bloody vengeance upon harmless calves and lambs and sheep and bullocks as punishment for inconsequential trespasses committed by their proprietors."

West's source, however, is Dostoevsky, whose evocation is part of the *donné* of Miss Lonelyhearts. Miss Lonelyhearts is patterned on Raskolnikov, moving aimlessly from his cupboard of a room to a tavern, meeting someone, going into someone's grubby room, eating or drinking with someone, and always returning to his cupboard. (Already in *The Dream Life of Balso Snell* of 1931, West named a character John Raskolnikov Gilson).[47] Miss Lonelyhearts's dreams parody Raskolnikov's, in particular that of the tortured animal, his little horse becoming the even more resonant sacrificial lamb. But the significant reference is to *The Brothers Karamazov* and the story of the Grand Inquisitor and the Problem of Evil. At bottom there is Jesus' refusal (as the Christ) to change stones into bread, appropriate to the Marxist thirties.

West's form is parodic and satiric, the dialogic form of Menippean satire: a short prose passage; a snatch of verse; a series of letters; the dreams and the various encounters—their typicality, the "chosen" quality of the scenes, suggested by the titles of the chapters, like the stories characters tell in *Don Quixote* (or in the *Satyricon* at Trimalchio's dinner), in particular Shrike's parody litanies, commentaries, and speeches (which recall the monologues of Groucho Marx).[48]

Surrealism is part of West's parodic mode, one source for the grotesquerie of the images: the dream of the sheep, the doomed pregnant woman, the noseless girl, the raped deaf-and-dumb girl, the rapes of the girls who are out of place, all the images of cruelty and gratuitous torture of the sort found in the novels of Bataille, out of the novels of the Marquis de Sade. And then, equally surrealist, the image of Miss Lonelyhearts as Christ the Redeemer.

As Jude Fawley said of himself, "what a poor Christ he made."[49] In terms of the English tradition, West is recovering (again, probably out of Eliot's recovery of Pope and Dryden) the mock-heroic mode of satire: Christ is reduced (the comparison made by Shrike) to the Miss Lonely-hearts of a big city newspaper—a secular version of Christ or a priest, mediating between God and man. Or is Miss Lonelyhearts raised, via the mock-heroic of Shrike's litany, to the proportions of Christ? In fact, Miss Lonelyhearts as Christ is the object of Shrike's satire (Shrike, a bird with hooked beak, preys on insects, impales its prey on is beak). And the man who assumes the Miss Lonelyhearts role in the newspaper comes to think of himself as the Savior, comes to think he really is Miss Lonelyhearts; thereafter, reading the letters, he thinks he is the Savior. As our Christ he goes to Delehanty's speakeasy "for a drink," and "the shadow of a lamp-post . . . pierced him like a spear"—this in the passage evoking Eliot's "April is the cruelest month" (70).

Therefore, like another Gulliver, he goes mad—in terms of the conventions of satire, he is the satirist satirized, in this sense another Captain Ahab pursuing his whale: Miss Lonelyhearts (the man who becomes Miss Lonelyhearts) is satirized because he can no longer bear the reality around him, must become a Savior (Knight Errant) in the Quixote situation. He is the man with the obsession who can't cope. The satire reflects on the Christ-type in our society, the man who tries to take upon himself the burden that only Christ could, and so is guilty of hubris. And yet West's idea is that in this world all we have to intercede for us, to redeem us, to die for our sins (as Miss Lonelyhearts in fact at the end appears to do) is the Miss Lonelyhearts of the local newspaper. The situation, however different, is a twentieth-century reprise of the "atonement" of Mary Hack-about, the Harlot.

The satire is directed against the horror (noseless children)—and those responsible, beginning with God but including particular people and the religion of Christ, the Rock, and the Redemption. But, in the case of Miss L., the satire is also against the man who lets the horror warp his attitudes (the Gulliver, or the Governess in *Turn of the Screw*). Even the hero and heroine in West's *A Cool Million* (1934), who are raped and dismembered, are painfully naive, memories of what would happen to Horatio Alger in the real world of 1930s America. The Marquis de Sade made the same point, on a painfully extended scale, in his parody of Richardson's *Pamela: or Virtue Rewarded* in his *Justine* and *Juliette*.

As satire, *Miss Lonelyhearts* calls for an ideal or norm against which to judge the evil with which Miss Lonelyhearts tries to come to terms. But vainly. (1) Shrike adjusts to this world—by irony and by the pragmatics of his easy relationship with his wife: Let another man (Miss Lonelyhearts) do the foreplay and then get home just in time to consummate. Shrike is the cold realist, cynic, joker, and pragmatist: hardly an ideal or norm. (2) Mary Shrike and Betty follow an old-fashioned moral code: Mary draws the line at adultery, and Betty holds out until the proper moment to give herself to Miss Lonelyhearts. Memory and nostalgia for an ideal in the past comes closest. (3) Miss Lonelyhearts has fond memories of the past as order, beauty, the music of Mozart, and his younger sister's dance to the music—a harmonious union of nature and art; but the memory is interrupted by a punch in the mouth (the Shrikean reality principle). There is a recovery of such memories in the chapter called "Miss L. in the Country," Miss L. and Betty in Arcadia, but the country is now the place where "yids" aren't allowed (even there he finds lovelorn cases), and the visit is followed by his return to the city, where he is the same Miss L.; the interlude hasn't helped. Nevertheless, it was good while it lasted—or at least in combination with Betty. But not sufficient: He is too far gone by this time into his role of Christ the Rock. (4) Betty comes to represent a nice mix of order-disorder ("her arms full of bundles," 105) and memories of her childhood on the farm—but then Shrike bursts in, offering his list of remedies, beginning with country, then South Sea islands, and the rest. Betty is a kind of compromised ideal associated with party dresses, strawberry sodas, and babies (136–37), which dissolves when brought into contact with Christ and Miss Lonelyhearts as the Rock.

Jesus is humility and Christ is the Rock: one house built upon earth and another upon rock (Luke 6:48–49), which is reminiscent of Walt Disney's contemporary Depression allegory in his animated cartoon of the three little pigs. But weakly opposing the rock and bread, and somehow distinct, are Betty and love and earth: to which as Jesus Miss L. listens, but he sees himself as in fact the other Jesus, Christ the Rock. Betty remains thoughtful and loving; she would have married him, and she comes for him at the end, just moments too late. It is a satiric convention that she should come too late—all that matters is that she was there; just behind madness, but there.

Miss Lonelyhearts is Jesus among the wine-bibbers and harlots and the Jesus of love thy neighbor as thyself—as opposed to the other Christ of the rock/stone to be preferred over bread. But if Miss Lonelyhearts "is" Christ, in what does his Atonement/Redemption consist? (In compensation for the evils of this world?) It is never—even in the adages of Shrike—the promise of an afterlife of eternal happiness. Shrike's solutions are always escapes here and now (into travel, art, retirement, pursuit of pleasure, etc.)—as Betty's is also (escape from the city into the country, party dresses, and strawberry sodas). Miss Lonelyheart's solution is only the idea that Christ suffered for us, and that (suffering, not heaven) is his heritage: "He died nailed to a tree for you. His gift to you is suffering and it is only through suffering that you can know him. Cherish this gift, for . . ."—but then, having typed so far, he "snatched the paper out of the machine. With him, even the word Christ was a vanity" (116).

Miss Lonelyhearts "atones" by his sacrificial death. In his epiphany he becomes "Christ," having given up the more realistic (pragmatic, moral?) role of "Jesus." But there is no indication of what result his atonement will have for Desperate, Broad Shoulders, and Sick-of-it-All.

The first time he accepts Fay Doyle's embraces, he is accepting not love but lust, though he may in some sense be easing her suffering. When, the second time, he is the Rock and refuses her—he is being Christ—he gets himself killed: a sacrifice to her unsatisfied desires and to Mr. Doyle's resentment against the world for his crippling. He atones for the cripple with his own suffering/death. Period.

Christ is not a stable entity. West places Miss Lonelyhearts between the idea of God/Christ and Christian Atonement for sins and the other, the Jesus, aspect, of love thy neighbor as thyself and forgive. He is reverting to the mock-theology of Blake and the cosmic satire of the Romantics in which God is at fault. In the eighteenth century satire was ordinarily directed against man (as in Pope's *Essay on Man*); in the nineteenth, Romantic satire turned away from man's responsibility to accept and make the best of things to the God who permitted such an unhappy situation. Humans' futile attempts to overcome their environment, whether by dreaming or damning, were no longer funny, as they had been a century earlier.

Thus children abandoned in a dangerous world by their parents do whatever is called for in order to survive *in this world;* Dr. Moreau's animals and Dr. Frankenstein's monster rebel; and young Cain's murder of Abel is his answer to the demand of his creator-god for a sacrifice, a substitution that reverses the story of Abraham, Isaac, and the ram. Creatures driven from Mars attempt to colonize another planet, and when this fails presumably another. Finally, in the 1930s, a lovelorn columnist tries to deal with little girls, noseless and raped, and a sacrificial lamb by trying to become himself the Lamb, Christ atoning for the Original Sin, a situation in which the Problem of Evil is coped with by being reduced (as Twain reduces it) to black comedy. By the end of the century doing-evil, like suffering-evil, has its responsibility assigned to God or the state, and this means that coping with evil amounts to a turn against authority, whether it is a parent, a brother (who has aligned himself with God), God's Leviathan, or God himself. The original sin in these cases is in fact (as with Cain) the original evil, the result of being in a fallen world of evils.

Scapegoating: McEwan, The Comfort of Strangers

What was sin to Freud? There is no reference in the index of the Standard Edition to sin (nothing between *Simultaneity* and *Sinai Desert*); under *evil*, only *Evil, Problem of* and *Evil eye*. Sin had no meaning for Freud, nor does the term *depravity*, although notoriously he demonstrated the "evil" of children, by which he meant their sexuality; and the pious, unable to accept Freud's assumptions about children, meant by sexuality, sin. Freud replaced Original Sin with the Oedipus (or Electra) Complex, the boy's reaction against his father, the girl's against her mother. This is neither sin nor evil to Freud but simply the way people are, a given. The neurosis or psychosis causes unhappiness and can sometimes have consequences that are evil in the sense of "Evil, Problem of."

In the Problem of Evil Freud in effect replaced the existence of evil in the world with the dread we feel at the thought and anticipation of that evil, at the memory of the first evil in childhood. All of these, from the dread of death and the other evils to the feelings of guilt and the creation of a god, he internalizes in the human consciousness. He replaces Adam and Eve and God with a man, his mother, and his father; he replaces the situation of a sin of offense or disobedience to God with the murder of the father—ontogenetically in wish, phylogenetically (he believed) in fact—followed by feelings of guilt.[50]

Freud's theory was based on "a longing for the father" (13.148). It was not based on coming to terms with evil in the world as experienced; rather it drew on the child's dread before he yet knows of death, when he relies heavily on mother and father—and so, in this situation, he invents a god in the image of the father; then, based on his first reliance on his mother, he develops what Freud calls the Oedipus Complex, jealousy of the father and guilty wishes to supersede and eliminate him.

> When the growing individual finds that he is destined to re-
> main a child for ever, that he can never do without protection
> against strange superior powers, he lends those powers the fea-
> tures belonging to the figure of his father; he creates for him-
> self the gods whom he dreads, whom he seeks to propitiate,
> and whom he nevertheless entrusts with his own protection.
> Thus his longing for a father is a motive identical with his need
> for protection against the consequences of his human weak-
> ness. The defence against childish helplessness is what lends
> its characteristic features to the adult's reaction to the helpless-
> ness which he has to acknowledge—a reaction which is pre-
> cisely the formation of religion.[51]

In 1917 Freud described the three breakthroughs (he calls them blows or wounds) that destabilized men and left them available to the revaluation of the Problem of Evil: the cosmological blow was the Copernican revolu-tion that removed man from the center of the universe; the Darwinian was the biological blow, which destroyed the pride that led him to make "claims to a divine descent which permitted him to break the bond of community between him and the animal kingdom. . . . Darwin and his collaborators and forerunners put an end to this presumption on the part of man. Man is not a being different from animals or superior to them; he himself is of animal descent, being more closely related to some species and more distantly to others."[52]

"The third blow," he continues, "which is psychological in nature, is probably the most wounding": Freud attributes his "blow" to two discov-eries—"that the life of our sexual instincts cannot be wholly tamed, and that mental processes are in themselves unconscious and only reach the ego and come under its control through incomplete and untrustworthy perceptions—these two discoveries amount to a statement that the ego is not master in its own house" (17:143). In short, sex and the subconscious, terrifying taboos to the Victorian superego, were translated into evolution, devolution, regression, repression, and so on.

In Ian McEwan's novel *The Comfort of Strangers* (1981) a man picks up a total stranger, cultivates his friendship and kills him, slashing his wrist in a mock sacrifice. But the gratuitous act is given a motive. It is Robert's problem with his father that leads him, initially, to the Original Sin—in his case, as a child, Eve's sins of gluttony and pride, but essentially disobedience to the father—and punishment; subsequently to commit acts of evil, repeating the act of punishment (the evil) his father inflicted on him. Robert is a psychiatric case history, made in the film of the novel even more prominent by Christopher Walken's opening voice-over, and the closing reprise, of his story of his father and his Original Sin. His evil act is explained by an original evil, his childhood trauma at the hands of his father and sisters—"I never forgave them," he says of his sisters, meaning women. He has never forgiven his sisters for their humiliation of him—and so he continues to take it out on his wife, Caroline (who, up to a point, enjoys the pain), and, in misogynist words, on women in general. As Freud put it, "As the child passes over from the passivity of the [traumatic] experience to the activity of the game, he hands on the disagreeable experience to one of his playmates and in this way revenges himself on a substitute" (i.e., not the father who punished him and whose role he has assumed).[53]

After breaking her back what more was there left for Robert to do to Caroline except kill her? The Englishman Colin, the innocent tourist visiting Venice, serves as the scapegoat, fulfilling the need for a victim to reanimate the Robert-Caroline relationship, which has itself this reanimating effect on Colin and his girlfriend (not yet wife) Mary. Thus Colin and Mary are absorbed into their SM game by Robert and Caroline, and bloodily sacrificed. It apparently requires all four of them—Mary must hear the story, must watch and witness. But punishment proves the crime: Robert and Caroline have to be caught and punished, as in the Original Sin against Robert's father, for their pleasure to be consummated.

Colin serves as the (beautiful, desirable, plus having a girlfriend named Mary) scapegoat of John 11.47–53: Caiaphas, the high priest, tells the priests and Pharisees "that it is better for one man [Jesus] to die for the people, than for the whole nation to be destroyed . . . to gather together in unity the scattered children of God" (and so back to Genesis and the father's substitution of himself with his son, then with a lamb)—which secularizes and politicizes the reality of Christ's sacrifice of himself for

the sins of all men: Thus the difference too between the Gospel story of
the Atonement and Robert-Caroline's obscene parody of it.

Robert and Caroline are psychopaths in need of a surrogate or scapegoat. They choose to sacrifice Colin and Mary in order to keep their marriage intact. This supposes Robert and Caroline having run out of games
and now being at odds, perhaps about to break up: an evil that has to be
coped with. The situation is what René Girard has referred to as putting an
end to the vendetta, the continuing cycle of violence, by producing "an act
of violence without risk of vengeance," in which "the role of sacrifice is to
stem this rising tide of indiscriminate substitutions and redirect violence
into 'proper' channels": on an outsider as scapegoat, someone whom both
factions (in this case Robert and Caroline) can agree upon, a foreigner but
one with a sympathetic character. "The aim," Girard writes, "is to achieve
a radically new type of violence, truly decisive and self-contained, a form
that will put an end once and for all to violence itself."[54] In this case, to
renew pleasure, and Robert's plan includes, built into the scenario, its
denouement, his apprehension and punishment.

Why, if Colin is the scapegoat, is it important that Mary participate—
be a witness to the "sacrifice" (slashed wrist in the novel, throat in the
film, but in either case reminiscent of the sacrifice of a lamb or goat)?
Voyeurism is apparently required—Robert of Colin to begin with, then at
the moment of the "sacrifice," of Caroline and the witness, Colin's lover
Mary.[55] More significantly, in the ritual Robert is the substitute for the
father (or, in Atonement terms, the Father), Colin for the young Robert
who was beaten by his father (the Son), and Mary for the sisters; and the
effect in their sexual satisfaction (most obvious in the film where they
retire to the bedroom).

As Caroline tells Mary: "Colin brought us together."[56] The relationship
is, however, symmetrical. The Robert-Caroline relationship had also fallen
into the doldrums before the lucky day when Robert saw Colin and Mary
arrive. Robert and Caroline release the passion in Colin and Mary, who
become, as they began as, their doubles. If there is the "love" of Robert and
Caroline, there is also the love of Colin and Mary—one passionate, alive,
but deadly and evil; the other faded into friendship (5.62), not making love
and hardly talking—and outside their hotel room they "keep getting lost."

McEwan uses the idea of Venice (4.49)—without maps a place in
which it is easy to get lost—the Venice of Poe's "Assignation" (a double

suicide, as Pinkie projects in *Brighton Rock*), the Venice of Thomas Mann's "Death in Venice" and of Nicholas Roeg's *Don't Look Now* and a place easily associated with love and evil. Geographically, Robert lives opposite the cemetery of San Michele, where his father and grandfather are buried; from his apartment and from the barbershop they frequented he can keep the cemetery in sight; their possessions decorate his flat. Colin and Mary, the English unmarried tourists, and Robert and Caroline are on opposite sides of the island—the first looking across the Grand Canal to the church of San Giorgio Maggiori (some sort of a religious norm or ideal presumably), the second looking across at the cemetery, at the past and death.

Colin and Mary, quite unaware of their roles in the fantasy of their acquaintances until Robert glancingly shows Mary one of his photographs of Colin, are powerfully if subliminally affected by their contact with the demonic Robert and Caroline: after returning to their hotel, they immediately become passionate lovers—they don't leave their room for four or five days; and with strong suggestions of the sadomasochistic. They fantasize handcuffing themselves together and throwing away the key:

> They took to muttering in each other's ear as they made love, stories that came from nowhere, out of the dark, stories that produced moans and giggles of hopeless abandon, that won from the spellbound listener consent to a lifetime of subjection and humiliation. Mary muttered her intention of hiring a surgeon to amputate Colin's arms and legs. She would keep him in a room in her house, and use him exclusively for sex, sometimes lending him out to friends. Colin invented for Mary a large, intricate machine, made of steel, painted bright red and powered by electricity; . . . Once Mary was strapped in, fitted to tubes that fed and evacuated her body, the machine would fuck her, not just for hours or weeks, but for years, on and on, for the rest of her life, till she was dead and on even after that, till Colin, or his lawyer, turned it off. (8.81–82)

These fantasies, comic versions of Robert's, may derive from Mary's talk with Caroline, an SM prisoner with an injured back, or, subliminally, from the aura of the Venice that is shared by both Mary and Colin. Then Mary remembers the photograph, connects it with Robert standing on the balcony one morning—they are only a part of Robert and Caroline's game. Accident is involved (Robert's first view of Colin), and a fatalism that directs Colin and Mary to the vaporetto stop opposite San Michele, to decide to walk across the island rather than ride the vaporetto around. Or (parallel to their increased love-making) their secret desire to join in, be drawn in. Thus the somewhat supernatural aura, more than naturalistic reality, surrounds the "evil" couple—which further sets them off from the innocent couple, who are nevertheless (from some inner compulsion) drawn to them, like Geraldine, with Christabel "inviting them in."

A young English couple, as innocent as the albatross, is preyed upon in the sinister Venice of Mann's "Death in Venice"; but is the exploiter, Robert, evil-doer or himself the original-sinner? His evil acts are explained by his "sin" against his father, and the English couple represents in one sense innocence exploited, in another complicity in the sacrificial ceremony with which the story culminates. Doing-evil, in short, becomes interchangeable with suffering-evil, here as in the case of Adam and Eve.

In McEwan's *Black Dogs* (1992) the innocent animal has turned vicious: the black dogs are animals who are not exactly mistreated; they have been corrupted, trained (in our terms, "created") by SS men during the Occupation to rape women suspected of terrorist activities, but when the Nazis retreat they are abandoned to wander the countryside, now foragers as well as trained torturers. The scene is France in 1944, the situation the Nazi occupiers and the Resistance. When they threaten the female protagonist, June, we are left to judge whether the attack would have been sexual or merely from hunger—or training—whether she would have been raped or eaten. They are, in a sense, "man's best friends" transformed so as to invoke the wolves of the Grimm brothers' fairy tales. The attack on June and the mayor's story of the Gestapo dogs follow upon (as in *Comfort of Strangers*) the account of her and Bernard's passionate love-making—a potential rape if we believe the mayor's story, but dark deadly animal violence in any case, and for June (a Communist at the time) there is the awareness of what had come in France just before—and the sense of God that follows for her, turning the attack into a conversion experience. But in the story of the Gestapo dogs, there are also the other perpetrators—the mayor and the men of the village, the ordinary folk who distrusted the woman as an alien, therefore made her another scapegoat, and love to tell the stories of how she was raped by the dogs. Thus, their way of dealing with the ambiguity of the Occupation.

CHAPTER EIGHT

Modern Sin and Evil

The problem of evil will be the fundamental problem of postwar intellectual life in Europe—as death became the fundamental problem after the last war.

—*Hannah Arendt, 1945*

1. IDEOLOGY

Private and Public Evil: "Murder and More"
In the 1920s, in the aftermath of World War I, Ernest Hemingway described in *A Farewell to Arms* (1929) how Frederic Henry leaves the deathbed of his beloved Catherine Barkley, goes for a walk, and remembers an earlier time:

> Once in camp I put a log on top of the fire and it was full of ants. As it commenced to burn, the ants swarmed out and went first toward the center where the fire was; then turned back and ran toward the end. When there were enough on the end they fell off into the fire. Some got out, their bodies burnt and flattened, and went off not knowing where they were going. But most of them went toward the fire and then back toward the end and swarmed on the cool end and finally fell off into the fire. I remember thinking at the time that it was the end of the world and a splendid chance to be a messiah and lift the log off the fire and throw it out where the ants could get off onto the ground. But I did not do anything but threw a tin cup of water on the log, so that I would have the cup empty to put whisky in before I added water to it. I think the cup of water on the burning log only steamed the ants.[1]

Frederic Henry is the Twain demiurge (Satan-Traum) as a suffering soldier, his personal suffering explained by the dying Catherine, his public
suffering by the so-called Great War from which he has emerged. He assumes the role of God and hurries the ants (Twain's "collection of ants")
to their doom. The ants are his scapegoat, his response to the Problem of
Evil. Yet it is not he or God but the generals far behind the trenches who
are randomly killing millions.

In the twentieth century the two distinctive evils were war and genocide. These were public evils, not that there was a dearth of private. Public
evil is a matter of magnitude, as if the death of Catherine Barkley—or the
rape of Temple Drake—had spread to all the citizens of the United States
and the world. The killing of Poe's black cat was private and personal,
as were the crimes of the James, Faulkner, and Greene novels, though
the guilt may spread from two to four, from four outward into the public
domain. The Mariner's killing of the albatross has public repercussions,
as does Ahab's attack on the whale: Both are personal acts, but the crews
of both ships are wiped out. Up to this point, evil was one on one, one
horse, one bird, one cat, or one whale. Now whole armies and races are
destroyed—30 million Russians, 6 million Jews, 140 thousand Germans
in Dresden, 75 thousand Japanese in Hiroshima; and by one man, as if
Popeye had violated all the women of Mississippi. The random killings
in Twain's *Mysterious Stranger* were a watershed, followed by the overpowering slaughter of World War I, grounds for Hemingway's image of
Frederic Henry destroying the ant colony. Every kind of evil was writ large,
including the scope and nature of vengeance as the Russian armies swept
toward Berlin.

These are all public evils, comparable in magnitude to the so-called
natural evils of the Lisbon Earthquake and the tsunami of 2004, equally
incomprehensible in a theistic world. They all derive from the will of
one man or a small group. From a single man, a single control center—the Chancellery in Berlin, the war room in London and Washington—the word was passed down to the executioners, those who cut the
throats or fired the shots and dropped the bodies into mass graves; to the
bombardiers, and finally the slaughter of noncombatant civilians on the
ground.

The Holocaust, above all, was a conscious act conceived and ordered
by a single man, whose order from almost any human perspective was a

usurpation of God's function. (Another example was Stalin's starvation of the kulaks and his purge trials that wiped out a large part of the Soviet elite—or, in Asia, Mao's Cultural Revolution and Pol Pot's cleansing.) Evil lies ultimately in the absolute power of one party over another, in the Nazi (and Russian) case, the power of the totalitarian state: "immense life-and-death power . . . in the hands of a few unelected leaders who were not accountable to those whose lives they controlled, and right and wrong was defined in terms of a single unquestionable set of beliefs as interpreted by these leaders."[2] In other words, more than the psychology of an individual is at stake—a huge toy and a child's mentality, that of a Hitler, Stalin, Pol Pot, Saddam Hussein, to play with it.

These phenomena helped to correct the growing emphasis we have noted in chapter 7 on God as the chief perpetrator of evils, discovering one or more humans who came close to equaling him and then demonizing them. Susan Neiman has argued that after Lisbon moral evil was distinguished from natural disaster—and Edward Rothstein has noted, apropos of Hurricane Katrina, that "it is remarkable how this natural disaster has almost imperceptibly come to seem the result of human agency, as if failures in planning were almost evidence of cause, as if forces of nature were subject to human oversight. . . . [This theodicy] doesn't really explain catastrophe, but it attempts to explain why we are forced to experience it: because of human failings."[3] Rothstein, referring to "global warming" and irresponsible violations of the environment, is giving an up-to-date version of Rousseau's explanation of the Lisbon earthquake as the result of the planners who laid out their city in an area liable to earthquakes and packed it with too many people in shoddy houses. Or, put differently, Auschwitz had an impact on T. W. Adorno similar to the Lisbon earthquake on Voltaire, for whom it had discredited any (in particular Leibniz's) theodicy.[4]

By twentieth-century war we mean what was modern and unprecedented: vast numbers killed; but in fact, part of the war (permitted by the war) was the systematic killing of specified ethnic, national, religious groups: the Armenian genocide of 1915, the Jewish genocide of the 1940s, the Cambodian genocide of the 1970s, the Bosnian genocide of the 1990s, and the current genocide in Darfur. As noted, genocide was characterized by Senator Javits as "murder and more," "more" being in this case not only quantity but, if we apply Hannah Arendt's words, a "crime against the human status"; or against the particularity of a culture, as the Israeli court declared of Adolf Eichmann, "an actual act of murder in addition to acts of destroying whole Jewish communities."[5] The first resolution on genocide passed by the United Nations General Assembly declared that "genocide is the denial of the right of existence of entire human groups, as homicide is the denial of the right to live of individual human beings."[6]

The key words that describe (and derive from) this "modern" evil are *radical, absolute, total* (as in "total war"), *without exception*. The instrumental terms are *system* and *modernization*—not just killing or "diplomacy by other means," but in the wars by aerial bombs and weapons of mass destruction, in the Holocaust by train schedules, itemized lists, and the vast bureaucracy of the German Reich.

The Holocaust in Germany was also, of course, a gigantic case of scapegoating. The perpetrators of genocide "stigmatize[d] the potential victims or enemy as the embodiment of evil: non-human, diseased, unclean, diabolical."[7] This involved first *dehumanizing* the victims, calling them rats and bedbugs (then "exterminating" them by poison gas); packing them in stock cars, leading them to slaughterhouses in scenes that recalled the cruelty-to-animals topos we have followed in the literature of the Enlightenment. As Andrew Delbanco writes, "The purest expression of the characteristic form of evil in the modern world: the ability to erase the humanity of other beings and turn them into usable and dispensable things" (soap, lampshades).[8]

Another disturbing element of that ultimate evil, the Holocaust, was the question (Adorno's question), How could such things have happened in Germany, a highly civilized country (the country of Bach, Mozart, Beethoven, Schubert, Brahms; Goethe, Hegel, Nietzsche, Mann), a symbol of Western Civilization?[9] The worst atrocities of the twentieth century were committed by the most civilized of European people. The possibly laudable principle of euthanasia, for example, was corrupted by German doctors into the Holocaust (not to mention the cruelty of Josef Mengele's medical experiments carried out on children). Germanic efficiency and system were put to the most appalling ends. The language of Goethe was debased by the Nazi euphemisms for these crimes, "special treatment," "evacuation," and "final solution."

Sin as Ideological Deviation: Koestler, Darkness at Noon

The two great evils of the last century were war and genocide, but the encompassing evil was ideology. Arendt defined *ideology* as "—isms which to the satisfaction of their adherents can explain everything and every occurrence by deducing it from a single premise. . . . it is the logic of an idea . . . [characterized by its] claim to total explanation," the capacity to be "independent of all experience" (it "emancipate[s] thought from experience and reality"), a system "with a consistency that exists nowhere in the realm of reality"—that is completely self-enclosed. "Not before Hitler and Stalin," she adds, "were the great political potentialities of the ideologies discovered."[10]

We can single out for the practical operation of ideology, *persecution,* meaning to pursue with the intention of injuring, to cause another to suffer because of belief. Hogarth showed the persecution of a sinner, the Harlot, but sin as a public issue was always in the plural (Swift's intention in the *Tale of a Tub* was to persecute sinners, the heretic dissenters). The aim of persecution was to submerge the personal in the type—a harlot (M. Hackabout or Hester Prynne) or an orphan (Oliver Twist) or a Jew or a Gypsy or a homosexual. In chapters 3 and 4 we saw the situation of sinners persecuted by evil as representatives of the "holy" who echoed the image in the *Beggar's Opera* paintings of the wicked Peachum assuming a *Noli me tangere* (a holier-than-thou) pose vis-à-vis his fornicating daughter Polly, refusing to reprieve the sinner Macheath. Peachum and Lockit, like the priests and magistrates of the *Harlot's Progress,* were representatives of the law, church, and government (the Great Man and his cohorts).

An orthodoxy or ideology persecutes all of the type without exception—from Puritan London or New England to Nazi Germany or Croatia or Rwanda. Persecution is evil characterized by persistence, consistency, relentlessness, totality, as opposed to a single personal act. Persecution is always Murder One, premeditated and planned.

If the Romantics recovered religion as superstition and devil-worship (and worship of the pagan gods), the Marxists replaced religion with ideology. The process had gradually taken place from the Reformation onward, nationalism replacing sin with treason against the king and the state. In the writings of Hegel and Marx, religion was replaced by ideology, sin and heresy were replaced by rebellion against the ideology (or against History, secularized religion). Finally, the secularization of the sacred recovered sin as ideological deviation, the evil being the Stalinist suppression of the heresies.

Arthur Koestler, for example, makes this abundantly clear in the vocabulary of his essay "The Initiates" and his novel *Darkness at Noon* (1941). The essay appeared in the collection of essays by ex-Communists called *The God that Failed* (1949). As the title of that book suggests, the vocabulary is of "faith" and "conversion"; becoming a Communist was to "enter the womb of a church."[11] Koestler writes,

> Nothing henceforth can disturb the convert's inner peace and serenity—except the occasional fear of losing faith again, losing thereby what alone makes life worth living, and falling back into the outer darkness, where there is wailing and gnashing of teeth. (22 [cf. Matt. 8:12])
>
> Renegades of the Party were lost souls, fallen out of grace; to argue with them, even to listen to them, meant trafficking with the Powers of Evil. (33)

Louis Fischer employs in his essay the same discourse of "worship," "crisis of faith," and the idea that "the angels of this morning might be declared devils by evening"; the Party "in the requirements of austerity and dedication . . . resembled a monastic order" (217, 202); Stephen Spender, in his essay, refers to "the almost mystical faith" of the Party (245).

In Koestler's *Darkness at Noon* the Old Bolsheviks like Rubashov believe (or are made to believe by the "priesthood") that they are sinning and so must accept the evil (suffering, death) that is their punishment in the name of the greater cause, or No. 1 (Stalin).[12] (Or is the analogy with martyrdom rather than heresy? But unlike martyrs, the Old Bolsheviks recant and repent—the central event is "confession"—before being put to death.) Rubashov and his interrogator Ivanov share the common Christian discourse in which ideology is "all he had believed in, fought for and preached."[13] At one point No. 1 is "the high priest celebrating the Mass" (3.3.127);[14] at another, Lenin "was revered as God-the-Father, and No. 1 as the Son" (1.12.48). Except that No. 1 is not the atoning Son, only a continuation of God-the-Father, the unknowable god of wrath who visits suffering-evil on the disobedient "sinners": "The Party knew only one crime: to swerve from the course laid out [the original sense of *sin*]; and only one punishment: death. Death was no mystery in the movement;

there was nothing exalted about it: it was the logical solution to political divergences" (1.13.57).

Therefore we must punish wrong ideas as others punish crimes: with death (2.1.74), as in Christianity death was the logical punishment for the disobedience of Adam and Eve, the consequence of Original Sin. Rubashov goes on to explain History (with the same irony as above): "History knows no scruples and no hesitation. Inert and unerring, she flows towards her goal. At every bend in her course she leaves the mud which she carries and the corpses of the drowned. History knows her way. She makes no mistakes. He who has not absolute faith in history does not belong in the party's ranks" (1.9.36). Only in terms of such definitions can the arbitrary judgment of a No. 1 make any sense—and then only in a Calvinist way, positing an unknowable deity in whom one can only have faith. The worst that can happen to you (as when Rubashov deals with Richard) is to be expelled from the Party—and this is for "deviation."

In the dialectic of *Darkness at Noon* Rubashov, not No. 1, becomes the scapegoat—the lamb, and so the Lamb/Christ—the analogy Gletkin explains: Not only, Gletkin tells Rubashov, have there always been scapegoats, a fact he has learned from his late superior Ivanov, himself now turned into another scapegoat, but "there are also examples in history of voluntary scapegoats." He learned from "the village priest that Jesus Christ called himself a lamb, which had taken on itself all sin. I have never understood in what way it could help mankind if someone declares he is being sacrificed for its sake. But for two thousand years people have apparently found it quite natural." Gletkin is setting up his own (or the Party's) analogy between the Party and Christianity, noting that "in the outline of history published by the Party for the evening classes for adults, it is emphasized that during the first few centuries the Christian religion realized an objective progress for mankind. Whether Jesus spoke the truth or not when he asserted he was the son of God and of a virgin is of no interest to any sensible person. It is said to be symbolical, but the peasants take it literally. We have the same right to invent useful symbols which the peasants take literally" (3.4.161).

The old porter Wassilij (a relic of pre-Revolutionary Russia) makes the connection with Rubashov explicit as he listens to his daughter read the transcript of Rubashov's trial. What runs through his mind is a memory of the *Ecce Homo* scene of Christ's trial, the words of Mark: "And they clothed him with purple and they smote him on the head with a reed and did spit upon him; and bowing their knees worshipped him."[15] Rubashov himself, as he waits for the executioner, remembers the drawing of a Pietà he looked at on the wall of the art gallery where he condemned the young Communist Richard "to outer darkness" (4.2.181). He kept looking at it over Richard's head but could see only "the Madonna's thin hands, curved upwards, hollowed to the shape of a bowl, and a bit of empty sky covered with horizontal pen-lines. More was not to be seen as, while speaking, Richard's head persisted immovably in the same position on his slightly bowed, reddish neck." The point in the last minutes of his life is: Richard then, filling the empty space (filling the eucharist "bowl") where the body of Christ appears; Rubashov now. And what first made Rubashov recall the Pietà on his first day in prison was the mental image of the clasped hands of the Czarist in the neighboring cell—and this in the context of his memory of the champagne-glass breasts of his lover Arlova. It is only later that we learn how he betrayed Arlova in order to stay alive himself, in order, he reasons, to continue his work for the Party—another example of the end justifying the means.

The End Justifies the Means

The principle of evil in *Darkness at Noon*—for which Rubashov "atones"— is the motto "the end justifies the means."[16] For this principle he recants but by continuing to worry and think up to the very end about Arlova, Richard, and other individuals, he retains some trace of his identity, which is presented as the Old Bolshevik identity and exceeds the bare needs of Gletkin and No. 1. In this sense he fits the epigraph Koestler attaches to "The Third Hearing": "But let your communication be, Yea, yea; Nay, nay; for whatsoever is more than these cometh of evil" (3.1.119; Matt. 5:37).

Rubashov had questioned the doctrine in his last dialogue with Ivanov: "Do you remember 'Raskolnikov'?" he asks Ivanov. "If Raskolnikov had bumped off the old woman at the command of the Party," replies Ivanov, "—for example, to increase strike funds or to install an illegal Press—then the equation would stand, and the novel with its misleading problem would never have been written, and so much the better for humanity."

"I don't approve of mixing ideologies," Ivanov continued.

"There are only two conceptions of human ethics, and they are at opposite poles. One of them is Christian and humane, declares the individual to be sacrosanct, and asserts that the rules of arithmetic are not to be applied to human units. The other starts from the basic principle that a collective aim justifies all means, and not only allows, but demands, that the individual should in every way be subordinated and sacrificed to the community—which may dispose of it as an experimentation rabbit or a sacrificial lamb." (2.7.114)

From the Party's perspective, Richard, Arlova, and Rubashov are all lambs sacrificed to the greater good (means to an end); by the older generation, which can remember Christianity, they are regarded as sacrificial atonement to the God/No. 1. If No. 1 anticipates Big Brother, for the Gletkins and the porter's daughter the memory is as faint as that of the old song "The Bells of St. Clements" in George Orwell's *Nineteen Eighty-Four* (or of Christianity in Swift's *Argument against Abolishing Christianity*).

The Communist heretics do recant and confess to heresies of which they are innocent. They accept the greater Good, subordinate themselves to it—a recovery of Augustine's doctrine of the part-whole. Ironically we may notice a reaffirmation of Swift's Christian ecclesiastical norm in *A Tale of a Tub*, in which he satirized the part that will not subordinate itself to the whole. "The individual was nothing, the Party was all; the branch which broke from the tree must wither," and the "I" was forever replaced by "we" (1.14.62). The villain of Stalinist ideology was Swift's spider or Modern or Gnostic. Koestler attaches to "The Second Hearing" an epigraph from Dietrich von Nieheim, a twelfth-century bishop of Verden, which concludes, "For all order is for the sake of the community, and the individual must be sacrificed to the common good" (71). Only the bishop's intransitive "be sacrificed" sets off the passage from Augustine and Swift, who would have phrased it differently.

Ivanov expresses about institutional Christianity, without irony, Blake's notion of what happened to Christ's Atonement—as analogous to what has happened to Communism: "Do you know, since the establishment of Christianity as a state religion, a single example of a state which really followed a Christian policy? You can't point out one" (2.7.114). Ivanov uses the Blakean angel-devil reversal: God has "the double chin of industrial liberalism," while Satan "is thin, ascetic and a fanatical devotee of logic":

"He is damned to become a slaughterer, in order to abolish slaughtering, to sacrifice lambs so that no more lambs may be slaughtered, to whip people with knouts so that they may learn not to be themselves whipped" (2.7.108–09).

Atonement-sacrifice for the Christian is the supreme symbol of salvation; for another it is a symbol of evil, or at least of evil as the institutionalization of sacrifice, either as appropriating it after the fact or as using it as a way of rationalizing or mystifying the liquidation of dissent or heresy: the fiction the Party member is persuaded to accept, rendering himself (in Swift's terminology) a fool to the Party's knave.

Stalinism and the Christian church, Koestler is noting, are both regimes based on dogma, censorship, heresy, deception, bureaucracy, hagiography, and personality cults. The parallels with Christianity work both ways: they show Communism as a corruption of Christianity, a parody religion, but also a parallel in terms of its institutionalization (though put in the mouth of Gletkin). This emphatically reverses Swift's formula (see chapter 2) and shows how sin as deviation/heresy (as of the scandalous Miles, Jekyll, and Dorian) could be regarded as a virtue in the context of ideology or what we are calling the system. The same society that Wilde opposed to Dorian's sexual transgressions was now totalitarian.

Stupidity

We may recall Peter in Swift's *Tale of a Tub* when Koestler writes in *The God that Failed*, "Faith is a wondrous thing; it is not only capable of moving mountains, but also of making you believe that a herring is a race horse" (44)—or that a loaf of bread is beef and claret. Koestler is, of course, writing his own modern *Tale of a Tub*, where heresy has become "deviation": "once the Party has decided to adopt a certain line regarding a given problem, all criticism of that decision becomes deviationist sabotage" (49). But this stupidity can apply as well to the ideologue who kills Rubashov.

In the end-means category, one element is stupidity; and perhaps the strongest sense of Augustine's definition of evil as good-minus is the stupidity of ideology: Stalin's purges almost lost him the war. (Koestler did not see stupidity—not the comedy of stupidity but the tragedy of ideology idolized. Only in the aftermath of the war and after the collapse of Soviet Russia did the ironies become apparent: the folly of Stalin's purges, which murdered his best generals.)[17] Stupidity itself is presumably one of the many evils consequent upon the Fall; it is an evil (like the crippled leg) from which sin follows. Ideology is the stupid acceptance of an orthodoxy, for example, the exclusion of heretics and deviants on the basis of ideological correctness, whatever the evil consequences (as doing- and suffering-evil).[18]

There is the fact that Hitler's ideology—his obsession with cleansing the world of Jews—cost him the scientists who could have made him the atom bomb, the Jews who were gassed rather than used as a labor force, the trains that should have been carrying troops to the front but were transporting Jews to death camps. The consequence of stupidity was certainly an evil, from the German point of view the losing of the war.[19] The German files were "filled with memoranda written by the military complaining that the deportations of millions of Jews and Poles completely disregarded all 'military and economic necessities.'"[20]

But Hitler's serious intention, at the time of defeat, was to destroy the German people who had failed him as well as the Jews—his object being the winnowing that would produce a pure Aryan race. Genocide was primary, the war secondary. Taking into consideration the primacy of the ideological goal—racial cleansing—we find stupidity only in a profounder sense, the principle of nonutilitarianism, the "supreme disregard for immediate consequences," "contempt for utilitarian motives," and an "idealism" that Arendt calls an "unwavering faith in an ideological fictitious world," which replaces lust for power or wealth or any other end.[21] In the singlemindedness that subordinated all else to the final solution, permitting the ideology of racial purification to undermine the war effort, evil and stupidity coincided.

One stupidity of Christian ideology has been the doctrine of "Right to Life"—no contraceptives permitted or masturbation or anything that is not directed to procreation; and yet the millions of adults and children who have consequently died of AIDS. A related irony is that the layman's sin of abortion or masturbation was complemented by the privileged release available to priests—molestation of the boys in their congregations.[22] The Church's cover-up of this evil was justified by the doctrine that only a priest can say Mass, can turn the bread and wine into Christ's body and blood, and therefore (as in The Power and the Glory) it is of secondary importance that he is a sinner, an alcoholic and fornicator, or for that matter evil, a seducer or rapist of young children. Greene would have understood the notorious cover-up by the Church as a means to a greater end, one's own salvation.

Ideology and Pragmatism

The opposite of ideology, the complementary evil, is pragmatism—exploitation of (or accommodation to) the ideologues. Once past the originator and a few others, there were, among the perpetrators, all the individual agents with their own motives—of advancement, preferment, and financial profit; whose systematic, businesslike efficiency (trains, gas chambers, furnaces), while in its own terms horrible and incomprehensible, was in *their* terms less ideological than utilitarian. And, though less spectacular than the evil itself, there were also the fellow-travelers—the hundreds of thousands of non-Jews who, while not participating in their murders, appropriated their businesses, homes, and goods; the French collaborators who turned in Jews and then after the war claimed they had been heroes of the Resistance and massacred Algerians on the streets of Paris; and those who for practical purposes ignored their neighbors' guilt (as, for that matter, the Allied forces who used Nazi war criminals for their own purposes).[23]

If Eliot and Yeats spoke for the evils of World War I, Arendt spoke for the evils of World War II, summed up in the Holocaust. The pragmatism of the hotel keeper Schomberg prefigured the "banality of evil" described by Arendt in *Eichmann in Jerusalem*:

> Eichmann was not Iago and not Macbeth, and nothing would have been farther from his mind than to determine with Richard III 'to prove a villain.' Except for an extraordinary diligence in looking out for his personal advancement, he had no motives at all. And this diligence in itself was in no way criminal; he certainly would never have murdered his superior in order to inherit his post. He *merely*, to put the matter colloquially, *never realized what he was doing*. (287)

Schomberg might have "murdered his superior in order to inherit his post," but otherwise he foreshadows this version of evil, which Conrad sets off against the melodramatic grotesques of the infernal trio. Arendt goes on to say that it was not, with Eichmann, even stupidity: "It was sheer thoughtlessness—something by no means identical with stupidity—that predisposed him to become one of the greatest criminals of that period. And if this is 'banal' and even funny, if with the best will in the world one cannot extract any diabolical or demonic profundity from Eichmann, that is still far from calling it commonplace."[24]

The Hitler-Eichmann dualism (the demonic—the banal, the burning—the rotting) can be interpreted as supplementary, one balanced by the other, or as the real banality beneath the myth of evil. The romantic figure of the ideologue requires power (though, of course, he must behave pragmatically until he has power), with which he can commit evil with a capital E; the mere pragmatist represents the evil of everyday experience.

2. WAR

Evil, Internal: Golding, The Lord of the Flies
Another word like *moral turpitude* or *cruel and unusual punishment, atrocity* (from the Latin *atroc-, atrox,* meaning gloomy—extremely wicked, brutal, or cruel—barbaric, savage) in warfare replaced rules, honor, camaraderie, the Geneva Convention; atrocity was another aspect of the corruption of an ideal. Obviously atrocities were committed throughout history, but the modern sense of *atrocity* connected with warfare dates back to the so-called German atrocities of World War I—the indiscriminate killing of civilians—and forward to the Japanese army in Nanking and in some of the POW camps, the actions of both sides in the Balkans or Rwanda, the Turks' role in the genocide of the Armenians—individual acts that exceeded the ideology of genocide: rape, cruelty to children (starvation, torture, mutilation) that violated previous conventions of warfare (bombing "open cities" was another).[25]

William Golding's *Lord of the Flies* (1954) is about a group of public school boys—once again, children—dropped on a deserted jungle island and their different ways of coping with the experience. Jack's torture and killing of a pig—the impaling of its head (eating its body) and its penumbra of hungry flies—is the central image of Golding's novel; but juxtaposing the innocent pig with the supposedly (the assumption of pre-Freudians) innocent boys who, reverting to a state of nature, do these things to the pig, projects another story of how to deal with the evil of nature, which is Hobbesian war, by scapegoating and sacrificing the weaker. The killing of the pig—and of "Piggie" and young Simon—is the compensation for the threatening evils of death and natural decomposition, a conflation of doing-evil and suffering-evil. The pig is the sacrifice to placate the "Beast" (the body of a dead flier), followed by the "sacrifice" of Simon, "another head for the beast," and finally Piggie.

There are different prisms through which we can understand the novel; first, Golding's own words, in which he situates it in the midst of the war in the Pacific. At the end the boys' regression back into civilized bestiality is taken for granted by the air force pilot who rescues them—"Jolly good show"—as he, in Golding's words, "having interrupted a man-hunt, prepares to take the children off the island in a cruiser which will presently be hunting its enemy in the same implacable way."[26] This is a fable of World War II.

But second, the boys relive the Problem of Evil: beginning with their isolation on the island, then fear of a beast in the jungle (never actually encountered), to placate which they sacrifice a pig and at the same time—for Simon at least—create a sacrificial god, the pig's head encased in a mass of hungry flies (a parody halo): The lord of the flies—or Beelzebub, a devil, who presides over the hunters—convinces Simon that he and it are one, prefiguring the hunters' second, this time human, sacrifice, of Simon. The World War intrudes in the figure of the dead parachutist, parallel to the head of the pig and invoking the offstage macrocosm. But just what does the "lord of the flies" represent? the hunters who killed it? the beast in the jungle they fear? the degenerative process they illustrate? It is partly scapegoat, ritual sacrifice, but it is also food for the hungry boys.

Golding's innocent pig (actually a sow) is no threat (though the boys associate her with the beast in the jungle); she is tortured and killed along with her piglets, and yet she serves as a talisman for Jack and his hunters, a symbol of both doing-evil (Jack) and suffering-evil (the pig itself, Simon, "Piggie").[27] The same might be inferred from the parachutist who hangs nearby, her human equivalent: He has been shot down but before that he was shooting down enemy aircraft.

This scenario seems to portray a stage later than that of the Original Sin. Ralph and the seekers after rescue and return to the civilized world, whose motto is "Keep the fire going," using fire for light and outreach, are contrasted with Jack's hunters, who use fire for cooking food and turn from hunters of animals into hunters of human prey. The first leads forward, the second points backward. But essentially both point back to the state of nature that Ralph keeps trying to emerge from by his talk of his election as chief, the conch for calling conclaves, and a fledgling social contract. (And yet, we can also fit this story into the Cain–Abel relationship: Abel was the hunter who sacrificed blood to Jehovah, and Cain, the farmer who offered instead vegetables, had his offering rejected.)

Since neither of these scenarios fits terribly well, in one sense *The Lord of the Flies* is merely a rewriting of *The Heart of Darkness*,[28] as Golding's later novel about evil, *Rites of Passage* (1980), is a rewriting of *Billy Budd*.[29] Jack goes into the darkness and is transformed, as Kurtz was before him.

Finally, behind Golding's fiction are Peter Pan's children in Neverland—a remote island where they can live their fantasies of pirates and Indians. There were "threats" but entirely external ones. These boys and girls did not revert to their images of evil—Captain Hook and his pirates (the crocodile is only after Hook)—as Golding's boys do, though at the end all are whisked back to London, as in *Peter Pan,* by air. The Problem of Evil was, in that play (1904), which was known to all English children, implicit in the anxiety of growing up, the threat of the figure with an abbreviated scythe, whose nemesis is the crocodile with the clock in his belly, ticking away to indicate that the evil of death is inexorably approaching: in the first case toward Peter (avoided), in the second toward Hook (not avoided). Further back is the military code celebrating the comradeship of soldiers and Boy Scouts, subverted in the evils of modern warfare.[30]

Evil, External: Heller, Catch-22

In *Lord of the Flies* and Joseph Heller's *Catch-22* (1955) the two central images are of doing- and suffering-evil—the severed fly-blown head of the pig and the airman Snowden's body (the "secret") bursting with entrails: "The grim secret Snowden had spilled all over the messy floor. It was easy to read the message in his entrails. Man was matter, that was Snowden's secret. Drop him out a window and he'll fall. Set fire to him and he'll burn. Bury him and he'll rot like other kinds of garbage. The spirit gone, man is garbage. That was Snowden's secret. Ripeness was all."[31] The emphasis on entrails and their secret (as classical priests read the entrails of their sacrificial animals), however, tilts toward suffering-evil. The burst entrails are the sign of Snowden's mortality, as the passage suggests. The name Snowden refers not only to the cold, the pallor of his body (recalling the "soldier in white" in the hospital), and Mount Snowden, but also to François Villon's "Où sont les neiges d'antan?" (Where are the snows of yesteryear?) Nazi firepower (doing-evil) has killed Snowden, but he serves Yossarian as a symbol of God's "playfulness" (suffering-evil). Thus we read the passage that finally describes the burst entrails in the context of Yossarian's earlier opinion of God:

> "And don't tell me God works in mysterious ways. . . . There's nothing so mysterious about it. He's not working at all. He's playing. Or else He's forgotten all about us. That's the kind of God you people talk about—a country bumpkin, a clumsy, bungling, brainless, conceited, uncouth hayseed. Good God, how much reverence can you have for a Supreme Being who finds it necessary to include such phenomena as phlegm and tooth decay in His divine system of creation? What in the world was running through that warped, evil, scatological mind of His when He robbed old people of the power to control their bowel movements? Why in the world did He ever create pain?" (18.184).

The children of *Lord of the Flies* have agency, doing things to each other. Youth once again is corrupted or corruptible; evil is internal, Original Sin or natural depravity. Snowden is pure victim, and the evils are external. The characters in *Catch-22* also act like children—they are all young and about to die; but their acts are childish because there seems to be no other way of dealing with what threatens them every day they go up in their airplanes.

How to cope with the war is a primary subject of the post–World War II novels: *Catch-22* is about Yossarian's ways of dealing specifically with the death of Snowden: you go naked and climb up into a tree, you hide yourself in a hospital, you prove you're crazy; you have to deal not only with the war and death but with Catch-22, which relates the army to the evils of God's created world, both irrational and ending in death (5.46–47).

Active, responsible evil equals the army, the totalitarian but also incompetent structures of authority and power and stupidity. The Problem of Evil is set against the evil of particular men in a particular system (the army, in wartime, and the army as microcosm of the state). A hospital, for example, can be—as seen by Yossarian at least—an escape from the world outside it: "There was a much lower death rate inside the hospital than outside the hospital, and a much healthier death rate. Few people died unnecessarily. People knew a lot more about dying inside the hospital and made a much neater, more orderly job of it. They couldn't dominate Death inside the hospital, but they certainly made her behave. They had taught her manners. They couldn't keep death out, but while she was in she had to act like a lady" (17.170)—this as opposed to Snowden spilling his guts all over the inside of the airplane. And Dr. Stubbs asks what is the point in "saving people's lives . . . since they all have to die anyway." To which Dunbar answers,

> "The point is to keep them from dying for as long as you can."
> "Yeah, but what's the point, since they all have to die anyway?"
> "The trick is not to think about that."
> "Never mind the trick. What the hell's the point?"
> Dunbar pondered in silence for a few moments. "Who the hell knows?" (10.113–14).

Elsewhere Dunbar comments, "'Just for once I'd like to see all these things sort of straightened out, with each person getting exactly what he deserves. It might give me some confidence in this universe'" (175).

So also Colonel Cathcart and Milo Minderbinder and ex-Pfc. Wintergreen, all of whom cope with—some exploit—the war, which is summed up in the rule Catch-22, which says you can be exempted if you are crazy, but if you say you're crazy (knowing the war to be what it is) you are obviously sane and therefore cannot be exempted.

The mess that is the army was the subject of the most powerful postwar novels. Another novel about the army at war—though not in combat—was James Gould Cozzens's *Guard of Honor* (1948): "All This Crap—the Army's arbitrary regulations and discipline"—"mess after mess" is his version of *Catch-22*, in his case dealt with not satirically but analytically and with sympathy for the reality of that great complex organism, the army. It is all about, in great detail, how Colonel Ross but also General Beal, and Colonel Mowbray, Captain Hicks, and the rest, deal with that mess—which stands in for combat, offstage or glimpsed in flashbacks. How, in Cozzens's terms, the air force deals with the ultimate mess, death, is very different from Heller's answer: "To face the endless risks of aerial flight a man must have a sanguine, happy-go-lucky habit of thought; but replaceable instantly, at need or at will, by its very antithesis—a freezing into precision as the controls were taken. This was the condition of survival; the only way to put off sudden realization of all those risks in sudden death."[32]

The System

In newspapers and speeches World War II was commonly described as a just war. In World War II novels the Nazis and Japanese are evil and the Americans good—a fact presumably not in dispute but seldom dwelt upon.[33] The distinction between "enemy" soldiers and "War" can be illustrated in that very popular between-wars novel *Goodbye Mr. Chips* (1934): Mr. Chips's Brookfield students remark when Chips reads off among the dead the name of a Brookfield German master: "Seems funny, then, to read his name out. With all the others. After all, he was an enemy."[34] In the *Iliad* the reader's sympathy was balanced between Hector and Achilles, in the *Aeneid* between Aeneas and Turnus. In both the evil was the disorder that goes back ultimately to the adultery of Helen and Paris.

During World War I the evil was depicted in atrocity images of the kaiser or a simian or Hunnish representative of the Germans killing and raping innocent civilians.[35] After the war, in retrospect at least, evil was attributed not to the Germans or the French but to the old men of Kipling's couplet ("If any question why we died, / Tell them, because our fathers lied"), the statesmen, politicians, and generals: the image of the Great, going back to the Great Man Walpole, but by this time including God the Creator, contrasted with all the little men who served as cannon fodder. Recall the passages in books like Hemingway's *Farewell to Arms* in which "the words sacred, glorious, and sacrifice . . . glory, honor, courage, or hallow"—"obscene" words—are played against the ugly realities, which presage the passage I have quoted in which Frederic Henry kills the ants, reflecting his feelings about what has happened to Catherine Barkley but also the power of statesmen and generals, surrogates of this dumb god, and the millions they have just killed as Frederic kills the ants.[36]

The major World War I novels and memoirs did focus on combat—horribly and definitively in Robert Graves's *Goodbye to All That* (1929), Hemingway's *Farewell to Arms,* and in Germany Ernst Jünger's *Storm of Steel* (*In Stahlgewittern,* 1920) and Erich Maria Remarque's *All Quiet on the Western Front* (1928). Jünger saw the war as a source of fraternity and solidarity, a crucible for German rebirth; Remarque as a hell. But Jünger takes note of the mechanization of war—the fact "that war in the era of machines could not possibly breed virtues like chivalry, courage, honor, and manliness, that it imposed on men nothing but the experience of bare destruction together with the humiliation of being only small cogs in the majestic wheel of slaughter."[37] It is easy to see how this view—of industrialized murder—became the idea of army and nation as merely another, the *great*, system.[38]

These works seemed definitive indictments, leaving not much to be said except to shift the focus onto the army itself, its "world" of false order, confusion, corruption, and stupidity. James Jones's *From Here to Eternity* and Cozzens's *Guard of Honor* are about not combat but the bivouac situation of army camps and army infrastructure—about system, although including (for Heller) all or (for Cozzens) some stupid officers. True also of *Catch-22*, which almost entirely takes place in an army installation—combat is far up in the air, above anything like the hand-to-hand slaughter of the two novels that focus on combat, Norman Mailer's *The Naked and the Dead* and Irwin Shaw's *The Young Lions* (both 1948). In Evelyn Waugh's three volumes of *Men at Arms* (1952), later called *Sword of Honour* (1965), combat is constantly deferred while Waugh describes in great detail the malfunctioning of army and army bases, war plans and their execution.

The evil explored in the major works of the imagination that followed World War II was system and the army itself, the machine for killing. As Waugh put it in *Men at Arms*, "Guy [Crouchback] had caught sight of that vast uniformed and bemedalled bureaucracy by whose power alone a man might stick his bayonet into another, and had felt something of its measureless obstructive strength."[39] Shaw's sympathy in *The Young Lions* is equally with Christian Diestl, his German soldier, and his two Americans, Michael and Noah, Gentile and Jew. The evil (wrongdoing raised by a World War to evil) is the general "eighty miles away." Shaw pauses in his account of the horrors of combat to generalize:

Battle exists on many different levels. There is the purely moral level, at the Supreme Headquarters perhaps eighty miles away from the sound of the guns, where the filing cabinets have been dusted in the morning, where there is a sense of quiet and efficiency, where soldiers who never fire a gun and never have a shot fired at them, the high Generals, sit in their pressed uniforms and prepare statements to the effect that all has been done that is humanly possible, the rest being left to the judgment of God. . . . The men on the scene see the affair on a different level. They have not been questioned on the proper manner of isolating the battlefield. They have not been consulted on the length of the preliminary bombardment. . . . They see helmets, vomit, green water, shell geysers, smoke, crashing planes, blood plasma, submerged obstacles, guns, pale, senseless faces, a confused drowning mob of men running and falling, that seem to have no relation to any of the things they have been taught since they left their jobs and wives to put on the uniform of their country.[40]

All the man on the ground can cry is, "Oh, God, it is all screwed up." The enemy—the fool or the knave—is not the German (or, to the German, the American) but one's own officers. War up close was not evil but about camaraderie and survival, sometimes (most often in stateside scenes) about bad sergeants, bad officers; at a distance, the sacrifice engineered by the tyrant or the ruling class. We might say the animus is not against "God and Country" (except perhaps as a concept, Hemingway's "obscene" words like "glory") but against the equivalent of clericalism.

World War II was "the just war" in that the division of good and evil was fairly clear; but once it was over, the virtue of the Allied side began to be questioned. With Korea, and more with Vietnam, the idea of *us* and *them* (International Communism and the "domino effect") became truly ambiguous. The responsibility for the deaths and suffering was less easy to pin down—historically attached to the 1960s but with the literary precedents of Golding, Heller, and others (though, as I note, with precedents that go back to World War I, to Kipling, Graves, and Hemingway).

Evil, Low and High: Greene, The Third Man
Greene's *Third Man* appeared first as a film in 1949, then as a short novel a year later. Although the title became associated with the "third man," the spy who supplemented Burgess and Maclean—that is, the man who turned out to be Kim Philby—it began as another of Greene's allusions

to Eliot's *Waste Land,* to part V, which opens with echoes of the taking of Christ in the Garden of Gethsemane and the Passion. A few lines later he evokes the disciples on the road to Emmaus:

> Who is the third who walks always beside you?
> When I count, there are only you and I together
> But when I look ahead up the white road
> There is always another one walking beside you. (ll. 359–62)

A dozen lines later Eliot even makes a reference to Vienna: "Jerusalem Athens Alexandria / Vienna London / Unreal" (ll. 375–76). Harry Lime is the third man who carries the body of "Harry Lime" and so is a parodic Christ or anti-Christ "resurrected"—a demonic figure like Pinkie Brown. Greene, as he was writing it, referred to *The Third Man* as "the risen-from-the-dead story."[41] But it is another of the Eliot-Greene stories in which "He who was living is now dead / We who were living are now dying / With a little patience" (ll. 328–30), now in the devastated post–World War world.

What does it do to Harry Lime to compare him with Jesus resurrected and joining his disciples at Emmaus? First, as usual for Greene, it raises the stakes for the representation of the "evil." It does not elevate Harry, as Hogarth did his Harlot and Tom Nero; it is another Eliot ploy, contrasting our cultural heritage, specifically the Christian religion, with the ruins of Vienna, its sewers, its blackmarketeers and exploiters, with a memory too of the war that brought this about—the ruin and the scavengers and opportunists like Harry. But, as Michael Shelden has pointed out, in the film Carol Reed conveys something Greene cannot suggest so well in the book: "In the film the devastation [of Vienna] is visible in frame after frame, constantly reminding us of an evil far greater than Lime's little racket. Lime is responsible for the suffering of a relatively small group in the city; the bombers and tanks that invaded Vienna have not only hurt thousands of people but also destroyed large portions of one of the great cultural capitals in the Western world. With their good intentions the Allied armies have helped to reduce a city of splendid beauty to a sad collection of damaged buildings and piles of rubble."[42]

The view from the Prater Ferris wheel reminds us of the similar view from the World War II bombers: "[A] for 20,000 pounds a dot, Lime thinks that anyone would be willing to eliminate one dot after another.

By itself this seems a singularly monstrous comment, but the ruins of Vienna serve to remind us that 'good' bombardiers destroy countless dots and get medals for doing so. [B] Because Harry Lime is such a charming villain, we want to like him. When he speaks of killing dots, we see the evil lurking behind his smile. But Greene does not want to allow us the leisure of feeling morally superior. With the help of Carol Reed's camera, he surrounds Lime with the overwhelming evidence of a far greater evil done in the name of justice—the destruction of Vienna"—and indeed of Europe (275). We might add Harry's own detachment from the vantage of the Ferris wheel: He never sees the children he ruins, and he keeps at a distance from Anna—but beyond him are the bombardiers and the Bomber Harrises and Winston Churchills who sent them to bomb cities like Dresden and Hamburg. In other words, Greene, like so many of the satirists with whom we have dealt, implies the greater evil behind/beyond these evil people in the foreground. In the 1930s, in *It's a Battlefield*, Greene had observed of the murderer whose commutation is the object sought by most of the characters: "They hanged this man and pardoned that; one embezzler was in prison, but other men of the same kind were sent to Parliament" (39), words that echo a text Greene probably knew well, John Gay's *Beggar's Opera*, which Bertolt Brecht had adapted in *Die Dreigroschenoper* to Berlin in the 1920s. Another film, released two years before *The Third Man*, that made the same point, was Charles Chaplin's *Monsieur Verdoux*. What Greene adds is the aerial perspective—the view from the Ferris wheel and from the bomber plane.

On either side of *Brighton Rock* were *A Gun for Sale* and *The Confidential Agent* (1936, 1939), in which local evil was contextualized by a larger, more successful one. Pinkie is the small fish in the bigger pond of Colleoni and his gang. Raven is a professional killer who skillfully carries out his mission (job, duty, and profession recalling Conrad and his account of the company accountant) on a war minister in an unstable Balkan country; when he returns, the middleman Davis pays him in marked bills, betraying him, and so he tracks down Davis and his master: There is the agent, intermediary, but the real evil is the intentions of the steel company's owner, who intended the killing of the minister to start a war, which would increase the sale of steel. In *The Confidential Agent* there is the leftist ex-professor-philologist D., who is trying to buy coal for his party, and there is the old, conservative government, with all the money and influence, represented by L., and beyond these the stupid English officialdom and the greedy coal mine owners.[43]

Greene also uses the contrast of accessory and principal, distance and proximity, and foreground and background as mitigation for D. or Raven. In the foreground, as in *The Beggar's Opera*, is a love story—Polly's true love contrasted with the mercantile values of her elders and the Great Men who do not hang but die in their beds; Greene's story is of love and friendship against the larger picture of the system.

My Country or My Friend: Le Carré, Tinker, Tailor, Soldier, Spy

In *Darkness at Noon* Rubashov's sin was general in that he could well be interchangeable with his old friend Ivanov—as was demonstrated by Ivanov's being himself purged and executed before Rubashov. But the guilt that is most telling—to the reader and to Rubashov himself—was the personal betrayal of his mistress, Arlova; which connects Koestler's story with Orwell's *Nineteen Eighty-Four* (1948), which also focused on a love affair: Like Rubashov, Winston Smith was distinguished by his love for Julia but then betrayed her to save himself (as she mutually betrayed him) and adjusted to the ethos of Big Brother, but without the Christian parallels (the part vs. the whole) or the Party logic. As opposed to ideological, the act was personal, pragmatic, and self-serving.

Harry Lime's crime is the blackmarketing of penicillin and, to increase profits, diluting it with disastrous results for the patients; the evil is the suffering of children. He also betrays his lover Anna to the Russians, with whom he collaborates when it is to his advantage, passing on information to them. But it is the children, in the hospital, that convince his friend Holly Rollins to betray Harry—and that have some effect on Anna as well: appropriate in that Harry himself is childlike, an adept at games in which he comes out on top, and who ends like another frightened child hunted down in his underground hidingplace.

So there is the obvious evil of Lime's greed, which kills or maims many children; and there is what Anna regards as his betrayal by his old friend Holly, who has been shown the consequences of Harry's evil in the children's hospital. Is this Greene's study of evil or rather of overriding love? Or the conflict of love with friendship compromised by duty and a sense of right and wrong: Do you turn in your friend Kim Philby? Greene's concern with betrayal was personal ("I've betrayed so very many people in my life") and public (his obsession with Philby) and may go some way to explain his greater stress on betrayal of a friend than violence against neighbors or country. Recall Dante's three betrayers of their masters: Judas betrays his God, Cassius the head of his state, and Brutus that plus his master/father/friend, even though it might be virtuous to murder a tyrant.

Harry, like Pinkie, is another schoolboy who has not grown up. In fact, he's another "boy," but unlike Pinkie, Harry is happy, charming, cheerful. He "made everything seem like fun," he was beloved of his cat, and seems to be one of those children of James who "want to see more life." The viewer of the film feels sympathy during the chase through the sewers when he is hounded by the police; and, at the end, it is Holly whom Anna rejects, showing that she is still in love with Harry despite his crimes, despite his betrayal of her—another, more sophisticated Rose. And it is Holly who fills the role of Ida the detective. He gets the porter killed, gets Lime killed, and alienates Anna; in his case not because he has a sense of justice or *lex talionis* but because he is a novelist who writes popular stories of action and adventure in the Old West; a writer who turns Old Vienna into the Old West.

The same situation, faintly suggested in Greene's *The Third Man*, occurs in John Le Carré's *Tinker, Tailor, Soldier, Spy* (1974), a thriller about geopolitical hostility that is in fact a story of friendship; where the "mole" Bill Hayden's real evil lies not in his betrayal of the British Empire but in his betrayal of his best friend, Jim Prideaux. The story of George Smiley and Bill Hayden is written as if by the Conrad of *Lord Jim:* Smiley becomes Marlow (better, the Marlow of *Heart of Darkness*) and the story is really about Hayden and his relationship with Karla at the expense of his friend Prideaux and his colleague Smiley.

While there are references to the agents betrayed by Bill Hayden, who were "rolled back"—taken and executed—the Russians, the evil of treason, or even the betrayal of his colleagues in the "Circus," is subordinated to the betrayal of his old school chum Prideaux. The echo is of Forster's notorious "If I had to choose between my friend and my country . . . ," for Hayden and Prideaux were not only best friends and colleagues but apparently, as students at Oxford, lovers. Le Carré is drawing on the Burgess-Maclean affair and the Philby case, but the connection with *Darkness at Noon* and *Nineteen Eighty-Four* is also evident.

Already in *The Spy Who Came in from the Cold* (1963) Le Carré sets the deadly pragmatism of the "Circus" (MI5, represented in this case by Smiley) against the love of Alec Leamas and Liz Gold and the friendship of the Cold War opponents, Alec and his Communist opposite, Fiedler. All three are destroyed by the organization in order to preserve the double agent and killer Mundt.

The old equation of god and king, of church and state, which served primarily to support kingship, no longer applies. When sin no longer has substance in re either deity or monarch, all that is left is interpersonal relations. Then one can say: If I had to choose between my friend and my country, between the part and the whole, the individual and the ideology. . . .

MI5 and the "Military-Industrial Complex"

In the spy novels of Le Carré (as opposed to the "entertainments" of Greene, in which one side is plainly worse than the other), while the Russian spy-chief Karla goes to extremes of brutality to protect himself, the evil—which is largely evildoing—is finally (as emerges at the denouement of each novel) the systems in which, and for which, both Karla and Smiley are working. These systems exist independently of them, each as much a "mess" as Yossarian's army or God's creation. Le Carré's Cold War novels are about treason—betrayal of one's friends or master: but it is the state—the flimsy, bungling ruthless system of MI5—which betrays its own operatives (means) to the larger end, whatever that may be (fictions of "Cold War")—as opposed to betrayal of a friend; and with that dichotomy the choice is obvious. Already in the Cold War novels the ultimate evil is the system, against which friendship stands out as a sacrificed ideal.

The end justifies the means—or doesn't—but the sides are balanced: as if we were to see Smiley's story from Karla's point of view. *Interchangeability* is a term that finally applies to Smiley and Karla.

Le Carré's *The Constant Gardener* (2001) shows what has become of his spy subject since the end of Communism and the Soviet "threat": there is still a love object. Tessa Quayle is gang-raped; her throat is cut, and her black friend Dr. Arnold Bluhm is "tortured" for two days before being killed—by "the pharmaceutical chaps," that is, "the House of ThreeBees, Third World venturers"—ThreeBees Nairobi and KVH, whose "wonder drug" Dypraxa kills hundreds of children in India and will kill untold numbers in Africa.[44] But the evil is extended to "American tobacco companies who spike their cigarettes in order to create child addicts, to Somali warlords who drop cluster bombs on undefended villages and the arms companies that manufacture the cluster bombs" (12.275–76). The emphasis on the suffering of children and, secondarily, of women, summons up once again Ivan's formulation, "I refuse to believe in the existence of a God who permits the suffering of innocent children" (11.259). Beyond the pharmaceuticals is the medical profession itself, bought off with money, professorships, etc., by the pharmaceuticals (12.267–68).

Le Carré's subject, ultimately, is political systems, the British High Commission, or Great Britain the colonial power in Kenya—referred to appropriately as "Chancery" (e.g., 12.270). Chancery is represented by, above all, Sandy Woodrow, the "five star megacreep" as Tessa writes to Ham. But implicated also are "the Kenyan authorities," "the tentacles of Moi's empire" (11.261), which the High Commission for prudential reasons tolerates, including the profits from ThreeBees and KVH. And "The Great American Hydra," "the 'Master Capital'" (13.297). Money, not inherent cruelty or desire to destroy, is the source of this complex—not cruelty but indifference to the consequences of the profit motif, the means to what is taken as a good end (ultimate health of African natives).

Le Carré's specific case of drug companies is morally ambiguous compared to the arms industry or even the United States: their ostensible aim is to cure people, ease pain, and preserve life, but they also must make money (for themselves and their shareholders). Thus "the great crime" is the passing off of Dypraxa by all of these systems on the innocent children of Africa—evil in its original sense of death and suffering—a "cure" for a tubercular pandemic, or death—referred to as "the White Plague, the Great Stalker, the Great Imitator, the Captain of Death" (13.309).

So one subject of evil is system—from the Court of Chancery in *Bleak House* to Marx's Capitalism, in the twentieth century the army, the totalitarian state in politics, and what Dwight Eisenhower denounced as the "military-industrial-academic complex."[45] Earlier there were Freemasonry and the Jesuits—secret societies dominating the world by means of a gigantic conspiracy; in the Far East, "the Great Game," capitalism, imperialism, the nation-state system, and now the economic and industrial complex—based on (in Arendt's words) a "politics of expansion for expansion's sake" based on "the limitless pursuit of power after power that could roam and lay waste the whole globe with no certain nationally and territorially prescribed purpose."⁴⁶ From the beginning of the last century there were the "Protocols of the Elders of Zion" and the myth of a Jewish secret society that has ruled, or aspired to rule, the world since antiquity—seen as agents of Satan and devil-worshipers. The protocols served as Hitler's model for world domination: the difference being that the Nazis possessed instruments of violence.⁴⁷

On the theological level, in the discourse of sin, was the Catholic Church—and now the evangelical sects joining it on the issues of homosexuality (a strange choice given the scandal of priests' homosexuality) and same-sex marriage, contraception, and abortion. In the long run system even produced 9/11 and Katrina and into the future more powerful hurricanes and more threats of terrorism in the United States (the result of the ideology of "Iraq Freedom/Democracy"). And there were also, of course, MI5, SIS, and the spy system, "the intimate traditional connection between imperialist politics and rule by 'invisible government' and secret agents."

Arendt has claimed that what characterizes system in the state is "bureaucracy or the rule of an intricate system of bureaus in which no men, neither one nor the best, neither the few nor the many, can be held responsible, and which could properly be called rule by Nobody."⁴⁸ This rings true of Le Carré's MI5 and his multinational companies, but Enron and Al Qaeda and the "Bush Administration" are all identified by the names of their CEOs.

There is the system and the individual wrongdoer or evildoer, the demonic figure at the center of the system (in Juvenal's and Swift's terms, the knave) and the banal figures (the fools) who carry out his orders. But the CEO, an Eichmann and not a Hitler, is unaware of the pain suffered by Tessa and Arnold Bluhm, is "above" it and as unaware as the bombers of the suffering of those "below." His only ideology is profit and power for its own sake; he is even, possibly, submerged in a system that is system for its own sake and beyond anyone's control (as seems the case with MI5).

Terrorism: Conrad, The Secret Agent

Conrad's *The Secret Agent* (1910) had at its center a terrorist act: the destruction of the Greenwich Observatory, from which time around the globe is marked; this was the symbol of England's control of the sea and the trade routes, indeed of the British Empire. But it is an act that involved no innocent civilian casualties, and furthermore an act that never takes place. *The Secret Agent* is, however, a spectrum of the terrorist act, guilt at one end and innocence at the other: Mr. Vladimir, the Russian ambassador, gives the order, for the sake of persuading England to oppose anarchists, but for the specific advantage of his own government. He is the instigator, safe at a distance from the terrorist act. In one sense, the obvious, criminal villain (Verloc, Fagin, and Sikes) is supplemented by the respectable representative of society (Bumble, the ambassador, the Congo Company accountant). Mr. Verloc, the bomber, needs the money; he could otherwise lose his job as secret agent and/or be turned in to the police. Therefore to carry out the job he exploits his feebleminded brother-in-law Stevie, but with no intention of hurting anyone with the bomb—though to keep himself at a safe distance from the bomb. Indeed, neither he nor Vladimir *intends* a fatality, only the destruction of a symbol of Great Britain. But Verloc (a stupid, careless man) neglects to note that he is dealing with a mentally deficient youth, incidentally a total innocent. The explosion kills Stevie—who stumbles over a root while merely carrying out orders—and does not even damage the Greenwich Observatory, the symbol. Is Verloc evil? His wife, Winnie, thinks he is and kills him, and finally herself. Ideology (or anti-ideology) is present in the intention of the ambassador; ideology itself, absent in Verloc, hovers in the background of his milieu, primarily in the figure of the anarchist professor with dynamite strapped to his body awaiting detonation.

"Evil," I have said, tends to apply most unequivocally to power; David's killing of Goliath was regarded as a defensive act, or as a conventional single combat that replaces a battle, based on the rules of warfare. With the advent of terrorism a situation has arisen in which the supposedly powerless commit atrocities on the powerful that must be considered to be—at least insofar as they randomly kill innocent civilians—no less evil because they are acts of apparent desperation.

In the discussion of *The Golden Bowl* I posed the question of who really had the power, Milly or Charlotte? In the long run, the Ververs, but in the short run Charlotte and the Prince, who, in a modern sense, were rebels against the law of adultery and the financial power of the Ververs. 9/11 too was a question of perspective: From *their* point of view, it was the American devils (or the military-industrial complex, the system) who had the power; but from *our* point of view, it was the terrorists who coopted the airplanes, rendering innocent individuals prisoners, and flew them into the World Trade Center and the Pentagon who at that moment had the power. So it can be

any other citizen who is in the power position, and in this case over innocent people randomly chosen—if any are guilty of crimes it is a coincidence.

Terrorism can be explained as the desperation of the powerless against
the powerful—and this is a rationale that would also apply to the gangsters
who were rebelling against (to them and, at least, many others) an oppressive government when in the Depression thirties they robbed the banks that
were foreclosing mortgages and during Prohibition "bootlegged" whiskey.

Of the lone terrorist, without backing, we can say that all he/she needs
is the position of momentary power (the Columbine students needed only
weapons against unarmed students). However, insofar as these atrocities
include the suicide of the terrorist, we must conclude that the degree of
evil increases upward toward the mastermind who planned the terrorist
attack and watches it from some remote hideaway. And this figure—
an Osama bin Laden—represents power in the sense that he has large
reserves of money for bankrolling the act of terrorism and most likely
behind him a network called Al Qaeda, and behind that a Middle East
country or a religious orthodoxy (the same chain-of-command Le Carré
shows in *The Constant Gardener*), though possibly not as powerful as the
country being attacked.

Terrorism is not in fact carried out by "loners, socially marginalized
persons acting out of pathological sadness or economic desperation,"
but rather "acting in the name of organizations conducting campaigns
designed to achieve specific political goals." "An organization recruits,
indoctrinates, and trains the bomber; an organization picks the targets
and later makes the case for the legitimacy of the attacks by distributing
promotional literature or 'martyr videos,' recorded by the bomber before
death."[49] In short, the fact that they killed (or sacrificed) themselves in the
process only indicates the truth we first saw in Juvenal and Swift, later in
Koestler, that evil requires a fool as well as a knave, the suicide bomber
and his/her ideological instructor.

3. HOLOCAUST

The Metaphor of the Holocaust
The phenomenon of the Holocaust has been called—and probably is—be-
yond the capabilities of literature or art, unredeemable by words or images.
The philosophical debates about the Holocaust, first raised by Adorno,

Paul Celan, and George Steiner, were about its unrepresentability—the morality of artists' attempts to depict an "unimaginable ordeal," the impossibility of rendering it into art.[50] It is perhaps true, as W. G. Sebald notes in *Campo Santo* (2005), that an experience that surpasses all imagination is best approached through the most matter-of-fact reports, such as letters. A mere recitation of the facts is sufficient.[51] The film *Shoah* comes closest to defining the whole process of the extermination in the words of a great many survivors, and the two films made from the transcript of the Wansee Conference offer a chilling chart of the planning. The major Holocaust memoirs certainly indicate and describe a process of evil, but, like the spiritual autobiography of the Puritans, they are more about survival, the Crusoe narrative (Primo Levi's *Se questo è un uomo* [1958; *If This Is a Man*]), or how to save a number of Jews (Thomas Keneally's *Schindler's List* [1982]). Elie Wiesel's *Night* (1958) epitomizes the Holocaust in one vivid scene, an angelic little boy hanging and still alive after half an hour.

In practice, *Holocaust* comes to mean anything that is beyond description, beyond the power of imagination. Where I wish to indicate the model of the Holocaust is in the elements that have been transferred to post-Holocaust subjects. On a trivial level Sylvia Plath used the Holocaust to describe her adulterous husband by way of her German father—her mother possibly with Jewish blood. She takes the most generally accepted case of evil of her time and makes it a metaphor for her treatment at the hands of her husband. The gist of attack on Plath was the remoteness of the tenor from the vehicle: Not only because she "was not a Jew," as Steiner noted, but "she had no personal connections with the holocaust [except her father's German origins] . . . she was a child, plump and golden in America, when the trains actually went"—this more than the fact that "those who are Jewish or closely acquainted with someone who experienced the camps might legitimately identify with the 'actual survivor.'"[52] Her experience of Ted-Hughes-as-Holocaust was a metaphor that, seen from any distance, had a mock-heroic effect.

A. Alvarez unconvincingly defended Plath by arguing that writing under the threat of nuclear war, Plath could have regarded the Holocaust as "a small-scale trial run for a nuclear war," since in an instant a bomb could destroy as many people as the Nazis destroyed in five years—we all suffer the threat of sudden annihilation.[53] On a higher level, or one in which the tenor and the vehicle more closely correspond, are the cases of the major war novels, written in the decades following the Holocaust, in which the Holocaust defined World War II and the postwar world. Writing of the Vietnam War, Wendy Steiner has noted that "as the reportage of that war increased, Americans felt themselves implicated in events of equal horror to the holocaust, surpassing the ugliness of any fictional imaginings"—repeating the way "in Nazi Germany the imaginable became real."[54] The evils of World War II were conflated with the particular horrors of the Holocaust; at the same time, some equated the evil of the Holocaust with the evil of the contemporary saturation bombing of Germany, the atom bomb, and the ambiguities attendant upon their use.

On yet another level of reference, combining the idea of magnitude (sheer numbers) and apocalypse, Evangelical Christians have referred to the AIDS epidemic as a "gay holocaust," in Old Testament terms punishment for an abomination, same-sex sex. The only continuum between *Holocaust* and the AIDS epidemic is the scale of suffering-evil. But *Holocaust* has also been applied to the consequences of the Church's doctrine of abstinence, the suffering and death of millions of Africans, distinct from the Jewish Holocaust only in that the consequence was unintended. The first was in fact sin, the second evil.

The Bomb: Vonnegut, Slaughterhouse-Five

Kurt Vonnegut's *Slaughterhouse-Five* (1969) is about another holocaust, but one inflicted not by the Nazis but by the Allied bomber command: Billy Pilgrim and his author are both suffering the Dresden bombing and the traumatic aftereffects, but they are victims, not the perpetrators, of the fire-bombing—though little distinction is made between friends and enemies. They suffer *with* the Germans.

The story of *Slaughterhouse-Five*, like that of *Catch-22*, is about the ways people deal with traumas—Billy Pilgrim and the Tralfamadorians, Roland Weary and the Three Musketeers. But the traumas include war as only one of man's suffering-evils; besides wars there are glaciers and "plain old death," accidental and natural, and the Holocaust. The odor of Billy's breath when drunk, "mustard gas and roses," turns out to be the odor of the decaying bodies in Dresden bomb shelters, and the description of naked feet, whether of dead soldiers or the living Billy Pilgrim, as "ivory and blue," equates the living with their inevitable death. And there is the veteran who after surviving the war becomes an elevator operator, catches his wedding ring in the elevator's ornamental iron lace, and "the car squashed him. So it goes."[55]

At the outset, Vonnegut makes clear that *Slaughterhouse-Five*—his own experience in Dresden—is about the Problem of Evil. Roland Weary is a fat, stupid, smelly youth who compensates for his intolerable situation first by his fantasy of the Three Musketeers, which soon ends when the other two are killed; then he falls back on his fantasies of sadistic torture—cruelty, or a form of scapegoating, as compensation for natural evil (30–32). Is cruelty one consequence of the Problem of Evil? "Is the panic resulting from the consciousness of death the cause of cruelty?" Is cruelty compensation for suffering the evil (ultimately of death) in the world?

Paul Lazzaro, as unfortunate as Weary, carries on for Weary when he dies; he is pledged to kill Billy, which eventually he does. He is characterized by suffering "many plagues of boils" (72), recalling one of the plagues God visits upon the Egyptians (Exod. 9.9) as well as Job's sufferings at the hands of the Lord, and his name suggests the beggar Lazarus (or the picaro Lázaro de Tormes). But it is also Lazzaro who, in *Slaughterhouse-Five*, does the act of cruelty upon an animal—a dog, whom he feeds steak filled with steel springs: "he tried to bite out his own insides. I laughed," says Lazzaro, explaining that his motive was revenge—the dog had bitten him (120–21).[56] There are also horses, in this case pulling the American POWs out of Dresden. Billy hears a keening that reminds him of "the friends of Jesus when they took His ruined body down from His cross," but it is the Germans who are aware of the horses, whose "mouths were bleeding, gashed by the bits," and their "hooves were broken, so that every step meant agony," and "the horses were insane with thirst. The Americans had treated their form of transportation as though it were no more sensitive than a six-cylinder Chevrolet" (169).

"So it goes" is the most general way in which Vonnegut—or Billy Pilgrim—deals with the Problem of Evil, that is, death—all sorts of death: even when champagne is "dead," it's "So it goes," and when water is "dead" (63, 88). Like so many other locutions in the novel, the phrase is eventually explained, its source given—or one source: It is "what the Tralfamadorians say about dead people" (38). But there is the bird's equivalent—"All there is to say about a massacre, things like '*Poo-tee-weet*'" (17). The bird's song makes "So it goes" sound upbeat, positive, and this is the word with which the novel ends.

Christianity does not seem to be a solution. For Billy's mother compensation for the evils of the world is the crucifix she buys and for some reason hangs on Billy's wall (33). Billy Pilgrim is a chaplain's assistant and has "a weak faith in a loving Jesus which most soldiers found putrid" (26). Billy looks through a Gideon Bible he finds in a hotel room for "tales of great destruction," Old Testament stories of rewards and punishments, which he finds in profusion. "A visitor from outer space," Vonnegut tells us, "made a serious study of Christianity, to learn, if he could, why Christians found it so easy to be cruel" (94). Like West, he invokes *The Brothers Karamazov:* "But," says Eliot Rosewater, who is making the allusion, "that isn't enough anymore" (87), by which he means war, Dresden and Hiroshima.

Billy's particular way of dealing with death after the war and Dresden is by way of the extraterrestrials, the Tralfamadorians. Their solution is to believe that people die but keep on living: "The most important thing I learned on Tralfamadore was that when a person dies he only appears to die. He is still very much alive in the past, so it is very silly for people to cry at his funeral. All moments, past, present, and future, always have existed, always will exist" (23). We can see them "all at one time" (76).

Here we learn that he came at the (we might say, to use Twain's term) "dream" of the Tralfamadorians by way of Kilgore Trout's science fiction, a novel called *The Big Board* (173–74).

But there is the further question, What do the Tralfamadorians do about "their wars," according to one Tralfamadorian, "as horrible as any you've ever seen or read about." "There isn't anything we can do about them, so we simply don't look at them. We ignore them. We spend eternity looking at pleasant moments—like today at the zoo [where Billy is on display]" (101). And so back once again to the dream and perhaps the true sense of "So it goes."

And "coming unstuck in time" is another way to explain the Tralfamadorian dream. The first time Billy is alone in the snow, isolated from his unit in the Battle of the Bulge, and the swing is to the YMCA swimming pool and his being dropped in by his father to sink or swim (later repeated in a visit to the Grand Canyon [86]). The second time takes him to his mother in a nursing home: "How did I get so old?" (38). The process, which involves going forward as well as back in time, illustrates the Tralfamadorian belief in "how permanent all the moments are" (23).

Another way is Billy's politeness ("Excuse me" and "I beg your pardon"

[48]), and the American POWs—when they are fed by the Germans, "the human beings were quiet and trusting and beautiful. They shared" (61). They are now, therefore, "human beings." And politeness is summed up existentially by the English POWs: "What the Englishman said about survival was this: 'If you stop taking pride in your appearance, you will very soon die.' He said that he had seen several men die in the following way: 'They ceased to stand up straight, then ceased to shave or wash, then ceased to get out of bed, then ceased to talk, then died. There is this much to be said for it: it is evidently a very easy and painless way to go.' So it goes" (126). In other words, one way is discipline, another giving up—something presumably this side of "So it goes" and closer to Satan's "dream" and Swift's Grub Street hack's happy "delusion." But the Englishman's English solution is undercut by Vonnegut's irony, and later by the reductio ad absurdum of Billy's son Robert, who is a total dropout and petty thief until he enlists in the Green Berets: "His posture was now wonderful and his shoes were shined and his trousers were pressed, and he was a leader of men"—by which Vonnegut means that he is a killing machine in Vietnam (163–64).[57]

Vonnegut's own way of coping is the same as Mark Twain's. In *The Mysterious Stranger*, sandwiched in as almost an aside, Twain offers his solution to the Problem of Evil—laughter. True laughter—presumably satire—is a quality Satan denies to human beings, who have, he says, only "a mongrel perception of humor, nothing more." "This multitude see the comic side of a thousand low-grade and trivial things—broad incongruities, mainly; grotesqueries, absurdities, evokers of the horse-laugh. The ten thousand high-grade comicalities which exist in the world are sealed from their dull vision." It is precisely laughter of a higher sort—presumbly Satanic—that is the "one really effective weapon" which can take "power, money, persuasion, supplication, persecution" and "blow [them] to rags and atoms at a blast. Against the assault of laughter nothing can stand" (10.735).[58] Life, Melville noted in chapter 49 of *Moby-Dick*, "The Hyena," is "a vast practical joke": "And as for small difficulties and worryings, prospects of sudden disaster, peril of life and limb; all these, and death itself, seem to him only sly, good-natured hits, and jolly punches in the side bestowed by the unseen and unaccountable old joker," that is, God. This as opposed to Twain's satire as the human way of dealing with the evils of the creator.

The form death takes in Dresden is its ruins: the black ghetto of Ilium (Billy's hometown and ancient Troy) "looked like Dresden after it was fire-bombed"; and one way to deal with the "fighting in Vietnam" is to bomb it "back into the stone age" (51). An Englishman tells Billy and his colleagues, "You needn't worry about bombs, by the way. Dresden is an open city. It is undefended, and contains no war industries or troop concentrations of any importance" (127). Dresden is presented as a place of total innocence, emblematized in the treatment of the dog and the horses. The cases of the Dresden and Hiroshima bombings were distressingly similar, based on proper political (enemy vs. friend) or ideological motives—hypotheses about shortening the war. The Allies' authority for the bombing of German cities, Vonnegut suggests, was Genesis 19:24, that "the Lord rained upon Sodom and upon Gomorrah brimstone and fire from the Lord out of Heaven; and He overthrew those cities" (the bombing of Hamburg was designated Operation Gomorrah).[59]

The Scapegoat: O'Brien, In the Lake of the Woods

Following the Vietnam War, Tim O'Brien's *In the Lake of the Woods* (1994) does, in Michael Herr's words, contrary to viewing from the bomber's-eye view, "go out to the grungy men in the jungle who talked bloody murder and killed people all the time," but it uses these scenes to get at the point O'Brien wants to make, which is about the nature of both the evil and the trauma of atrocity—a memory of the My Lai massacre.[60] He poses the questions: How could American soldiers have committed atrocities? And how did they respond to the peculiar nature of their enemy, who engaged in guerilla warfare? The novel is about what caused American soldiers to commit an evil act comparable to those atrocities of World War II, and what were the consequences to them of their act.

What did they do? One soldier, cited by O'Brien, testified, "That day in My Lai, I was personally responsible for killing about 256 people. Personally. Men, women. From shooting them, to cutting their throats, scalping them, to . . . cutting off their hands and cutting out their tongues. I did it."[61] O'Brien's explanation: "They were young, all of them. Calley was twenty-four, T'souvas was nineteen, Thinbill was eighteen, Sorcerer [John Wade] was twenty-three, Conti was twenty-one, young and scared and almost always lost. The war was a maze. In the months after Thuan Yen they wandered here and there, no aim or direction, searching villages and setting up ambushes and taking casualties and doing what they had to do because nothing else could be done" (26.267). The typicality—or American typicality—of these soldiers, especially John Wade, who later runs for the senate, is emphasized by the parallels in the chapters called "Evidence" with successful American politicians—Lyndon Johnson, Woodrow Wilson, and Richard Nixon. Look what happened to them! A memory of the contrasts used by Gay, Fielding, and others between the ordinary thief, who suffers for his crime, and the Great Men, who do not.

The cause in the case of O'Brien's protagonist John Wade is primarily anger—"Kill Jesus," he cries in moments of stress. He suffers from what is ordinarily thought of as one of the Seven Deadly Sins, wrath. The confusion of evil and sin emerges momentarily in Wade's ("Sorcerer's") realization: "This was not madness, Sorcerer understood. This was sin" (13.107). The deadly sins are, in existential terms, vices, psychological states, that either are or are not controlled by the will. In Wade's case his supposed sin, his inability or unwillingness to control his wrath, we are shown in great detail, is determined by his genes, mind, neuroses, psychoses, and conditioning; for John Wade, by the childhood trauma of his father's suicide, but also his father's genes, his retreat into magic tricks (his "sorcery," his ability to manipulate reality), the utter mess in Vietnam, his electoral defeat, and the Lake of the Woods to which he retreats, which is another Vietnam and leads to another My Lai, the murder of his wife, Kathy. O'Brien gives a psychological explanation of the massacre and the murder, a commentary that extends the explanation to the author himself, who also served in Vietnam and subsequently retraced Wade's footsteps through those "woods."

This is what he *says*. What O'Brien demonstrates, however, is different. In one of the footnotes that extend Wade's case to the author's, he describes his own walk through the villages. "I know what happened that day," he writes of the massacre. "I know how it happened. I know why":

It was the sunlight. It was the wickedness that soaks into your
blood and slowly heats up and begins to boil. Frustration,
partly. Rage, partly. The enemy was invisible. They were ghosts.
They killed us with land mines and booby traps; they disappeared into the night, or into tunnels, or into the deep misted-
over paddies and bamboo and elephant grass. But it went

beyond that. Something more mysterious. The smell of incense, maybe. The unknown, the unknowable. The blank faces.
The overwhelming otherness. This is not to justify what oc-
curred on March 16, 1968, for in my view such justifications
are both futile and outrageous. Rather, it's to bear witness to
the mystery of evil. (20.199)

His sin of wrath and bad genes, the *mystery of evil:* O'Brien is describing
the enemy on whom the American soldiers' act of evil was perpetrated
as, in the terms of writers on the nature of evil from James to Conrad to
Greene, that mysterious thing called "evil." Except, of course, that it is
perpetrated not on the "unknown, the unknowable" itself, which is inaccessible, but on the innocent villagers of Thuan Yen, My Khe, Co Luy,
or Pinkville (or My Lai). They were the "evil" that the American soldiers
were flailing out at that day: the "evil" *them* being killed by the American
soldiers, who have no other way to deal with the actual Vietcong soldiers,
the simple wrongdoers—whether we regard them as soldiers or gueril-
las or whatever. Confronted with "evil," all you can do is act irrationally,
become evil in your own way; and you therefore *become* the enemy, the
evil, in all or more of his real or only imagined savagery.

Put in a less Conradian or mystified way, Allen J. Boyce of First Pla-
toon, Charlie Company, testifies, "We were all psyched up because we
wanted revenge for some of our fallen comrades that had been killed prior
to this operation in the general area of Pinkville" (256).

This can be called generalizing: "When we first started losing members of the company, it was mostly through booby-traps and snipers.
. . . You didn't trust anybody. . . . [I]n the end, anybody that was still in
the country was the enemy." "They was all VC and VC sympathizers
and I still believe they was all Viet Cong and Viet Cong sympathizers"
(25.259–60).

Them and Us: The Demonic Other

It could be argued that the otherness to which the soldiers were responding applies equally to others who only seem to be a threat—or to manu-
factured threats. O'Brien quotes General William Tecumseh Sherman
about the Native Americans: "We must act with vindictive earnestness
against the Sioux, even to their extermination, men, women, and children"

(25.257). This is the "evil" we have seen emerge in the works of Conrad and Greene—as opposed to mere wrongdoing—the "evil" which is mysterious and unknowable, to which you react madly and irrationally (with wrath: "Kill Jesus"), whether the evil/enemy is the Vietcong (invisible, manifest only in land mines and booby traps or snipers) or, in earlier times, "Indians" or witchcraft or the Black Death, any of those terrifying because unknowable evils—in fact, examples of the Problem of Evil (why "we," the good and innocent, suffer in this God-made world); and so you seek out scapegoats, torturing and murdering them in ways that (psychologically at least, but probably ideologically as well) are identical with what was done at My Lai. Going back to O'Brien's remark that the "unknown, the unknowable" is "to bear witness to the mystery of evil": It is rather to the soldiers' mystifying of evil. As Alford said of the "experience of dread," "We defend ourselves against unbearable experience by projecting it into others."[62] Put differently, by Morton in *On Evil*, "evil" participates in a discourse "of hatred, dismissal, or incomprehension. We call acts or people evil when they are so bad that we cannot fit them within our normal moral and explanatory frames," but this is a discourse that can reflect paranoia and offers "permission . . . for reprisals, witch-hunts, protective or preemptive atrocities. . . . Thinking in terms of evil can, if we are not careful, make us accomplices in atrocity."[63]

The mystifying of evil is part of the trauma of evil, which means the denial of evil, the original need for displacement from the invisible enemy to some other, and the subsequent denial and attempt to falsify that outrage, first applied by Sorcerer Wade to the massacre at My Lai and then applied to his killing of Kathy: "This could not have happened. Therefore it did not. . . . He would both remember and not remember" (13.109). ("The ordinary response to atrocities is to banish them from consciousness.")[64]

Ultimately the illusion includes Pfc. Weatherby and eventually Kathy—by which time Wade's "evil" is his own past and the consequent loss of the senate election. The illusion of Kathy-as-evil, that is, as scapegoat for the election fiasco (which included the revelation of Wade's part in the massacre and his falsification of the records), has to be boiled out with scalding tea and denied. "Not a monster, he thought. Certainly not. He was Sorcerer" (28.278)—someone who transforms reality, for example, innocent people into guilty, X into Y, or a murder into a disappearance ("perform his masterly forgetting trick," 30.298n.).

How do you deal with a trauma like the evil of My Lai if you are one of the perpetrators? You go into denial. (And you cannot admit to yourself what you did to your wife ten years later.) It didn't happen, or at least not that way. Even the author O'Brien remains in denial, quoting Freud: "Whoever undertakes to write a biography binds himself to lying, to concealment, to flummery. . . . Truth is not accessible" (291)—although in a footnote O'Brien admits to having himself done what Wade did in Vietnam (298n.).

O'Brien quotes from Judith Herman's *Trauma and Recovery:* "To study psychological trauma is to come face to face both with human vulnerability in the natural world and with the capacity for evil in human nature."[65] For "trauma" we can substitute "evil," and for "vulnerability," the Problem of Evil, for "capacity" the nature of evil. Whereas Cain coped with evil (death, suffering, God) by killing his brother; Ahab by pursuing an animal (a Leviathan); Mark Twain by projecting a Manichaean god; and West by supposing a world without God; the Americans at My Lai cannot cope with "evil" in any other way than to destroy an innocent village.

My Lai illustrated the evil that results from attacking the incomprehensible, the designated "evil" as in "Axis of Evil," when 9/11 became difficult to deal with. The invisible bin Laden, the allusive Al Qaeda from any moral perspective evil, proves inaccessible—somewhere in Afghanistan, or somewhere else. So bin Laden is replaced by the visible Saddam Hussein, who is substituted for him and labeled evil. The destruction of the World Trade Center was, of course, carried out with the intention of bringing down a godless nation, in their terms evil (in our terms, sinners).

How do you cope with evils such as the death or prospective death of children or husbands or wives in Iraq?—by believing that they are fighting "Evil" and dying for America and Democracy if not (in the discourse of sin) God; by denial of the obvious reality that they are dying for nothing more than the ideology of a few Neocons around the president, for a radical Christian idea of good and evil, for an inappropriate (to Muslim belief) ideology of democracy, or for the Halliburton Company and for American oil interests in the Middle East.

The suicides of 9/11 were ostensibly acting more rationally than the American soldiers at My Lai. The "evil" of 9/11 reaches back from the men, who used their bodies, suiciding themselves in order to kill the people on the planes and the thousands of invisible people on the ground, to

Osama bin Laden, who convinced them to do so, and so back to those who interpreted the Koran to this end, and back to the Koran itself insofar as it carried substance for such lethal interpretations and then back to the power inherent in religious texts and priests who, for their own advantage, convinced people of this.

Distance and Proximity

The question is whether a certain kind of combat unleashed these animal qualities or whether it was encouraged by *them* at the top. In the court martials of Lt. William Calley and others, the issue of orders was raised: Did Lt. Calley give a direct order to his men? was he given a direct order from above? This linked the perpetrators of the My Lai massacre to the perpetrators of the Holocaust, who claimed only to be following orders. Were they part of a system or a mob of independent, vengeful soldiers? O'Brien makes only glancing references to statements of Lt. Calley, no reference to a direct order to massacre the villagers. What he does have Calley order is that no one say anything about what has happened.

In the 1940s, C. S. Lewis argued that cruelty is not gratuitous: "People are cruel for one of two reasons—either because they are sadists, that is, because they have a sexual perversion which makes cruelty a source of sensual pleasure to them, or else for the sake of something they are go-ing to get out of it—money, or power, or safety."[66] In the situation of My Lai "revenge" and "safety" were factors, and so the necessity of "power"; but the sense of "getting back" at the invisible enemy, teaching them a lesson, in the heat of the atrocities could graduate into the gratuitous, or inflicting pain for its own sake—though on *these* to punish *those*. The Nazis' treatment of Jews may have had the same effect, but in general what would seem gratuitous was part of the systematic and ideological dehumanization. Still, as at My Lai there would also have been the sense of sheer power ("because I *could*") as well as being part of a mob, say a lynch mob—encouraged by one's companions, those friends Augustine cited to explain his own excesses.

Even the Nazi "evil" of the extermination camps was not quite the same as that of the soldiers in Vietnam in that the Nazis tried hard to avoid trauma: the Nazi cleansing units followed an ideology and orders from the top, behaving (as Himmler instructed them) rationally and, so far as possible, distancing themselves from the horror of the dying and deaths, the need to look their victims in the face and feel some kind of sympathy or empathy. The German soldiers, as Himmler told his officers, were to be distanced from the physical contact with the killing by employing gas chambers and furnaces and using other prisoners to conduct the executions and the burning of the bodies—as Hitler and Himmler and Heydrich were themselves spared by even further distancing from the physical acts.

In the same way the World War II bombings were carried out on London, Tokyo, Dresden, Hamburg, Coventry, and Hiroshima and Nagasaki by men who never saw the carnage and, further away, by Goering in Berlin, Bomber Harris in London, General Marshall in Washington. In retrospect, World War I (called the Great War) had offered a foretaste of II in the introduction of air warfare and bombs as well as in the unprecedentedly massive killing fields directed by generals and politicians from far behind the lines (more than "eighty miles away"), whose aplomb in the face of the casualty figures can only be explained by detachment and some theoretical, ideological, pragmatic rationale. The twentieth-century innovations were the use of gas in the trenches of World War I, the atom bomb of World War II, the napalm of Vietnam, white phosphorus of Iraq—in general the "weapons of mass destruction," death on a vast scale—technologically in the 1940s advanced by bombs and airplanes, which "if used on the 'enemy,' were okay."

The detachment of the bombardiers is caught in the beauty of the napalm drops imagined by Kilgore Trout in one of his novels—"of burning jellied gasoline on human beings": "It was dropped on them from airplanes. Robots did the dropping. They had no conscience, and no circuits which would allow them to imagine what was happening to the people on the ground" (144). Being on the ground, Billy Pilgrim has a different experience of the bombing. Like Gulliver speaking to the king of Brobdingnag, he tells the horrified Tralfamadorians, "I myself have seen the bodies of schoolgirls who were boiled alive in a water tower by my own countrymen, who were proud of fighting pure evil at the time" (100). He also notes the death camps and the "candles from the fat of human beings who were butchered by the brothers and fathers of those schoolgirls who were boiled"; and, indeed, the slaughterhouse in which he experiences the Dresden bombing has a relationship to the slaughterhouses where the Jews were butchered.

Burke, we recall, defined the sublime by the criterion of distance. Death, suffering, a public execution, a disaster of some sort—feared but distant enough to be experienced without risk—is terror, for example the bomber's experience as opposed to that of the people on the ground. The bombardier of the plane that dropped the atom bomb on Nagasaki recalled his experience as the "greatest thrill of my life."[67] Horror, by contrast, is touching the half-decomposed body of the pregnant nun who has been left to die in the vaults of the convent—or participating in the massacre of My Lai.

So, first, quantity and second, distance: both terms of the Burkean sublime. This war combined horror and terror based on the experience on the ground of a bombing and the expectation of more and worse. In a totalitarian dictatorship such as Stalin's *anyone* could be apprehended, tortured, and murdered. Terror was the crucial fact, or rather threat, based on the reality of horror (of the auto-da-fé, of the purges, above all, of hell). Indeed, *terror* is a term that describes war in the twentieth century and returns at the end of the century in *terrorists,* individuals who attack randomly and function as sources of fear. But for the terror to be effective, it has to be based on horror, the horror of experiencing 9/11 or the London underground bombings.

But the significant juxtaposition is of "the bodies of schoolgirls who were boiled alive" and "my own countrymen, who were proud of fighting pure evil at the time" (destroying Sodom and Gomorrah)—Vonnegut's reflection of what was happening in Vietnam at the time of his writing *Slaughterhouse-Five* and recovered in detail by O'Brien in *In the Lake of the Woods.* The close-up, hand-to-hand slaughter of My Lai (and perhaps also the guerilla warfare of Iraq) has become the latest metaphor of Evil, of the reality beneath the myth of Good: "The idea was to hasten the end of the war" (155), or cruelty justified by expediency.

There are three senses of *distance:* the use of Jewish Kapos in the death camps to distance the Nazi soldiers from the immediate experience of the gas chamber and crematorium; the employment of bombers a mile above the devastation they are carrying out; and ourselves in relation to the AIDS epidemic, the famine, and the genocides of Africa.

Evil in the Eye of the Beholder?

The atom bomb also introduced—or led to a focus on—the question of justifiable evil. *Justifiable* very soon becomes *justified* evil (bullying and, if necessary, killing other people for their own good, or for the higher "good" of racial purity), as in the cultural purification of Pol Pot's Khmer Rouge or Mao's Cultural Revolution: Then we might see Pol Pot on a continuum with the Aztec human sacrifices to appease the sun with human blood, or the 150 million natives dead as a consequence of the Christianizing Spaniards in the New World, or those dispensed with by the Manifest Destiny of the American colonists.

Evil called permissible or justified might apply to the case of the bombing of Hiroshima—in the absolute or pure sense of evil, a huge disaster, incomprehensible (at least at the time) in a theistic world, but in this case morally ambiguous. Perhaps the moral ambiguity is as important an aspect of the evil with a capital E as the gratuitous. Without the bombing of Hiroshima and Nagasaki a million American soldiers (plus Japanese soldiers and civilians) would probably have lost their lives. All evidence suggests that the Japanese would have fought to the death protecting the home islands.[68] Whether or not they were on the point of surrendering only shifts the dilemma slightly. On the same continuum was the bombing of Dresden, the pragmatic rationale for which was that the bombing would help bring about the end of a war against an evil tyranny. Just as Aztec sacrifices did not seem as evil to the Aztec chiefs as they did to the victims, so these bombings did not appear as evil to the Americans and English as they did to the Germans and Japanese victims.

Is it no longer possible to conclude that evil means are justified by a virtuous end? Is the end-means category evil per se, as with Hiroshima compared to the Holocaust?—seen from the perspective of the United States or of Japan—or of Nazi Germany? Intuitively, the end of shortening the war with Japan seemed less evil than killing all the Jews in Europe for a principle of racial cleansing. For one thing, the first was pragmatic, the second ideological. The Japanese had initiated the war (by a "sneak attack" that would "live in infamy") and were known to be fanatics who would defend their homeland to the last man and woman. The bomb which killed 75,000 innocent Japanese would save the lives of perhaps a million Americans.

Slavery, the model for evil in the United States prior to the Holocaust, denoted the possession and objectification, the dehumanizing of human beings by southern cotton planters: their power of life and death over other humans. At best it was designated an extended family, called paternalism, the means to a good end (cotton production); at worst, evil with the largest capital E: thus the paradigmatic figure of John Brown, hero in the North, demonic madman in the South.

Then, after the Civil War, there was *lynching:* To the Ku Klux Klan, the word denoted just punishment for a black man's ignoring racial and class boundaries (like Hogarth's Harlot's attempt to be a lady); most often punishment for interracial sex—or merely a black boy's whistle at a white woman. This, though often designated evil, was to Bible-readers the sin of miscegenation, a Levitical abomination. In reality, the word covered for male envy and the threat of black virility (a white man coupling with a black woman was acceptable). James Baldwin's short story "Going to Meet the Man" (1965) describes in detail a lynching, the punishment of castration, roasting over a slow fire, and hanging, with emphasis on the size of the black man's member.[69] A black man coupling with a white woman was in the South evil, while in the North evil was what was done to him.

Only with the radicalism of the 1960s, however, and the Vietnam War was the metaphor of "slavery" plausibly extended from the Confederate states to the Founding Fathers and American "imperialism." *Colonialism* is another term the meaning of which, depending on the speaker, can extend from paternalism (as now either a positive or negative term) to genocide. Ten years before *In the Lake of the Woods,* Cormac McCarthy published *Blood Meridian, or, The Evening Redness in the West* (1985), which dramatizes in excruciating detail the bloodshed that paid for, or brought about, the American dream of empire, the westward movement: the reality under the myth of Manifest Destiny (and Frederic Remington's idealized paintings of the frontier, Zane Grey's purple sage). Robert Penn Warren had made the point in *Brother to Dragons* (1953, 1979),[70] but now, in *Blood Meridian,* everyone is a hardened killer, Americans, Mexicans, and Amero-Indians. McCarthy's story is another *Moby-Dick,* written on the same panoramic scale, with Ahab replaced by the demonic Judge, the whale by the Indians the troop of Americans is killing for their scalps, and the sea by the land, the Malpais, the desert, and the mountains. The Indians (and Mexicans), like the whale, fight back, eventually killing all the scalp-hunters except "the kid" and the Judge. But the kid, like Ishmael, is pursuing the Judge as much as—or more than—he is the Indians: The Judge (in appearance seven feet tall, hairless, smooth-skinned, huge but babylike, and the "enormous dome of his head when he bared it was blinding white") is the whalelike symbol of evil, at the end surviving and apparently eternal ("He says that he will never die").

As this strange novel progresses *Moby-Dick* becomes Twain's *Mysterious Stranger:* The Judge is in the same relation to the kid and the other characters as Philip Traum was to Theodor and his friends. He saves two orphaned puppies only to drop them into the river to drown; he rescues an Apache child only to scalp him. He is a draughtsman who, like Lewis and Clark and the other explorers of the West, obsessively represents copies of his surroundings—of creatures he then kills. Echoing Traum, he regards the world as "a hat trick in a medicine show, a fevered dream, a trance bepopulate with chimeras having neither analogue nor precedent, an itinerant carnival, a migratory tentshow," made livable only by what he calls "the dance," which we see him engaged in as the novel comes to an end.[71]

For McCarthy (and less radically, Warren), the U.S. has *always* been, and is, beneath the idealistic talk of progress, a slave country, racist, sexist, antilabor, genocidally expansionist. The word *slavery* (the characteristic American evil) is extended to the slaughtering of Native Americans and American "holocausts" (lowercase once the term has become general).

In the preceding chapters, examining a sequence of Anglo-American fictions, I have sketched a history of evil, a history of sin. There has been no basic disagreement over what is an evil act, whether gratuitous cruelty, slavery, plague, earthquake, or genocide. But "Evil" *has* been simulated—by adding an aesthetic or a theology, by demonizing or superimposing sin (which reintroduces God, not as the author of evils but the object of worship or betrayal) or abomination, by scapegoating the melodramatic (or allegorical) figure of the witch, the harlot, the heretic, the homosexual when the real evil is in the auto-da-fé. There were Edwards's hell and the witch trials, and the "witches"; and then there were the lying witnesses and the merciless and/or corrupt judges, who believed *sinners* were *evil*.

Throughout I have followed most of my authors in conflating evil and evils, but in the end there is a difference. Only conflicting ideologies disagree about the evils of the modern period, large and small, public and private. The adjective *evil*, however, refers to an agent and the assignment of personal guilt: the judges-witnesses and/or the witches. God, like individual humans, is blamed or defended depending on one's stake in one's own god. It will usually be someone else's who is blamed. The adjectival evil has ultimately to be judged on a scale from one upward, and there is probably no zero (no one is without evil); the degree of guilt, not the evil itself, is ultimately in the eye of the (shall we say?) unprejudiced beholder, whether the critic of Kate Croy or Charlotte Stant, or of current political figures here and abroad. The disagreement has not been over the "evil" of an evil act but its agency: not the *what* but the *who* and the *why* were the questions asked; *who* is guilty and *who* is innocent—American or Muslim, Muslim or Israeli—and to what degree and *why,* under what justification, was the evil carried out? Such questions point to the true sense of the term "moral values," which has been attached reductively to the discourse of sin.

Whether or not evil is in the eye of the beholder, sin certainly is. The Holocaust, like Edwards's and Calvin's hell, predicated no sin, only evil. Except to fanatics, the Holocaust invalidates the hypothesis of sin. "Sin" is a weak and evasive word applied to the responsibility for either Holocaust or Hiroshima (or Katrina, where Rousseau's explanation for the Lisbon Earthquake becomes relevant). "Sin" has taken its place with Hemingway's "words sacred, glorious, and sacrifice" and Goebbels's "special treatment," "evacuation," and "final solution." Sin was the biblical concept used by the religious to explain both senses of evil and evils, but also frequently to cover what many regard as goods. The words all became interchangeable, but sin has been the added flavor and, in many arguments, the trump card. Sin was one fictive lens through which ideologues saw the actions of their opponents. Alongside the monstrous evil/evils of the twentieth century, sin appeared trivial—a diversion from harsh realities of enormous death and suffering; but it has, unfortunately, been slipped back into discourse under the guise of evil. Much of what is *called* evil is only sin. Sin is the term for the large gray area covered by custom and ideology: whether a woman's head should be covered, or her breast; whether members of the same sex should marry. We must conclude that evil as an act has remained a constant, sin a variable.

NOTES

CHAPTER 1. EVIL, SIN, AND WRONGDOING

1. Donald Bloxam, in *Firestorm: The Bombing of Dresden, 1945,* ed. Paul Addison and Jeremy A. Crang (London: Pimlico, 2006), quoted, Ian Garrick Mason, "Logics of War," *TLS,* 28 April 2006, 26.

2. James, *Golden Bowl* (New York: Grove Press, 1952), 1:394. Cf. Adam Morton's term "extreme wrongdoing" (*On Evil* [London: Routledge, 2004], 3).

3. S. H. Butcher, *Aristotle's Theory of Poetry and Fine Art,* trans. Butcher (New York: Dover, 1951), 43, 47, 51.

4. Cf. German *übel* (vs. *böse*).

5. One such formulation adds humiliation: "acts that impose death, pain, or humiliation on others" (Morton, *On Evil,* 1).

6. Elaine Pagels, *The Gnostic Gospels* (New York: Random House, 1979; Vintage ed., 1989), 143.

7. *Oxford Companion to the Bible,* ed. Adrian Hastings, Alistair Mason, and Hugh Pyper (Oxford: Oxford University Press, 2000), 208; Robert Alter, trans., *Genesis: Translation and Commentary* (New York: Norton, 1996), 28.

8. See also Jer. 4:6; Mic. 2:3; Eccles. 11:2; 1 Kings 1:20.

9. See Barbara Neiman, *Evil in Modern Thought: An Alternative History of Philosophy* (Princeton University Press, 2002); also Joseph F. Kelly, *The Problem of Evil in the Western Tradition: From the Book of Job to Modern Genetics* (Collegeville, Minn., 2002). I was also inspired by, but have reacted against, Robert Lowell's interesting essay "Art and Evil," in Lowell, *Collected Prose,* ed. Robert Giroux (New York: Farrar Strauss Giroux, 1987), 130–44.

10. Ecclesiastes lists the evils of this world, which are of God's making, but internalizes them in men: "This is an evil among all things that are done

under the sun, that there is one event unto all: yea, also the heart of the sons of men is full of evil, and madness is in their heart while they live, and after that they go to the dead" (9:3).

11. Kierkegaard, *The Sickness unto Death* (1849), trans. Alastair Hannay (London: Penguin, 1989), 38.

12. Alford, *What Evil Means to Us* (Ithaca: Cornell University Press, 1997), 3.

13. We can posit, if we like, a God who first created these people evil in an evil world but appears to have left them to it; in that case God created their minds a *tabula rasa* (no inherent idea of God), and it was the evil in which they lived that led them to posit a deity.

14. Augustine, *De Civitate Dei*, xi, 22, trans. Henry Bettenson, *Concerning the City of God against the Pagans* (London: Penguin, 2003), 454.

15. In the words of Psalm 51:5, "Behold, I was shapen in iniquity, and in sin did my mother conceive me."

16. A third possibility is polytheism, which postulates many forces of nature at odds with or compensating for each other: in many ways the most satisfactory solution. The old Romans attached their gods to trees, groves, rivers, and so on.

17. Alter, *The David Story: A Translation with Commentary of 1 and 2 Samuel* (New York: Norton, 1999), 13.

18. Another Hebrew root, *pesha'*, suggests the dimension of rebellion, against a human such as a king (1 Kings 12.19) or against God (Isaiah 1.2). See Paul Ricoeur, *The Symbolism of Evil*, trans. Emerson Buchanan (Boston: Beacon Press, 1967), 9, 72–73; also Isaiah 43:27 and Job 34:37. I notice that in Jewish prayer books the word is translated as "sin," and in Judaism we "atone" for our wrongdoings on Yom Kippur. In Christianity God atones for our sins (and presumably our evil deeds as well).

19. Ricoeur, *Symbolism of Evil*, 52, 74.

20. Amos, 5:7, 5:21, 6:12; Hosea; Isaiah, 6:1–13. See Ricoeur, *Symbolism of Evil*, 56 ff.

21. Douglas, *Purity and Danger: An Analysis of [the] Concept of Pollution and Taboo* (London: Routledge, 1966), 76.

22. The sin of wrath/anger, if exacerbated into hatred, could lead to victimage and evil, as with anti-Semitism and misogyny. See André Glucksmann, *Le Discours de la haine* (Paris: Plon, 2005).

23. Chaucer, "The Parson's Tale," in *The Canterbury Tales*.

24. *Secularization* is a term that calls for definition: to transfer from ecclesiastical to civil or lay use, possession, or control. Originally it was a word in canon law "for the release of a cleric from his order into the status of a secular priest," and subsequently it designated "the juridical act of seizing assets from ecclesiastical custody" (Joseph Leo Koerner, *The Reformation of the Image* [Chicago: University of Chicago Press, 2004], 61).

25. Nietzsche, *On the Genealogy of Morals*, III.20, trans. Walter Kaufmann and R. J. Hollingdale (New York: Vintage, 1969), 140–41. Kenneth Burke makes

the chronology: "Order leads to Guilt / (for who can keep commandments!) / Guilt needs Redemption / (for who would not be cleansed!) / Redemption needs Redeemer / (which is to say, a Victim)" (Burke, *The Rhetoric
of Religion* [Berkeley: University of California Press, 1970], 4–5). I am arguing that evil precedes the rest.

26. *Varieties of Religious Experience* (New York: Modern Library, 1929), 197–98,
    205, quoting J. H. Leuba and E. D. Starbuck; and James himself, 132, 208;
    see in general Lectures 6 and 7.
27. Alford, *What Evil Means to Us*, 58, 3, 15.
28. Douglas, *Purity and Danger*, 66–71 and xv–xvi; Tony Tanner, *Adultery in the
    Novel: Contract and Transgression* (Baltimore: Johns Hopkins University
    Press, 1979), 12.
29. Dale Keiger, "Crafting Sound," *Johns Hopkins Magazine* (April 2004),
    42–43.
30. Ricoeur, *Symbolism of Evil*, 33–40.
31. Quoted, Amélie Oksenberg Rorty, ed., *The Many Faces of Evil: Historical
    Perspectives* (readings) (London and New York: Routledge, 2001), 40.
32. C. S. Lewis, *Mere Christianity*, rev. ed. (London: Collins/Fontana, 1952), 44;
    Tom Shippey, "Orcs, Wraiths, Wights: Tolkien's Images of Evil," in *J. R. R.
    Tolkien and His Literary Resonances*, ed. George Clark and Daniel Timmons
    (Westport, Conn.: Greenwood Press, 2000), 184.
33. Augustine, *Confessions*, trans. William Watts (Cambridge, Mass.: Loeb
    Library, 2002), 1:77–79.
34. Latin *malum* meant both apple and evil, a coincidence the Church Fathers
    used to support the story of Adam and Eve with the classical story of the
    Judgment of Paris—and its consequences in the Trojan War.
35. Quoted, J. B. Russell, *Satan: The Early Christian Tradition* (Ithaca: Cornell
    University Press, 1981), 96n.50.
36. Lewis, *A Preface to "Paradise Lost,"* 6th ed. (Cambridge: Cambridge Univer-
    sity Press, 1949), 68. See also Lewis, *Mere Christianity*, 48.
37. Gaca, *The Making of Fornication: Eros, Ethics, and Political Reform in Greek
    Philosophy and Early Christianity* (Berkeley and Los Angeles: University
    of California Press, 2003), 125, 127, 129–31, 137. See also Merry E. Wiesner-
    Hanks, *Christianity and Sexuality in the Early Modern World: Regulating
    Desire, Reforming Practice* (New York: Routledge, 2000).
38. Ricoeur, *Symbolism of Evil*, 28.
39. Gaca, *Making of Fornication*, 179, 292.
40. Plato, *Laws* 773e5–74a1.
41. Gaca, *Making of Fornication*, 181.
42. Rorty, *Many Faces of Evil*, 88.
43. Meier, *Oxford Companion to the Bible*, ed. Bruce M. Metzger and Michael D.
    Coogan (New York: Oxford University Press, 1993), 208.
44. King Saul: 1 Sam. 16:14–16, 18:10–11, 19:9–10; Ahab: 2 Chron. 18:18–22;
    plagues: 2 Sam. 24:1–25, 13–16, and 1 Chron. 21:1–30.

45. Lucifer ("Fire-bearer" from Latin) in Hebrew is *Helel ben Sahan*, "Bright Son of the Morning."

46. Pagels, *The Origin of Satan* (New York: Random House, Vintage ed., 1996), chap. 2.

47. De Rougemont, *The Devil's Share: An Essay on the Diabolic in Modern Society* (1944), trans. Haakon Chevalier (New York: Meridian, 1956), 23–24. These myths are what C. S. Lewis calls "those queer stories scattered all through the heathen religions [and, he should have added, the Christian religion] about a god who dies and comes to life again and, by his death, has somehow given new life to men"; or "pictures [that are] there only to help you to understand the formula [man is evil, man is redeemable]. They are not really true in the way the formula is; they do not give you the real thing but only something more or less like it" (*Mere Christianity*, 50, 55). They are, in other words, signs or etiological fables representing great universal truths.

48. Max Weber defined the state as "the rule of men over men based on the means of legitimate, that is, allegedly legitimate, violence" (Weber, *Politics as a Vocation* [1921], 1, citing Trotsky's remark in Brest-Litovsk, "Every state is based on violence"). Voltaire: "Power consists in making others act as I choose"; "All politics is a struggle for power; the ultimate kind of power is violence." See also C. Wright Mills, *The Power Elite* (New York, 1956), 171; quoted, Hannah Arendt, *Origins of Totalitarianism* (New York: Harcourt, 1968; ed. Harvest Bks., 1976), 135, 134.

49. *Wickedness* implies craft, slyness, something less than evil—perhaps less destructive, less major.

50. Morrow, *Evil: An Investigation* (New York: Basic Books, 2003), 51.

51. Blackstone *Commentaries on the Laws of England: A Facsimile of the First Edition of 1765–69* (Chicago: University of Chicago Press, 1979), 4:9.

52. A page later it applies to a situation similar to eye-for-eye (unmediated) punishment or retaliation for a wrong.

53. Javits quote, 1977, cited Amy Hungerford, *The Holocaust of Texts: Genocide, Literature, and Personification* (Chicago: University of Chicago Press, 2003), 7.

54. Among the moral terms: *flagitious*—L. *flagitiosus*, from *flagium*, whip; a shameful thing (for a Roman the shame of being whipped), and so an outrageous or scandalous crime or vice.

55. Hammond, *OePs* cxix, 137–8 Paragraph 609.

56. See Colin (Joan) Dayan, "Cruel and Unusual: The End of the Eighth Amendment," *Boston Review* 28, no. 5 (2004), 24–31; "Legal Slaves and Civil Bodies," in *Materializing Democracy*, ed. Russ Castronovo and Dana Nelson (Durham: Duke University Press, 2002), 53–94.

57. Eliot, *After Strange Gods* (New York: Harcourt, 1934), 43.

58. Eliot, "The Church's Message to the World," *Listener*, 17 Feb. 1937; cited, Christopher Ricks, *Eliot and Prejudice* (London: Faber, 1988), 8.

59. I am quoting in this paragraph from Jackson Lears, "Sanctimonies," a review of James A. Morone, *Hellfire Nation: The Politics of Sin in American His-*

tory (New Haven: Yale University Press, 2003), in *New Republic,* 30 June 2003, 27–32.

60. Stephen King's example, *Danse Macabre* (New York: Everest House, 1981), 71.

61. Joseph F. Kelly, *The Problem of Evil,* 20.

62. Schneewind, *The Invention of Autonomy: A History of Modern Moral Philosophy* (Cambridge: Cambridge University Press, 1998), 19; to which I am indebted in this section on morality.

63. Cicero, *De Officiis,* trans. John Higginbotham as *Cicero on Moral Obligation* (Berkeley: University of California Press, 1967).

64. Cited, Gordon Rupp, *The Righteousness of God: Luther Studies* (London, 1953), 370–71; Schneewind, *Invention of Autonomy,* 28. Cf. Augustine, *City of God,* XI.34; XIV.13, 28.

65. Hogg, *The Private Memoirs and Confessions of a Justified Sinner,* ed. John Carey (London: Oxford University Press, 1969), 102.

66. Schneewind, *Invention of Autonomy,* 31.

67. Cited, Schneewind, Introduction, ed., *Moral Philosophy from Montaigne to Kant* (Cambridge University Press, 2003), 8. "Voluntarism," Schneewind writes in *The Invention of Autonomy,* "held that God created morality and imposed it upon us by an arbitrary fiat of his will"; "intellectualism" believed that God's morality was "guided by his intellect's knowledge of eternal standards" (8–9).

68. Schneewind, *Moral Philosophy,* 8. It was Calvin's view that "God's will is so much the highest rule of righteousness that whatever he wills [i.e., earthquakes], by the very fact that he wills it, must be considered righteous."

69. Schneewind, *The Invention of Autonomy,* 4.

70. Hobbes, *De Corpore* (1655), 1.7.

71. Morality and ethics have the same etymological source in habit and custom; ethics (as in Aristotle's *Nicomachean Ethics*) more properly designates a study of the moral virtues (courage, temperance, friendship, justice) and seems to have accrued the more exalted associations, perhaps because its derivation is Greek—*ethikos,* based on *ethos,* a person's character; while morality comes from the Latin *moralis.* Schneewind repeatedly uses ethics and morality interchangeably; e.g., on p. 10, though at one point he writes that "ethics tended to be associated with extreme conceptions of morality"—he is discussing voluntarism, and so the sentence is completed with: "as obedience to God." Citing Mill's *Utilitarianism* and the "Art of Life" in his *System of Logic,* Alan Ryan writes, "What we now call 'narrow morality' was described by Mill as the regulation of the 'business' aspects of life, and the consideration of the ends of human existence was to be the task of 'aesthetics,' or as we now say, of 'ethics.'" Citing Anthony Appiah's *The Ethics of Identity,* Ryan writes that ethics asks the "question, 'What should I make of my life?' This is not the moral question 'What do I owe to everyone else?' nor is it the political question 'What are the proper functions of the liberal state?'" ("The Magic of 'I,'" *New York Review of Books,* 28 April 2005, 36). So

ethics seems to be the third element, corresponding to soteriology: What do I owe to God? What do I owe to others? What do I owe to myself?

72. See Lewis, *Mere Christianity*, 72–74, 92. "I may repeat," Lewis writes, "'do as you would be done by' [i.e., Jesus' teaching, his morality] till I am black in the face, but I cannot really carry it out till I love my neighbour as myself: *and* I cannot learn to love my neighbour as myself till I learn to love God: and I cannot learn to love God except by learning *to obey* Him. And so, as I warned you, we are driven on to something more inward—driven on from social matters to religious matters" (emphasis added) (87).

73. Sabourin, *Oxford Companion to the Bible*, 696.

74. Aquinas, *On Evil*, in Rorty, *Many Faces of Evil*, 89.

75. Niebuhr, *The Children of Light and the Children of Darkness* (New York: Scribner's, 1944), 9.

76. Pascal, *Pensées* 618, trans. A. J. Krailsheimer (London, 1967). Schneewind draws attention to Pascal's use of the Pauline-Augustine part–whole metaphor: "We would see ourselves as members of an organism. Each part, while aware of its own existence, would subordinate its 'individual will' [*volonté particulière*] to the 'primal will [*volonté première*] governing the whole body'" (citing Pascal's fourth letter to C. Roannez, *Oeuvres*, 360, 368–74) (Schneewind, *The Invention of Autonomy*, 273).

CHAPTER 2. CLASSICAL AND CHRISTIAN EQUIVALENTS OF SIN AND EVIL

1. Cleanth Brooks and W. K. Wimsatt, *Literary Criticism: A Short History* (New York: Knopf, 1957), 41. They are citing Aristotle's commentator, S. H. Butcher, *Aristotle's Theory of Poetry and Fine Art* (New York: Dover, 1951). In his *Ethics* Aristotle wrote that "incontinence . . . is blamed not only as a fault (*hamartia*) but as a kind of vice (*kakia*)," the last word combining senses of evil and vice but distancing intention and agency (Aristotle, *Ethics*, VII.4). In this context, *kakia* is equivalent to the word for vice, *mochtheria* (see *Ethics* V.8).

2. *Aristotle's Theory of Poetry and Fine Art*, trans. Butcher, 43, 47, 51.

3. See Butcher, *Aristotle's Theory*, 319–20.

4. See W. H. Auden, "The Christian Tragic Hero," *New York Times Book Review*, 16 Dec. 1945, 1.

5. Latin synonyms for *malus* were *pravus*, crooked, misshapen, deformed, perverse, vicious; the noun *pravitas* denoted, bad, vicious, or perverse conduct; from which came the English *depravity* (*deprave*—to make bad or corrupt, make crooked, debase, pervert). The adjective *improbus* meant bad, wicked, impudent, dishonest as well as excessive, presumptuous (the verb *improbo* meant to disapprove or condemn).

6. For Virgil's readers Dido recalled her contemporary analogue, another foreign queen whose hold on a great Roman was disastrous; the past was a

model (a prefiguration) for the behavior of the modern Aeneas, Octavius (later Augustus), from which Antony, following the ethos of Dido, fell short.

7. In canto V of Dante's *Inferno* Dido suffers with Paolo and Francesca for her passion for Aeneas, but specifically for her betrayal of her late husband, Sichaeus, not of her city, Carthage.

8. The story was further developed in the iconography of poets and artists of the sixteenth and seventeenth centuries. (See Dora and Erwin Panofsky, *Pandora's Box: The Changing Aspects of a Mythical Symbol* [Princeton: Bolingen, 1956; ed., New York: Harper, 1965], 12; see 10–13.)

9. Rolfe Humphries, trans., *Ovid Metamorphoses* (Bloomington: Indiana University Press, 1955), 20.

10. Syrinx, like the Belinda of the 1712 *Rape*, simply "aspired to be, one like Diana," "virgin always"; and, we are told, "She might, sometimes, be taken for the goddess" (Humphries, 24). But the purpose of the story, told by Mercury to Argus, is to put the latter to sleep (at Jove's order) so that Mercury can kill him and release Io from his surveillance, returning her from heifer to nymph.

11. And this story is followed by the story of Niobe and so to the story of Pelops and his shoulder—"an ivory substitute" (p. 142)—to which Martial alludes and Pope, again, when he quotes from Martial in his epigraph to the *Rape*.

12. In this section I draw on materials in my *The Fictions of Satire* (Baltimore: Johns Hopkins University Press, 1967), 20–30.

13. Smith Palmer Bovie, trans., *Satires and Epistles of Horace* (Chicago: University of Chicago Press, 1959), 37, 35.

14. These pages draw upon my "Fool-Knave Relation in Picaresque Satire," *Rice University Studies*, 51 (1965), and *The Fictions of Satire*, chap. 1.

15. The Latin words are many: besides *monstrum* and *scelus* (or *scelero*, to defile), there are other overlapping terms referring to various degrees of crimes—*flagitium, crimen, delictum, maleficium*, etc.

16. See, e.g., Northrop Frye, *Anatomy of Criticism: Four Essays* (Princeton: Princeton University Press, 1957), 183.

17. The quotation is from the Strassburg Fragment (97A), trans. G. L. Hendrickson, "Archilochus and the Victims of His Iambics," *American Journal of Philology* 46 (1925), 115.

18. Especially notable in the followers of Juvenal, who produced satires in England around the turn of the sixteenth century. See Alvin Kernan, *The Cankered Muse* (New Haven: Yale University Press, 1959).

19. Jeffrey Burton Russell, *Satan: The Early Christian Tradition* (Ithaca: Cornell University Press, 1981), 45.

20. In Hebrew the word *Sheol*, translated as "Hell," is essentially a "grave" or "pit," where the body in death will be placed. (*Gehenna*, sometimes translated as "Hell," was the valley of Hinnom, a dumping ground for garbage and the bodies of animals and criminals—a place far from Yahweh.)

21. In England, Dante's *Commedia* was known to Chaucer, Milton, and the

Renaissance Italianists, but to others before the mid–eighteenth century only secondhand. Aside from the episode of Ugolino, described by Jonathan Richardson in *An Argument on Behalf of the Science of a Connoisseur* (1719) (which Joshua Reynolds followed in his *Ugolino and His Children* of 1773), and the story of Paolo and Francesca, only the general structure (the nine circles) would have been familiar to English writers. Richardson and Thomas Gray taught themselves Italian in order to read Dante. Swift and Pope make only vague allusions. The first complete English translation was by William Huggins in the 1750s. Huggins published some passages of his translation, but the MS. was lost at his death, and the first published Englishing of Dante was by the Rev. Henry Boyd (1802), beginning with the *Inferno* in 1785; this was followed by Henry Cary's better-known translation in 1814. Blake's illustrations were begun in 1825, based on these texts plus Blake's attempt to learn Italian. Huggins's *Inferno*, however, had been read in manuscript by his friend Hogarth in the late 1850s. Hogarth declined Huggins's invitation to make illustrations, but the influence of his reading was apparent in *The Cockpit* and *Enthusiasm Delineated*, where Hell is associated with English politics and Methodism. See Milton Klonsky, *Blake's Dante* (New York: Harmony Books, 1980), 7; Paulson, *Hogarth: Art and Politics, 1750–1764* (New Brunswick: Rutgers University Press, 1993), 291–93. My text for the *Inferno* is *The Divine Comedy: Volume 1, Inferno*, trans. and commentary by Mark Musa (New York: Penguin, 2003).

22. On Erasmus's *Praise of Folly*, see Kathleen Williams, ed., *Twentieth-Century Interpretations of "The Praise of Folly"* (Englewood Cliffs: Prentice-Hall, 1969).

23. Adams, "The Modern Relevance of *The Praise of Folly*," in Williams, op. cit., 69, 70.

24. Erasmus, *The Praise of Folly*, trans. John Wilson (1668) (Ann Arbor: University of Michigan Press, 1958), 48. Subsequent citations are to this text.

25. Cf. Charles A. Knight's argument that *The Praise of Folly* divides into two types of satire, what he calls incarnational and eschatological, the first with its emphasis on nature (Christ's-Folly's taking on nature, the body), the second with its emphasis on heaven, as when Folly says, "A priest should be free from all worldly desires and think of nothing but heavenly things" (121). (Knight, *The Literature of Satire* [Cambridge: Cambridge University Press, 2004], 20–24.)

26. Swift, *A Tale of a Tub*, ed. A. C. Guthkelch and S. Nichol Smith, 2d ed. (Oxford: Clarendon Press, 1958), 9.171, 174.

27. Folly speaks only for credulity when she uses the example of the stage and the curiosity that strips the actor "of his disguise and show[s] him to the people in his true native form": "But to discover this were to spoil all, it being the only thing that entertains the eyes of the spectators. And what is all this life but a kind of comedy, wherein men walk up and down in one an-

other's disguises and act their respective parts, till the property man brings them back to the attiring house" (44).

28. John Wilmot, earl of Rochester, "Artemesia to Chloe" (ll. 256–57), spoken by the "lady," who is another source for Swift's Grub Street hack.

29. That the *Tale* focuses on heresy, in particular the Gnostic heresy as it was expounded by Irenaeus, is a thesis I proposed in a book published in 1960, but it was a thesis that met at the time with little enthusiasm; since then, with the work of Elaine Pagels and others, some Swift scholars have taken note, but I feel I must outline the evidence once again. See Paulson, *Theme and Structure in Swift's "Tale of a Tub"* (New Haven: Yale University Press, 1960).

If we need more than the internal evidence of the text, we can refer to Swift's sermons of 1717 ff., which use the same terms as his satire. In "On Brotherly Love," he wrote, "The first Dissentions between Christians took their Beginning from the Errors and Heresies that arose among them; many of those Heresies sometimes extinguished, and sometimes reviving or succeeded by others, remain to this Day; and having been made Instruments to the Pride, Avarice, or Ambition of ill designing Men, by extinguishing brotherly Love, have been the Cause of infinite Calamities, as well as Corruptions of Faith and Manners, in the Christian World" (*Irish Tracts and Sermons,* ed. Herbert Davis [Oxford: Blackwell, 1948], 171). The terms— "dissentions" that "revive" and "succeed" others, remaining to this day, all "extinguishing brotherly love"—allow us to feel that Swift is saying, among other things, that the whole theology of sin has destroyed interhuman, interpersonal ethics; which, in a way, he demonstrates by what happens to the three loving brothers when they find themselves in the heart of fashion (a metaphor for theology and heresy). In both *Tale* and sermon Swift is writing about "the great Want of" brotherly love (172).

In the sermons he makes the same connection as in the *Tale* between church and state: "This Nation of ours hath for an Hundred Years past [i.e., back to the Civil Wars], been infested by two Enemies, the Papists and Fanaticks, who each, in their Turns, filled it with Blood and Slaughter, and for a Time destroyed both the Church and Government" (172). It is the "Memory of these Events" that he invokes in his reference to "the Fanaticks [who] revile us, as too nearly approaching to Popery; and the Papists [who] condemn us, as bordering too much on Fanaticism." As in the *Tale,* and formulated in the "Apology" he added to the fifth edition of 1710, Swift "celebrates the Church of England as the most *perfect of all others* in Discipline and Doctrine" (emphasis added) because it is based on a middle way that avoids the extremes of popery and fanaticism, even though it lacks the perfection of Apostolic Christianity, forever lost with the ravages of popery and reformation.

30. Irenaeus, *Libros Quinques Adversus Haereses, Praefatio* 2.

31. Irenaeus, *Libros Quinques,* 1.13.6.

32. Tertullian, *De Praescriptione Haereticorum,* 42, 37.

33. Swift also, for example in his account of the Banbury Saint, follows Irenaeus, who notes that women were especially drawn to heretical enclaves ("many foolish women," in his words), and that the preacher, Marcus or some other, determined to "deceive, victimize, and defile" them, "address[ing] them in such seductive words" that they were corrupted into accepting his heresy, in some cases becoming what were later called "families of love" (Irenaeus, 1.13.5; 1.13.5, 3. See also Tertullian, *De Praescriptione Haereticorum* 41).

34. Pagels, *The Gnostic Gospels* (New York: Random House, 1979; Vintage, 1989), xxii.

35. The evil is division in its special form of schism ("the Sin or Danger of Schism")—disturbance/"zeal"/"where Party hath once made Entrance with all its Consequences of Hatred, Envy, Partiality, and Virulence, Religion cannot long keep its hold in any State or degree of Life whatsoever." Here no one understands the "meaning of the Word Moderation; a Word which hath been much abused, and bandied about for several Years past" (Pagels, *Gnostic Gospels,* 175).

36. See Walter Bauer, *Orthodoxy and Heresy in Earliest Christianity,* ed. Robert A. Kraft and Gerhard Krobel (Philadelphia: Fortress Press, 1971), 111–240.

37. Bunyan, *The Pilgrim's Progress,* ed. James Blanton Wharrey and Roger Sharrock, 2d ed. (Oxford: Clarendon Press, 1975), 10.

38. Emile Durkheim, *The Elementary Forms of the Religious Life* (1917), trans. J. Swain (Glencoe, Ill., 1961), 61.

39. See Greenacre, *Swift and Carroll: A Psychoanalytical Study of Two Lives* (New York: International Universities Presses, 1955), 99.

40. The subject was not new: In *Publick Employment and an Active Life prefer'd to Solitude* (1667) John Evelyn was echoing traditional arguments against solitude when he warned, "He ought to be a wise and good man indeed that dares trust himself alone; for Ambition and Malice, Lust and Superstition are in Solitude, as in their kingdom." See Thomas Laqueur, *Solitary Sex: A Cultural History of Masturbation* (New York: Zone, 2003).

41. Rousseau, *Emile,* quoted, Taylor, "Too Much," *London Review of Books,* 6 May 2004, 22.

42. See Hugh Kenner, *The Counterfeiters: An Historical Comedy* (Bloomington: Indiana University Press, 1968), 130–31.

43. Gaca, *The Making of Fornication: Eros, Ethics, and Political Reform in Greek Philosophy and Early Christianity* (Berkeley and Los Angeles: University of California Press, 2003), 184. "There is nothing like it," Gaca writes, "in either the Septuagint or the tradition of Hellenistic Jewish polemic against polytheism" (185).

44. As Douglas says, "Just as it is true that everything symbolizes the body, so it is equally true (and all the more so for that reason) that the body symbolizes everything else" (*Purity and Danger: An Analysis of [the] Concept of Pollution and Taboo* [London: Routledge, 1966], 151).

45. Augustine, *De Civ. Dei*, xiv, 11, 13, 568, 571–74.

46. I am quoting Pope Nicholas V in 1449, but the assumption is clear in Hooker and Anglican divines; quoted, Henry Kamen, *The Spanish Inquisition* (New York: Meridian, 1975), 40.

47. *Confessions*, IV.16.200–01. The second quotation, which I have not located, is cited without reference by Kenneth Burke, *Rhetoric of Religion*, 81–82.

48. Cudworth, *The Intellectual System of the Universe*, 875–76; cited, Martin Battestin, ed., Fielding, *Amelia* (Middletown: Wesleyan University Press, 1983), 31n. 2.

49. Ricoeur, *Symbolism of Evil*, trans. Emerson Buchanan (Boston: Beacon Press, 1967), 74.

50. If the Irenaeus epigraph refers to both its author—whom Swift is imitating in the manner of Irenaeus—and its object of parody, satire, and attack, the second, Lucretian epigraph refers only to the atheist, materialist object of attack, the Aeolists—though we might read it slightly differently: as the author, like Lucretius, seeing the Aeolist/enthusiast realistically in Lucretian (or Hobbesian) terms, spirit as flatulance, etc.

51. The windmill, *Moulinavent*, certainly alludes to *Don Quixote*, but also to the figure of Satan (and this is a "devil") in the last canto of Dante's *Inferno*.

52. The words are Taylor's, op. cit., 24. See Jon Mee, *Romanticism, Enthusiasm and Regulation* (Oxford: Oxford University Press, 2003).

53. This is a solution that corresponds closely to the message of Dryden's *Religio Laici* (1682), his statement of a layman's faith at the moment when he was still spokesman for the Church of England (before he converted to Catholicism)—which concludes very much as the *Tale* does:

That private Reason 'tis more Just to curb,
Than by Disputes the publick Peace disturb.
For points obscure are of small use to learn:
But *Common quiet* is *Mankind's concern*. (ll. 447–50)

CHAPTER 3. SIN AND EVIL REDEFINED: THE ENLIGHTENMENT

1. David Riggs, *The World of Christopher Marlowe* (London: Faber, 2004); the quotation is from Michael Dobson's review, "Posthumous Gentleman," *London Review of Books*, 29 Aug. 2004, 12.

2. Marlowe, *The Works of Christopher Marlowe*, ed. Alexander Dyce (London: Edward Moxon, 1858), 80a.

3. Also, following from the predestination of damnation, and opposed to the Roman belief, *Doctor Faustus* precludes the possibility of intercession; and thus the inevitability of Faustus's damnation in act 5 ("Christ cannot save thy soul, for he is just . . ."); see Alice Turner, *The History of Hell* (New York: Harcourt Brace, 1993), 168.

4. According to Jonathan Dollimore, "Faustus' transgression becomes

subversive in being submissive yet the reverse of propitiatory" (*Radical Tragedy* [Durham: Duke University Press, 1993], 281n.6).

5. Seneca, *Medea*, trans. Frank Justus Miller, in *The Complete Roman Drama*, ed. George E. Duckworth (New York: Random House, 1942), 2:584.

6. The exertion of power is perhaps most powerfully stated in *Thyestes*: "Herein is greatest good of royal power: / The populace not only must endure / Their master's deeds, but praise them" (Seneca, *Thyestes*, trans. Ella Isabel Harris, in *Roman Drama*, 2:759).

7. For Horner the consequences of sex are disease: "Why, 'tis as hard to find an old whoremaster without jealousy and the gout, as a young one without fear of the pox.

As gout in age from pox in youth proceeds,
So wenching past, then jealousy succeeds
The worst disease that love and wenching breeds.

(Wycherley, *The Country Wife*, ed. Thomas H. Fujimura [Lincoln: University of Nebraska Press, 1965], 24.)

8. Norman Holland, *The First Modern Comedies: The Significance of Etherege, Wycherley and Congreve* (Cambridge: Harvard University Press, 1959), 75.

9. See Markley, *Two-Edged Weapons: Style and Ideology in the Comedies of Etherege, Wycherley, and Congreve* (Oxford: Clarendon Press, 1988), 15, 164.

10. Brown, *English Dramatic Form, 1660–1760* (New Haven: Yale University Press, 1981), 167.

11. *Paradise Lost*, 5.860.

12. Jonathan Richardson, *Explanatory Notes and Remarks on Milton's "Paradise Lost"* (1735), 71–72.

13. *Confessions*, II.6.86–87. I have substituted "perversely" for the Loeb "awkwardly," which I think corresponds more closely to the Latin *perverse*, which would be Milton's sense.

14. Italics added. Etherege, *The Man of Mode*, 2.2 and 5.2, in *The Plays of Sir George Etherege*, ed. Michael Cordner (Cambridge: Cambridge University Press, 1982), 245, 320.

15. In the game of wit played by Horner and his friends, fornication is compared to the satisfaction of hunger; but his own elegant performances (based on his fiction of impotence) are compared to china: plain appetite, or a plain earthen dish, is heightened by the artful decoration of Dresden or Meissen, we might say painted and decorated to conceal its earthy origins, and displayed in a glass case, Horner's "collection." Lady Fidget, and later Marjorie Pinchwife, are additions to his collection.

16. Wycherley, *The Country Wife*, ed. Fujimura, 64, 81, 83, 31.

17. In the terms of high and low, the rake, as portrayed on the popular stage, is an aristocrat, a social model in Restoration society, a representation of the "high"; but in terms of the court, and the tradition of court masques, he is a

low equivalent of the monarch, who was the central performer in the masque, the real center of patronage.

18. Cited, Eve Borsook, *The Companion Guide to Florence,* 5th ed. (New York: Harper Collins, 1991), 112.

19. *Poems on Affairs of State: Augustan Satirical Verse, 1660–1714,* vol. 6, ed. Frank H. Ellis (New Haven: Yale University Press, 1970), 407. The high-low relationship includes even the low and weak, who are inclined not to attack the high, only people lower in the system than they.

20. Robert Darnton, "Peasants Tell Tales: The Meaning of Mother Goose," in *The Great Cat Massacre and Other Episodes in French Cultural History* (New York: Basic Books, 1984), 31.

21. The high-low topos, which includes Gay, depends on a somewhat different sense of power from Satan's or God's. In Hannah Arendt's words, "Power is never the property of an individual; it belongs to a group and remains in existence only so long as the group keeps together. When we say of somebody that he is 'in power' we actually refer to his being empowered by a certain number of people to act in their name. The moment the group, from which the power originated to begin with (*potestas in populo,* without a people or group there is no power), disappears, 'his power' also vanishes"—as when Walpole finally lost the confidence of Parliament (Arendt, *The Origins of Totalitarianism* [New York: Harcourt, 1968; ed. Harvest Bks., 1976], 143).

22. See William Empson's crucial essay, "The Beggar's Opera: Mock-Pastoral and the Call of Independence," in *Some Versions of Pastoral* (1935; repr. Norfolk, Conn.: New Directions, n.d.), 195–252.

23. For Tundal, see Turner, *History of Hell,* 98, 153. Parts of this chapter appeared in my essay, "Pictorial Satire: From Emblem to Expression," in *A Companion to Satire,* ed. Ruben Quintero (Oxford: Blackwell, 2007), 293–324.

24. Swift's image of the "modern" world as hell echoes the Gnostic belief that Hell is the world we live in, created by the wicked demiurge—the irony is that to get more spirit (and escape this evil world) Jack's followers pump air into themselves, thus making themselves into the grotesques of a Bosch or Brueghel.

25. E.g., Martin Schongauer's engraving, c. 1470, in Paris, Bibliothèque Nationale.

26. *Letters of St. Jerome,* trans. C. C. Mierow (London: Longmans, 1963), Letter 22, "To Eustochium," sec. 7, p. 140.

27. Trying to give a sense of what he called "the satiric scene," Alvin Kernan turned to examples of graphic satire. Daumier's *The Incriminating Evidence* (1865–68) shows a row of grim magistrates seated under a picture of Christ on the cross; only his feet nailed to the cross are visible—the rest is cut off by the top horizontal of Daumier's picture space. This corresponds, as Kernan suggests, to the "scene" of the Roman *satura* of Horace and Juvenal, indeed to most narrative satires as well: a great many examples of folly or knavery crowded threateningly around, crushing or drowning, a single

disappearing indication of virtue. Kernan traced this "scene" back to Christian paintings, most notably North European (specifically by Bosch, Massys, and Brueghel), of Christ being mocked, flagellated, and crucified, where he is a tiny idealized figure surrounded by—almost, in some cases, lost among—ugly, brutal, torturing or mocking figures of Jews, Romans, soldiers, and priests. See Kernan, *The Cankered Muse: Satire of the English Renaissance* (New Haven: Yale University Press, 1959), 8–10.

28. Paintings and prints of the Massacre of the Innocents operated in the same way, showing many innocent surrogates for the Christ child being killed by savage soldiers.

29. See Bosch's *Christ Mocked* in the National Gallery, London, and Massys' *Ecce Homo* in the Prado, Madrid.

30. *Hogarth's Graphic Works*, ed. Paulson (London: Print Room, 1989), cat. no. 36.

31. Lady Fidget described Horner's unmanning of himself for sex-starved wives as an analogue to Christ's Atonement for the sins of men: "But, poor gentleman, could you be so generous, so truly a man of honour, as for the sakes of us women of honor, to cause yourself to be reported no man? No man! And to suffer yourself the greatest shame that could fall upon a man, that none might fall upon us women by your conversation?" [II.i].

32. Cf. Faustus's allusion to Christ's Atonement and the Duke's words in *Measure for Measure* as he prepares to return to his proper role as duke: "Look, the unfolding star calls up the shepherd." On "sacred parody," see Paulson, *Hogarth's Harlot: Sacred Parody* (Baltimore: Johns Hopkins University Press, 2003).

33. At the hands of his father, Richard Hogarth: See Paulson, *Hogarth: The Modern Moral Subject, 1697–1732* (New Brunswick: Rutgers University Press, 1991), chap. 2.

34. See Paulson, *Hogarth's Graphic Works*, cat. nos. 121–26; and Paulson, *Hogarth's Harlot*, but this was an argument that originated in *Hogarth's Graphic Works* (New Haven: Yale University Press, 1965 ed.) and *Hogarth: His Life, Art, and Times* (New Haven: Yale University Press 1971).

35. I deal with its "uniqueness" in *Hogarth's Harlot*. As to its scandalousness: Edmund Burke believed that graphic images were more precise, less open to obscurity and ambiguity than words. In fact, graphic images are more indeterminate than words—like Empson's ambiguous words, they invite multiple readings, therefore permitting the spectator choices. As Freud recognized, the meaning of images is always multivalent and therefore in dreams serves as a censoring mechanism, which seeks to conceal the motivating desires behind the dream. Where the possibilities for meaning are multiple, a forbidden one can easily be hidden and overlooked. The picture is this or that, an obvious metaphor or not, depending on how you choose to look at it. Censorship can be thwarted, as Hogarth demonstrated in *A Harlot's Progress*.

36. The following passage draws on the concluding pages of *Hogarth's Harlot*.

37. "Creed of the Savoyard Vicar," *Emile*, in bk. 4.

38. As also in *The Sleeping Congregation*, where God has been replaced by the royal arms (*Dieu et mon droit*). See *Hogarth's Graphic Works*, cat. nos. 158, 140.

39. Gaca, *The Making of Fornication: Eros, Ethics, and Political Reform in Greek Philosophy and Early Christianity* (Berkeley and Los Angeles: University of California Press, 2003), 129–31, 137.

40. Ibid., 13, 138–39.

41. A recent issue of the *Johns Hopkins Magazine* (Sept. 2005) was devoted to "The 7 Deadly Sins and why they are not always so bad"—a comic performance which was received with some violently negative responses from Hopkins alumni.

42. Anthony Ashley-Cooper, third earl of Shafesbury, *Inquiry concerning Virtue or Merit* (1699), in *Characteristics* (1711), ed. John M. Robertson (New York: Dutton, 1900).

43. Hogarth, *The Analysis of Beauty*, ed. Ronald Paulson (New Haven: Yale University Press, 1997), 59.

44. Shaftesbury's argument for the Choice of Hercules as the model for history painters was made in his *Notion of the historical Draught or Tablature of the Judgment of Hercules*, published in 1713. The Harlot's name appears as "Md. Hackbout" on a letter in an open drawer in the third scene, and on her coffin in the final scene is "M. Hackabout." For the likenesses, recognized by contemporaries, see Paulson, *Hogarth: The Modern Moral Subject*, 247–55.

45. See Neil Kenny, *The Uses of Curiosity in Early Modern France and Germany* (Oxford: Oxford University Press, 2004).

46. Hobbes, *Leviathan* VI.58, VII.16.

47. Rowlandson in effect produced comic versions of the "grotesque" style that had originally been developed by Raphael in his decorations for the Loggia of the Vatican, based on the grotesques—forms that merged plant, animal, and human shapes—in the newly excavated Golden House of Nero.

48. Ernst Gombrich, "The Cartoonist's Armoury," in *Meditations on a Hobby Horse and Other Essays on the Theory of Art* (London: Phaidon, 1962).

49. David V. Erdman, *The Illuminated Blake* (New York: Doubleday, 1974), 139–40; I discuss this subject at greater length in *Representations of Revolution* (New Haven: Yale University Press, 1983), chap. 4.

50. There is no God, therefore no Satan, in Hogarth's world. There are echoes of the former as a conceptual framework for the way things *work* in eighteenth-century England, but Satan makes only one appearance: in the painting *Satan, Sin, and Death*, where he appears not in a parody Trinity, as he does in Milton and in Hayman's illustrations, but rather in the Macheath role in Hogarth's *Scene from "The Beggar's Opera"*—the gestalt in which Polly tries to mediate between her lover and her father (see fig. 16).

51. In "The Everlasting Gospel": "He mockd the sabbath & he mockd / The Sabbaths God & he unlockd / The Evil spirits from their Shrines / And turnd

Fishermen to Divines" (*The Poetry and Prose of William Blake*, ed. David V. Erdman, *Poetry and Prose* [New York: Doubleday, 1965], 794).

52. Blake, *The Last Judgment* (1810), Erdman, *Poetry and Prose*, 549. For Mary-Jesus, see above, n. 34.

53. See *Marriage of Heaven and Hell* 9 and *America* 8.13.

54. Bataille, *Literature and Evil*, trans. Alistair Hamilton (New York: Urizen Books, 1973), 5.

55. Vonnegut, quoted, A. O. Scott, "God Bless You, Mr. Vonnegut," *New York Times Book Review*, 9 Oct. 2005, 31.

56. The Marquis de Sade—as good an example as we have of gratuitous evil—is nevertheless an aestheticizer of evil: first, because he is writing about it, representing it rather than experiencing it; second, when he did experience it, the "sadism" was less extreme, less ideal, tainted by the real world; third, even in his representations, he is, like Bataille and Breton, defying a deity—at his most blatant, in *Juliette* in the mock-crucifixion of one of the victims.

57. Andrew Sullivan, "Atrocities in Plain Sight," *New York Times Book Review*, 23 Jan. 2005, 8.

58. "The Khmer Rouge cadre who cut open the woman's stomach to prove she had stolen rice did so because of a fatal convergence in his mind of political rationale (stealing rice was a crime against the regime, the People), empowerment (he held the authority, and the knife), and sheer stupidity (he was probably an overindoctrinated country boy who knew almost nothing except the year-zero cant of the political overlords)" (Morrow, *Evil*, 85).

59. Alford, *What Evil Means to Us* (Ithaca: Cornell University Press, 1997), 58.

60. *Crime and Punishment*, trans. Constance Garnett (New York: Modern Library), 56–57.

61. Although he cites Nikolai Nekrasov's poem "Before Evening," from the cycle *About the Weather* (1859), which includes the crucial detail shared by Hogarth of the *overloaded* wagon, it is not unlikely that both may also have seen Hogarth's print.

62. *Brothers Karamazov*, trans. Richard Pevear and Larissa Volokhonsky (San Francisco: Northpoint, 1990), 5.4.241. Cf. Peter Singer's *Animal Liberation* (1998), which gives moral standing to animals on the criterion of their capacity to suffer—the basic fact being, again, cruelty.

63. On the evils of both reactionary and liberal attitudes to punishment and the law—the evil of the punishment and of the punishers—his example, Kafka's "In the Penal Colony," see Robert Boyers, "Thinking about Evil," *Raritan* 23, no. 2 (2003), 1–23.

64. With features that (if we accept Battestin's attribution of the British Museum portrait) are suspiciously close to Fielding's own (Paulson, *Hogarth: Art and Politics, 1750–1764* [New Brunswick: Rutgers University Press, 1993], 3:30–31).

65. In the Corsham Court Collection, now in the City of Bristol Museum and Art Gallery. There are at least three versions: besides Bristol, in the Prado,

Madrid, and the Minneapolis Institute of Arts (the latter could have also been in an English collection before it surfaced in the nineteenth century in Lord Egremont's collection—sold 1896). See *Anthony van Dyck,* ed. Arthur K. Wheelock, Jr., et al. (Washington: National Gallery, 1991), cat. nos. 13 and 14.

66. He also wears a hat that simulates the triangular halo that often appeared in the iconography of God the Father. Cf. also the figure of God in Judgment in Brueghel's *Last Judgment* (the print). In *Stages of Cruelty,* plate 1, the torture Nero is imposing on the dog is taken from the torture inflicted on a sinner by one of the devils in Jacques Callot's *Temptation of St. Anthony,* an image of hell that is supported by the image of the magistrate in the fourth plate.

67. Is it significant that Nero kills his own child, bringing an end to the cyclic nature of the *lex talionis,* emphasized in "The Reward of Cruelty" with its circular forms and reading structure (see Paulson, *Hogarth: Art and Politics, 1750–1764* [New Brunswick: Rutgers University Press, 1993], 28–29)?

68. Kenneth Burke, *The Rhetoric of Religion* (Berkeley: University of California Press, 1970), 7.

69. Edmund Burke, *A Philosophical Enquiry into the Origin of Our Ideas of the Sublime and Beautiful* (1757), ed. J. T. Boulton (London: Routledge, 1958), 62; see also Joseph Grixti, *Terrors of Uncertainty; The Cultural Contexts of Horror Fiction* (London: Routledge, 1989), esp. 50–51.

70. Burke, *Philosophical Enquiry,* 64–65.

71. Burke opposes love, the social virtue, to power and the fear and pain of the sublime; but love also involves a kind of power, especially in its *loss* (comparable to the vacuity of the sublime), and thus "the violent effects produced by love, which has sometimes been even wrought up to madness" (41). Burke is grudging in his account of love (later he describes the grotesque facial signs that accompany passion), but he does acknowledge that the "object" is "the *beauty* of the sex. Men are carried to the sex in general, as it is the sex, and by the common law of nature; but they are attached to particulars by personal *beauty*" (42). And (in 3.10) he seems to agree with Hogarth, contra Shaftesbury, that there is no clear relationship between beauty and virtue (112).

72. Paulson, *Representations of Revolution* (New Haven: Yale University Press, 1983), 68.

73. In the 1760s Hogarth accurately and presciently parodied Burke's sublime: in *Enthusiasm Delineated* he associated it with ideas of the sacred (hell and damnation) and sexual ecstasy; in *Tail Piece, or The Bathos,* his final print (1764), with violence, ruin, and the end of the world. See *Hogarth's Graphic Works,* nos. 210 (*Enthusiasm Delineated*), 210A (*Credulity*), 106 (*Cunicularii*), and 216 (*The Bathos*).

74. This painting also appears to have been one of the inspirations behind Burke's *Philosophical Inquiry* (see Paulson, *Hogarth: Art and Politics,* 242–46).

CHAPTER 4. SIN/EVIL AND THE LAW: THE NOVEL

1. For the phrase, see *Amelia*, ed. Martin Battestin (Middletown: Wesleyan University Press, 1983), e.g., 4.8.185, 5.1.194. Parts of this chapter draw upon my essay "Fielding, Hogarth, and Cruelty," in *Henry Fielding (1707–1754), Novelist, Playwright, Journalist: A Double Anniversary Tribute*, ed. Claude Rawson (Newark, Del.: University of Delaware Press, 2006).

2. The paradigm of the Good Samaritan was central to the story of *Joseph Andrews* (1742), in which Joseph is put in the situation of the wounded man, the coachload of respectable folk represent the priests and Pharisees, and the postillion (the lowest of the low) is the only one to offer Joseph assistance.

3. Fielding, *Contributions to the Champion and Related Writings*, ed. W. B. Coley (Oxford: Clarendon Press, 2003), 243–44.

4. Fielding, *An Enquiry into the Causes of the Late Increase of Robbers and Related Writings*, ed. Malvin R. Zirker (Middletown: Wesleyan University Press, 1988), 90, 83, 92.

5. Fielding, *Enquiry*, 98–99. Fielding may have been acknowledging Hogarth's prints two years later in *A Journal of a Voyage to Lisbon* (1754), in which cruelty (largely to Fielding himself) is a chief subject. The work offers "a lively picture of that cruelty and inhumanity, in the nature of men, which I have often contemplated with concern; and which leads the mind into a train of very uncomfortable and melancholy thoughts" (*Journal*, ed. Harold Pagliaro [New York, 1963], 45; Paulson, *Hogarth: Art and Politics*, 26ff.).

6. Fielding, *Enquiry*, 164.

7. Fielding, *The Covent-Garden Journal*, ed. Bertrand A. Goldgar (Middletown: Wesleyan University Press, 1988), 312 and n.

8. An example is the contrast between the laws of felony and perjury: the capital crime of the poor vs. the misdemeanor of the rich, perjury "with an Intention of taking away the Life of an innocent Person by Form of Law." As Robinson, the speaker of the above, adds, "What is taking away a little Property, from a Man compared to taking away his Life, and his Reputation, and ruining his Family in the Bargain" (*Amelia*, 1.4.34–35).

9. Not always: Dr. Harrison, probably accurately, accuses Booth of the sin of vanity or pride when he purchases an expensive equipage (4.3.165).

10. *Amelia*, 4.6.177.

11. See, e.g., *Amelia*, 4.6.177, 4.8.185.

12. We are reminded of Black George, who "loved" Tom Jones but, when his self-interest was at stake, betrayed him.

13. The metaphor is, as befits the profession of the male characters (but also typical of Restoration comedies), of warfare: "A triumphant Passion is an active Conqueror, never failing to improve the Victor, nor stopping, 'till it hath perfectly subdued and rendered itself absolute Master of the Mind"—better stopped in the first trench than the last. Cf. *Amelia*, where you must immediately stop and retreat, and the *Champion* essay of a decade earlier: "No

Passion attacks us at first with that Violence, which it afterward assumes. It steals imperceptibly into our Minds, and seldom declares itself 'till certain of the Victory" (4.2.155, 157).

14. See Paulson, *Popular and Polite Art in the Age of Hogarth and Fielding* (Notre Dame: University of Notre Dame Press, 1979), 172–89. The hydraulic model appears elsewhere as well, e.g., in Miss Matthews, 1.6.42–43, and earlier in *Tom Jones* when, thinking he has lost Sophia, he encounters Molly Seagrim.

15. Tanner, *Adultery in the Novel: Contract and Transgression* (Baltimore: Johns Hopkins University Press, 1979), 14.

16. Amelia's term for Colonel James's actions is "villainy": "For sure all Mankind almost are Villains in their Hearts," she tells Dr. Harrison, speaking of James, whose designs to seduce her were "artfully disguised under the Appearance of so much Virtue." But Harrison, obviously more a Pelagian than she, replies, "The Nature of Man is far from being in itself Evil. It abounds with Benevolence, Charity and Pity, coveting Praise and Honour, and shunning Shame and Disgrace. Bad Education, bad Habits, and bad Customs, debauch our Nature, and drive it Headlong as it were into Vice." That he is speaking for Fielding is confirmed when he adds, "The Governors of the World, and I am afraid the Priesthood, are answerable for the Badness of it. Instead of discouraging Wickedness to the utmost of their Power, both are too apt to connive at it." And he turns his attention to "the great Sin of Adultery . . . this monstrous Crime . . . protected by Law and countenanced by custom" (9.5.374–75), which is the subject of *Amelia*. Harrison, by no means the model clergyman that Parson Adams was, in this instance at least is on a wavelength with his author.

17. Adultery, as defined by Blackstone (3.8.3.p. 139), falls under the category of private property and "the *rights of things*" as a "civil injury, (and surely there can be no greater) the law gives a satisfaction to the husband for it by an action of trespass *vi et armis* against the adulterer, wherein the damages recovered are usually very large and exemplary." He does not draw attention to the fact that it is an analogue of treason (IV.6), a private wrong vs. a public (betrayal of the king). Blackstone does imply an analogy between adultery and treason when he describes treason as breaking allegiance: "the tie which binds every subject to be true and faithful to his sovereign liege lord the king, in return for that protection which is afforded him" (ibid.).

18. See Blackstone, 3.8.3.139.

19. One of the punishments Fielding cites is the Egyptians' for the adulterous lady: "to have her nose cut off: for they thought it reasonable . . . to deprive lascivious Women of those charms which they used to the Purpose of unlawful Lust" (*Covent-Garden Journal*, 353; again, 358). The tongue-in-cheek reference is to the controversy over his forgetting to replace Amelia's shattered nose in the first edition of the novel: The charms of Amelia, the emblem of chastity, were only increased by the surgery to her nose. A joke, I presume, like others in the essays: "Two Punishments of the Women,

I cannot omit. The one was by prohibiting them to dress themselves in any Manner of Finery, the other was by forbidding their Husbands to have any future Converse with them under the Penalty of Infamy and Loss of freedom. The former of these may possibly by some be thought the more grievous Penance" (355).

20. Coley, ed. *Champion*, 136–38, 220. Cf. the solution of transmigration of souls in *Trivia* and the *Champion* essay on horses, a comic equivalent like the ducking of adulterers.

21. My thanks to Richard Quaintance for drawing my attention to the tree, which I had ignored. The tree appears in the engraving and the drawing but not in the woodcut of plate 3. I presume that the drawing, engraving, and woodcut corresponded, and that after the woodcut had been made Hogarth added the tree to the engraving—an easy process for an engraver, but impossible at this point for a woodcut artist.

22. Evident from the advertisements and Hogarth's own comments in his "Autobiographical Notes." See in Paulson, *Hogarth: Art and Politics*, 17–26; Joseph Burke, ed., Hogarth, "Autobiographical Notes," in *The Analysis of Beauty* (Oxford: Clarendon Press, 1955), 226.

23. See *Hogarth's Graphic Works*, cat. no. 139.

24. NB the economic significance of gin in this context; see *Hogarth: Art and Politics*, 23–25.

25. Hardy, *Jude the Obscure* (1895), ed. Robert Heilman (New York: Harper and Row, 1966), 1.11.114. Again, Jude, urged to give up drink, replies, "I could avoid that easily enough, if I had any kind of hope to support me" (2.7.170).

26. *Beer Street* substitutes for gin the more expensive beer, the escape for the somewhat better off. Hogarth may be suggesting that beer invigorates while gin deadens.

27. Alford, *What Evil Means to Us* (Ithaca: Cornell University Press, 1997), 58, 3, 15.

28. Márai, *Memoir of Hungary 1944–1948* (1972), trans. Albert Tezla (Budapest: Corvina Books, 2000), 211, 212.

29. Dickens, review of Cruikshank's "The Drunkard's Children: A Sequel to the Bottle," in *The Examiner*, 8 July 1848.

30. Arnold Kettle, *An Introduction to the English Novel* (New York: Harper, 1960), 2:124–25.

31. *Oliver Twist*, ed. J. Hillis Miller (New York: Holt, Rinehart, 1962), 4.35; cited, Kettle, *Introduction to the English Novel*, 126. For a good account of Hogarth's influence on Dickens and his illustrators, see J. R. Harvey, *Victorian Novelists and Their Illustrators* (New York: New York University Press, 1971), *passim*.

32. Inevitably, the scene of the death of Bill Sikes at the end of *Oliver Twist*, being pursued and howled at by the mob of citizens who made him the felon and murderer, recalls the third *Stage of Cruelty*. Bill Sykes has incidentally

killed, as Tom Nero did, his girlfriend, but the sympathy momentarily shifts to Sykes. In the case of Nancy, however, she has taken upon herself the role of atoner, sacrificing her life for the salvation of Oliver; in the case of Tom Nero's girlfriend, she betrayed her master in order to satisfy Nero's greed.

33. Bumble has "inwented" Oliver's name, as was the practice in the Foundling Hospital in Hogarth's time; which recalls the terrible names such as Nero imposed on the poor in Hogarth's prints.

34. The parallels or borrowings seem endless: Bumble also wears a button showing "the Good Samaritan healing the sick and bruised man," presented to him by the parish board: This recalls Hogarth's painting of the scene on the staircase of St. Bartholomew's Hospital (later engraved) and Fielding's use of the parable, applied to the victimization of Joseph, in *Joseph Andrews*.

35. As with Dickens's slippery use of "great man" and "gentleman," "Atonement" appears only in the title of chapter 27, which "Atones for the unpoliteness of a former chapter . . ." (27.194). I am not arguing that Dickens consciously set out a program of atonement in *Oliver Twist*, or indeed that he was thinking very consciously of Atonement when he had Sidney Carton atone for his sins by sacrificing his life for Charles Darnay in *Tale of Two Cities*. But the Christian story was clearly in his mind, or at least the story Hogarth told in *A Harlot's Progress*.

36. What Kettle refers to as her "genuine humanity" means that, as in most interpretations of the Atonement, while totally human, she does not share humankind's (Sikes's and Fagin's) ineradicable sin: she has a virtue that, as Dickens says in the preface, is "the last fair drop of water at the bottom of the weed-choked well" (xxxiii).

37. P. 60 and title to Chap. 18.

38. The Artful Dodger, in the great trial scene, is legally guilty and condemned to transportation for life for the theft of a watch, but derives from that young pickpocket in *Trivia*, the "subtil Artist" who "with practis'd Slight, / And unfelt Fingers make thy Pocket light," and is pursued ("Hounds following Hounds, grow louder as he flies") caught, and ducked:

Seiz'd by rough Hands, he's dragg'd amid the Rout,
And stretch'd beneath the Pump's incessant Spout:
Or plung'd in miry Ponds, he gasping lies,
Mud choaks his Mouth, and plaisters o'er his Eyes. (II.54, 69–76)

In Gay's terms, he is a figure more playful than dangerous, brutally punished. (Another of Fagin's boys, "Master Bates," may be Dickens's memory of Swift's pun.)

39. *The Works of Charles Dickens*, ed. Andrew Lang, 16 vols. (New York: 1899): 1:19.329.

40. Karl Marx and Frederick Engels, "Manifesto of the Communist Party, in

Selected Works(Moscow: Progress Publishers, 1969), 1: 112. The "Manifesto" was published in London in 1848 and translated into English in 1850.

41. Marx, *Selected Works*, 1:109.

42. See above, n. 24.

43. Hawthorne, *The Scarlet Letter* (London: Walter Scott, n.d.), chap. 2, pp. 57–58.

44. See chap. 18, p. 241, for the various synonyms for Law ("regulations," "principles," "prejudices," "crime," etc.).

45. In retelling the story in part 2 of *The Age of Reason* (1795) Paine wrote, "Were any girl that is now with child to say, and even to swear it, that she was gotten with child by a ghost, and that an angel told her so, would she be believed? Certainly she would not." (Paine, *Age of Reason*, ed. Foner, 52, 160.) For Paine and Blake's more elaborate version in "The Everlasting Gospel" and *Jerusalem*, see Paulson, *Hogarth's Harlot*, 79, 83, 328.

46. NB also that Hester sets out, in the words of the final line of *Paradise Lost*, "with the world before her"—a line Henry James uses more than once in his novels, e.g., in *Portrait of a Lady* and *Wings of the Dove*.

47. See above, 88–89.

48. Lawrence, *Studies in Classic American Literature* (1922; repr. New York: Doubleday Anchor, 1953), 92–110.

49. Fiedler, *Love and Death in the American Novel* (New York: Criterion Books, 1960), 497.

50. Of course, by this time Greuze and other artists, and especially in England the illustrators of Dickens's novels, had followed Hogarth's practice.

51. See *Hogarth's Graphic Works*, cat. no. 126.

52. I don't know how far we can push the connection with Hogarthian aesthetics; but her hair certainly recalls Hogarth's emphasis on the beauty of untrammeled hair—drawing on Virgil's description of Venus's hair in *Aeneid* I and Milton's of Eve's in *Paradise Lost*. See Hogarth, *Analysis of Beauty*, title page, 34–35, 39, *et passim*.

53. My thanks to Brenda Wineapple for her splendid biography, *Hawthorne, A Life* (New York: Knopf, 2003), and for useful exchanges on e-mail.

54. Melville, *Billy Budd, Sailor*, in Melville, *Billy Budd and Other Stories* (1924; corr. ed., 1962; repr. New York: Penguin, 1986), 16.336, 13.328, 2.299. Melville notes that "as a class, sailors are in character a juvenile race" (337).

55. He is also compared to the nature boy Caspar Hauser (302).

56. For background, see Hershel Parker, *Reading Billy Budd* (Evanston: Northwestern University Press, 1990).

57. One wonders if Melville, describing Claggart's treatment of Billy, was remembering the scene in *The Confessions of a Justified Sinner* in which the diabolic Robert Wringhim does his best to destroy his classmate M'Gill, who excels him at school: "I told a lie of him. I came boldly up to the master, and told him that M'Gill had in my hearing cursed him in a most shocking manner, and called him vile names. He called M'Gill, and charged him with

the crime, and the proud young coxcomb was so stunned at the atrocity of the charge, that his face grew as red as crimson, and the words stuck in his throat as he feebly denied it. His guilt was manifest, and he was again flogged most nobly, and dismissed the school for ever in disgrace, as a most incorrigible vagabond" (Hogg, *The Private Memoirs and Confessions of a Justified Sinner,* ed. John Carey [London: Oxford University Press, 1969], 148. 111).

58. Customary procedure allowed that any sailor in Billy's position could have been judged at a later time by a properly convened panel on land. The ship's surgeon thinks Vere has gone mad to interpret the law so strictly, and the other officers of the *Bellipotent* find Vere's verdict equally unusual.

CHAPTER 5. THE DEMONIZING OF SIN

1. Originally published in *The Three Imposters* (1895); my text is based on the 1922 edition: Machen, *Tales of Terror and the Supernatural,* ed. Philip van Doren Stern (New York: Knopf, 1948), 116–18. (The title *The Three Imposters* refers to the blasphemous text of the seventeenth century *Traité des Trois Imposteurs.* The three imposters were Moses, Jesus, and Mohammed.) In our own day, C. S. Lewis recalls dismissing those Christians (like Machen) who "talk about mere sins of thought as if they were immensely important: and they talk about the most frightful murders and treacheries as if you had only got to repent and all would be forgiven. But I have come to see that they are right. What they are always thinking of is the mark which the action leaves on that tiny central self which no one sees in this life but which each of us will have to endure—or enjoy—for ever" (*Mere Christianity* [1952; repr. New York: Harper, 1980], 92).

2. Walter Stephens, *Demon Lovers: Witchcraft, Sex, and the Crisis of Belief* (Chicago: University of Chicago Press, 2002).

3. Susan J. Navarette, *The Shape of Fear: Horror and the Fin de Siècle Culture of Decadence* (Lexington: University of Kentucky Press, 1998), 188; see her illuminating chapter on Machen, 178–201.

4. Stern, "Preface," Machen, *Tales of Terror and the Supernatural,* 175.

5. Machen, "Out of the Earth," *Tales of Terror and the Supernatural,* 290–91.

6. Bataille, *Literature and Evil,* trans. Alastair Hamilton (New York: Urizen Books, 1973), 8.

7. The story was published in the London *Evening News,* 29 Sept. 1914, following the retreat from Mons; its effect was not unlike that of Orson Welles's Mercury Theater production of H. G. Wells's *War of the Worlds.*

8. Zola, *Nana,* 2:312, 336; quoted, Navarette, *Shape of Fear,* 194; see 194–95.

9. "The Dunwich Horror" in *Best of H. P. Lovecraft* (New York: World, 1941), 114.

10. Chambers, *The King in Yellow and Other Horror Stories* (New York: Dover, 1970), 18. For the idea of the "poisonous text," see Navarette, *Shape of Fear,* 46–47.

11. King, *Danse Macabre* (New York: Everest House, 1981), 73.

12. Stoker, *Dracula,* ed. Maurice Hindle (London: Penguin, 2003), 18.251–52.

13. See, e.g., Paul Murray, *From the Shadow of "Dracula": A Life of Bram Stoker* (London: Jonathan Cape, 2004).

14. Le Fanu, "Carmilla," in *The Penguin Book of Vampire Stories*, ed. Alan Ryan (London: Penguin, 1987), 83.

15. Cf. Stoker, *Dracula*, 18.255: "He may not enter anywhere at the first, unless there be some one of the household who bid him to come; though afterwards he can come as he please."

16. Bate, *Coleridge* (New York: Macmillan, 1968), 68, 71.

17. LeFanu, "Carmilla," 89.

18. Delbanco, *The Death of Satan: How Americans Have Lost the Sense of Evil* (New York: Farrar, Straus, 1995), 63; quoting Carol F. Karlsen, *The Devil in the Shape of a Woman: Witchcraft in Colonial New England* (New York: Norton, 1987), 41.

19. Freud, *The Standard Edition of the Complete Psychological Works of Sigmund Freud*, ed. James Strachey (London: Hogarth Press, 1966–74), 21:31.

20. James, *The Turn of the Screw* (New York: Modern Library, 1930), 12.73.

21. In Shirley Jackson's *Haunting of Hill House* (1959), Eleanor takes off from the governess in *The Turn of the Screw*. In her case the baggage she brings with her to Hill House is her imprisonment with her mother, whom she cares for until her death—a day on which she failed (or refused) to hear the mother's cries for help. Approaching Hill House, she has fantasies of what she wishes for—projections that are absorbed in the life of Hill House, including bonding with the lesbian Theodora and associating herself with the companion of the bedridden Miss C., with the nursery where Miss C. and her sister once idyllically played—ultimately the enclosed garden where they picnicked—and the library where the companion, having gotten the property away from the other sister, hanged herself. Eleanor ends by becoming the ghost that haunts Hill House—in order to find a home there, or anywhere (all her other "homes" are projections), both before she dies and after. The novel would have been written out of a reading of Edmund Wilson's well-known essay on *The Turn of the Screw*, in which he does a psychoanalytical treatment of the governess. "The Ambiguity of Henry James," *Hound & Horn* 7 [1934]: 385–406; reprinted, *The Triple Thinkers* (New York: Oxford, 1938). On James and the ghost story, see J. Hillis Miller, *Literature as Conduct: Speech Acts in Henry James* (New York: Fordham, 2005), 299–307.

22. *Henry James: Literary Criticism*, vol. 1: *Essays, English and American* (Library of America, 1984), 742.

23. James, *The Sacred Fount*, ed. Leon Edel (New York: Grove Press, 1953), 2.29, 14.300.

24. E.g., "in possession of the scene," in "possession of the room" (*The Sacred Fount*, 2.6, 20, again 4.53, 68; 5.74); "aggrandizement" (2.25), "'he takes everything. He just cleans her out'" (3.35), "depletion" (2.28), "bloated" vs. "shrunken" states (4.67), "eating poor Briss up inch by inch" (5.71). Posses-

sion as the work of a collector: He "adds" another "to my little gallery—the small collection" he is gathering (2.22).

25. Cf. Leon Edel's interpretation, in Edel, ed., *The Sacred Fount*, v–xxxii.

26. Before *The Sacred Fount* there were variations on the female vampire: Mary Elizabeth Braddon's "Good Lady Ducayne" (1896), in which the rich old lady lives off the blood of her young female companions that is transfused by her doctor—leading to their deaths; or, shortly after, the eponymous lady of Mary E. Wilkins-Freeman's "Luella Miller" (1903), who, though she may or may not be literally a vampire, battens off the lives and bodies of all the men and women who are drawn to this helpless woman. A rewriting of *The Sacred Fount* was Algernon Blackwood's "The Transfer" (1912), in which the "Forbidden Corner," a patch of infertile ground, seizes the energy of a vampirish human who tends to absorb everything from the people around him—and is about to absorb his young nephew—and leaves him as drained as "poor Briss" or Mrs. Server.

27. For a comparison of *Turn of the Screw* and *Dracula*, see Navarette, *The Shape of Fear*, 126–28.

28. As many critics have noted, the plot of *The Portrait of a Lady* recalls (partly derives from) George Eliot's *Daniel Deronda*: Grandcourt anticipates Osmond, in particular in his seduction and appropriation of Gwendolyn Harleth; Lydia Glasher and Mme. Merle are both former, cast-off lovers of, respectively, Grandcourt and Osmond.

29. James, *Portrait of a Lady* (London: Penguin, 2003), 34.396, 42.482.

30. James, *The Wings of the Dove* (New York: Modern Library, 1946), 1: 3.5.139. See Matthew 4.

31. Millicent Bell, *Meaning in Henry James* (Cambridge: Harvard University Press, 1991), 294.

32. James also more than once applies the words of the last line of *Paradise Lost*, as Hawthorne did in the reference to Hester in *The Scarlet Letter*. Lionel Croy is associated with the devil himself, the seedy negative figure Dostoevsky had shown in conversation with Ivan Karamazov.

33. Earlier Lord Mark had visualized Milly among people "in Veronese costumes" (1:4.7.162).

34. In Bell's words, "Like Christ, luminous but remote in the background of the crowded painting, Milly is seen from a distance 'diffus[ing] in wide warm waves the spell of a general, a beatific mildness'" (296). Veronese's *Christ in the House of Levi*, originally painted as a Last Supper, was renamed to accord with the criticisms of the Inquisition.

35. Charles Anderson has pointed out that the Bronzino portrait James had in mind, of Lucrezia Panciatichi in the Uffizi, shows the subject holding a book, the Latin text of which is a hymn to the Virgin (Anderson, *Person, Place, and Thing in Henry James's Novels* [Durham: Duke University Press, 1977], 185–88).

36. James, *Sacred Fount*, 4.55.

37. James, "The Third Person," *The Ghostly Tales of Henry James*, ed. Leon Edel (New Brunswick: Rutgers University Press, 1948), 656. The ghost of Sir Edmund Orme also brings about the "redemption" of his old girlfriend through her daughter (above, 179).

38. James, *The American*, in *Selected Novels of Henry James* (New York: Caxton House, 1946), 24.281.

39. For a subtle analysis of the morality in *The Golden Bowl*, and especially of Maggie, see Martha Nussbaum, "Flawed Crystals: James's *The Golden Bowl* and Literature as Moral Philosophy," and "'Finely Aware and Richly Responsible': Literature and the Moral Imagination," in *Love's Knowledge: Essays on Philosophy and Literature* (New York: Oxford University Press, 1990), 4–167.

40. Maggie's discovery gives her empowerment, matures her, turns the novel around: The second volume, which begins with her first impression, as Amerigo returns from the day in Gloucester with Charlotte, that something is wrong, shifts from the perspective of Charlotte, Amerigo, and the Assinghams to Maggie and never for long leaves her. With the discovery of the golden bowl, she takes over agency. She recalls Catherine Sloper, who after her catastrophe also emerges as an agent capable of exercising choice and wielding power. These are really, perhaps, stories of coming out, variants of the story of Isabel Archer. One danger of reading *Golden Bowl* after a reading of *Wings* is to endow Charlotte at least, if not equally Amerigo, with the agency of Kate and Merton—when in fact the anomaly is Maggie and her father Adam's relationship, into which the other two fit themselves naturally to enjoy their affair.

41. Greene, *Collected Essays* (New York: Viking, 1983), 53, 116.

42. James, *The Golden Bowl* (New York: Grove Press, 1952), 1:24.394.

43. Caleb Crain notes, "No awe surrounds evil in [the novels of] Howells. He would never have cast the spell of mystification around Gilbert Osmond's vanity that James did"; a clergyman in Howells's *Annie Lilburn* (1888) suggests that "it was not a wholly meritorious thing to hate evil. . . . He said it was a good deal more desirable to understand evil than to hate it, for then we could begin to cure it." (Caleb Crain, "Hazards and Fortunes," *New Republic*, 15 Aug. 2005, 33.)

44. Greene, "The Private Universe," in *Henry James: A Collection of Critical Essays*, ed. Leon Edel (Englewood Cliffs: Prentice-Hall, 1963), 111–22.

45. James, *The Ambassadors* (New York: Harper Classics, 1948), 4.47, 5.56, 11.149–50.

CHAPTER 6. DEMONIC AND BANAL EVIL

1. D. Punter, *The Literature of Terror: A History of Gothic Fictions from 1765 to the Present Day* (London: Longman, 1980), 232.

2. King, *Danse Macabre* (New York: Everest House, 1981), 290.

3. In James's "The Jolly Corner" (1907) again, the ghost, the figure of the other, is only *other*, the shadow double, the projection of what Spencer Bryden

might have ended up as—in other words, like Quint and Jessel a figment of the susceptible mind of the living protagonist. In fact, Bryden's is a story of doubling, but his demonic other is sad, wounded, and unthreatening—in short only a ghost, not a demon. Another sort of double appears in "The Private Life" (a short story of 1892): the great novelist Clare Vawdrey is in fact in public the "bourgeois" who tells long, boring anecdotes and in private the "genius" who stays in his darkened hotel room writing masterpieces. There is also Lord Mellifont, dazzling in public but nonexistent when no one else is around: "He's there from the moment he knows somebody else is" (240).

4. Hogg, *The Private Memoirs and Confessions of a Justified Sinner,* ed. John Carey (London: Oxford University Press, 1969), 148.

5. The first applies Barton's criticism of Robert for uttering "sickan sublime and ridiculous sophistry I never heard come out of another mouth but ane," which Robert repeats as referring to his father Wringhim, whereas it presumably referred to the prince of liars and sophisters, Satan; but the two are, once again, doubles—when Barton refers to Satan, he is also referring to old Wringhim.

6. See C. G. Jung, *Four Archetypes* (reprinted from H. Read, M. Fordham, and G. Adler, eds., *The Collected Works of C. G. Jung* [1956; repr. London: Routledge, 1972]); Otto Rank, *The Double: A Psychoanalytic Study,* trans. H. Tucker (Chapel Hill: University of North Carolina Press, 1971).

7. Stevenson, *Dr. Jekyll and Mr. Hyde and Other Strange Tales* (Ann Arbor: Borders Classics, 2004), 10.59.

8. And so, in Patricia Highsmith's *Strangers on a Train* (1950), Bruno is the bad double who carries out the murder the other could not otherwise have committed but wished for.

9. I am indebted in this discussion to Joseph Grixti, *Terrors of Uncertainty: The Cultural Contexts of Horror Fiction* (London: Routledge, 1989).

10. Cited Navarette, *Shape of Fear,* 188 and n. My text is Wilde, *The Picture of Dorian Gray,* ed. Robert Mighall (London: Penguin: 2001), 11.124, 20.213. Cf. Colin McGinn, *Ethics, Evil, and Fiction* (Oxford: Clarendon Press, 1997), especially the chapter on *Dorian Gray.*

11. In terms of Dorian's commitment to Lord Henry's nature–art dichotomy Sibyl's mistake is to choose nature (herself) over art (her role in a Shakespeare play). On the relationship between *Dorian Gray* and Wilde's earlier story "The Model Millionaire" (and James's "the Real Thing"); and Maturin's *Melmoth the Wanderer* (the mirror in the attic and the Faustian pact); see Edouard Roditi, *Oscar Wilde,* 2d ed. (New York: New Directions, 1986), 71–72, 77–82.

12. See Roditi, *Oscar Wilde,* 87—as opposed to where Conrad's *Heart of Darkness* leads.

13. Dorian later believes that "Basil would have helped him to resist Lord Henry's influence, and the still more poisonous influences that came from his own temperament" (115).

14. Hogarth, *The Analysis of Beauty*, ed. Ronald Paulson (New Haven: Yale University Press, 1997), 59. There is only one reference to Hogarth in the index to Ellmann's biography of Wilde—to Wilde's attendance at the Hogarth Club. But there is evidence of his knowledge of earlier aestheticians—Lessing, for example, and Shaftesbury, and the friend and sponsor of Aubrey Beardsley cannot have not known Hogarth's works, graphic and written.

15. See Machen, above, 168; for Rowlandson, see Paulson, *Rowlandson: A New Interpretation* (London: Studio Vista, 1972), 31–37.

16. As to another object, the painting itself, this only embodies Dorian's decline and is not seen by anyone else, does not contaminate. I am arguing here with Navarette, who drew my attention to the significance of the "poisonous text" (Wilde's term) but includes under this category the portrait (46). See also William E. Buckler, "*The Picture of Dorian Gray*: An Essay in Aesthetic Exploration," *Victorian Institute Journal* 18 (1990): 158.

17. Chambon, "Inventing Sherlock Holmes," *New York Review of Books*, 10 Feb. 2005, 17. See also the second part, "The Game's Afoot," in the issue of 24 Feb. 2005, 14–17, for an interesting essay on the literary quality of the Holmes saga.

18. My text is *The Complete Sherlock Holmes* (New York: Garden City, 1938), "The Final Problem," 544.

19. *A Study in Scarlet*, in *Complete Sherlock Holmes*, 9.

20. In 1889, J. M. Stoddart, the American editor of *Lippincott's Magazine*, over lunch with Oscar Wilde and Arthur Conan Doyle, proposed that each author write a long story for him. Wilde produced *The Picture of Dorian Gray* and Conan Doyle wrote *The Sign of Four*, his second Sherlock Holmes novel, but of course his first, *The Study in Scarlet*, had already appeared in 1887.

21. In *A Study in Scarlet*, Holmes remarks that "it is a mistake to confound strangeness with mystery. The most commonplace crime is often the most mysterious, because it presents no new or special features from which deductions may be drawn," but most of his cases do have "*outré* and sensational accompaniments" (44).

22. Cf. the girl in *A Study in Scarlet*, who describes the Utah landscape in which the Mormons—a religious sect calling themselves "His own chosen people" —have settled and asks if God made all this barrenness: "'He made the country down in Illinois [from which they had started their journey], and He made the Missouri. . . . I guess somebody else made the country in these parts. It's not nearly so well done. They forgot the water and the trees'" (50).

23. Conrad, *Heart of Darkness*, ed. Robert Kimbrough (New York: Norton, 1963), 3.57, 65.

24. I have not mentioned Simon Legree's beating of his slave Uncle Tom, but this is another link in the chain (Harriet Beecher Stowe, *Uncle Tom's Cabin*, 1852).

25. From 1867 Doré's works were on permanent exhibition at the Doré Gallery in Bond Street. The illustrated Dante was one of his most popular works.

26. Kurtz's essay for the suppression of savage customs is another of the poisonous texts referred to above, 169, 206.

27. Guerard, *Conrad the Novelist* (Cambridge: Harvard University Press 1958), 168.

28. Lilian Feder, "Marlow's Descent into Hell," *Nineteenth-Century Fiction* 9 (Mar. 1955), 184.

29. Conrad, *Victory*, in Conrad, *Complete Works* (New York: Doubleday, 1924), 15:4.5.329.

30. *Brothers Karamazov*, trans. Richard Pevear and Larissa Volokhonsky (San Francisco: Northpoint, 1990), 11.9.634–39.

31. "Meditations in Time of Civil War," dated 1923, in *The Tower* (1928), in W. B. Yeats, *The Poems: A New Edition*, ed. Richard J. Finneran (New York: Macmillan, 1983), 200–06.

32. "Nineteen Hundred and Nineteen," *Poems*, 210 and n. 607.

33. "The Circus Animals' Desertion," "Crazy Jane Talks with the Bishop," *Poems*, 347–48, 259–60.

34. Cf. Blake's cycle: youth overthrows age, the son kills the father, but then he *becomes* the father; whereas in Yeats's *Purgatory* the father kills the son to stop the cycle (or is merely afraid the son will kill him?).

35. Yeats, *Purgatory: Manuscript Materials Including the Author's Final Text*, ed. Sandra F. Siegel (Ithaca: Cornell University Press, 1986), 195.

36. "A Statesman's Holiday," *Poems*, 583.

37. In the first encounter, only Temple's description of the first visit of Popeye the night before, and his foreplay, appear.

38. See William S. Kubie, "William Faulkner's *Sanctuary*," in R. P. Warren, *A Collection of Critical Essays* (Englewood Cliffs: Prentice-Hall, 1966), 139.

39. Faulkner, *Sanctuary* (New York: Modern Library, 1932), 25.298–99.

40. I am grateful to Lawrence Kenney for drawing my attention to Popeye's corncob pipe.

41. *Faulkner at Nagano*, ed. Robert A. Jeliffe (Tokyo: Kenkyusha, 1962), 104.

42. O'Donnell, "Faulkner's Mythology," in *Kenyon Review* 1, no. 3 (1939), reprinted, Robert Penn Warren, ed., *Faulkner*, 25–26. O'Donnell, however, sets aside *Sanctuary* as a failed allegory on this theme: "Southern Womanhood Corrupted but Undefiled (Temple Drake), in the company of the Corrupted Tradition (Gowan Stevens, a professional Virginian), falls into the clutches of amoral Modernism (Popeye), which is itself impotent, but which with the aid of its strong ally Natural Lust ("Red") rapes Southern Womanhood unnaturally and then seduces her so satisfactorily that her corruption is total, and she becomes the tacit ally of Modernism. Meanwhile Pore White Trash (Godwin) has been accused of the crime which he, with the aid of the Naive Faithful (Tawmmy), actually tried to prevent. The Formalized Tradition (Horace Benbow), perceiving the true state of affairs, tries vainly to defend Pore White Trash. However, Southern Womanhood is so hopelessly corrupted that she wilfully sees Pore White Trash convicted and lynched; she is

then carried off by Wealth (Judge Drake) to meaningless escape in European luxury. Modernism, carrying in it from birth its own impotence and doom, submits with masochistic pleasure to its own destruction for the one crime that it has not yet committed—Revolutionary Destruction of Order (the murder of the Alabama policeman, for which the innocent Popeye is executed)" (28).

43. As Lawrence S. Kubie has described it, *Sanctuary* is "a dramatization of the impact between the forces of instinctual evil . . . represented as rising up out of the pits of the underworld through Popeye and Temple [to which we can add Narcissa, Gowan, etc.]" and the code of respectable upper-class society. Psychoanalytically, Faulkner dramatizes the struggle of the *Id* ("the reservoir of instincts," Popeye and to a lesser extent the other inhabitants of the Old Frenchman's Place), the *Superego* ("the all-but-blind forces of a conscience whose operation is by no means always rational and clear"), in Narcissa, Gowan, etc., but also the blind rage of the Jefferson mob acting on its version of the code, which is the sanctity of Southern Womanhood, especially virgins, and the "much-battered" intermediate *Ego* (Horace Benbow). (Kubie, "William Faulkner's *Sanctuary*," 142.)

44. See his remarks in *Journey without Maps,* his attempt to recreate Marlow's quest up the Congo River (Norman Sherry, *The Life of Graham Greene,* vol. 1, *1901–1939* [New York: Viking, 1989], 421).

45. Greene, *Brighton Rock* (London: Heinemann, 1940), 2.1.75.

46. Sherry, *Life of Graham Greene,* 1:635–36.

47. Cf. Pinkie on ghosts, *Brighton Rock,* 241.

48. Michael Shelden, *Graham Greene: The Enemy Within* (New York: Random House, 1994), 197.

49. Kite, incidentally, we learn in *A Gun for Sale* (1936), was killed by the protagonist of that novel, Raven, who presumably at that time worked for Colleoni. Raven's past is as traumatic as Pinkie's: his father was hanged, his mother commited suicide, he was stuck in an orphanage, and he was born with a harelip (which is bungled by a surgeon).

50. Sherry, *Life of Graham Greene,* 1:637.

51. Greene, *Graham Greene on Film,* ed. John Russell Taylor (New York: Simon and Schuster, 1972), 72.

52. Bataille, *Literature and Evil,* 9.

53. Greene, *Collected Essays,* 204–05.

54. Greene, *It's a Battlefield* (1934; repr. London: Heinemann, 1948), 2.89–90.

55. Letter to Melanchthon, *Epistolae M. Lutheri* (Irenae, 1556), 1:345.

56. Eliot, *Selected Prose,* ed. John Hayward (London: Penguin, 1953), 194.

57. *Collected Essays,* 181.

58. On Greene's conversion, see Shelden, *Graham Greene,* 102 ff., and on his spying and double agenting, see Shelden, *passim.*

59. Quoted, Sheldon, *Graham Greene,* 9.

60. Shelden, *Graham Greene,* 183. I think he carries the analogy beyond the

limits of Christmas when he calls Raven "Judas . . . who is willing to fight back, to betray others before they can betray him." Or take Greene's anti-Semitism: Greene's Jew is in fact evil, a background and controlling figure —"a dark alien sowing corruption in society" (ibid., 130; and 123–30 on Greene's anti-Semitism). Colleoni refers to the Italian mercenary, but Greene labels him Jewish—leader of a Jewish gang taking over Brighton (cf. in *Confidential Agent* [1939], Forbes née Furtstein—recalling Eliot's "Rachel née Rabinovich"—the Eliot of "Burbank with a Baedecker").

61. Shelden, *Graham Greene*, 109, 184.
62. Father Harold Gardiner, quoted Shelden, *Graham Greene*, 108.
63. Shelden, *Graham Greene*, 181.
64. Ibid., 107.
65. Machen, *Tales of Terror*, 290.
66. Shelden's description of Greene's theology sounds in fact more like Blake's than Eliot's: "God is tyrannical, the soul must assert its independence, sin can have its charms, easy virtue can corrupt, evil can be overwhelming, and damnation can be a noble act of defiance. What Catholicism gave to all this was the right background. It gave him rules to break and props to knock over. . . . He could subject it to one indignity after another, turning its good points into bad ones, making its God a devil and Lucifer a saint. He could ridicule its priests and parody its rituals." (Shelden, *Graham Greene*, 106–07). Shelden could be describing the Greene of the much later novel *The Honorary Consul* (1973), in which the excommunicated priest, "Father" Rivas sounds more like Dostoevsky's Ivan. As if recalling the noseless girl of *Miss Lonelyhearts* (below, p. 289), Greene has Rivas comment on "a child born without hands and feet": "A duty to love a God who produces that abortion? It's like the duty of a German to love Hitler. Isn't it better not to believe in that horror up there sitting in the clouds of heaven than pretend to love him?"; but he adds, "He made us in His image—and so our evil is His evil too. How could I love God if He were not like me? Divided like me. Tempted like me" (New York: Penguin, 1973), 217–19.
67. Greene, *The Power and the Glory* (London: Heinemann, 1951), 2.1.93, 3.3.251–52.

CHAPTER 7. THE ORIGINAL EVIL AND THE ORIGINAL SIN

1. Edwards's term is "wickedness." The *OED* cites Coverdale's translation of Genesis 13:13, "Ye men of Sodome were wicked, and synned exceedingly agaynst the Lorde," cites the usage of Satan as "the Wicked One," and derives it from "f. Wick *a.* as *wretched* from *wrecche* Wretch," i.e., once again, initially suffering, subsequently doing.
2. *Jonathan Edwards: Basic Writings*, ed. Ola Elizabeth Winslow (New York: New American Library, 1966), 153.
3. R. C. Bald notes that Coleridge indicated as a topic for a projected poem "The Origin of Evil, an Epic Poem" (Gutch memorandum book, f. 21a; Bald,

"Coleridge and *The Ancient Mariner:* Addenda to *The Road to Xanadu,*" in *Nineteenth-Century Studies* [1940], 16). Bald also quotes from a letter to Coleridge from Charles Lamb, early 1797: "I have a dim recollection that, when in town, you were talking of the Origin of evil as a most prolific subject for a long poem" (*Letters of Charles Lamb,* ed. E. V. Lucas [London, 1935], 1:95).

4. Robert Penn Warren, "A Poem of Pure Imagination: An Experiment in Reading," originally published in 1946 as preface to an edition of *The Ancient Mariner;* reprinted in Warren, *New and Selected Essays* (New York: Random House, 1989), 335–423.

5. *Table-Talk,* 3 May 1830, cited in Warren, "A Pure Poem," 355. Warren writes that it is "a story of crime and punishment" and that Coleridge has "refrained from using the word sin," but his argument makes it plain that sin is precisely what he means—Original Sin.

6. Walter Jackson Bate, *Coleridge* (New York: Macmillan, 1968), 219. He cites Coleridge's discussions in the *Aids to Reflection* and *Opus Maximum.*

7. The quotations are from Bate, *Coleridge,* 58.

8. *The Statesman's Manual,* in Bate, *Coleridge,* 458.

9. What follows the Mariner's "accident" is externalized guilt, an equivalent of the internalized "evils" of God's punishment as described by Coleridge five years later in the poem "The Pains of Sleep": "For all seemed guilt, remorse or woe, / My own or others—still the same / Lie-stifling fear, soul-stifling shame," in which he concludes, "Such punishments, I said, were due / To natures deepliest stained with sin,—/ For aye entempesting anew / The unfathomable hell within, / The horror of their deeds to view, / To know and loathe, yet wish and do!" (ll. 30–33, 43–48).

10. Quoted, Bald, op. cit., 26–27.

11. Warren, "A Poem of Pure Imagination," 361. Warren himself fits into the tradition of beating-the-innocent animal. In *At Heaven's Gate* (1943) Ashby Wyndham, in his interpolated narrative, describes his wanton beating to death of a mule—in a drunken rage, like Poe's "perverse" narrator in "The Black Cat" (which Warren also cites). Ashby is, like the Mariner, on a quest for salvation, but his treatment of the mule is closer to Wordsworth's in *Peter Bell.*

12. In terms of Coleridge's intention to write an epic on the "Origin of Evil," Christabel evokes an equivalent of the Mariner. He killed the albatross, she invited Geraldine into her house and her bed—both mistakes, corruptions of the will rather than malicious acts. But the parallel is obviously between Christabel (with her *Christ*-like name) and the albatross, "which had come so hospitably to the ship and was then slain. Similarly, this hospitality on the part of the 'dove' Christabel is violated" by the serpentine Geraldine (Bate, *Coleridge,* 71).

13. Warren, *Brother to Dragons* (Baton Rouge: Louisiana State University Press, n.d.), 117, 119.

14. Although written c. 1797, Wordsworth did not publish the poem until 1819, when he added the long story of the little boat. Mary Jacobus argues that Wordsworth uses "the human heart" to correct Coleridge's use of "super-natural agency"; Alan Bewell argues that Wordsworth supplants Coleridge's Christian narrative of redemption with a syncretic myth drawn from the "hypothetical histories" common to Enlightenment historiography (Jacobus, *Tradition and Experiment in "Lyrical Ballads"* [Oxford: Clarendon Press, 1976], 262–72; Bewell, *Wordsworth and the Enlightenment* [New Haven: Yale University Press, 1989], 109–41).

15. It is possible that Wordsworth remembered Sterne's mules drawing the nuns of Andouillet in volume 7 of Sterne's *Tristram Shandy*. The mules will not proceed; the muleteer gives them "a sound lash" and "a second good crack"—but, if (as is likely) Sterne was responding to Hogarth's print, it is the demotic word *bouger* (*bou-ger*) recited by the nuns of Andouillet that gets them up and going.

16. In his *Ecclesiastical Sonnets* he makes plain his belief in the inefficacy of the Roman rites of confession, penance, and indulgences (see l. 20).

17. Poe, "The Black Cat," in *Tales of Edgar Allan Poe* (New York: Random House, 1944), 552.

18. Warren, "A Poem of Pure Imagination," 23; *Brother to Dragons*, 116, 67.

19. Hardy, *Jude the Obscure*, ed. Robert B. Heilman (New York: Harper and Row, 1966), 6.1.367.

20. Heilman, "Introduction," *Jude the Obscure*, 1.

21. *Hogarth's Graphic Works*, cat. nos. 140, 210.

22. Heilman's words, "Introduction," *Jude the Obscure*, 10.

23. Mary Shelley, *Frankenstein*, ed. M. K. Joseph (London: Oxford University Press, 1969), Letter 4. 28, 54.

24. He also echoes Milton's line at the end of *Paradise Lost* as he sets out: "'And now,' he says, 'with the world before me, whither should I bend my steps?'" (139).

25. Wells, *The Island of Dr. Moreau* (New York: Bantom, 2005), 22.138.

26. The Brando film invoked Freud's *Totem and Taboo*—the father killed/sacrificed by the son.

27. Wells, *The War of the Worlds* (New York: New York Review of Books, 1960), 1.13–14.

28. Wells subsequently wrote other invasion fantasies: *The War in the Air* (1908) and *The World Set Free* (1914). The latter predicts the atom bomb, and, as Tom Reiss notes, "The book's main character is [as in *War of the Worlds* it was the coming "Great War"] the nuclear chain reaction itself: a phenomenon portrayed in such intimate and creepy detail that it seems almost like a living thing" ("Imagining the Worst," *New Yorker*, 28 Nov. 2005, 168).

29. Johnson, "Review of 'A Free Enquiry into the Nature and Origin of Evil,'" *Literary Magazine*, nos. 13:171–75; 14:251–53; 15:301–06 (1757), in *Johnson: Prose and Poetry*, ed. Mona Wilson (Cambridge: Harvard University Press, 1951),

364–65. See Richard B. Schwartz, *Samuel Johnson and the Problem of Evil* (Madison: University of Wisconsin Press, 1975).

30. Twain, *The Mysterious Stranger,* in *The Portable Mark Twain,* ed. Bernard DeVoto (New York: Viking, 1946), 2.642.

31. There are many verbal echoes of Swift, who is probably Twain's chief model in *The Mysterious Stranger;* in a number of places Theodor and Satan recall Gulliver and the King of Brobdingnag (644, 649), but the primary source seems to have been the *Tale*—and, in one striking instance, its supplement, *The Mechanical Operation of the Spirit.* Satan describes humans as "notwithstanding they were so dull and ignorant and trivial and conceited, and so diseased and rickety and such a shabby, poor, worthless lot all around . . . ," which recalls: "Who, that sees a little paultry Mortal, droning, and dreaming, and drivelling to a Multitude, can think it agreeable to common good Sense, that either Heaven or Hell should be put to the Trouble of Influence or Inspection upon what he is about?" (*Tale of a Tub,* ed. A. C. Guthkelch and S. Nichol Smith, 2d ed. [Oxford: Clarendon Press, 1958], 276).

32. Swift, *Tale,* 171.

33. Published in *The Bible According to Mark Twain,* ed. Howard G. Baetzhold and Joseph B. McCullough (Athens: University of Georgia Press, 1995), 319.

34. Bettelheim, *The Uses of Enchantment: The Meaning and Importance of Fairy Tales* (1976; repr. New York: Random House, Vintage 1977), 166–83. The first edition of the Grimm brothers' *Children and Household Tales* was published in 1812.

35. Darnton, "Peasants Tell Tales: The Meaning of Mother Goose," in *The Great Cat Massacre and Other Episodes in French Cultural History* (New York: Basic Books, 1984), 9–74. Note the numerous examples of hunger in the examples we have examined, from Oliver Twist's request for another bowl of porridge to the mouths in *Enthusiasm Delineated.*

36. Bettelheim, *Uses of Enchantment,* 44.

37. On the folk tale in the *Lazarillo de Tormes* and specifically hunger and the priest, see Fernando Lázaro Carreter, *"Lazarillo de Tormes" en la picaresca* (Barcelona, 1972); Harry Sieber, *Language and Society in "La Vida de Lazarillo de Tormes"* (Baltimore: Johns Hopkins University Press, 1978). My text is *Lazarillo de Tormes,* trans. Mack Hendricks Singleton, in *Masterpieces of the Spanish Golden Age,* ed. Angel Flores (New York: Rinehart, 1957).

38. Paul Cantor, *Creature and Creator* (Cambridge: Cambridge University Press, 1984), 135.

39. Byron, *Cain,* in *The Complete Poetical Works,* ed. Jerome J. McGann and Barry Weller, 6 vols. (Oxford: Clarendon Press, 1981), 1.1.249–52, p. 240.

40. *Cain,* 1.1.358–60, 363–64, p. 245.

41. Again, Lucifer speaking ironically of God's temptation of Adam: "Did *I* plant things prohibited within / The reach of beings innocent, and curious / By their own innocence? I would have made ye / Gods, and even He who

thrust ye forth, so thrust ye / Because 'e should not eat the fruits of life, / And become gods as we'" (1.1.200–05).

42. Melville, *Moby-Dick,* ed. Charles Feidelson (New York: Bobbs-Merrill, 1964); see, e.g., 24.154. For some of the conflicting interpretations, see Giles Gunn, ed., *A Historical Guide to Herman Melville* (New York: Oxford University Press, 2005).

43. Why does Melville bring in Hogarth's whale in his illustration for Lewis Theobald's harlequinade, *Perseus and Andromeda* (1729/30), which in the mid–nineteenth century would have been a very rare item—presumably seen by Melville on his visit to London, either in the original pamphlet or in a Hogarth collection, possibly in a printseller's (55.347)? His reference to the Cock Lane Ghost suggests that he had seen Hogarth's famous print *Credulity, Superstition, and Fanaticism* of 1762 (403). Both of these references suggest that when he refers to "lines of beauty" (481), and a page later to the Belvedere Hercules in the Vatican, he is recalling *The Analysis of Beauty* and its plate 1. See Paulson, *Hogarth's Graphic Works* (London: Print Room, 1989), cat. nos. 116 [118], 210A, and 195).

44. For example, his chapter 55, on the impossibility of painting a sublime whale without making it look silly is Burke's, an attack on Hogarth.

45. I cannot improve upon Charles Feidelson's words: "If we begin with the natural world—the nonhuman environment that bulks so large in the book—we may see it as merely indifferent to men, who read human moral values into it. Or we may see it as an eternal mystery, incomprehensible to men but ordered by God. Or we may view it through Ahab's eyes, as primarily evil *because* it is incomprehensible, whether or not it is ruled by God. Or we may side with Ishmael, the pantheist, who wants to identify nature with divinity. Or we may combine the visions of Ahab and Ishmael, as Ishmael is always forced to do, into an ambiguous union of natural good and evil, divinity and neutrality, meaning and nothingness" (*Moby-Dick,* xxii).

46. *The Complete Works of Nathanael West* (New York: Farrar, Straus, 1957), 67.

47. Etienne Gilson was the French Thomist theologian, a name evoking fashionable religious thinking in the 1930s. West was also writing in the wake of the rediscovery of Melville and *Moby-Dick* in the twenties and thirties.

48. West's brother-in-law was S. J. Perelman, who wrote some of Groucho's monologues.

49. *Jude the Obscure,* ed. Heilman, 2.7.166.

50. In *Totem and Taboo* (1913) murder and incest are the "only crimes" or taboos—both in Christian terms sins because murder is originally of the father (worship only God, Honor thy father and mother). In its original sense, as with murder, the crime was against the father, who possesses the woman, his wife, to himself. Parricide was "the great crime" and "the two driving factors [of religion], the son's sense of guilt and the son's rebelliousness, never became extinct" (*The Standard Edition of the Complete Psychological*

Works of Sigmund Freud, ed. James Strachey [London: Hogarth Press, 1966–74], 13:150, 152).

51. Freud, *The Future of an Illusion* (1927), in *Standard Edition*, 21:24.
52. Freud, "A Difficulty in the Path of Psycho-Analysis" (1917), *Standard Edition*, 17:140–41.
53. Freud, *Beyond the Pleasure Principle* (1921), *Standard Edition*, 18:17.
54. Girard, *Violence and the Sacred*, trans. Patrick Gregory (Baltimore: Johns Hopkins University Press, 1977), 10–14, 27.
55. Cf. Faulkner's *Sanctuary*, in which voyeurism is central: Benbow and Popeye looking at each other, the town boys watching the college girls and Popeye's of Temple.
56. McEwan, *The Comfort of Strangers* (New York: Penguin, 1981), 9.115–16.

CHAPTER 8. MODERN SIN AND EVIL

1. Hemingway, *A Farewell to Arms* (New York: Modern Library, 1932), 5.41.350. Cf. Wells's version of the same topos: "But the Martian machine took no more notice for the moment of the people running this way and that than a man would of the confusion of ants in a nest against which his foot has kicked" (*War of the Worlds*, 12.89).
2. "It is clear why a totalitarian state has immense rescources [*sic*] for evil." See Morton, *On Evil*, 79; see Arendt, *The Origins of Totalitarianism* (1968; repr. New York: Harvest Bks., 1976), *passim*.
3. Neiman, *Evil in Modern Thought: An Alternative History of Philosophy* (Princeton: Princeton University Press, 2002); Rothstein, "Seeking Justice, of Gods or Politicians," *New York Times*, 8 Sept. 2005, Arts, 5.
4. For Adorno, "Auschwitz destroyed what had replaced that theodicy: the transformation of the idea of providence into the idea of social progress. It was not just that industrial capitalism had produced human beings who could see it as quite normal to create factories for mass murder; it had undermined the basis of belief in a society as a collective enterprise in which each individual has an intrinsic value" (Michael Rosen, "Being German," *TLS*, 30 Sept. 2005, 6).
5. Javits quote, 1977, cited in Amy Hungerford, *The Holocaust of Texts: Genocide, Literature, and Personification* (Chicago: University of Chicago Press, 2003), 7; the following quotation is Hungerford, *The Holocaust of Texts*, 7.
6. Lawrence J. LeBlanc, *The United States and the Genocide Convention* (Durham: Duke University Press, 1991), 22.
7. Helen Fein, *Genocide: A Sociological Perspective* (Newbury Park: Sage Publications, 1993), 50.
8. Delbanco, *The Death of Satan: How Americans Have Lost the Sense of Evil* (New York: Farrar, Straus, 1995), 183, 181.
9. Adorno's chief points about the Holocaust are (1) the dehumanizing and (2) the fact that this could have happened of all places in Germany.
10. Arendt, *The Origins of Totalitarianism*, 468–71.

11. *The God that Failed,* ed., Richard Crossman (New York: Bantam, 1951), 14, 13.

12. Koestler's basic assumption "was wrong—as we now know. . . . The confessions were not made because the instigators of the trials appealed to the iron Party discipline of old Bolsheviks, their belief that the Party is never wrong and that the Party demanded their sacrifice. The interrogators were far less subtle and sophisticated: they were torturing, beating and blackmailing the victims to get their confessions. But if Koestler's theory was wrong with regard to those appearing in the trials, it still applied to a large extent to many other Communists in the Soviet Union and the West, who continued to justify the show trials for many years" (Walter Laqueur, "A Bully and a Classic," *TLS,* 4 Nov. 2005, 5).

13. *Darkness at Noon,* trans. Daphne Hardy (New York: Penguin, 1941), 1.14.61.

14. NB the description of the Soviet spy-chief Karla in Le Carré's spy novels, in which he is compared to a priest.

15. Mark 15:17–20, paraphrased.

16. See Arendt, *Origins of Totalitarianism,* 153; also Arendt, *Crises of the Republic* (New York: Harcourt Brace, 1972).

17. Of the Soviet apparatchik, Edward Crankshaw remarked, "I have had to work with such officials in war and peace. Their sycophancy, their cowardice, are so blatant, their ignorance so stultifying, their stupidity so absolute, that I have found it impossible to convey it with any credibility to those fortunate enough never to have encountered it" (*Putting Up With the Russians,* quoted, Robert Conquest, "When Goodness Won," *New Republic,* 12 Sept. 2005, 38).

18. Not only the twentieth century. One can note a parallel between the Holocaust and the Spanish expulsion of the Jews (and then the Inquisition) in the 1400s–1600s: Both were based on the idea of purification, repectively, of the German race and of the Spanish Christian faith. Both were counterintuitive. The chronicler Hernando del Pulgar wrote that "since the absence of these people depopulated a large part of the country, the Queen was informed that commerce was declining; but setting little importance on the decline in her revenue, and prizing highly the purity (*limpieza*) of her lands, she said that the essential thing was to cleanse the country of that sin of heresy, for she understood it to be in God's service and her own." On the introduction of the Inquisition and the consequent flight of the conversos and the ruining of his country's economy, a twentieth-century historian writes, "The King maintained that spiritual reasons were more important than mere material considerations of the national economy." The chief difference is that the Spaniards only expelled the Jews, anticipating the Nazis' Madagascar plan and entailing great suffering short of immediate death; the Inquisition's killing—extensive enough—was of conversos who remained observant Jews. Hernando del Pulgar, *Crónica de los Reyes Católicos* (Madrid, 1943), 5:337; quoted, Henry Kamen, *The Spanish Inquisition* (New York: Meridian, 1975), 45, 18.

19. As a kind of reductio ad absurdum, in George Steiner's *The Portage to San Cristóbal of A. H.* (Chicago: University of Chicago Press, 1979) the principle has become the proposal that the end of banishing anti-Semitism is worth the killing of six million Jews. Steiner's satire is based on a Swiftean irony, reminiscent of *A Modest Proposal,* arguing that Hitler invented the Holocaust in order to rid the world of anti-Semitism. Cf. the nonsatiric theory that Stalin's and Hitler's "ethnic cleansing" made possible the neat ethnic divisions that made possible the amazing European postwar recovery following (Tony Judt, *Postwar: A History of Europe since 1945* [New York: Penguin, 2005]).

20. Léon, "The Weapon of Antisemitism," *The Third Reich* [London, 1955], 321, cited by Arendt, *Origins of Totalitarianism,* 348n.

21. Arendt, *Origins of Totalitarianism,* 417–19. Arendt: "Stalin's methods of rule succeeded in destroying whatever measure of competence and technical know-how the country had acquired after the October Revolution." Of Hitler as well as Stalin: "political forces that cannot be trusted to follow the rules of common sense and self-interest—forces that look like sheer insanity, if judged by the standards of other centuries" (*Origins of Totalitarianism,* xxxiv, vii). For "the relationship between stupidity and evil," see Lance Morrow, *Evil: An Investigation* (New York: Basic Books, 2003), 103–07: "everyday stupidity, inattention, convenience, cowardice, peer pressure, momentary entertainment, or idiot ideology" (106).

22. See Garry Wills, "Fringe Government," *New York Review of Books,* 6 Oct. 2005, 46–50.

23. On the "passivity of the onlookers" to acts of evil, see Robert Boyers, "Thinking about Evil," *Raritan* 23, no. 2 (2003), 13–14.

24. Arendt, *Eichmann in Jerusalem: A Report on the Banality of Evil* (New York: Penguin, 1964; ed. 1992), 288. See also, Arendt, *Origins of Totalitarianism,* 338.

25. On atrocity and the gratuitous, see Morrow, *Evil: An Investigation,* chap. 9.

26. Quoted, E. L. Epstein, in "Notes on *Lord of the Flies,*" in his edition, *The Lord of the Flies* (New York: Perigree, nd.), 204.

27. The other main character, Ralph's wise adviser "Piggie," is on the one hand the voice of smart common sense, whose spectacles (gradually dismantled) are his synecdoche, as they were for another Enlightenment hero, Gulliver; but on the other, he is the intellectual scapegoat, the other pig, who is sacrificed by the hunters in place of Ralph, who, though he uses and tolerates Piggie, consistently disdains him, turning him into a joke.

28. Golding revered Conrad's story, and at the climax of Simon's dialogue with the "Lord of the Flies," the pig's head covered with hungry flies, which he has made a god, it sounds very like Conrad: "There was blackness within, a blackness that spread. . . . Simon was inside the mouth. He fell down and lost consciousness" (the Lord of the Flies has told him, "You knew, didn't you? I'm part of you?"—or you are part of me). The echo is clearly of Kurtz's

death: "I saw him open his mouth wide—it gave him a weirdly voracious aspect, as though he wanted to swallow all the air, all the earth, all the men before him"—a passage that eerily recalls those visual images of Goya of mouths, from priestly to feminine to architectural and natural (and Christ's own mouth), that do not eat the Eucharist but swallow worshipers. (Epstein draws attention to the Conrad parallel, "Notes on *Lord of the Flies*," 208n.)

29. Golding's *Rites of Passage* (1980) is an extension of the situation of Simon and Piggie into a plot reminiscent of *Billy Budd*. This stylish pastiche recovers the same period as Melville's novella, but the ship is going to Australia and the Billy character is a young clergyman, despised by the anticlerical Captain Anderson and by the snobbish narrator Edmund Talbot. First we see him from Talbot's point of view—a figure of fun and folly who lets himself be totally humiliated by drinking too much. Then we see him through his own eyes, where he becomes another Billy Budd, killed by two Claggarts, whose motivations are more closely scrutinized than Claggart's. Talbot's Lordship—his godfather—fills the role of Captain DeVere insofar as he is the deity, for whom Talbot seems to see himself as a sort of mediating Son with the ship's crew.

30. Closer to Golding's time was Richard Hughes's popular novel *High Wind in Jamaica* (1929), another corrective parody of Barrie's fantasy, in which children go native.

31. Heller, *Catch-22* (New York: Dell, 1961), 41.450.

32. *Guard of Honor* (Garden City: Perma-book ed., 1952), 2.2.161, 182, 2.6.223.

33. There are, of course, novels with evil Japs/SS men, about the war and atrocities (e.g., Robert Bowen, *The Weight of the Cross* of 1951).

34. James Hilton, *Goodbye, Mr. Chips* (1934), in Ernest Hemingway's collection *Men at War* (New York: Avon, 1942), 580. This collection gives a good idea of how war was depicted by writers over the nineteenth and early twentieth centuries.

35. See, for example, the graphic images of Louis Raemaekers, the Belgian political cartoonist.

36. *A Farewell to Arms*, 196. *A Farewell to Arms* is, however, about (to cite some of the categories Hemingway used in his collection of essays, *Men at War*) "the province of danger, and therefore courage above all things is the first quality of a warrior," "War is the province of physical exertion and suffering," "War demands resolution, firmness, and staunchness," and so on.

37. Arendt, *Origins of Totalitarianism*, 329.

38. Stanley Kubrick's film *Paths of Glory* (1957) was another reflection on the military high command of World War I, a particularly stringent example of the pacifist films of the thirties—King Vidor's *The Big Parade* (1925), Lewis Milestone's *All Quiet on the Western Front* (1930), in which soldiers risk their lives for a bad cause.

39. Waugh, *Men at Arms* (New York: Little, Brown, 1952), 18.83–84. Waugh, however, even more than Cozzens, sees the positive side of the army's order.

Using Hemingway's metaphor of ants but pushing it in an opposite direction, he writes, "Shake up a colony of ants and for some minutes all seems chaos. The creatures scramble aimlessly, frantically about; then instinct reasserts itself. They find their proper places and proper functions. As ants, so soldiers" (18.224).

40. Shaw, *The Young Lions* (New York: Signet, 1950), 28.416–18 (it is a long passage of which I quote only a short part).

41. Sherry, *The Life of Graham Greene*, 2:242.

42. Shelden, *Graham Greene: The Enemy Within*, 225.

43. The religious parody is one point at which *The Third Man* (film 1948, novel 1950) picks up where *Brighton Rock* left off; there is also another proposed double suicide pact—Harry and Anna Schmidt, who, like Rose, says, "I want to die," after Harry's "death." The Marlow "lie" returns, now applied to both Holly and Anna, in Kurtz's construction of Harry's last words as reported—and, of course, Holly Martins' guide into the puzzle of Harry's death is named after Marlow's guide into the heart of darkness. (I am referring primarily to the Carol Reed film and Greene's screenplay.)

44. Le Carré, *The Constant Gardener* (New York: Scribner, 2001; ed., Pocket Bk., 2001), 11.251–52.

45. See the review of the film of *The Constant Gardener* by Marcia Angell, *New York Review of Books*, 6 Oct. 2005, 23–26.

46. Arendt, *Origins of Totalitarianism*, xvii–xviii.

47. Ibid., 358–60. Cf. Arendt's description of the Nazi movement—"international in organization," "global in its political aspirations"—but how much is power or ideology and how much profit for the multinational companies? (Power as the means toward that end?) As also of the pharmaceutical company, it is not clear how "all-comprehensive is its *ideological* scope?" (ibid., 389, italics added; see also 376–81).

48. "If, in accord with traditional political thought, we identify tyranny as government that is not held to give account of itself, rule by Nobody is clearly the most tyrannical of all, since there is no one left who could even be asked to answer for what is being done. It is this state of affairs, making it impossible to localize responsibility and to identify the enemy, that is among the most potent causes of the current worldwide rebellious unrest, its chaotic nature, and its dangerous tendency to get out of control and to run amuck" (Arendt, *Origins of Totalitarianism*, 138–39).

49. Christian Caryl, "Why They Do It," *New York Review of Books*, 22 Sept. 2005, 29. Another, as cogent an example as *The Secret Agent*, would be James's *The Princess Casamassima* (1886), in which Hyacinth Robinson, compared to one key on a piano keyboard, is assigned an act of terrorism by a remote mastermind—but commits suicide rather than carry it out.

50. George Steiner, "In Extremis," *Cambridge Review* 90:2187 (1969): 248; quoted, Hungerford, whose response is the second quotation (Hungerford, *Holocaust of Texts*, 25). Aside from Hungerford's useful book, see Lawrence

Langer, *The Holocaust and the Literary Imagination* (New Haven: Yale University Press, 1975); Sidra Ezrahi, *By Words Alone: The Holocaust in Literature* (Chicago: University of Chicago Press, 1980); Martin Jay, *Probing the Limits of Representation: Nazism and the "Final Solution"* (Cambridge: Cambridge University Press, 1992).

51. More effective than the melodrama of Edward Lewis Wallant's *The Pawnbroker* (1961), D. M. Thomas's *The White Hotel* (1981) and *Pictures at an Exhibition* (1993), and William Styron's *Sophie's Choice* (1979). The details one remembers from these novels are the atrocities, tortures, and abominations: forcing a daughter to have sex with her father in order to save herself but then made to fellate him as he is being hanged (*Pictures at an Exhibition*); or the husband accidentally sees his wife forced to fellate a Gestapo torturer (*Pawnbroker*); or the mother forced to choose between the lives of her two children.

52. George Steiner, cited Wendy Steiner, "Postmodern Fictions, 1960–1990," in *Prose Writing, 1940–1990*, vol. 7 of *The Cambridge History of American Literature*, ed. Sacvan Bercovitch (Cambridge: Cambridge University Press, 1990), 434.

53. Alvarez, "The Literature of the Holocaust," *Commentary* 38.5 (1964): 65–66.

54. Wendy Steiner, "Postmodern Fictions," 434.

55. Vonnegut, *Slaughterhouse-Five or The Children's Crusade* (New York: Delacorte Press, 1969), 8.

56. When he recalls the bombing of Dresden, Lazzaro "did not exult," because he had nothing against the Germans. "'Nobody ever got it from Lazzaro,' he said, 'who didn't have it coming'" (121).

57. As Vonnegut was well aware, Freud described order as "a kind of compulsion to repeat which, when a regulation has been laid down once and for all, decides when, where and how a thing shall be done. . . . It enables men to use space and time to the best advantage while conserving their psychical forces [but] on the contrary, human beings exhibit an inborn tendency to carelessness, irregularity and unreliability in their work"—what he calls in *Civilization and its Discontents* (1930) "goals of utility and a yield of pleasure" (*Standard Edition*, 21:93–95).

58. In a separate essay, "To the Person Sitting in Darkness," Twain writes a satire on colonialism focused on the role of Christian missionaries in the exploitation of these countries.

59. Note also the disproportionate number of children killed in saturation bombings. See *Firestorm: The Bombing of Dresden, 1945*, ed. Paul Addison and Jeremy A. Crang (London: Pimlico, 2006), in which the maximum number of deaths in the Dresden bombing is set at 40,000.

60. Herr, *Dispatches* (1968; repr. New York: Avon, 1978), 43.

61. O'Brien, *In the Lake of the Woods* (New York: Penguin, 1995), 25.257. Cf. a similar novel, Ward Just's *A Dangerous Friend* (New York: Houghton Mifflin, 1999): "The men, women, and children of Song Nu were as anonymous as

farm animals," and they are "incinerate[d]" (146). As to the war itself, citing Conrad, Just writes, "You can't resign from it any more than you can resign from a typhoon. . . . When you go back to the world you'll still be in the war. It's nature's way, and we've given our word" (252).

62. Alford, *What Evil Means to Us* (Ithaca: Cornell University Press, 1997), 15.

63. Morton, *On Evil*, 5–6.

64. *In the Lake of the Woods*, 16.138, citing Judith Herman, *Trauma and Recovery* (New York: Basic Books, 1992), 1.

65. Citing Herman, *Trauma and Recovery*, 26, 7.

66. Lewis, *Mere Christianity* (1952; repr. New York: Harper, 1980), 43–44.

67. Quoted, David Bromwich, in "Maenads and Jihadis," *The New Republic*, 23 Jan. 2006, 29 (where he also discusses Burke's sublime).

68. Vonnegut quotes Air Marshal Saundby, "Those who approved it [the Dresden bombing] were neither wicked nor cruel, though it may well be that they were too remote from the harsh realities of war to understand fully the appalling destructive power of air bombardment in the spring of 1943" (162). Though, when he quotes an American, President Truman's statement on the Japanese and Hiroshima, "They have been repaid many-fold" (160), he is aware of the assumption of revenge given in Old Testament cadences. And behind these statements is the idea of the general somewhat more than "eighty miles away." For the latest word on the issue of the Hiroshima bombing, see Tsuyoshi Hasegawa, *Racing the Enemy: Stalin, Truman and the Surrender of Japan* (Cambridge: Harvard University Press, 2005). He places most of the blame on Japan—then on Stalin's double dealing and Truman's talk of revenge.

69. Baldwin, *Going to Meet the Man: Stories* (New York: Vintage, 1995), 229–49.

70. In Warren's *All the King's Men* (1946) Cass Mastern's story, containing the vivid scene of the slave market, the slave woman stripped and checked over by her prospective master, is followed later by Jack Burden's stripping and sexual submission of Ann Stanton: another "slave" situation.

71. McCarthy, *Blood Meridian* (1985; repr. New York: Vintage, 1992), 245.

INDEX